D1447125

# INTRODUCTION TO
# MEDICAL PSYCHOLOGY

# INTRODUCTION TO MEDICAL PSYCHOLOGY

## James C. Norton, Ph.D.
Veterans Administration and
Albert B. Chandler Medical Centers
University of Kentucky

THE FREE PRESS
*A Division of Macmillan Publishing Co., Inc.*
NEW YORK

Collier Macmillan Publishers
LONDON

The Free Press
A Division of Macmillan Publishing Co., Inc.
866 Third Avenue, New York, N.Y. 10022

Collier Macmillan Canada, Ltd.

Library of Congress Catalog Card Number: 81-69223

Printed in the United States of America

printing number
1   2   3   4   5   6   7   8   9   10

Library of Congress Cataloging in Publication Data

Norton, James C.
    Introduction to medical psychology.

    Includes index.
    1. Medicine and psychology.   I. Title.   [DNLM:
1. Psychology, Clinical.   2. Psychosomatic medicine.
3. Preventive medicine.   WM 90 N885i]
R726.5.N67          616'.001'9 .         81-69223
ISBN 0-02-923290-2                       AACR2

This book is dedicated to my parents.

# Contents

# Preface

Profound forces for change in American medicine are at work. Some of them are internal to the medical profession; others come from outside. From within the profession, technological and therapeutic innovations offer mixed blessings: new forms of treatment may prolong life without offering hope for cure or improvement. At the same time, an ever larger knowledge base makes it difficult to determine what is essential in the training of physicians. Finally, the doctor's role has come under question as preventive medicine takes its place alongside the traditional healing function. Among external forces, consumers and their representatives in government are surely the most vocal and potentially powerful. Their demands run the gamut of issues: from the type of health services available to the cost of these services; from the training of medical personnel to the deployment of people so trained. Oftentimes, these demands conflict. Expanded services and cost containment are difficult to achieve simultaneously. And demand for highly specialized services is challenged by a widely perceived need for more primary care physicians. Calls for greater use of paraprofessionals are met by pleas for quality control. Medicine thus is beset by economic, social, and political forces to which the profession must find ways to respond.

Conceptual, scientific, and philosophic influences also are affecting the intellectual climate of the field. Behavioristic psychology is one such force, and its impact is increasing. For example, an experimental and clinical literature examining the relevance of behaviorism to medicine is fast accumulating. This literature addresses a wide range of issues but points to a common conclusion: the laws of behavior play an important role in health. Studies looking at topics as diverse as compliance with medical prescription, the effects of exercise on health, and the operant conditioning of heart rate all lead inevitably to the view that to be maximally effective medicine must incorporate not only the laws of physiology but those of behavior as well.

A unique opportunity for innovation and collaboration is created by the confluence of ferment in medicine and increasing knowledge about behavior. Behaviorism offers the medical profession new ways to look at old problems at a time when the latter field is seeking solutions to changing demands. Some advocate a shift in priorities from heroic to preventive health care strategies. Many of these strategies involve behavioral changes. New modes of health service delivery, such as the family practice clinic or the health maintenance organization, are being explored; maximizing their efficacy is a problem in behavioral engineering. Likewise, technologic advances such as renal dialysis, may require massive behavioral change. Finally, as life expectancy lengthens, the special problems of the aged—in large measure behavioral—call for answers. Thus, physicians, psychologists, nurses, nutritionists, and other health care professionals have a natural, common interest in behavior, for it permeates every aspect of professional activity. New models for system design and for care must continuously address behavioral variables. Psychologists in particular ought seriously to examine the partnership of their discipline with medicine.

Medical psychology involves application of the principles of the science of behavior to problems in health. This field is concerned primarily with the role of behavior in health and disease. The idea that behavior and health are related is not new and is, in fact, almost self-evident. Exercise has been a prescription for the maintenance of health for a very long time, as has rest for the relief of illness. What is relatively new is the notion that behavior can be studied scientifically. Newer still is the idea that such a science might be applied to medicine. Indeed, this idea is young enough that the interface between psychology and medicine is not yet completely clear. A major purpose of this book is to explore this interface and to suggest some useful lines of pursuit.

Medical psychology is an applied science. Its procedures and postulates are based on data and subject to objective test and verification. Medical psychology proceeds mainly from laboratory based behaviorism, in this way differing markedly from traditional clinical psychology, which developed in the context of Freudian psychiatry and its permutations. The paradigm that guides this text assumes that behavior is caused and that its causes are at least theoretically knowable. The topic is thus the role of the laws of behavior in the treatment and prevention of disease.

The text is divided into four sections. First, there are several introductory chapters. In order to operate effectively in a medical setting, one must appreciate the medical way of thinking, which requires familiarity with the evolution of the discipline. A survey chapter on history introduces the field, then surveys contemporary practice in terms of the metatheory of medicine. A chapter on medicine as a social institution follows, with a chapter on behaviorism rounding out part one. The second section deals with interventionist medicine, or the process of attempting to cure disease. Chapters 4–10 outline the role of scientific psychology in the management and diagnosis of a variety of disorders. Part three addresses issues of prevention and such behavioral health hazards as smoking and substance abuse.

This book is directed first to psychologists and psychology students. Traditionally, they are the practitioners most likely to apply behavioral strategies to health. In addition, however, physicians are increasingly involved in this endeavor, a trend reflected in an increasing number of physician authored articles on behavioral topics. Physicians and medical students thus make up an equally pertinent audience. Other professional health care workers such as nurses, administrators, paramedics, and social workers, also will find this book relevant.

A few words must be spent here on terminology. This book is entitled *An Introduction to Medical Psychology,* though it might as easily have been called *An Introduction to Behavioral Medicine;* in fact, in the United States the latter title might be deemed more timely. Though the two terms have been used interchangeably, the latter, behavioral medicine, seems to be carrying the day. I think the trend is unfortunate and have chosen the less popular term, medical psychology, because it more accurately delineates the realm of endeavor denoted by the two: the clinical activities making up the field, and the supporting theories and paradigms, represent types of psychology, not types of medicine. Medicine is the province of physicians, and in common practice adjectives used before the term "medicine" define the activities of particular types of physicians.

The field of medical psychology is new and its boundaries are unclear. A major purpose of this book is to help define an emerging, exciting discipline. The relevance of behavioral principles to both intervention and prevention will be illustrated, I hope convincingly. A second purpose of the book is to introduce the uninitiated to medicine as a way of thinking, a social system, and a technical enterprise. Medicine represents one of the most fascinating products of our culture, filled at once with arcane rituals and dazzling technology, petty jealousy and great courage, astonishing folly and profound wisdom. Medicine is only partly understood from within and widely misconstrued from without. I hope after reading this book the nonphysician will have a clearer perception of the nature of medicine—a respect for its strengths and an understanding of its weaknesses. Finally, for the physician, the book may demonstrate the very rich possibilities for collaboration with psychology in the effort to improve health and function among the ill and to maintain health among the well.

# Acknowledgments

This book has been a very long time in development; hence, I have a great many people to thank. One hesitates to begin for fear of either running on for pages or omitting someone. With apologies to anyone I have neglected, I would like to express my gratitude first to people who critically read chapters. At the same time I would like to exonerate them from responsibility for any errors of fact or thought that survive, in all probability the result of not incorporating all their comments. The readers are Drs. John Dougherty, Jane Kotchen, Arnold Ludwig, Charles Matthews, Robert Straus, Dan Tynan, and an anonymous reviewer whose comments, early in the process, were of immeasurable benefit—thank you, whoever you are. While the text is fairly liberally referenced, I would like here to express a debt to several writers whose works were especially influential: Drs. René DuBos, Neal Miller, Edmund Murphy, E. Mansell Pattison, Hans Selye, B. F. Skinner (of course), Anne and Herman Somers, and especially E. A. Esper, whose *History of Psychology* should be much more widely read than it is. A scholar certainly cannot be blamed for the use others make of his efforts, but if there is anything of value in the pages to follow, these writers deserve much of the credit.

I would also like to thank colleagues at the University of Kentucky College of Medicine and the Veterans Administration Medical Center, Lexington, Kentucky, whose interest and support rendered the project achievable. I am grateful also to Mss. Betty Lawson, Juanita Vornhold, and Mildred Neal, whose clerical efforts were essential. Finally, I would like to express a special thanks to Dr. David B. Clark, who taught me, and a great many others, the realities of clinical medicine and, in my case, in a way non-physicians rarely experience. It is a privilege to work in his presence.

# PART I

# Introduction to Medicine and Psychology

This section is designed to orient the nonphysician to the discipline of medicine and the physician to a psychological approach to illness. The psychological approach favored is that of behaviorism (chapter 3 discusses this paradigm in detail). In subsequent sections, deviations from this point of view appear, but its relevance to many issues will be illustrated and it serves as the primary psychological focus.

The other two chapters making up this section address the field of medicine from different points of view. Chapter 1 briefly reviews the evolution of medicine to give the reader a sense of from whence the field has come, then addresses medical logic to help the reader appreciate the medical way of thinking, or the underlying paradigm. Chapter 2 likewise serves to orient the reader, but more in the area of practical patient-doctor behavior variables than in conceptualization or theory.

# 1

# History and Logic of Medicine

## History

The contemporary practice of medicine is the product of a very long evolution, beginning in prehistory. During this evolution a number of trends in medical thinking can be discerned and present practice shows their vestiges. For example, historical periods have differed in their relative reliance on empirical observation or on authority as determinants of acceptable practice. Emphasis on prevention of disease or curative technologies likewise has waxed and waned. Medicine is always bound to culture, and the prevailing philosophic winds affect the way doctors view their patients, patients their doctors, and how both conceive of disease. Finally, concepts of singular versus multiple causality of disease have preoccupied the medical establishment variously. This last point is especially pertinent to medical psychology because the variables it addresses form part of multiple causality models of disease.

In the present chapter, the logic of medicine as currently practiced is explored. To understand this logic or paradigm, some historical antecedents must be mentioned. Medicine began as a religious, priestly pursuit. The great Hippocrates advocated scientific or naturalistic views of disease, but models more spiritually colored held sway throughout most of the world until relatively recently. When we speak of medical science, then, we are discussing a product mainly of the last century. Before that time, effective procedures for curing illness were unknown and causal hypotheses were largely fantastic. The physician of the Middle Ages bore scant resemblance to his contemporary counterpart. Mettler describes the training of physicians as follows:

> The peculiar nature of medicine, through the twelfth to sixteenth centuries, can be understood only by realizing that the training of physicians was almost completely theoretic. There was no such thing as a laboratory and practically no contact with the sick. There was only one recognized method of treating a patient and that was according to the teachings of the three recognized medical authorities [Hippocrates, Galen and Avicenna]. No disagreement with their dicta was permissible. In place of observation and experiments, the appeal to authority and the use of logical method governed the teaching and practice of medicine. (Mettler, 1947: 361)

To single out a particular event as heralding the dawn of contemporary medical science is probably a vain pursuit. Harvey's demonstration of the circulation might be chosen, or Morgani's description of organ pathology, but the advance of scientific understanding in physiology and biology was a slow process of fits and starts. As regards the practice of medicine, however, the discovery of infectious agents and methods of treating the conditions they appeared to cause seems to occupy a very special position because it was here that the physician first tasted success in treating illness. In many ways, the experience with infectious disease set an agenda for years to follow and the contemporary logic of medicine owes much to the work of Pasteur, Koch and the other pioneers.

## THE MODERN THEORY OF INFECTIOUS DISEASE

Since antiquity people have recognized the phenomenon of contagion. Precisely how disease spreads remained a mystery until the nineteenth century, yet effective strategies of treatment and prevention were used long before mechanism was understood. In the mid-1800s, Ignez Semmelweis, working at the Vienna General Hospital, observed that maternal death from fever was much more frequent in one of the maternity wards than in the other. The process through which he solved this problem stands as a classic example of empirical method (Hempel, 1966). Semmelweis submitted a variety of hypotheses to experimental test by altering procedures in the affected ward. A chance event gave him the critical clue. One of his colleagues accidently cut himself on a scalpel that had been used during autopsy; he died of a fever quite like the one that was carrying off so many delivering mothers. Semmelweis reasoned that some aspect of the cadaveric matter introduced into his friend's bloodstream caused the illness. Since Semmelweis and his colleagues frequently came from the autopsy room to the delivery room, he concluded that the disease was being carried by staff. Accordingly, he required that anyone delivering babies first wash his hands in a solution of chlorinated lime. The maternal death rate dropped to the level of the other ward, which was staffed by midwives, who did not perform autopsy. What we see, then, is successful control of infection without knowledge of microorganisms and behavior change that eliminated an environmental contributor to illness.

The existence of microscopic organisms had been known for some time before their role in contagion was discovered. In the seventeenth century, Anton van Leeuwenhoek developed the microscope and recorded his observations of protozoa and bacteria. The role of such organisms in disease did not emerge all at once, though the possibility had occurred to a number of men over the years and speculation along these lines appears even in pre-Christian writing. In 1844 Agostino Bassi published *On Contagions*, which outlined his experiments with infection and sterilization and attributed smallpox and plague to "living parasites, animal or vegetable." Ten years later, Jacob Henle described tha anthrax bacillus in the blood of dead sheep and showed that organisms could be found in the stool of cholera victims. The elucidation of the role of bacteria in disease, however, made its greatest leap forward in the work of Pasteur and Koch.

> Until late in the nineteenth century disease had been regarded as resulting from a lack of harmony between the sick person and his environment; as an upset of the proper balance between yin and yang, according to the Chinese or among the four humors, according to Hippocrates. Louis Pasteur, Robert Koch and their followers took a far simpler and more direct view of the problem. They showed by laboratory experiments that disease could be produced at will by the mere artifice of introducing a single specific factor—a virulent microorganism into a healthy animal.
>
> From the field of infection the doctrine of specific etiology spread rapidly to other areas of medicine; a large variety of well-defined disease states could be produced experimentally by creating in the body specific biochemical or physiological lesions. . . . The ancient concept of disharmony between the sick person and his environment seems very primitive and obscure indeed when compared with the precise terminology and explanations of modern medicine. (DuBos, 1959: 21)

Pasteur demonstrated that certain diseases followed the introduction of microorganisms into the body. His early work in fermentation convinced him that these organisms could be transmitted by air and did not spontaneously generate in the fermenting substance. Relying on Pasteur's work, Joseph Lister introduced sterilization into the field of surgery. Toward the end of his life, Pasteur developed the treatment for rabies, isolated the microbial agents of anthrax in sheep and cholera in chickens, and introduced vaccinations against these diseases. Following Pasteur, Koch isolated the tubercle bacillus in 1882 and developed an antibiotic treatment for this disease in 1890. He demonstrated that the body is able to form antitoxins to certain bacterial toxins and thus to protect itself from the ravages of infection. Immunization against tetanus and diphtheria proceeded from this discovery.

As the nineteenth century drew to a close, a great number of specific etiologic organisms were isolated and the field of bacteriology came to great prominence. Mass immunization against infectious disease became possible and ever more effective antibiotic drugs were developed for treating infected persons. In a general way, one can say that microorganisms came to be viewed as the cause of disease and therapy was directed at their destruction.

The success in treating infectious disease resulted in an emphasis on singular, specific causes for disease and a search for cures specific to those causes. A naive formulation suggests that for any given disorder there must be one cause analogous to the tubercle bacillus. Such a formulation is naive for two reasons: first, the lesson of infectious disease is *not* that diseases have singular causes; second, even if they did, there is no reason to assume that other sorts of disease must have similar mechanisms. Let us look at both these propositions in more detail, first at the lessons to be learned from the infectious disease example.

It is popularly believed that the health of Western man is improving and that he is living longer. It is also generally believed that scientific medicine is responsible for this happy circumstance. Both these views are suspect (Powles, 1974). In the first place, though the incidence of infectious diseases has declined in the West, it began to do so long before the introduction of antibiotics or immunization. Outbreaks of infectious diseases are associated with crowded conditions and poor sanitation, circumstances that were rife during the early stages of the industrial revolution. In England, around the middle of the nineteenth century, social reformers mounted an attack on these problems for esthetic and humanitarian reasons having nothing to do with bacteriologic theory; a decline in death from infection followed immediately and continued downward. Likewise, increased longevity is largely an artifact of drastically reduced infant mortality: though in England and Wales life expectancy at birth increased from around 40 years in 1870 to around 65 years in 1970, life expectancy at age 45 has increased only slightly and, for men, has leveled off; moreover, this downward trend in infant mortality—from 150 to 20 per 1000 live births—began long before efficacious inoculation or antibiotic treatment, though the overwhelming bulk of infant deaths were caused by infection. All of this suggests that infection was on the wane before modern medicine began effectively to attack microbes: ''The introduction of inexpensive cotton undergarments easy to launder and of transparent glass that brought light into the most humble dwelling, contributed more to the control of infection than did all drugs and medical practices'' (DuBos, 1959: 220).

These historical examples should remind us that a wide range of environmental factors play a very significant role in the incidence of infectious disease. What Pasteur demonstrated in the laboratory is thus only partly analogous to what happens in the world. It is now clear that the microorganism is a necessary but not a sufficient cause of clinical disease, and Pasteur was aware of this constraint. Many people are exposed to the tubercle bacillus, but only a relative few contract TB. It is therefore incorrect to argue from the experience of infectious disease that diseases have singular causes. On the contrary, observation suggests that diseases are multiply caused. In the heydey of what came to be called the germ theory of disease, however, insufficient attention was paid to the issue of multiple causation as efforts toward identifying hypothesized singular causes were pursued.

What of other categories of disease? With the decline of infection in the West, the bulk of deaths have other causes, most notably cardiovascular disease and cancer. As a greater and greater proportion of the population survives to middle age, these diseases loom ever larger as problems with which medicine must deal. For these, the so-called chronic diseases, hypotheses of singular causality seem fruitless. The existing research has already identified a wide range of risk factors associated with these disorders. In the case of infection, it proved possible at least to identify a necessary cause, the agent. The chronic diseases may well have no single necessary cause and a very complex multifactorial model may be required. Different treatment implications follow from these ideas: for an infection like TB, identification of the necessary cause leads to an effective treatment even though complete understanding of cause is not attained; identification of a treatment for conditions lacking a necessary cause seems less likely, and in such disorders a preventive strategy based on risk factors identified epidemiologically may be more fruitful.

The naive formulation of infectious disease does not characterize the thinking of modern physicians. Yet there is a tendency in medicine to stress cure over prevention, and the training of practitioners, characteristically provided in tertiary care centers, serves to reinforce this notion. Even more worrisome is the prevalent belief that cures for various serious diseases are only a matter of time. The great health fantasy is a pill to cure cancer, high blood pressure, or whatever, and this fantasy proceeds quite naturally from the striking effects of medicines that control infection. Unfortunately, the man who says he does not intend to stop smoking because by the time he gets cancer there will be a cure reflects a naive faith in the universal applicability of the germ theory of disease, and this absurd faith is reinforced by an endless media glorification of the "miracles" of modern medicine. The reality is rather more sobering: the so-called miracles are confined in the main to diseases that collectively pose a relatively minor threat to contemporary man. Most of us will die of heart attacks, cancer, or a poorly understood entity called old age—miracle cures for these conditions are a long way off.

An awareness of multiple causality bears directly on the relationship between psychology and medicine because behavioral phenomena such as diet, exercise, and stress figure prominently in emerging multidimensional models of causality. Preventive medicine is behavioral in many respects. Immunization, a biological intervention, plays a major role in preventing infection, but the prevention of cancer seems likely to entail changes in population behavior patterns. Smoking cigarettes is one such parameter and abuse of the environment is another. There is evidence that pollution of the air is more than unsightly; it may be a risk factor in various diseases. Thus, a broad range of behavioral variables bear a relationship to health status and this link becomes increasingly evident as medicine becomes ever more dominated by chronic disease.

The idea that behavior relates to health is certainly not new. For as long as there have been doctors, there has been awareness that remedies require patients to take them. However, we have lacked a scientific approach to the problem of compliance with medical advice. It seems likely that to some degree the historical preoccupation with biological mechanisms of causation and with intervention at that level has reflected the important fact that knowledge of biology has vastly outstripped knowledge of behavior. Not surprisingly, therefore, systematic treatment of the behavioral aspects of medicine is largely a twentieth-century phenomenon for it had to await development of a science of behavior.

The physician thus began as a priest, invoking the Gods in hopes of curing the sick. In Hippocratic times, natural causes were suspected, but cures remained in the hands of fate. With Pasteur, action became possible and the impulse to identify the organism and wipe it out became characteristic of the physician. Contemporary medical thinking derives from this initial success. The impetus to act is very strong and this impetus interacts with the accumulation of knowledge in complicated ways. The following discussion of medical logic should bring to light some of these complexities.


LOGIC

In this century medicine is viewed as a scientific undertaking, and in the public mind the distinction between medical science and medical practice is nonexistent. This perception is inaccurate for two general reasons, one inevitable, the other not.

Medicine is first an art rather than a science because illness does not await scientific solutions. Doctors deal with sick patients whose conditions are not fully understood. In this situation, physicians may employ procedures that are not always firmly grounded in physiologic or pharmacologic science. Relying on the diagnosis, the doctor prescribes treatment whose efficacy is usually less than perfect and whose mechanism is often unknown. That some doctors seem better at this than others attests to the artistic, creative character of the process of medicine.

There is a second aspect to the artistic character of medicine. In the absence of perfect knowledge, one has no choice but to muddle through, yet it is essential to acknowledge just what one is doing and not assume that more is known than is, in fact, known. While scientific precision may be unattainable in medicine, it can be approximated to greater or lesser degrees in most clinical situations. Nevertheless, this goal is often not even attempted. This second reason that medicine is not scientific has to do with the attitudes characteristic of doctors, the clinical mentality; hence, it is important to understand this way of thinking and its social determinants. To this end I shall outline the logic of medical practice in somewhat idealized terms, then turn to the determinants of deviation from this ideal that occur in the day-to-day activities of clinicians.

## Ideal Logic of Medicine

### DIFFERENTIAL DIAGNOSIS

The heart of the practice of medicine is differential diagnosis. Characteristically this process is initiated by the patient's presentation of symptoms or complaints. The patient says, "There is something wrong with me." The doctor tries first to find out what is the matter, then to treat the condition. Next he observes the effects of the treatment. If the diagnosis is correct, the problem will go away. Otherwise, the doctor begins again and arrives at a new diagnosis, which leads to additional treatment and observation. This process continues until the patient is cured or dead. That, in simplistic outline, is how medicine is done. (I am assuming, for the sake of illustration, that the condition, A, can be cured with treatment provided that A is correctly identified. In many cases, of course, A may be known, treated in the best possible way, but persist.) A moment's reflection reveals that this process is not unique. The television repairman does roughly the same thing. Auto mechanics proceed similarly and the analogy is explicitly acknowledged by service stations that refer to diagnostic equipment and the like.

The diagnostic process has several sequential steps and generally parallels a single-subject A–B–A research design. The first step is information gathering, which entails listening to the patient's complaints, examining him to identify signs of disease, and ordering routine laboratory tests. The second step is formulating the differential diagnosis. Here the physician itemizes the various diagnostic possibilities. What known diseases could give rise to the symptoms of which the patient complains and to the signs the physician discovers through examination? The third step is diagnosis itself. Here the clinician applies a variety of laboratory tests or treatments, the outcome of which favor one or another of the diagnoses listed in the differential. This is an important distinction between expert and mediocre practice (and cost efficient versus wasteful practice). Diagnostic studies ought to be logically bound to the differential possibilities which should be evident from reading a well-kept medical record.

Once diagnosis is established, treatment follows; the results of the treatment feed back to the physician information about the diagnosis. In the analogy to the single-subject design, B is the treatment phase, whose consequences are the results of the experiment. If the treatment is ineffective, the hypothesis is not confirmed; that is, the diagnosis was incorrect and the doctor and patient find themselves still at A. Accordingly, another hypothesis is offered and a second treatment, C, is begun. This procedure is more or less protracted (A–B–A–C–A–D) depending on the complexity of the condition and the skill of the physician. In medicine, the consultation mechanism is the customary response to repeated disconfirmation of the diagnosis. That is, the physician will turn to someone with particular expertise once he realizes that the condition he faces goes beyond his knowledge base. Further hypotheses are then elaborated in consultation.

The procedure just outlined differs in an important respect from the single-subject design of experimental psychology. In general, the single-subject design assumes reversibility. That is, the application of treatment B leads to some change that will reverse once B is withdrawn. In medicine, this circumstance does not always obtain. If the suspected ailment is pneumonia, the treatment, B, is penicillin. If the treatment is effective, the condition is cured and removal of penicillin does not lead to relapse (reversal). In other circumstances, the analogy is closer. If the doctor suspects diabetes, the treatment may be insulin, but in this case removal of the treatment does lead to symptom recurrence. This difference in outcome reflects the peculiarities of different diseases and serves to remind us that biological events need not be isomorphic with conceptual schemas; at the same time, good fit between appearances and explanatory models may encourage us to draw incorrect conclusions about the disease process.

In the case of pneumonia, our single-subject outcome, the alleviation of the disorder with penicillin leads to the conclusion that penicillin is an effective treatment for this disease. Is this conclusion justified? On the basis of this single-subject paradigm, it actually is not because the treatment is confounded with an important variable in medicine, the passage of time. There is danger of the post hoc, ergo propter hoc fallacy in any A–B–A model in which A changes over time, independently of B; fortunately, this process characterizes a great many disease states. The biological reality is that the body, left to its own extraordinary devices, tends to fix itself. This fact has led to a great many incorrect inferences of therapeutic efficacy, and today controlled trials of any treatment are deemed essential in documenting its effectiveness.

MEDICAL SCIENCE

The discussion thus far has focused on the logic of the single clinician-patient transaction. This dyad fits into a broader enterprise and plays an essential role in it. In brief, the logic of medicine has as its ultimate goal etiologic diagnosis, or an ever more complete understanding of the mechanisms of disease. From such an understanding, treatments are offered that correct the underlying mechanisms and disease is cured or prevented. The process by which this result happens is evolutionary in character and is facilitated by some aspects of clinical practice and impeded by others. The facilitating and impeding variables have social as well as logical-scientific origin, but ideally the process entails a continual interplay between clinical procedure and basic science, with science verifying hypotheses arising in the clinic and clinical practice changing in response to scientific advance.

Clearly, the problems to be addressed emerge in the clinic in the day-to-day practice of medicine. The individual clinician, seeing patient after patient, notes commonalities. At various points in history, especially astute clinicians have noted commonalities that had not previously been described. When this happens, and the observations are published, a new diagnosis is born. George Huntington, for example, noted an unusual neurological syndrome that ran through certain families in his practice in New York. Benefiting from the experience of his father with these families, as well as from his own observations, he was able to see how this disease progressed through the life of the sufferer and how it afflicted a percentage of his offspring. In 1872, Huntington published a description of this disorder, calling it ''hereditary chorea''; we now call the condition Huntington's disease. Because of Huntington's observations, this malady is easily recognized by clinicians today, but description was the necessary precursor to identification of a distinct disease. Crisp comments on the activities of the clinician as follows:

> [T]he clinician, whatever his approach, cannot escape from doing research. His working life is spent accumulating and sifting information from case to

case and accordingly . . . shaping his approach to the classification and manipulation of the diseases he is encountering [1977, pp. 447-448].

In addition to having a descriptive function, clinical medicine generates treatment hypotheses. A physician may note that a particular drug is especially effective in one subgroup of persons having a disease but less effective in another group. Similarly, clinicians may note unexpected beneficial effects of a drug: prescribed for condition A, the medication may lead to improvement in condition B in some patients, causing the clinician to hypothesize a new treatment mechanism for condition B. Finally, theoretical considerations or clinical hunches may prompt doctors to try a treatment long before there is experimental evidence to support its use. This, in fact, was the only mechanism through which new treatments came into being until recent years.

All three of these routes have been followed in clinical medicine, but the next step—validating treatment efficacy through the more objective mechanism of the controlled double-blind study—is a late development. This method allows us to determine whether the treatment is effective for the targeted condition; then, highly specific indications and contraindications of the treatment are worked out. Experimentation can reveal under what conditions the treatment is effective. For example, treatment may be very effective in a percentage of the cases but ineffective in others, an outcome with important implications.

Syndromes are descriptions of signs and symptoms. They do not define etiology. In fact, the same syndrome may have very different causes. One way this circumstance is brought to light is the demonstration of differential effectiveness of a drug in the syndromatic population. This outcome allows us to identify subdivisions of the syndrome, one reactive to the treatment, the other not. With this information, clinicians are alerted to signs and symptoms that might differentiate the two subtypes. In this way, diagnoses change over time and are brought in closer and closer approximation to biologically meaningful categories. The ultimate result of this evolution is the etiologic diagnosis, that is, identification of a specific cause or collection of causes.

## Approximations to the Ideal

### CLINICAL URGENCY

Of course, this outline is not a perfect description of actual practice. Clinicians address practical and not abstract problems in facing the patient. The hypothesis, the diagnosis, is not reached in the relative leisure of scientific inquiry but in the sometimes frantic circumstances of human suffering. This urgency requires that a hypothesis of some sort be formulated even if the data are inadequate. Inevitably, some of these hypotheses are going to be incorrect or inadequate. The hypothesis, for example, may lead to an effective treatment whose mechanism of action is unknown or poorly understood. These clinical realities affect the quality of diagnoses as scientific hypotheses.

The aptness of the hypothesis is a function of the patient's symptoms and the state of knowledge about those symptoms. Symptoms and symptom complexes vary in their specificity and frequency. For example, acute pain in the right lower abdomen, with tenderness, fever, and overlying muscle spasm, leads quite readily to the hypothesis that the patient's appendix is infected; that is, this group of symptoms is rather rare in the absence of appendicitis. On the other hand, the symptom of headache is associated with encephalitis, brain tumor, poor reading light, and flu. Headache, then, is a nonspecific symptom. Clearly, the range of possible diagnoses, or hypotheses, and their associated probabilities of being correct are quite different in these two examples.

Diagnoses derived from symptoms differ also as to what they convey about etiology, or cause. This point is important because to the extent that the cause of a disease yielding the symptoms is known, treatment is likely to be facilitated. This general principal of medicine has exceptions but, theoretically the most efficacious treatments proceed from an understanding of etiology. For example, we know that tuberculosis is caused at least in part by the presence of the tubercle bacillus. This information resulted in a specific antibacterial treatment for TB. In the case of multiple sclerosis, on the other hand, the diagnosis does not lead to etiologic treatment because we do not know the cause. In this disease, in fact, diagnosis may lead to no treatment at all. Administration of morphine derivatives for the alleviation of pain associated with a vast array of conditions is an example of palliative, or symptomatic, treatment pursued independently of etiology; the use of psychotropic agents in psychosis is another. Though in general etiologic specificity is necessary for maximally effective treatment, this is not always the case. Some varieties of viral encephalitis have no treatment although the infectious agent is known. On the other hand, anxiety is a symptom very amenable to chemical modification though its etiology is mysterious. Finally, certain conditions of known cause are best treated symptomatically. Cholera, for example, is effectively treated by replacing depleted fluids and allowing the infection to run its course; antibiotics may be helpful but are not essential (Mann, 1975).

Thus, as scientific hypotheses, diagnoses vary considerably in the degree to which they fit a theoretical framework. The etiologic diagnosis represents the most elegant formulation in clinical medicine but in many practical situations is impossible to achieve. Accordingly, the clinician diagnoses in a syndromatic way and prescribes treatment that does not necessarily address etiology. At an even less theoretical level, the clinician may be able to offer only a palliative for the symptom. This symptomatic level of diagnosis is clearly of little scientific merit since it merely restates the patient's complaint in more abstruse language (the patient who has a headache may be diagnosed as showing cephalagia). Nevertheless, relief of symptoms is a useful goal. In general, then, practical utility rather than scientific elegance is the determining factor in diagnosis, and as scientific hypotheses diagnoses are variably useful.

## CLINICAL MENTALITY

The press of practical problems is one source of deviation from the ideal logic of medical practice and science. Another is the clinical mentality, which refers to both the cognitive style and the personal values of the typical clinician (Freidson, 1972). These characteristics have a discernible effect on the scientific status of medicine as practiced day to day, inevitably producing deviation from an ideal flow of information and modification of procedures in response to new information.

Freidson listed five cardinal attributes of the clinical as opposed to the theoretical-scientific mentality (1972). First, the clinician is prone to act, to intervene. This is what he is trained to do and in doing so he feels most fully realized in his professional role: "Successful action is to be preferred, but action with very little chance of success is to be preferred over no action at all" (p. 168). Second, the practitioner must believe in what he is doing. In fact, skepticism and detachment are antithetical to clinical work because so many clinical problems are ambiguous. One must believe in order to move ahead in a context of ambiguity. Implicit in both these attributes is a third: the clinician is a thoroughgoing pragmatist, much more interested in results and bottom lines than in theoretical explanations for results. Furthermore, he is more interested in results he has personally witnessed than in reported results of scientific studies. This emphasis on firsthand experience is a fourth clinical attribute and it is connected with the fifth. Clinicians tend to emphasize indeterminacy and uncertainty in work as opposed to lawfulness and regularity: "Whether or not that idea faithfully represents actual deficiencies in available knowledge or technique, it does provide the practitioner with a psychological ground from which to justify his pragmatic emphasis on first hand experience" (p. 169).

This description of the clinician is admittedly stereotypic, as are all such sketches, but it identifies tendencies common to a significant proportion of practitioners. These tendencies encourage resistance to change and a strain of self-justification in practice. In other words, to the extent that firsthand knowledge is essential, each practitioner is limited to an idiosyncratic subsample of the population, his own patients. If he has seen a treatment method work, he is reluctant to abandon it for an alternative therapy he has only read or heard about. Furthermore, because he relies on firsthand experience, selective perception is inevitable and can lead to erroneous belief in efficacy. Since belief is an essential ingredient in clinical function, the reliance on firsthand, subjectively assessed knowledge and the need to believe in his remedies combine to bias the clinician in the direction of exaggerated faith in his efficacy. This faith in turn mitigates against change proceeding from the basic sciences, particularly since the basic scientist lacks, by definition, the firsthand experience that the clinician values so greatly.

At their worst, these clinician attributes generate a totally unscientific medicine based on faith and lacking self-correction. Fortunately, such medicine is not characteristic of Western society. In general, medicine does progress in response to scientific advance and discovery, but the rate of change in clinical practice is probably slower than it could be and the clinician's tendency to trust his experience contributes to the perpetuation of less than optimal intervention. Murphy characterized this as superstitious thinking:

> In their attitude toward the pre-scientific era, scientists with the arrogance of the under furnished mind have been almost all guilty of . . . the bland assumption that anything seen, reported, done or argued about a long time in the past has automatically been discredited by the passage of time. One of the commonest accusations made against the common man in all ages up to what is pretentiously referred to as the age of reason (i.e. the eighteenth century) was that they were superstitious. The criticism is a fair one. But if it implies that we have emancipated ourselves from this defect, then there is a good deal more to say about the matter. . . .
>
> The lack of rigor in the evaluation of [scientific] evidence has meant that . . . the practice of medicine is riddled with superstitions both positive and negative in nature. . . . There must be countless thousands of doctors treating the common cold with penicillin (oral penicillin, because it troubles both doctor and patient less). Surgery for the peptic ulcer seems to be a matter of cyclic fashion and there is an implicit belief that by repetitions of the same four or five procedures . . . the new enthusiast may succeed where the older one has failed.
>
> Any new procedure does work well provided the proponent does not make the cardinal error of studying the subsequent fate of his patients.
>
> If we could take one of these practices, the use of penicillin for the common cold, as an example, the scientist would want to know if this procedure is rational. Is there any evidence that the organism is sensitive to the drug? No. Failing this, is there any empirical evidence from clinical trials that it has aborted the disease or reduced complications? No. Is there any evidence that the patient's morale is improved by the thought that something is being done for him? No. Why is it being used? A harsh critic might accuse those who use

it of professional, if not actual commercial, dishonesty. But could it be that those who use it do so to be on the safe side? This is surely the essence of superstition. Many do not believe that sitting 13 at a table causes misfortune, but they will not do it. Just to be on the safe side. But the medical superstition is worse. There is no evidence that any harm results from avoiding odd numbers of guests at table and, indeed, even numbers promote companionable dinner conversation. But there is a great deal of evidence that any treatment yet invented, starting with distilled water by mouth, may be harmful. Penicillin, in particular, has a small but definite risk attached to its use. It is a poor consolation when a patient dies of, or is made ill by, penicillin unnecessarily used, that he was the victim of an attempt of dubious value to protect him from some danger unspecified. (1976: 162–167)

Murphy's point lies at the heart of the clinical mentality. There is little doubt that much of physician behavior is superstitious (so, incidentally, is much of psychologists' behavior). It is superstitious in that it is based on selective perception of the potentially relevant data, such that supporting facts are noted and nonsupporting ones are ignored. This mechanism is commonly described in social psychology; Allport's *Nature of Prejudice* (1954) comes to mind. It is unnerving, however, to see it operating as a matter of routine among those making decisions about health and treatment. Murphy's example is not an isolated one. There are many treatments administered for which the rational basis, the supporting scientific data and theory, is equivocal, extremely shoddy, or lacking altogether. Coronary bypass surgery may be a rather drastic case in point (Burch & Giles, 1976). The interesting question then arises, How does this happen?

Few physicians in either ancient or modern times have practiced research or have been trained in the discipline of experimental and statistical controls; if modern physicians were so trained, it would be impossible for drug firms to distribute a continuous stream of "miracle" drugs, of which many are presently found to be therapeutically ineffectual and some allergenic or even fatal. Most physicians, in modern as in ancient times, follow recipes and clinical demonstrations of manual and instrumental techniques. This situation is described by calling the practice of medicine an *art*, and speaking of anatomy, physiology, biochemistry, pharmacology, etc. as *supporting* or *basic medical sciences*. (Esper, 1964: 109)

Physicians tend to trust their clinical instincts, but the potential fallibility of this way of thinking is clear: "Over forty years ago, Lewis warned about 'the manifest tendency which is traditional, for the medical profession to exaggerate the accuracy of its subjective methods'" (Murphy, 1976: 172). This tendency remains, and Becker and associates' classic study of medical school teaching revealed that these attitudes are fostered very early in the training of physicians, with great emphasis placed on clinical experience, or firsthand knowledge of disease in individuals, as opposed to book knowledge (1961).

The clinical mentality, like any other, does not evolve in a vacuum. I have suggested that training encourages it, but there is a more fundamental generative mechanism. The clinical mentality is an adaptive response to social realities. In looking at the history of medicine we saw that the physician's role was traditionally associated with, and in fact derived from, the role of priest. The physician is consulted by persons in distress, who generally are not interested in the elegancies of scientific theory and who want to believe in the physician's remedies. Patients want help. This expectation serves to reinforce the clinician's tendency to do something, anything, in the face of patient demand. In fact, were the clinician perfectly scientific in his attitude, he would be immobilized since so little is known with surety about disease. The practical man, the clinician, applies treatments whether or not their efficacy is understood. The theoretical man, the scientist, goes back to the laboratory to ask why. But while he is exploring, the patient waits.

The evolution and maintenance of the physician's role represents an interesting bit of cultural history, the effects of which clearly are not entirely negative. Given, on the one hand, the huge estimated proportion of illness that is psychosomatic and, on the other, the documented power of such mechanisms as suggestion and self-fulfilling prophecy, untold quantities of human suffering no doubt have been alleviated through the delusion, maintained by both patient and doctor, that the latter knows what he is doing. The available data relative to this topic suggest that optimistic doctors who convey the notion that their remedies are efficacious get better results than do less enthusiastic users of the same remedies. Although some degree of selection bias cannot be ruled out here, the role of suggestion seems plausible.

## Implications for Psychologists

What do the vagaries of medical practice mean for the psychologist working in medicine? For clinicians trained in the traditional manner, the clinical mentality is familiar and they have little difficulty relating to the physician's frame of mind. Meehl gave the following example:

> A psychologist tells me that he is perfectly confident that psychotherapy benefits psychotic depression (a question open on available data), his reason being that his personal experience shows this. But this same psychologist tells me that he has never seen a single patient helped by shock therapy. (Such a statement that he has never seen a *single patient* helped by shock

therapy, can only be attributed to some sort of perceptual or memory defect on his part.) When challenged by the published evidence indicating that shock is a near specific for classical depression, he says that these experiments are not perfect and further adds, "you can prove anything with experiments. (Believe it or not, these are quotations!)" (1973: 265–266)

A psychologist of this type is not likely to be disturbed by such physician statements as "Often, in my experience, patients like this have responded well to . . . " since his Rorschach interpretations are identical in form. By contrast, the psychologist (physiologist, biochemist, or sociologist) trained along more experimental lines may find himself in turmoil as he tries to classify remarks by his medical colleagues into fact-speculation-fantasy categories. When a surgeon says, "I know that radical mastectomy is the best treatment for carcinoma of the breast," he is using "know" in a very different way from that of the sociologist who says, "I know that the frequency of below-subsistence income is greater among southern than among northern blacks." The difference has to do with the criteria of evidence and one can get into serious trouble when the parties to a discussion use disparate criteria for what is fact and what is not. Mutual sensitivity to this issue is essential to successful collaboration and such sensitivity is emerging as psychologists learn more about medicine and begin more seriously to address questions that touch on clinician concerns. The role of behavioral variables in disease is a borderline area between accepted clinical practice and basic research. And it is precisely at the border between medical science and practice that scientific psychology can play a useful role.

Ideally, the psychologist is trained in research and uses the criteria of evidence associated with basic science. Yet the subject matter renders psychologists who study behavioral processes at the macrolevel sympathetic to the clinician's notions of indeterminacy. If the subject matter is the behavior of organisms, the sort of precision expected in chemistry or even physiology is unattainable no matter how elegant the conceptual model. Psychologists live at the $p < .05$ level of certainty, which seems to be about the level of confidence that the practitioner, in moments of reflection, can place in his remedies. Thus, the behavioral scientist is unique among basic scientists in studying a subject matter whose level of complexity, particularly in terms of uncertainty, approximates that of the clinician. He also frequently employs the single-subject design, which, as we have seen, is an imperfect but approximate analogue to the clinician's day-to-day activity. Finally, the psychologist approaches problems that are central to health, problems of behavioral control. Thus, the emerging collaboration between psychologists and physicians seems natural and inevitably productive once the traditional language and paradigm barriers are overcome.

## Conclusion

This chapter began with a look at history, then outlined the logic of medicine in ideal terms and noted some causes for deviation from the ideal. The press of practical problems is a major source of such deviations; the clinical mentality, another. This way of thinking can be viewed as an adaptive response to clinical realities and to the social pressures these realities engender. Our understanding of disease is incomplete and the clinician must be willing and able to act on incomplete understanding. Psychologists also inhabit a domain in which knowledge is woefully fragmentary and thus they share the physician's dilemma. Collaboration between the two disciplines requires mutual appreciation of the limits of knowledge, the need to believe in practice, and the necessity to remain open to new data and to change practice accordingly. The emerging data on the importance of behavioral factors in disease are prime examples of developing knowledge suggesting practice change. The following treatment of interventionist and preventive medicine describes some of this evidence in detail.

# 2

# Medicine as a Social Institution

In discussing the field of medicine thus far, I have focused in the main on illness as a biological event and medical practice as a response to that class of event. Medicine views itself essentially in this way. Physicians see themselves as offering more or less concrete services in response to more or less clearly definable biological problems. That, however, is only part of the story. Medicine is also a social institution, and the variables determining its function are determined only partly by biological phenomena labeled diseases. Political, social, cultural, and economic factors play an important and often ignored role in medical practice and a complete understanding of the field must address these variables.

The social character of medicine can be discussed at two levels. First, the healing act is social in the sense that it involves a transaction between two people. Ample evidence suggests that a very significant proportion of the outcome variance in such transactions cannot be ascribed to the biological manipulations included in the medical paradigm. Placebo effects are an example at the clinical level of this social aspect of medicine. In addition, medicine is social in an institutional sense that transcends and systematically affects every one-to-one interaction between patient and practitioner. This institutional level of social influence operates in both formal and informal ways, formally via organizations such as county medical societies, licensing boards, and the American Medical Association and informally through patient referral networks and more or less organized group practice structures. These institutional variables have specific effects on the health care patients receive; for example, quality control exerted by licensing boards presumably protects the patient from incompetent practitioners.

In the following pages we shall explore medicine as it functions in our society. This discussion looks first at the social structure of medicine, the preeminence of the physician in that structure, and the economic implications of various delivery mechanisms. Second, the doctor–patient dyad is examined as a social phenomenon in which role expectations play an important part, independent of the biological factors of disease cure or prevention.

## Social Structure of Medicine

To understand contemporary medicine in the United States as a social institution, we must address two general questions: how is care delivered and how is it paid for? In answer to both questions we shall find a variety of arrangements, each of which uniquely affects the care delivered. Since the doctor is at the center of these issues, let us begin by briefly considering the evolution of his social role and his status today.

### THE DOCTOR AS A SOCIAL FIGURE

In contemporary Western society, health care and medicine are virtually coextensive. When one feels unwell, one calls the doctor, and the vast majority of us would never think of calling anyone else. This circumstance is a distinctly modern phenomenon. In earlier eras, physicians were but one class of healer and not the most popular. In medieval times, barber-surgeons, herbalists, and grocers greatly outnumbered university trained physicians, whose practice was confined largely to an elite class. Accessibility no doubt played a role in this situation, but an equally important factor was the inefficacy of medieval medicine. If the lord of the manor contracted pneumonia and survived while his serf did not, the difference in outcome was undoubtedly due to differences in diet and lodging. The bloodletting and purgatives of the physician were in no sense more effective than the herbs of folk practitioners and may have been worse.

With the development of scientific medicine in the nineteenth century, this circumstance changed radically. Once causative agents were discovered, treatment entered a new phase so that medical ministration began to affect the course of disease while folk medicine remained at the level of symptom alleviation: "Distinction between physician and so-called quack needed no longer to rest on the academic certification of the superiority of one superstition over another" (Freidson, 1972: 16). The increasingly evident superiority of medical over other sorts of treatment set the stage for the establishment of medical hegemony over health care.

A related development that began in the nineteenth century and accelerated dramatically in the twentieth was mass education. Medicine is a consulting profession. To survive economically, the doctor must be sought out by persons willing to pay for his services. Demonstrating that the services are effective and disseminating this information attracts clients. Historically, as the population became literate, increasing numbers of people were made aware of what doctors could do and the reputation of the profession increased.

The hegemony of physicians in health care thus reflects technical achievement and public awareness of such achievement. In addition, however, the procedure of professional licensing insures a monopoly of doctors over health care by aligning the profession with the state and outlawing practice by nonphysicians. The licensing statutes are usually defended as being in the public interest by preventing incompetents from practicing. To what extent they actually accomplish this end is the subject of considerable debate (Derbyshire, 1969; Gross, 1978; Krause, 1977). In many jurisdictions, for example, incompetence is not a stipulation for censure and "even where incompetence is specified in the law as a basis for disciplinary action, disciplinary procedures in nearly all states are so weak and so weighted in favor of the doctor that effective action is virtually impossible" (Somers, 1977a: 29). Whatever their quality control effects, licensing statutes serve the economic and status interests of the medical profession by restricting entry and by fine-tuning supply to demand. For example, in 1939 the Illinois licensing board enacted a citizenship requirement in response to the influx of physicians from Europe, a requirement bearing no obvious relationship to technical competence (Moore, 1961).

The argument that licensing protects the public from untrained practitioners implies that only the initiated are competent to judge the quality of doctors' services. It follows that the profession itself must monitor physicians, and self-regulation is one of the essential elements of professionalism. What we have then is a licensed (state protected) monopoly that is essentially free of state regulation, the state boards characteristically consisting almost exclusively of physicians. The regulated and the regulators are thus one and the same. The consumer is notably left out of this picture.

The medical monopoly also enjoys a unique flexibility in the area of fees. In other cases of licensure, fees are negotiated with and set by the licensing authority (e.g., public utility commissions), or they are competitively responsive to market forces. Neither circumstance obtains in

medicine. If the telephone company were to insist that the state not interfere with its fee structure, one can safely assume the request would fall
on deaf ears or elicit vigorous consumer protest. The argument has been
made that the situation with physicians is different because they are independent of one another (like private detectives), subject to market
forces, and hence not in a monopoly position. This is nonsense, of
course, since market forces are held off by bans on advertising doctors'
fees, which policy until very recently was enforced by medical societies
on rather vague grounds of ethics. As Somers commented, "It would be
hard to find another major United States industry (with the possible exception of organized crime) that has not had to submit to the discipline
either of the market place or public regulation. The result—uncontrolled
growth and pluralism verging on anarchy—should not be surprising"
(1977b: 19–20).

Medicine's peculiar status reflects the traditional view of physicians
as altruists to whom monetary gain is immaterial. This presumption
derived in part from the historical fact that the physician was traditionally a gentleman and thus sufficiently wealthy to be unconcerned with
money matters. Such men were, however, a small minority serving the
rich. With the rise of capitalism, mass education, broader distribution of
wealth—and improving medical technology—demand for physicians'
services increased throughout the social hierarchy. Physicians began to
be trained in larger numbers and to come from the middle class, and entrepreneurial medicine was born. The model of altruistic gentleman-
scholars ceased to fit reality, though licensing bodies operate as though
this situation still existed. I am not suggesting that physicians are con-
spiring to rob the public, but they are human beings, subject to the same
contingencies that control the behavior of other human beings and current licensing provisions—notably self-regulation—do not necessarily
work in the direction of the public good.

Another consequence of the preeminence of physicians in matters of
health is their professional control over health delivery mechanisms and
personnel, the paradigm case being the relationship between the doctor
and the nurse in the hospital setting (Stein, 1967). The relationship between doctors and other health care personnel would appear simple
enough at first glance, with doctors at the top of the pyramid and
everyone else occupying roles below them in terms of prestige, money,
and autonomy. That is, in fact, a fairly accurate description, but there is
a great deal of clouding in the system due first to the tendency for workers
throughout the medical care system to define themselves as professionals
and second to a psuedo-egalitarian development of recent years termed
the team concept (Freidson, 1972).

The professionalism of nurses, laboratory technicians, and other
health workers is in a fundamental sense a sham because the essence of

professionalism is self-regulation and autonomy. As I noted earlier, this privilege is accorded to doctors by the state, but for others in health delivery, the so-called allied health professionals and nurses, self-regulation is only partial and subject to physician review and supervision. Put very simply, only doctors can write orders for patient care and since patient care is what the whole system is about, physicians are clearly the ultimate authority. To the extent that, nurses and technicians operate autonomously, they do so at the discretion of the doctor and that mandate can be quickly withdrawn.

The health care team is a fairly recent innovation that nominally represents a diffusion of authority and a democratization of decision-making. In fact, this arrangement amounts to, at best, a benign, as opposed to an autocratic dictatorship and at worst a confusing mockery of group decisionmaking. Since the physician has all the prerogatives, it does not much matter what the team thinks unless the physician happens to agree. This is as it must be given the current institutional structure because along with ultimate authority comes ultimate responsibility: if the surgery fails, the team is not going to end up in court.

Within this hierarchical structure, clinical psychologists occupy a peculiar position. Since they generally carry the title doctor and may wear white coats, they enjoy some reflected glory and are in certain settings deferred to by other nonphysician staff. In outpatient solo practices, furthermore, they are licensed in some states as autonomous service providers, but the service is carefully defined as nonmedical. Even in hospitals, there seems to be a generally acknowledged collection of activities in which psychologists engage that are different from what M.D.'s do and, most important, are deemed sufficiently esoteric as to be beyond the evaluative ken of laymen—including physicians in this context. One ought not, however, to exaggerate the autonomy or power of psychologists in mental health. In outpatient practices, while autonomy is not obviously dependent upon physician goodwill, it is still clearly circumscribed; in hospitals, psychologists' autonomy is contingent. Clearly, medical hegemony in the area of mental health is not seriously threatened by psychologists or anyone else, for that matter, except perhaps by disgruntled patients or by psychiatrists themselves. Thomas Szasz comes to mind in the latter regard.

We see, then, that the physician has over the years come to occupy the preeminent position in matters of health and until lately he has exercised this role with virtually complete autonomy and almost no accountability for either quality of service or level of fees. In recent years an increasing federal presence has evidenced itself in three watershed statutes: Titles XVIII and XIX of the Social Security Act of 1965, Medicare and Medicaid; Public Law 93-641, the National Health Planning and Resources Development Act of 1974; and Public Law 92-603, which established within HEW an Office of Professional Standards Review to coordinate the establishment of formal professional standards review organizations (PSROs) to assess care delivery in all settings receiving money under Medicare and Medicaid. These statutes put a federal presence in the middle of the private health care delivery system via payment of professional fees and monitoring of services being paid for. In addition, PL 93-641 mandated the formation of regional planning bodies to oversee the allocation of resources into such functions as hospital construction or purchase of new technology.

In the next section, the overall structure of health care delivery in this country is described. In the process, some of the forces that led to the legislative initiatives just mentioned will become clearer. To anticipate, however, there is a serious problem with regard to distribution of services and cost increases. In the minds of many federal officials, a planning effort is needed; these laws represent the first steps in that direction.

## HEALTH CARE DELIVERY SYSTEMS

Health care in the United States generally follows a three-tiered structure of primary, secondary, and tertiary care. These three differ in persons delivering care, in locations where doctor-patient transactions take place, in types of services delivered, and in problems addressed.

Primary care, with which most people are familiar, includes prenatal checkups, deliveries, general pediatric care including inoculations, routine medical attention for adults, health monitoring via annual physicals and chest X rays, and the like. Doctors providing primary care include general practitioners and those in pediatrics, gynecology, obstetrics, family practice, and internal medicine. Services are offered in hospital outpatient clinics, neighborhood clinics, private offices, and private group practice settings.

A recent innovation in the area of primary care is the physician's assistant (PA) and the nurse practitioner. These are non-M.D. professionals trained to do a variety of tasks traditionally done by physicians. Reliance on such personnel evolved in response to the increasing demand for primary care in the face of increasing specialization among physicians. If one compares, for example, medical graduates in 1930 with graduates in 1955, the percentage specializing rose from about 30 to over 75 (Budde, 1973). The physician extenders hold promise, particularly in redressing the chronic problem of underserved populations in certain geographic locations. These professional roles, however, are still evolving and there is a good deal of professional rivalry between nurses and PAs. Also, training standards for PAs are in a state of flux and procedures for certification and licensure are wholly inadequate. The legal status and autonomy of both groups have yet to be clarified, a situation rendered urgent because of the current malpractice furor. At the present time the health care system is only beginning to use these people effectively. One anticipates that PAs and nurse practitioners will play an ever increasing role throughout American health care in coming years (Ford, 1975).

Secondary care addresses problems somewhat more complex than those seen by primary care providers. Generally, patients are referred for secondary care. One's family physician, for example, may find that surgery is needed and send the patient to a surgeon, who is the secondary care provider in this case. The community or general hospital is frequently the site of secondary care since these problems may require an initial period of hospitalization for diagnosis and/or treatment. Followup care may be offered by the secondary care provider on an outpatient basis or may be handled by the primary provider. Physicians involved in secondary care are specialists such as surgeons, urologists, and psychiatrists. The major difference between secondary and primary care is the more limited focus of the former on problems of relatively infrequent occurrence. Secondary care, by definition, is not care for the total patient. A frequent source of complaint is the increasing specialization of medicine so that often there appears to be no one who cares for the total patient. The growing present emphasis on primary care, particularly family practice, is in part a response to this awareness, as is the evolution of PA and nurse practitioner roles.

Tertiary care is the province of superspecialists. Here the care focus is extremely narrow and usually highly technical. The conditions treated are rare and complicated. Microsurgery and organ transplantation would be examples of tertiary care. The setting of tertiary care characteristically is a university hospital or one of the more eminent private hospitals such as the Mayo Clinic. Tertiary care is expensive and directed toward a relatively small fraction of the total population who have exotic illnesses or more common illnesses that require exotic therapy. Heart disease is virtually epidemic, but heart transplants are infrequent. One should also note that as tertiary procedures become better understood and information about them spreads, they tend to move into the province of secondary care. For example, renal dialysis may be available in general hospital settings in coming years.

These three levels of care form the structure of American medicine. The enterprise as a whole lacks anything even approximating a rational three-way allocation of resources. Heavy emphasis on secondary and tertiary care is at the heart of what is called the crisis in health care in this country. Stated very simply, very large segments of the population—particularly the poor, residents of rural areas, and people in cities experiencing suburban flight and inner decay—have insufficient access to primary care. While in 1973 the overall physician-patient ratio in the United States was approximately 150 per 100,000 population, the effective ratio in different locations ranged from fewer than 50 physicians in some rural areas to over 230 in urban locations (AMA, 1973). Even within urban centers, different populations are very unevenly served: in portions of New York City, for example, there is 1 private doctor for every 200 persons, while in other parts of the city the ratio is closer to 1 per 12,000 (Kennedy, 1972). Solving this distribution problem is perhaps the single greatest challenge facing medicine in the 1980s.

In addition to problems of distribution and overspecialization, rising costs are plaguing patients in the United States. The most frequent cause of personal bankruptcy in the United States is medical bills (Rosser & Mossberg, 1977), and cost increases in the health care sector over the past several decades have outstripped hikes in all other major costs. With these facts in mind, let us turn now to the issue of economics: who pays what to whom?

### Fee-for-Service Medicine

The traditional method of paying for health care in the United States is the fee-for-service system. Nearly 80% of all American physicians are paid this way (Parker, 1974). In fee-for-service practice, the patient pays the doctor a fee that theoretically reflects the amount of service he has received. The concept of amount of service is vague, encompassing time spent, the complexity of the procedure, the prestige and/or skill of the practitioner, and a range of medically irrelevant but personally important factors such as the decorations in the office or the location of the facility. The fee also reflects the doctor's overhead, which is itself determined by national, regional, and local economic factors, the location and appointments of the office or clinic, and the doctor's managerial skills as a small (or large) businessman. Finally, the fee may be adjusted by the doctor for a variety of personal, humanitarian, or other reasons: so-called professional courtesy is traditionally extended to other doctors and their families, for example, the lost revenue presumably being made up by nondoctors and their families, and physicians may charge reduced fees to patients who are in financial difficulty.

The fee-for-service system grew up under laissez-faire capitalism and reflects the conventional values and wisdom of the bourgeoisie. Just as one paid the blacksmith to shoe one's horse's, one paid the doctor (now the podiatrist) to cut off one's corns. This free market model never operated perfectly in medicine, however, because of the special relationship between doctor and patient and because, as noted earlier doctor's fees are not usually made public. The suitability of this model is now being questioned in many quarters.

Efficacious medicine is of very recent origin and much of what is efficacious is also expensive. In an attempt to defray rising medical costs, insurance programs sprang up under a variety of auspices. Some are profit-making ventures; others are nonprofit. Some are government run; others are privately operated. In general, health insurers reimburse the patient for some portion of his medical expenses or pay the provider directly. Insurance companies are thus an add-on to the traditional fee-for-service model and act to offset the spiraling costs of health care by spreading the financial burden.

A great deal has been written about U.S. health insurance and its prospects for the future. Hetherington and associates, for example, examined contemporary health insurance and discussed the extent to which the industry has lived up to its implicit promise to protect the individual from ruinous major medical expenses and to lessen the financial impact of routine medical care (1975). The performance of insurance in these regards is complicated to evaluate because health insurance refers to an extremely heterogeneous group of plans covering different types of people and different types of service. Perhaps the most important thing to note about the current fee-for-service plus insurance model is that a very significant proportion of the population has no insurance coverage. Surveying the situation in the early 1970s, Mueller reported that 41 million Americans under age 65 had no insurance covering hospitalization and 42 million had no coverage for surgery (1975). Looking at the problem from the point of view of dollar flow, in 1974 about 65% of all medical bills were paid by third parties, insurers of one sort or another (Worthington, 1975); thus, about a third of all health costs were paid out of pocket. As might be expected, the uninsured are not a random sample of Americans but tend to cluster among the poor, the rural, the marginally employed, and ethnic minorities—in short, the have-nots.

Health insurance holders themselves have widely different benefits. It is instructive to read a policy or two to determine just what the company will and will not pay for. The reality is that the coverage offered in most health insurance packages is not complete. There may be upper limits per annum; deductibles; exclusions; little or no coverage for routine physicals and other preventive services; or limited coverage for outpatient visits, drugs, and/or laboratory fees. Also, the amount paid for a health care delivery event is usually limited to what is "reasonable and customary," a figure complexly and, for the insured, mysteriously determined. In practical terms, if the doctor charges more than the amount the insurance company deems reasonable and customary, the patient makes up the difference. Since most patients have no idea what the doctor is going to charge them, when a discrepancy occurs it is almost always after the fact. The implication of partial coverage is clear: even for the insured, health care is not free after the monthly premiums have been paid. Senator Kennedy summed up the situation in the early 1970s: "The fact is that health insurance coverages in America are riddled with holes, and they all add up to the same thing for American families: less protection than they think they have and more expense than they can afford. Every story of financial hardship . . . involves a failure of insurance coverage" (1972: 55).

Proposals for national health insurance have been a part of the U.S. political scene since World War I and recent plans seem to be motivated largely by the problem of inadequate coverage. The enactment of Medicare and Medicaid in 1965, over the howling protests of organized medicine, was a step toward better coverage for people over 65 and those with incomes below the poverty line. The difficulties with these programs are legion and will not be discussed here. Instead, let me quote one critic of national health insurance proposals:

> The proposals for National Health Insurance take for granted the wisdom of our current approaches to the pursuit of health, and thereby insure that in the future we will get more of the same. These proposals will simply make available to the non-insured what the privately insured get now: a hospital-centered, highly technological, disease oriented, therapy-centered medical care. The proponents have entirely ignored the question of whether what we now do in health is what we should be doing. They not only endorse the status quo, but fail to take advantage of the rare opportunity which financial crises provide to re-examine basic questions and directions. The real irony is that real economizing in health care is probably possible only by radically re-orienting the pursuit of health. (Kass, 1975: 41)

Sponsorship Medicine

A second model of health care delivery in the United States is that of sponsored services. Here an institution provides health care to a defined population without cost to the recipients. The care provided may be complete or partial, inpatient or outpatient, limited to certain categories of disease or comprehensive. Certainly the largest domestic example of this model is the Veterans Administration, whose 171 hospitals, 84 nursing homes, 19 domiciliaries, and over 200 clinics provide care to eligible veterans and, with many limitations, their dependents. State and county hospitals in many localities perform a similar function for indigent patients. On a much smaller scale, some corporations have in-house physicians who care for employees, but such services usually are limited to job related illness and injury and do not cover dependents. Some labor unions have established medical care programs for their members, building and staffing their own hospitals and clinics.

The sponsorship mode has several key attributes that set it off from other approaches. First, the physicians and other care providers in these systems are employees of the sponsoring agency. They receive salaries or wages and usually do not have managerial responsibilities. Patients in these systems generally are covered completely and do not have other insurance. The quality of care provided is maximally dependent on the largesse of the sponsoring agency since the health care system itself has no way of generating revenue. If "the Veterans Administration is one of the most impressive health care systems in the world" (Rosser & Mossberg, 1977: 62), certainly county and state hospitals in many locales represent the worst. Powerful unions, for example, the Alaska Teamsters, have spent large sums to build what are reported to be exemplary health care facilities, but this form of sponsored health care is dependent upon the affluence of the sponsor. In state sponsored systems, shifting political winds and priorities translate very directly into increased or decreased staff-patient ratios, modernization or deterioration of facilities, and so forth.

### Health Maintenance Organizations

The health maintenance organization (HMO) is a modality for health care delivery that is growing in importance. The HMO has attributes of both fee-for-service and sponsored systems and takes a number of forms. Basically, however, the HMO concept involves voluntary subscription or membership and prepayment at a fixed rate for complete or nearly complete coverage of all health needs. The subscriber is entitled to outpatient medical care, usually at a clinic operated by the HMO, and to inpatient care either in a cooperating hospital at which HMO physicians have attending privileges or in a hospital owned and operated by the HMO. As with the sponsored modality, physicians and other staff are employees of the HMO; their income thus is not directly related to care delivery. Unlike the sponsored modality, however, the patient pays for services, but at a fixed rate rather than at a fee-for-service rate. The rate depends on the management expertise of the HMO personnel and the actual costs of delivering services to subscribers. As with any other type of insurance, the HMO spreads risk among subscribers. Unlike conventional insurance, however, the provider of care and the insurer are one and the same.

The idea of prepayment for medical care dates back to the 1930s in the United States. Organized medicine has consistently opposed prepayment plans, as well as all other types of health insurance, at least initially: "The AMA has opposed every change in health-care service, dating back to the formation of the Mayo Clinic in the 1870's when the Mayo doctors were not allowed to join the AMA because they dared to practice as a group" (Gumbiner, 1975: 19). Rosser and Mossberg noted that "for many years the AMA actively subverted Blue Cross by expelling doctors hired under group health plans and threatening to stop intern-training programs in associated hospitals, thus pressuring hospitals to turn away patients referred from physicians in group plans'' (1975: 64). This policy led to indictment of the AMA on criminal charges of conspiracy in 1938. More recently, lobbying by the AMA led to the passage of laws preventing the founding of prepayment plans without the support of 51% of the practicing physicians in the state; these laws still stand in many states.

The HMO movement gained momentum with passage of Public Law 93-222, the Health Maintenance Organization Act of 1973. Briefly, the law provided funds for feasibility studies and startup of HMOs by interested groups of physicians, consumers, or insurers. Perhaps the most important provisions, however, established the preeminence of federal law over restrictive state statutes in matters of health care delivery and mandated that employers of over 25 persons must allow an HMO alternative in employee funded health insurance if such an alternative is available in the region. Passage of this law ignited interest in HMOs, but their impact in absolute numbers of patients served remains small. About 5 million people currently receive health care through HMOs.

## ECONOMIC INCENTIVES

Let us take a moment here to look at how economic incentives operate in each of these care delivery models. Let us assume that, other things being equal, people—doctors, patients, insurance companies, and everyone else involved in health care—will tend to engage in behavior that brings money in and to resist behavior that causes money to flow out. Let us also assume that the goal of medicine is to keep people well. It is obvious that from the point of view of economic incentive, the various care delivery models operate differently vis-à-vis this goal.

In fee-for-service practice, the doctor's incentive is to do as many procedures as possible. The economics of the fee-for-service system is piecework. Since healthy people do not require services, the economics of fee-for-service medicine encourage illness. In situations where there is ambiguity, where the patient might or might not be ill, the incentive is to diagnose illness and treat it. Furthermore, the treatment to be rendered should be as expensive as possible. For the patient, the incentives operate in the opposite direction: it is best not to be ill. Staying well may include periodic visits to the doctor for checkups, inoculations, and so on, but these procedures cost money so there is a dilemma from the economic point of view. Since the bill for preventive services is a surety and the possibility of illness without them only a possibility, the economic incentive is against preventive health activities. Even when ill, the patient may tend to deny illness and hope it will go away. Thus, in fee-for-service medicine illness is economically advantageous from the doctor's point of view: from the patient's point of view, health is advantageous but preventive measures are disadvantageous. From a purely economic perspective, then, fee-for-service medicine is not optimally designed for health maintenance.

The introduction of health insurance into the fee-for-service system has had a number of economic effects. For instance, with few exceptions insurance packages cover inpatient treatment much more completely than they cover outpatient. This feature encourages hospitalization for services that could easily be provided on an outpatient basis. Such hospitalization is clearly to the economic advantage of the insured patient, but makes no direct economic difference to the doctor. It is, however, to the doctor's economic advantage to keep the patient happy lest he go to a different doctor; the patient is much more likely to be happy if the doctor admits him to the hospital for work-ups that the insurance company will pay for. A related constraint is the nearly universal non-coverage of preventive health care contrasted with good coverage for curative care or treatment for diagnosed illness. The economic message is clear: it is cheaper to get sick than to stay well. With regard to covered procedures, the doctor's economic incentive to order a lot of expensive procedures is, through insurance, joined by the hospital's need to pay for its equipment and the patient's desire to have the best money can buy, particularly since it is no longer his money that is flowing.

From the insurer's point of view, there is economic incentive to maintain health and to treat illness as economically as possible. Yet the carrier has little control over what doctors or patients do. Thus, while economic incentive from the carrier's side favors health and preventive care, the carrier has no easy way to affect care delivery events. One obvious way, of course, would be to cover preventive procedures but this route has not generally been followed, presumably because in the short run such coverage increases costs to the carrier; furthermore, the carrier always has the option of raising rates and passing on higher costs to the enrollees, which is precisely what happens.

The economics of sponsorship medicine are quite different. From the doctor's point of view, economics are largely irrelevant: his salary is at most only vaguely related to units of care delivery. There is no economic advantage to doing expensive procedures, but there is also no advantage to frugality. From the patient's point of view, the issue is complicated because disability may play a role in sponsorship care; in short, the need for care and the degree of economic compensation over and above care are correlated in many sponsorship programs, the VA being a prime example. Thus, if one is well enough to work and does so, one loses disability compensation, which can be sizable. In fact, for many unskilled persons it is virtually impossible to earn, after taxes, a salary remotely approximating that which is forthcoming so long as they remain sick. In such a situation the economic incentive is clearly in the direction of maintaining illness rather than encouraging health. In sponsorship systems, the only incentive to economy is mediated by the sponsor; that is, funding may go up or down as a function of political factors, deficits in the union pension fund, or whatever, but such events are many steps removed from the day-to-day activities of care delivery and thus have only an indirect effect.

When we look at HMOs, we see a rather drastic shifting of economic incentives. Here both doctor and patient profit from low use of expensive procedures, but the profit is diffused. That is, in most HMOs the individual doctor does not earn more by doing fewer procedures but the system itself, the collectivity, is enriched. From the patient's point of view, he is entitled to preventive care so he has no disincentive to use the system and some indirect incentive to do so. In contrast to the sponsorship model, there is no economic advantage to the patient in being sick because the HMO does not itself provide disability benefits. Finally, in contrast to the fee-for-service plus insurance situation, there is no economic advantage to anyone to favor inpatient over outpatient treatment and, in fact, the incentive operates in the opposite direction.

From a purely economic perspective the HMO seems uniquely designed to minimize costs and maximize health. This conclusion has been reached by persons of varying perspectives, including Richard Nixon, who said:

> "HMOs simultaneously attack many of the problems comprising the health care crisis. They emphasize prevention and early care; they provide incentives for holding down costs and for increasing the productivity of resources; they offer opportunities for improving the quality of care; they provide a means of improving the geographic distribution of care; and, by mobilizing private capital and managerial talent, they reduce the need for Federal funds and direct control. (1971: 31)

## Doctor-Patient Roles

Thus far we have looked at the evolution of the physician's role in U.S. society and seen how the fee-for-service model has become preeminent. I described the various health care delivery systems currently in place and examined briefly the three-tiered structure of American medicine. To conclude this discussion of medicine as a social institution, the roles of doctor and patient as they are characteristically acted out in our culture will be examined. What we shall see is that the physician has assumed (or been put in) a rather exalted position in relation to his patients and that this status affects both parties. Certainly the nature of the doctor-patient relationship is complicated and there are no doubt vast differences reflecting personal styles. The discussion to follow is thus admittedly stereotypic and based on argument rather than data (existing data tend to support this description, but they are meager and often tangential). To the extent that the discussion is accurate, it suggests some fertile ground for medical psychology because the doctor-patient relationship is determined only partly by the parameters of disease. It is also a social transaction and thus the proper province of psychological analysis and intervention.

In contemporary medicine, the typical doctor-patient transaction assumes passivity on the part of the patient. Once the patient completes the active process of seeking help, he shifts to a passive role. He is expected to listen to what the doctor says, then follow the prescribed treatment, and respond to the therapy. He ought not ask a lot of questions because, it is assumed, that he will not comprehend the answers anyway. Patients are also expected not to complain very much and to limit symptom manifestation to regular office hours. Individuals who do all these things are termed good patients by doctors. By way of contrast, patients who complain often and loudly, who show up at the emergency room on Sunday, who ask a lot of questions, and who, even without being asked, volunteer that the treatment is making them worse, are termed by doctors, "crocks" or "hysterics." They are often referred to public, teaching, or university hospitals by private practitioners, bearing the introduction, "interesting case." "Good patients" are never referred to university hospitals.

I am overstating the case in order to emphasize the point that active participation by the patient in his treatment is not widely encouraged by physicians. Patients are generally told as little as possible about their condition, their questions are often viewed as a nuisance, and patient records are closely guarded from nonprofessional eyes for vaguely stated ethical or procedural reasons. Yet the few available data suggest that patients do better and feel more content with service when there is an open flow of information.

The secrecy surrounding patient files reflects the presumption that the doctor's knowledge is incomprehensible to the layman and that patients do not need to know the little they could understand. What patients need is orders to follow. However, it is simply not the case that the average educated layman, given some help with terms, cannot comprehend the bulk of his medical record. The vast majority of medical care delivery events are routine and simple. To shroud them in mystery is both ludicrous and unnecessary. In addition, the data suggest that compliance with medical advice is increased when reasons are given for the regimen. Therefore, it is not only untrue to say that patients do not need to know, it is antithetical to the goal of medicine. Finally, from a purely philosophical perspective, placing the patient in a passive role insults his intelligence and runs counter to our traditional emphasis on free choice.

Somers and Somers discussed doctor-patient roles in historical perspective, noting that the generally authoritarian posture of physicians was probably more acceptable to earlier generations than it is at present (1977). As patients grow increasingly sophisticated about matters of health and disease, they are decreasingly likely to be satisfied with "doctor's orders." Furthermore, the authoritarian role may have been rendered more acceptable in an earlier time by the fact that patients experienced a lifelong personal relationship with one (fatherly) physician. With more and more specialization, care has grown fragmented and patients seem increasingly to feel abandoned in a large, impersonal system. When the persons manning that system assume an authoritarian posture but do not at the same time manifest a fatherly sense of responsibility and caring, they are likely to be rejected or at least resented by patients. The classic California study of malpractice actions suggested that precisely this combination of perceived high-handedness and lack of personal involvement eventuates in malpractice litigation—usually, and somewhat surprisingly, with revenge rather than money the major motive (Blum, 1958).

## Conclusion

Medicine as a social institution and medicine as a biological technology are not coextensive. The healing process is not simply a matter of biological manipulation. In fact, until fairly recently the role of healer had almost nothing to do with biology. As a social institution, medicine represents a licensed monopoly, which state of affairs influences quality control and fees, definitions of illness, and organization of health services delivery. At the level of the individual doctor-patient transaction, the social role of the physician interacts with that of the patient and encourages some behaviors and not others. All these variables enter into the health equation in ways that we are only beginning to comprehend. There can be no doubt, however, that these issues must be addressed if the health care system is to be optimally effective, realizing the greatest degree of well-being for the greatest proportion of society.

# 3

# Behavioral Theory

Perhaps the central idea underlying the practice of medical psychology is that what we think of as illness includes a large behavioral component—sickness must be understood in terms not only of what the patient *has* but also of what he *does*. Medicine traditionally has concerned itself almost exclusively with physiological mechanisms and interventions on the implicit assumption that normal behavior will take care of itself. Included in this notion is a mind-body dualism of the Cartesian sort and this dualism is expressed operationally in the practice of referral to psychiatrists when no pathology can be discovered. If the patient's problem is not physiological, then it must be mental in origin; these two categories of causation are viewed as exhaustive and distinct. Let us be clear this mind-body dualism is not merely a conceptual convenience: it determines practice. However, it is fundamentally wrong.

In cases of physiological disease, the patient's behavior can be explained by that disease only in the most primitive way. People with broken legs obviously do not run, but what they *do* do is certainly not explained by the broken leg. Where there is no physiological disease, nothing is explained by attributing the behavior to the mind unless the mind can be adequately described in terms of function. The various psychodynamic formulations that purport to do this have not been proven adequate either experimentally or clinically. Both formulations, physiological and mental, ignore a third category of influence on behavior: the environment. Environmental influences operate all the time, whether physiological dysfunction is present or absent and whether mental derangement, if there is such a thing, is present or absent.

The phrases "doing well," "getting better," or "responding nicely" are applied to events only partially understandable in physiological terms. If our friend with the broken leg never goes back to work and spends the rest of his life in bed, he is not "doing well" no matter how "nicely" his fracture has healed. To dismiss this behavior as a mental aberration neither solves the problem nor addresses its origins in a serious way. Adding the mental label "compensation neurosis" likewise avails nothing unless it helps us both to understand and to intervene in the process. Ultimately, the understanding and the intervention must be stated in environmental-behavioral terms. Let me illustrate with an anecdote.

A woman in her mid-forties was presented for diagnostic and treatment discussion at a high-level (in terms of number of tenured faculty) conference devoted to the study of patients with psychiatric and neurologic difficulties. Approximately 16 years earlier, she had had an attack of weakness that persisted several weeks. She was hospitalized and the diagnosis of multiple sclerosis (MS) was entertained. She then was declared partially disabled and began to receive a pension. The years following were punctuated by nearly 30 hospitalizations for symptoms of almost every possible sort—vomiting, ovarian pain, back pain, headache, weakness, blurred vision. The woman was operated on several times for genital complaints. Throughout these hospitalizations, diagnoses varied from multiple sclerosis to different psychiatric conditions to a number of acute problems such as infection. The patient's social history included a divorce from her first husband following a beating. She remarried and had two children but was in essence totally disabled, staying home and doing very little.

The woman was examined at the conference and showed a gait disturbance that did not appear to have a definable neurologic origin. In fact, she showed no neurologic deficit of significance. She appeared tearful at times, very concerned about her condition and very unhappy. She said she wanted to know what was the matter with her and added that doctors over the years had been vague in their discussions with her. The woman described with a mixture of fear and distaste her being poked with needles, operated on, and generally mishandled by hospitals and doctors. She said she wanted to be well.

The patient had been referred to the conference for a definitive statement about her condition. The possibility of increased compensation had been raised and the degree of disability had to be determined. After the examination, the faculty divided along the following lines. The neurologic side of the house, including myself, speculated that the woman's symptoms were psychiatric in origin and the diagnosis of hysterical conversion reaction was advanced. The psychiatric side of the house pointed out that the woman was not typical of patients so diagnosed since she was clearly not indifferent to her condition and lacked a hysteroid personality (flirtatiousness, cloying manner, etc.). In effect, the neurologists and the psychiatrists were arguing for a diagnosis in each other's camp by exclusion: the woman had no neurological problems so she must be hysteric; she lacked the cardinal symptoms of hysteria so she must have multiple sclerosis. In the midst of this interchange, a third-year medical student asked to what extent the patient's 16-year contact with the medical profession might have played a role in how she looked at present? Have we reinforced her illness behavior? he asked. This was acknowledged as a very interesting question by those of us on the figurative front bench as we resumed discussion of whether the patient represented a conversion reaction or Briquet's syndrome or MS in remission. The medical student had, of course, raised the most pertinent point.

Here we see a woman who had been dysfunctional for 16 years. She had been hospitalized, medicated, and operated upon repeatedly during this period, yet she remained disabled though she lacked sufficient neurologic disturbance to account for this condition. That is, even if she had had an attack of MS, it had left her neurologically intact. To turn to hysteria as an explanation missed the point. The real issue was what had happended in this woman's life to make her act this way? What environmental influences made disability her method of living? It is a general rule that patients do the best they can; that is, whatever behavior the patient shows is the best he can come up with under the circumstances. What the medical student student wanted to know—and what, in fact, all of us should have considered—was how the woman had come to be the way she was and what role health care personnel had played? This question is at the heart of medical psychology but falls outside our usual way of thinking about health by addressing problems that do not fit the disease model. Questions of this sort are asked with encouraging frequency by medical students and are responded to with discouraging frequency by their elders.

## Models of Illness

When we look at disease events, two general approaches are possible. The preceding chapters sketched the medical model. The social learning, or behavioral, model comes from social science. Many discussions present these points of view as clashing, and in some situations they do indeed seem to be at loggerheads. On the other hand, the case can be made that in general they are complementary ways of looking at phenomena.

Both approaches are useful in some circumstances but not in others, and in many circumstances they are applicable to different aspects of the same problem.

## THE MEDICAL MODEL

The medical model holds that observed symptoms and signs can be most parsimoniously explained by disease entities. These entities are biological or physiological circumstances operating in the patient and giving rise to what is observed. Treatment, it follows, should be directed at correcting the underlying process, the disease. Diagnosis entails identifying the disease; treatment entails eliminating, correcting, or modifying it. Correct treatment results in symptom abatement.

The key features of the medical model are that cause is placed inside the organism, that cause is thought to be biological in character, and that treatment should be directed at the underlying cause. The conceptual and therapeutic power of the medical model has been amply and dramatically demonstrated, particularly with infectious disease. It must be remembered, however, that the medical model is not limited to the single-cause pardigm of infectious disease but includes a wide range of etiologic paradigms differing in complexity. Autoimmune responses, for example, are categories of disease that imply exceedingly complicated mechanisms behind symptoms and illness. Therefore, it is inaccurate to say that the medical model assumes a singular cause for any given disease. Hypotheses are biological in the medical model but not necessarily singular.

I stress this point because social scientists tend to attack the medical model, particularly as applied to psychiatry, on the ground that it reasons by analogy from infectious disease to behavior deviance, seeking singular causes, either biological or mental, within the patient to explain psychopathology. To the extent that psychiatrists actually follow this route, the criticism is a fair one, but this particular use of the medical model ought to be criticized, not the model itself. Properly applied, the model exemplifies Baconian inductive science, and it works exceptionally well provided the assumption of biological cause is appropriate. The limitations of the model flow from the assumption of biological causality. When this assumption accords with reality, for example, in lobular pneumonia, the model works; that is, it leads to a specific and successful treatment. In other circumstances, however, the match is not so good.

Let us take a patient who has a myocradial infarction. The patient, usually a middle-aged man who appeared well, becomes ill all of a sudden. According to the medical model he receives intensive care and drugs to control his blood pressure, cardiac function, etc. Now let us assume that the patient's status from a physiologic point of view has returned essentially to normal. Is he well? Does he return to baseline? Experience with cardiac patients yields very mixed answers to this question. Some do well; others do poorly not in terms of physiology but in terms of lifestyle. Suppose our hypothetical patient fails to return to work and spends his time waiting for and avoiding, he thinks, through inactivity, a second heart attack. How is this problem addressed in the medical model? It is not. Treatment of the biological cause does not lead to return to baseline, except from a biological point of view, in our imaginary but not atypical case. This brings us to an alternative formulation.

## THE SOCIAL LEARNING MODEL

The social learning model grew up in the social sciences and its focus. is behavior. In the most general terms this model holds that behavior, what people do, is maximally determined by environmental events both present and past and that a major category of environmental events is social, involving interaction between and among persons. Scientific study of behavior from this point of view entails the demonstration of functional relationships between specific sorts of environmental events and behavioral events. Proponents of this model vary widely in the categories of events they see as important and in the sorts of behavior they choose to study. Social and environmental mechanisms postulated to influence behavior differ in the amount of empirical support offered by their advocates. The model thus is a broad framework whose assumptions leave a great deal of latitude in defining behavior and environment. Procedures as diverse as operant conditioning and psychotherapy can be subsumed under the social learning model.

At first glance the medical and social learning models seem to address totally different things. The medical model concerns biological events; the social learning model concerns behavioral events. In an ideal sense that is true, but while it may be conceptually convenient and in certain circumstances practically appropriate to view biology and behavior as distinct, they are closely related in fact. If one does not eat, one will starve and die. Though eating is a behavior and dying is a biological event, they are related. At a less obvious level, a diabetic who does not take insulin or eat properly will have disturbances in blood sugar level, leading to coma, vascular changes, and a host of other untoward biological events. The insulin taking behavior has biological consequences. At a still more subtle level, a lifestyle variable such as extremely high achievement striving may predispose one to cardiac disease. Behavior and biology again interact. Clearly, the medical model is too narrow for a host of apparently biological problems.

## Behaviorism

The social learning model stresses the role of environmental events in behavior. To illustrate, the particular variant emphasized in the rest of this text will be described. Although there are many ways to look at the relationship between environment and behavior or between behavior and illness, reinforcement theory, reviewed here, has found considerable success in medical contexts.

From a behavioristic perspective, what an organism does is explicable on the basis of a limited range of innate, or automatic, responses to stimuli and the organism's history of interaction with the environment. The key to this interaction history is reinforcement. This point of view has been most completely and eloquently expounded by Skinner (1972).

Responses are of two general types, respondents and operants. Respondents are behaviors elicited by, or in reaction to, some environmental stimulus. Pupillary constriction to bright light is an example. Operants act on the environment in some way. Going to work is an operant. In general, respondents are mediated by the autonomic nervous system and smooth muscles, while operants involve the skeletal muscles. Operants are described as voluntary while respondents are described as reflex. Respondents are controlled by the stimuli that precede them; operants are controlled by their consequences, which are called reinforcers.

From a behavioral point of view, then, if we wish to understand what someone is doing, we need to understand the consequences that follow what the person is doing or have followed it in the past. As regards autonomic activity, the question is, What stimuli elicit the autonomic behaviors or have elicited them in the past? Note that there is no recourse to either mind or internal processes in order to explain behavior. Behavior is controlled by the environment and the environment can be seen, measured, and manipulated. For this reason, it is possible to modify behavior. Behavior modification denotes a collection of maneuvers used to change behavior by altering the environment in some way. Modification of behavior is also called learning. When we say that someone has learned something, we mean that over time, through interaction with the environment, his behavior has changed in some way. Learning is an extremely powerful process: it accounts for just about everything we do.

## RESPONDENT CONDITIONING

In Pavlov's classic experiments on respondent conditioning he paired a neutral stimulus, the ringing of a bell, with an active stimulus, meat powder, which elicited a respondent, salivation. After a while, the bell came to elicit the respondent, too, provided it was occasionally reinforced by administration of the meat powder in conjunction with the bell. The meat powder is technically termed an unconditional stimulus (UCS) for salivation, the unconditioned response (UCR); the bell is termed a conditioned stimulus (CS). Once salivation occurs in response to the bell, we have a conditioned response (CR).

Over the years a great many interesting things have been learned about conditioning by Pavlov and others who followed him in this line of study. If the response to a CS is never reinforced, it will slowly decrease in intensity and go away. This process is called extinction. On the other hand, if the CS is presented again after a while, the response will recur, a phenomenon termed spontaneous recovery. If there continues to be no reinforcement, extinction proceeds, but more rapidly, and after a sufficient number of trials is complete.

Once a CR has been established in relation to a stimulus, another neutral stimulus can acquire CS properties if it is similar to the CS in some way. If a tone of 4000 cps is a CS, a tone of 5000 cps may also elicit the response. This phenomenon is called generalization. The other side of the generalization coin is discrimination. If there is a conditioned response to a bell, bells of different timbre will also elicit the response but will do so decreasingly as they differ from the CS. Through a careful pairing of UCS and CS, but not with other potential CSs, exquisite discrimination can be developed such that the CR occurs to one bell but not to another. To the extent that the CR is discriminated, it does not generalize. In another phenomenon frequently observed in animal experiments, second-order conditioning, a stimulus temporally associated with a CS may come to elicit the CR; for example, if a tone elicits a CR of salivation, a light paired with the tone will begin to function as a CS in its own right.

The phenomenon of respondent conditioning accounts for a good deal of behavior. When one's mouth waters at the mention of lobster Newburg or at the sight of Julia Child preparing this dish, that's respondent conditioning. In the latter case, the generalization is obviously mediated in very complicated ways, the tiny colored dots on the TV screen bearing no obvious stimulus similarity to the taste of lobster Newburg. Because the generalization process can follow complex routes, many undesirable respondents can become conditioned to stimuli to which one would prefer to respond neutrally.

Applications of respondent conditioning to problems in medicine are numerous. Perhaps the classic example is systematic desensitization for phobic behavior (Wolpe, 1969). A phobia can be conceptualized as a collection of respondent behaviors, sympathetic discharge labeled fear or anxiety, elicited by something that ought to be neutral, like dogs. The desensitization procedure entails a process of extinction so that the CS, dogs, ceases to elicit the CR, fear, sweating, etc. Desensitization also has had some success in the treatment of bronchial spasm in asthma (Cooper, 1964). Here the spasm functions as a CR to a wide variety of emotionally arousing stimuli, themselves conditioned stimuli that gained their eliciting power by a circuitous route.

When a CS is presented, a number of things happen. One is the CR. In addition, however, the organism may begin to do things that are not respondent but operant behavior. For example, the stimulus of Julia Child on TV may elicit salivation. However, one might also get up and go to the refrigerator, settling for a dill pickle or some other edible in the absence of lobster Newburg. These are operant behaviors occasioned by the respondent event. Going to the refrigerator is the operant; the pickle is the reinforcer. In the case of Pavlov's dog, the bell elicited salivation, along with motor behaviors such as perking of the ears and looking around—the orienting reflex, in Pavlovian terms—that we might conceive of as the generalized operant of getting ready to do something. The point is that respondent and operant behavior, while conceptually distinct, blend together in a continuous flow in organism-environment transactions.

## OPERANT CONDITIONING

Respondents are controlled by preceding stimulus events. In operant behavior, the stimulus event following the behavior is important. When a stimulus event that follows a response affects the frequency of that response, it is called a reinforcer. The simplest example is the pigeon in the Skinner box. When the pigeon pecks at a disc, a bit of food is presented; in a short time, the pigeon begins to peck very frequently, which behavior pattern demonstrates that pecking is now under the control of the food dispensing event, or reinforcer. In other words, the pigeon has learned the disc-pecking response; that is, his pecking behavior has changed over time from random pecks all around the box to disc-pecking.

There are two general classes of reinforcers: positive and negative. Positive reinforcers increase response frequency when they are presented after the response, as in the preceding example. Reward is a nontechnical word for positive reinforcers, but it has other meanings so it is better to use the more technical term. Negative reinforcers are defined by an increase in the frequency of a response when that response leads to the removal of a stimulus. An example might be taking analgesics to alleviate pain. Here cessation of pain is the negative reinforcer and taking morphine is the operant. Behaviors conditioned through this mechanism become very strong and are difficult to modify. Avoidance behaviors are created in this way, and for reasons that will be made clear in a moment they are very persistent.

Extinction has about the same meaning for operant and respondent behavior. If the reinforcing event that controls the behavior is withdrawn, the response gradually drops off in frequency and finally stops altogether. If the response is maintained by positive reinforcement, the situation is fairly straightforward. With negative reinforcement some complexities are introduced. In order to look at them, we need the concept of discriminative stimulus (SD).

## DISCRIMINATIVE STIMULI

An SD is a stimulus that tells the organism that a response is likely to be reinforced. In the case of our pigeon, the box and the disc are the SDs. Staying with the pigeon for a moment, we might modify the conditioning procedure so that a light goes on at times; when it is on, disc-pecking will be reinforced, but not when it is off. The pigeon in this circumstance quickly learns to peck only when the light is on; that is, the light has become an SD for disc-pecking. As a further refinement of this method, we might have the disc itself light up but with two different hues, reinforcing one and not the other. Say we began with red and blue, reinforcing red. Now what would happen if we introduced purple? One of two things might happen: the pigeon might generalize from red to purple and peck at purple or he might discriminate red from purple and peck only at red. If we continue to reinforce only red we are training the discrimination of red and purple, but for this procedure to be successful the pigeon must be able to appreciate the difference between red and purple. Obviously, what we have here is a method for determing spectral sensitivity in pigeons. Such experiments have been done and it turns out that pigeons have very good color vision, just about as good as humans (Blough, 1957).

The key point is that reinforcement can be used to create highly discriminated behaviors or operants. From a behavioral point of view, human behavior can be conceptualized as the result largely of generalization and discrimination of SDs through differential reinforcement.

To get back to the problem of negative reinforcement and avoidance, in the simplest case the SD for the operant is some aversive stimulus, the removal of which is the negative reinforcer. The pigeon can learn to peck a disc to shut off an aversive noise; the patient can learn to take morphine to stop an aversive pain. Through the mechanism of generalization, however, other stimuli can become SDs for the operant. In the case of the pigeon a light might be turned on before the sound, and turned off when the pigeon pecks. In this case the pigeon will quickly learn to avoid the sound by pecking when the light comes on. To the extent the response is successful, the original negative reinforcer is never applied. Extinction does not occur because the response is consistently reinforced by offset of the light, which has acquired negative reinforcing properties through the light's previous association with the noise, an example of respondent conditioning. Let us suppose that this conditioning procedure had been accomplished before we were introduced to the pigeon. We would see a pigeon who pecks furiously at the disc when the light comes on, yet we would never see an easily identified reinforcer for this event. Faced with a human being and this puzzling state of affairs we would be tempted to make up an explanation like ''He has a compulsion,'' a cause presumed to reside in the person. This would, of course, explain nothing, being only another way of saying that the person does what he does. To understand the behavior we must retrace the history of the individual, where we will find a reasonable reinforcement explanation.

A great many problems in medicine and psychiatry involve avoidance learning. Some patients are aware of what is being avoided; others are not. Such awareness itself seems to play a minor role in determining the power of the avoidance response. The snake-phobic patient is perfectly aware of what he seeks to avoid—snakes—but still seeks desperately to avoid them. At a more subtle level, patients may learn illness behaviors because they thereby avoid some aversive circumstances. A professional man may develop incapacitating back pain as an avoidance response because of a problem at work. If we think he is unaware of the mechanism, he is called a hysteric; if awareness is assumed, he is a malingerer. Both these labels are pejorative and unhelpful in elucidating the behavior and modifying it. They place the cause in the person rather than in the relationship between him and his environment.

## SCHEDULES OF REINFORCEMENT

I have discussed operant behavior in terms of general categories of reinforcement, SDs, and generalization. We need now to look at schedules of reinforcement. Skinner and his followers have worked out in exquisite detail the relationship between reinforcement and event frequency. As it turns out, the nature of the response-reinforcement contingency has dramatic and predictable effects on the response's resistance to extinction, or its strength. At the extremes, reinforcement can be given either every time the response occurs or never. In between are varying frequencies of reinforcement application contingent on the response. These response-reinforcement relationships are called schedules and each schedule has an expected pattern of response frequency. Schedules can be contingent either on time or on response frequency. The former are called interval schedules; the latter, ratio schedules. On interval schedules, reinforcement is given by the clock, provided the organism responds during the interval. On a fixed-interval schedule (FI) the reinforcement comes, say, every minute. On a variable-interval schedule (VI), it comes at apparently random intervals that average to some predetermined period. On ratio schedules, reinforcement is tied to response and occurs when the response occurs. On fixed ratios (FR) reinforcement occurs after every fourth or fifth or fifteenth or whatever response. On variable ratios (VR) it occurs apparently at random but on a fixed average. In shorthand notation, VR 30 means reinforcement follows every thirtieth response on the average; FI 20 minutes means that reinforcement is given every 20 minutes.

Reinforcement schedules have different effects on response frequency and resistance to extinction. Obviously, interval schedules are not very efficient ways to get behavior going. Since the reinforcement is not temporally contingent on the response, it is only by chance that reinforcement will follow the response one wishes to increase. Once a behavior has been established, however, interval schedules have the advantage of simplicity of administration. Paychecks, for example, are given on FI schedules and they seem to maintain a good deal of behavior. To establish a behavior, then, to bring it under the control of reinforcement, one begins with an FR 1 schedule, applying the reinforcer every time the behavior occurs. To stay with this schedule indefinitely, however, is dysfunctional and inefficient for two reasons. First, the organism may satiate on the reinforcer and it will lose its value (after a huge meal, food is not an effective reinforcer). Second, it is inefficient and troublesome to reinforce every response. A shift to higher ratio scheduling solves these problems. This process, called thinning the schedule, has predictable and useful effects.

Careful thinning can achieve extremely high rates of responding under ratio schedules. By shifting to higher ratio schedules one can generate more behavior with less cost to the reinforcing agent. Furthermore, behaviors maintained by higher ratio schedules are more resistant to extinction than are those maintained by lower ones. If we stop reinforcement of an FR 100 schedule, the response will persist for longer than if the response had been maintained on an FR 2 schedule. People prone to mentalistic formulations would probably say that the organism on the lower ratio realizes that there is not going to be any more reinforcement sooner than does the organism on the FR 100; this explains nothing and merely says that what happened, happened. The explanation lies in the schedule. Similar mechanisms operate with interval schedules. There is more behavior per reinforcement on longer than on shorter intervals, but the relationship is somewhat looser since the reinforcement is time, rather than response, contingent. The pattern of responding is quite sensitive to the fixed versus variable aspect of the schedule, as well as to its richness or thinness. In general, the variable schedules, both interval and ratio, yield more constant and higher rates of responding than do the fixed. In both types of fixed schedule, the records of responding show a scalloped effect, with response frequency rising just before reinforcement; in behavioral terms this pattern represents expectation, or anticipation.

Overall, then, VR schedules yield the highest rate of responding and the greatest resistance to extinction and FI schedules yield the lowest and least. These relationships have been repeatedly demonstrated in the laboratory in organisms ranging from flatworms to humans. Examples from everyday life are rife. A child's allowance given every Saturday morning (FI 1 week) will control little behavior other than allowance requesting. Making the same allowance contingent on lawn cutting will increase lawn cutting behavior (FR 1). Shifting to allowance every other lawn cutting (FR 2) will yield more behavior for the same reinforcement.

The use of a ratio schedule assumes, of course, that the behavior to be brought under control will in fact occur, that it is already in the repertoire of the subject. Often, however, learning involves new behaviors. The operant conditioning method of establishing new responses is called shaping. Shaping means reinforcing successive approximations to the desired behavior. Over time, very complex responses can be taught. In a related method, chaining, a series of discrete responses are taught and then reinforced only when they occur in a sequence, with the length of the reinforced sequence gradually increased. Thus, the first response becomes an SD for the second and the second an SD for the third and so forth.

## DEFINING REINFORCERS

Reinforcement is defined circularly and the term has no meaning outside its operational sense. A positive reinforcement is an event that increases the frequency of a given behavior. The event must have this effect to qualify as a reinforcer. The term "reward" designates something the subject is thought to want; the reward is defined not by its actual effect but by what the "rewarder" thinks the effect ought to be. This is not an operationally useful concept and, as I noted earlier, reinforcement is to be preferred. To repeat, the reinforcer has to be operationally defined, or shown in fact to increase the behavior upon which it is contingent. A couple of guidelines help us identify events that are likely to be reinforcing.

Primary reinforcers are tied to biological needs. Food, water, sex, and rest are all primary reinforcers and are likely to be effective at appropriate times in most organisms. Secondary reinforcers are events that have been connected with primary reinforcers in the past or are related to them by way of generalization. Money is the classic example of a secondary reinforcer. The relation between primary and secondary reinforcers is extremely complex and buried in the subject's history. In many cases secondary reinforcers seem to bear no relation to primary reinforcers. The rock collector finds rocks very reinforcing and will perform a good deal of behavior in an effort to acquire them, but their relation to primary need states is tangential in the extreme. For practical purposes, the circular nature of the definition of reinforcement insures finding a useful one, primary or secondary.

Another guide to identifying reinforcers is the Premack principle. Premack pointed out in 1959 that any high-frequency or high-strength response can serve as a reinforcer for a response of lower frequency or strength. That is, making the opportunity to do a high-frequency behavior contingent upon doing a lower frequency behavior will reinforce the latter and increase its frequency. Identifying reinforcers using the Premack principle is simply a matter of observing the subject to see what he does often. If he smokes a lot of cigarettes, cigarettes are by definition reinforcing and making them contingent upon some lower frequency behavior will increase the latter. Watching TV is another common high-frequency behavior that can be made contingent upon other behavior.

The relevance of these principles of learning to medical problems is diverse—obvious in some circumstances, elusive in others. In the chapters to follow some of these application will be explored, but here I want to map out the terrain. In the first place, learning and behavior play a central role in all health maintenance. Cigarette smoking is a behavior that must be changed using behavioral methods. There is no medical solution available. Compliance with medical advice is another behavioral problem. Medication taking behavior needs to be reinforced or shaped and maintained behaviorally. Again, there is no medical model alternative. In illness there is behavioral change and this change is a direct biological consequence of the illness to varying degrees. To the extent it is *not* a direct biological consequence, such change is best conceptualized as an essentially behavioral problem and the only intervention strategy is behavioral. Finally, there is the biological process of illness itself. I have been speaking as though behavior and biology were distinct, requiring separate approaches, but in health problems both the behavioral and the medical model have relevance. Since learning is itself a biological process, a characteristic of living things and not of rocks, learning principles may be involved in biological dysfunction, as ample evidence indicates. The whole realm of psychosomatic disease rests on this notion and has a long history. In recent years, a number of workers have approached psychosomatic illness using the principles of reinforcement. Disorders like hypertension, asthma, and peptic ulcer have been so studied and conceptualized and useful treatments have emerged in some cases.


OBJECTIONS TO BEHAVIORISM

The learning theory approach outlined in this chapter focuses almost exclusively on observable events, behavioral and environmental. Yet, our subject matter, illness, is inherently subjective in nature. At times, patients come to the doctor with observable difficulties, a rash or a fever, but more frequently they come because they feel ill—a vague, subjective assessment. To ignore this fact and focus on observables misses the point, and many would argue against a behavioral approach to medicine for this reason alone. This objection may be philosophical or methodologic in character and to understand the behavioral approach to medicine, a distinction must be drawn between behaviorism as a methodologic strategy and behaviorism as a philosophy of man. The position taken here is that methodologic behaviorism is a practical necessity if one wishes to *study* medical problems and not merely to talk about them. Reliance on this perspective does not, however, imply philosophical behaviorism.

To state the case most simply, one cannot study scientifically what one cannot observe. People who work in the area of health obviously are concerned with human suffering, but what they can *do* about human suffering is limited to the possible. The nurse can hear the patient's complaint but has no direct access to his pain. If one wishes to study pain, reality requires that one study behavior, not pain itself. This point is important. To the extent that health workers fail to acknowledge the distinction, they delude themselves into thinking they are studying things that cannot be studied. As a result, they reach conclusions that have no meaning and may engage in treatment procedures whose effects can never be assessed.

Let us take obesity as an example. A number of possible explanations can be offered for this condition. Relying on psychoanalytic theory, one can argue that early childhood experiences caused the obese person to be fixated at the oral stage of psychosexual development, producing a compulsion to eat. The problem, overeating, is thus explained by a mental process, the compulsion. It follows that to solve the problem the compulsion must be eliminated, and psychoanalytic psychotherapy is offered as a method for doing this. One obvious problem with this formulation is that the treatment does not work. From a behavioral perspective, the problem with the formulation is that it precludes scientific study. The putative explanation, the compulsion, lies outside the realm of observation and can only be inferred from its effects, in this case, eating. But since we want to explain eating, we are locked into a circular argument. One solution to this difficulty is operational definition, which entails translating the mental process, compulsion, into observable measures. A test for compulsiveness, for example, might be designed and validated by showing that overeating was correlated with the test. What has been accomplished here? One type of behavior, eating, has been related to some degree with another sort of behavior, test responses. Advocates of this approach argue that as more and more behaviors are correlated, the concept (in this case compulsion) accrues meaning and is thus shown to be useful.

Intelligence is offered as an example of a concept that has been made useful through vast numbers of correlational studies. However, one must ask, Useful for what? Useful for predicting success in American grammar schools or useful as a scientific explanation for behavior? These are very different criteria of usefulness, but they are typically viewed as equivalent. To say that children who do well on intelligence tests also do well in school is not the same as saying that children who do well in school do so *because* they are intelligent, yet that claim is made. This trend has an unfortunate consequence. To the extent that one believes school success is explained by intelligence, one sees little reason to pursue the matter. That is, there is little reason to look for other variables that might relate to school success since the causal question is deemed already to have been answered. To account for the not infrequent occurrence of high intelligence and poor school performance, a second explanatory entity is invoked, motivation. Taken together, these two concepts can account for every possible outcome. Stupid children who do well are, by definition, highly motivated. Bright children do well unless they entirely lack motivation. The child who is both dull and unmotivated is, of course, a lost cause, but this is not the school's fault since the characteristics of low IQ and poor motivation are intrinsic to the child, not the school. Although correlational data can yield useful predictions, there is a tendency to reify correlationally derived variables like intelligence. When that hapens, we have the illusion that something has been explained when, in fact, the phenomenon has only been described.

An analogy to the medical model may make this point clearer. In developing a scientific understanding of any disease, description of the disorder is an essential first step. Certain manifestations are seen to occur together and are given a name, the syndromatic diagnosis (Ludwig & Othmer, 1977). It would be a mistake, however, to think that the symptoms have been explained by attaching a label to them. The next step is the search for etiology, or cause: "Philosophically, cause is not easy to define but, in the context of medicine, one can feel operationally comfortable with the following proposition: A cause is something which, if prevented, removed, or eliminated, will prevent the occurrence of the event in question, and/or if permitted, introduced or maintained, will be followed by the event in question" (Mack, 1974: 39). The term "intelligence" is like a syndromatic diagnosis designating a collection of behaviors that are related to one another to some degree. However, these behaviors are not explained by the concept of intelligence any more than a disease is explained by getting a name.

If behavioral labels do not explain behavior, do behavioral concepts, particularly reinforcement, explain behavior? Many philosophers of science argue that behaviorism is devoid of explanatory power. Earlier I criticized the circularity of compulsion as an explanatory entity, but reinforcement is also circularly defined; that is, a stimulus is called a reinforcer on the basis of its effect on behavior and *only* on that basis. The critical issue is the meaning of the term "explanation." The explanation of an event may lie at various levels of abstraction from that event and may be articulated to varying degrees with other ideas that together explain not only the event in question but also other events. Let me illustrate with two extreme examples.

If we throw water on a fire, it will go out. At the simplest level of explanation, one could say the fire went out because water puts out fire. The statement is true as far as it goes but tells us nothing about other events and is not part of an explanatory system. In fact, it is simply an empirical observation that generalizes only to other very similar events. Einstein's theory of relativity lies at the other extreme of explanation. This theory is a collection of statements that brings together a vast array of events and explains them in a unified way. That is, phenomena ranging from planetary movements to nuclear fission can be understood or predicted on the basis of Einstein's theory. In contrast, the water on fire explanation predicts only that the next fire we encounter can be extinguished with water—unless it is a chemical fire, which points out a major problem with low-level explanations. Their limited applicability prevents us from making accurate predictions beyond a very small set of circumstances. For the science of behavior, then, a fundamental question arises: what should an explanation look like and what should be its terms?

One might say that behaviorism addresses the surface structure of human life, or what people do. It seeks to explain these events in terms of observables (environmental variables). Yet there is an abiding sense among philosophers, scientists, and other interested people that there must be factors operating within the organism that in some ultimate sense explain what is observed. These might be termed the deep structure of human life and formulations about this realm often are framed in mentalistic language, as in Freud, or in physiological language. In 1956 Carnap went so far as to suggest that behavior ultimately can be explained in terms of physics:

> Both these approaches (the introspective and behavioristic) in psychology will probably converge toward theories of the central nervous system formulated in physiological terms. In this physiological phase of psychology, which has already begun, a more and more prominent role will be given to qualitative concepts and laws referring to micro-states described in terms of cells, molecules, atoms, fields, etc. And finally, microphysiology may be based on micro physics. (P. 74)

This reductionistic perspective is countered by writers who hold that emergent properties in complex systems canot be explained on the basis of their components; for example, existentialists see consciousness as irreducible to physiology.

Another possibility can be raised. It may be that a general theory of behavior can be stated in environmental terms but that the nature of those terms and their interrelationships will be more complex than the descriptive statements of contemporary behaviorism. Certainly the word "environment" is used rather broadly in the argument that behavior is under the control of the environment. I have proceeded as though the environment were a relatively simple entity characterized mainly by being something other than the organism, which ignores environmental structure and complexity, particularly vis-à-vis behavior. The concept of reinforcement represents an initial structuring of the environment into elements that affect behavior frequency as opposed to those that do not. One suspects, however, that other, more finely grained concepts will emerge in a mature theory of behavior that retains environmental primacy. The theoretical systems found in sociology and political science may be rudimentary exemplars.

The reinforcement model thus is closer to the fire and water explanation than to relativity theory. Behavioral concepts do not explain why some stimulus is reinforcing or, more generally, why behavior is affected by reinforcement. The empirical observation and the explanation derived from it are not articulated with a more general theory (Hempel, 1966). Whether a more general theory should be mentalistic, physiological, environmental, or some combination of these remains to be seen. In the interim, however, practical problems persist. The following chapters trace some of their medical manifestations.

## Conclusion

This chapter has examined the traditional medical model of illness and a reinforcement based formulation of human behavior. These points of view are complementary in many situations because illness has both biological and behavioral components. In subsequent chapters, specific applications of the behavioristic point of view will be described and will be shown to operate at both the micro and macro levels. That is, reinforcement can be used to affect heart rate or to encourage excercise. It is a very useful paradigm in medicine whose value is only beginning to be realized.

# PART II

# Interventionist Medicine

American medicine has been, in the main, interventionist in focus. That is, doctors respond to illness or complaint with diagnosis and treatment. People thus served are patients and can be contrasted to the rest of the population, the well. It is the latter toward whom preventive efforts are directed and they will be addressed in Part III.

Medical psychology has similarly been maximally involved with intervention in defined illness and in this section, examples of behavioral treatment in the context of medical intervention will be discussed. These efforts run a wide gamut from highly specific, learning theory based treatment for abnormalities of heartbeat, to more general approaches to improve response to medical procedures such as surgery or renal dialysis. The behavioristic model outlined above will be found to have varying degrees of relevance as different problems are addressed.

The topics discussed in this section should be viewed as representative rather than exhaustive for this field is growing very rapidly. By surveying these chapters, however, the reader should come to appreciate the breadth and depth of involvement psychologists are beginning to have in the treatment of both acute and chronic illness.

# 4

# Medicine I: Cardiology

This discussion of cardiac disease focuses on three categories of illness. First, the acute episode of myocardial infarction (MI) will be described and the role of psychological variables before, during, and after acute attack will be explored. One frequent consequence of heart attack is hearbeat abnormality; the behavioral approach to such abnormalities is the second topic. Finally, hypertension, or high blood pressure, is a serious condition predisposing the patient to a vast array of other illnesses; behavioral management of this condition is the last topic.

Before addressing these clinical matters some general facts about cardiac function, must be understood, with more detailed information provided where necessary. The focus here is behavioral and other states that affect cardiac function and the dependent variables, or measures, used to assess these effects. The physiological mechanisms relating the two are exceedingly complex. The interested reader is referred to Guyton's 1976 text for a detailed discussion.

## Physiology

### THE HEART AS A PUMP

The heart and blood vessel network (vasculature) is in essence a closed hydraulic pumping system under pressure. The heart is the pump; blood is the fluid flowing through the arteries and veins. Since

William Harvey first documented this monumentally important fact in the seventeenth century, a great deal has been learned about how this system accomplishes its task of keeping the body nourished and oxygenated.

The heart is a four-chambered muscular mass whose contractions exert the pumping force. The two smaller chambers, the atria, receive blood; two larger chambers, the ventricles, force it out into the circulation. The left ventricle pumps blood to most of the body and the right atrium receives blood from the body. The right ventricle pumps blood to the lungs, where the blood takes up oxygen, and the left ventricle receives blood from the lungs. Thus, there is a continuous circulation of blood, which is kept in motion by the pumping contractions of the cardiac muscle. Arteries are the vessels that carry blood from the heart; veins are the route back.

The heart normally beats in a rhythmic fashion at a complexly determined rate. The average normal heart rate is about 72 beats per minute (bpm) and is intrinsic to the heart. That is, while external neural and hormonal influences can alter heart rate, the heart is constructed in such a way that it will continue to beat even if it is totally denervated. The sinoatrial node (SA node) is a region of heart muscle that has the capacity to depolarize and repolarize in a repetitive fashion. The normal heart beat is formed at this locus. From there, the electrochemical impulse is propagated throughout the heart in an orderly fashion, causing the coordinate muscular contraction that is the pumping action. There is, however, a failsafe mechanism that comes into play should the SA node cease to function: ventricular escape, a rhythmic ventricular contraction, much slower than the normal rate, occurs if the ventricles are not stimulated in normal fashion. This mechanism is important in behavioral studies of abnormal beat formation in cardiac disease.

The term "cardiac output" refers to the quantity of blood moved through the system per minute. Several factors determine it. First is venous return. The heart has mechanisms that adjust output to input and thus avoid the damming of blood in the venous system. Exercise is a second factor that affects output. With strenuous exercise, the well-conditioned athlete will have a cardiac output up to six times the resting level. Heat is a third factor leading to increased output as, for example, in illness with fever. From the psychological point of view, however, a fourth factor—neural influence on cardiac output—is of special interest.

The heart is innervated by both the sympathetic and the parasympathetic divisions of the autonomic nervous system. The parasympathetic innervation is via the vagus nerve to the SA node. This parasympathetic influence, which serves to decrease heart rate and thus to reduce cardiac output, is constant, normally slowing the heart rate below its intrinsic rhythm. Parasympathetic denervation causes the heart rate to rise from the normal level to around 160 beats per minute. As with other body systems, the sympathetic system has the opposite effect. Sympathetic nerves innervate the cardiac muscle diffusely and can raise heart rate to as high as 250 beats per minute. Like the parasympathetic, the sympathetic system exerts a chronic influence, and sympathetic denervation causes heart rate to drop from 72 to around 60 beats per minute. Finally, these systems affect contraction strength in opposed functional directions, the parasympathetic reducing it, the sympathetic increasing it.

In general, heart rate and contraction strength affect cardiac output synergistically so that factors that influence one property also influence the other. In some types of pathology, however, they work in compensatory fashion. Thus, if contractile strength is reduced, rate may increase in an attempt to maintain cardiac output at a sufficient level to sustain life.

The well-conditioned heart is hypereffective, increasing cardiac output; the diseased heart is hypoeffective, exhibiting decreased cardiac output. Regular exercise increases the size of cardiac muscle and thus its efficiency; that is, fewer beats per minute are needed to achieve the same cardiac output. Distance runners have resting heart rates far below the normal 72 beats per minute. In contrast, the diseased heart pumps inefficiently and must therefore beat faster to achieve the same cardiac output. With any degree of exercise this rate can be quite rapid, hence the experience of palpitation, or racing heart, in the person with cardiac disease who suddenly exerts himself.

Physicians and physiologists employ three tactics to monitor heartbeat. One is simply to listen through a stethoscope (ausculation), the second is to feel the pulse, and the third is to record the electrical activity inherent in the depolarization-repolarization sequences—this last technique is the electrocardiogram (EKG). Some familiarity with the EKG is necessary in order to understand the conditioning treatment of abnormal heart rhythms because this method is typically used to measure the dependent variable in such cases. Monitoring of the pulse by the patient also is useful in conditioning treatments.

Because heart contraction is an electrochemical phenomenon, appropriate sensing and amplification devices can document the waves of depolarization as they pass over the heart muscle. This procedure is much like that employed to observe brain activity with the EEG or skin activity through galvanic skin response. In all these cases, a measure is obtained by comparing electrical activity in one location with activity in another. As the polarity of the two positions changes, the activity giving rise to these changes can be monitored and locked in time. In the case of the EKG, the contraction of the heart is effected by a depolarization of the muscle, followed by repolarization. The record of these changes on graph paper is the clinical EKG. Fig. 4–1 shows schematically the

**Figure 4-1.** Recording depolarization and repolarization from cardiac muscle fiber. Reproduced, with permission, from A.C. Guyton, *Textbook of Medical Physiology* (5th Edition). Philadelphia: W.B. Saunders, 1976.

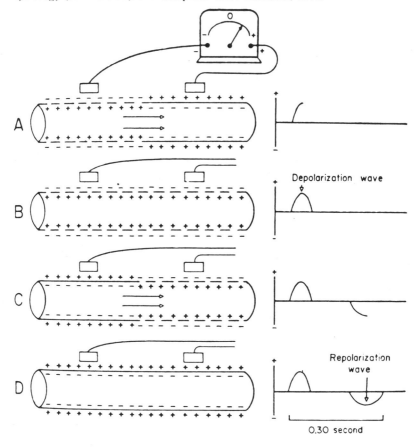

general principle of eletrophysiological recording of muscle activity. If we substitute axon for muscle fiber, the figure shows how single-neuron recording is done; if we substitute scalp under one electrode and earlobe under the other, EEG is schematized. In either case we are measuring polarity shifts.

Fig. 4–2 is a normal EKG, labeled with the conventional P–Q–R–S–T system. These letters mark prominent deflections in the line from the zero point. The direction in which the curves move is a totally arbitrary matter, dependent only upon which of the recording leads is negative and which is positive. The EKG's polarity can thus be reversed by reversing the recording leads and no information is lost. The temporal

**Figure 4-2.** The normal electrocardiagram (EKG). Reproduced, with permission, from A.C. Guyton, *Textbook of Medical Physiology* (5th Edition). Philadelphia: W.B. Saunders, 1976.

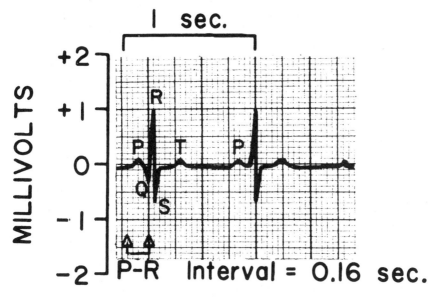

duration of the curves and their relation to one another, however, is not arbitrary and reflect intrinsic qualities of the myocardial response.

The physiological principles underlying the EKG are complex and one must understand them before employing EKG as a dependent variable. For present purposes, however, a simple appreciation of the measure is adequate. The waveform of the EKG reflects the contraction of the cardiac muscle, and clinicians examining the waveform are able to identify abnormalities of heartbeat in two dimensions. The first is rate. Heartbeat may be too rapid or too slow and interwaveform intervals, or the period of the EKG, can indicate abnormalities of rate. The second category of abnormality has to do with the physiology of the beat—how it is propagated through the heart and in what sequence the various regions of the heart contract. The morphology of the waveform may reveal abnormalities of beat. Behavioral techniques have addressed both categories of abnormality.

BLOOD PRESSURE

Movement of blood through the circulation occurs because the system is under pressure. The heartbeat is a major source of this pressure, but another is the elasticity of the system itself. In the clinical condition called hypertension, the pressure in the system is too high; this condition may occur as a result of a variety of factors, which are not completely understood. A very important point about hypertension, however, is that blood pressure is a continuously distributed variable, not a categorical one. An essentially arbitrary cutoff point has been clinically established as the operational definition of hypertension, but it is not correct to think that risk of death and disease is absent below and present above this limit. Rather, risk seems to increase monotonically along with blood pressure in a continuous fashion. For this reason, anything that lowers blood pressure to normal levels and does not engender other risks is good preventive therapy.

Blood pressure means simply the amount of pressure exerted in the arterial system at any point in time. A moment's reflection reveals complications with the operational definition of this parameter. In the first place, pressure varies throughout the system. Obviously, pressure measured at the ventricles is much higher than pressure measured at the atria. If it were not, there would be no pressure gradient and thus no circulation. Second, the heart is a repetitive, phasic pump, not a continuous machine. It follows that pressure will rise with heart contraction (systole) and fall during relaxation (diastole). Blood pressure is thus a complicated phenomenon and a great deal of work in basic physiology has been directed toward assessing it at different sites under varying physiologic conditions. For clinical purposes, however, a conventional method for measuring pressure has evolved that is widely used; typically, this measure is the dependent variable in behavioral studies of blood pressure control.

Blood pressure is conventionally expressed in millimeters of mercury (mm Hg) at sea level. Any pressure exerted on a column of mercury at the bottom will cause the mercury to rise. Blood pressure is expressed in the number of millimeters the column rises. Thus, if we say that the pressure in the blood vessel is 100mm Hg, this means that the pressure is sufficient to elevate the column 100mm at sea level. While the most accurate methods of measuring blood pressure entail introduction of the measurement device into the vessel, such procedures are impractical for routine clinical purposes. The auscultation method is well suited to clinical use, and all of us are familiar with it.

The procedure consists of listening to the artery in the lower arm while the upper arm is squeezed with an inflatable cuff. This cuff is attached to a column of mercury. First, the cuff is inflated to a pressure about 20mm Hg above arterial pressure. In this circumstance, no blood passes through the artery and the artery distal to the cuff collapses. As pressure in the cuff decreases, a point is reached at which pressure in the artery exceeds cuff pressure. When this happens, blood flows through the artery during systole, or when arterial pressure is greatest. During diastole, however, when pressure in the artery falls below cuff pressure, blood is dammed up again and the artery distal to the cuff collapses. When this happens, noises are generated called Korotkoff sounds; these sounds are audible through a stethoscope applied to the artery. As the cuff pressure continues to decrease, a point is reached at which the pressure in the artery exceeds cuff pressure even when arterial pressure is at its lowest level, or during diastole. When this happens, the artery ceases to collapse. The point at which sounds of alternating flow and collapse begin and cease can be collated with the elevation of mercury. The first reading is the systolic blood pressure; the latter is the diastolic.

Several factors affect pressure at any point in time. The heartbeat itself is a major one, the relative distensibility of the system is another, and the amount of fluid in the system is a third. If cardiac output rises, the system becomes less elastic, or the amount of fluid in the system rises, then blood pressure will rise. In the normal working of the system these factors operate in a complex system of checks and balances so that rises in blood pressure due to one factor are compensated by shifts in the others. These mechanisms and the various physiological events that underlie them are complex (Guyton, 1976), but hypertension can be thought of as a condition in which these factors cease to operate in a manner sufficient to keep pressure at normal levels.

Fig. 4–3 illustrates the distribution of pressures throughout the circulatory system. An important fact about regulation of blood pressure

**Figure 4-3.**  Blood pressures in different portions of the systemic circulation. Reproduced, with permission, from A.C. Guyton, *Textbook of Medical Physiology* (5th Edition). Philadelphia: W.B. Saunders, 1976.

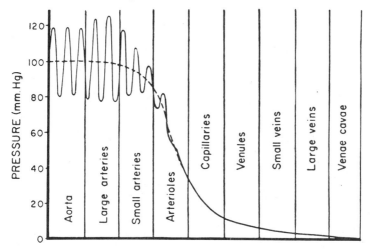

emerges from this figure. Pressure drops as blood moves from the left ventricle through the circulation and reenters the heart at the right atrium. Most notable here is the relatively abrupt drop in pressure in the arteriolar system, the vast network of minute vessels through which body tissues receive oxygen and nutrients. This illustrates great resistance to flow in this part of the circulation. The distribution of pressures suggests that a major determinant of total peripheral blood pressure is the state of the arteriolar system. To the extent that the system is compliant, total pressure will drop; to the extent that it is constricted, pressure will rise. The figure also illustrates the decrement of pulsatile pressure change as blood flows through the system. In the great arteries, pressure parallels the contraction and relaxation of the ventricles and is, in fact, exaggerated once the blood leaves the aorta. This pulsatile quality begins to diminish in the smaller arteries as resistance increases and vanishes completely in the capillaries. In the venous system, blood pressure normally is constant rather than pulsatile.

Given that about 50% of the total peripheral resistance lies in the arterioles, it is not surprising that they are a major determinant of peripheral pressure. This system has two general categories of control. The first, autoregulation, refers to the ability of local tissues to determine their own blood flow based on metabolic need. Exactly how this process is effected is not known, but the important point is that peripheral pressure is partly, a response to local factors with no known relationship to system-wide regulatory mechanisms. An example of autoregulation is reactive increase of flow to a region that has been briefly deprived of its blood supply. The second type of control of peripheral pressure in the arterioles is systemic, or achieved by factors that have general effects throughout the circulation. These will be discussed in a moment, but a point to be made first is that the *neural* control of peripheral pressure is exerted mainly at the level of the arterioles. There is sympathetic nervous system innervation of the entire vascular system, with major distribution to the kidney, intestines, spleen, and skin. In the skin, extremely powerful sympathetic control of blood pressure is effected by constriction of the regions of communication between the arterioles and capillaries (the arterial-venous anastomoses). Thus, a major site of neural regulation of blood pressure is the arterioles, where, given the large proportion of total peripheral resistance they represent, sympathetic discharge can greatly increase resistance and thus systemic pressure.

There are three basic sources of systemic regulation of arterial pressure: the kidneys, the endocrine glands, and the autonomic nervous system. From the psychological perspective, the last is of primary interest.

The neural control of blood pressure is achieved in the main by three mechanisms: increased sympathetic tone during exercise, decreased sympathetic tone in response to pressor receptors, and the central nervous system ischemic response. The third mechanism becomes active only in catastrophic circumstances—when mean arterial pressure falls to 50mm Hg or lower and the vasomotor center in the brain stem itself becomes ischemic. In this situation, however, the reaction is exceedingly intense, causing vasoconstriction throughout the body and greatly increasing heart rate in an attempt to protect blood supply to the brain and thus life itself.

In normal conditions the nervous regulation of blood pressure provides rapid response to exercise demands and changes in posture. In exercise, sympathetic discharge occurs along with motor activation of the skeletal system. These sympathetic effects include vasoconstriction throughout the body, raising blood pressure, and local vasodilatation at the muscles to facilitate metabolic exchange. This effect is initiated in the vasomotor center located in the brain stem. This center has a two-part organization: the lateral region initiates the sympathetic vasoconstriction response just described; the medial portion acts to inhibit the lateral portion and thus has an opposite effect at the periphery. These two centers also have complementary effects on heart rate. The lateral region acts to increase heart rate via the sympathetic innervation of the heart as it increases vasoconstriction peripherally. The medial region stimulates the dorsal motor nucleus of the vagus nerve while it inhibits the lateral region, leading to both vasodilatation and parasympathetic slowing of heart rate through vagal action at the SA node.

The vasomotor system is influenced by higher brain centers, particularly the hypothalamus, cingulate gyrus, temporal lobe, and orbitalfrontal regions. All these sites play a role in emotional expression and experience and thus figure in models of hypertension as a stress related disorder. Chronic states of emotional upset may include chronic sympathetic activation and result in hypertension. The relaxation approach to psychological treatment of hypertension can be conceptualized as entailing a decrease in emotional arousal and a resultant drop in sympathetic tone through inhibition of the lateral vasomotor centers. Decline in blood pressure should occur at the end of this chain of events.

The vasopressor reactions are reflex changes in arterial tone in response to stretching of pressor receptors located in the great arteries, especially the carotid sinus, aorta, and pulmonary arteries. When blood pressure increases, these receptors stretch and are stimulated to transmit impulses that inhibit the vasomotor center and excite the vagal center. This results in a drop in sympathetic tone and thus in vasodilatation and a rise in vagal activity and thus a drop in heart rate. The reverse effect is seen when blood pressure drops; this causes a decrease in pressoreceptor impulses, an increase in vasomotor center activity, and a decrease in vagal activity. The pressoreceptor reflex system thus acts as a buffer, opposing changes in pressure in either direction. Moreover, these reflexes are more responsive to change than to steady pressure; that is, a pressure of 60mm Hg will cause more pressoreceptor activity if it follows a previous pressure of 50mm Hg than if pressure is a steady state. This mechanism may be important in terms of the chronicity of hypertension in that if the reflex gets reset at a higher arterial pressure, efforts to lower pressure will be counteracted by reflex buffering around the current (hypertensive) steady state.

The pressor reflexes are important in postural adjustment. On rising from a reclining or sitting position, hydrostatic mechanisms tend to lower blood pressure in the head. In a standing person, all of the pressoreceptors are located at a level above the heart. This arrangement works nicely in that, on standing, pressure drops in the region above the heart while it rises in the region below and the reflex increase in sympathetic tone serves to increase cerebral circulation. Were the pressorreceptors located in the feet instead, fainting would be the usual consequence of standing up because the increase in pressure below the heart would elicit a reflex drop in blood pressure, cerebral ischemia, and collapse. Emotional fainting, incidentally, seems to reflect a strong and sudden sympathetic reflex, probably anterior hypothalamic in origin, that causes muscular vasodilatation and a drop in cerebral blood pressure and collapse. Restoration of consciousness is usually rapid once the person is recumbent because of hydrostatic redistribution of blood as well as a fall in sympathetic tone.

To recap, blood pressure regulation is a complex, ongoing process in which complementary mechanisms work in concert and in opposition. Furthermore, these various mechanisms work in a tonic fashion. Sympathetic tone is an ever present phenomenon whose intensity waxes and wanes. The vagus always inhibits the heart, but it does this more or less. Thus, when we speak activation of the vasomotor center, we do not mean that it is turned on like a light that has been off; rather, there is an increase in activity from some previous level. In turn, this increase alters the function of other parts of the system, which feed back their effects and so on and on in an unending flow. This fact has implications for the behavioral treatment of hypertension because such treatment entails intervention in a complex system of interactive mechanisms. The results of such intervention are not likely to be all-or-none phenomena.


## Myocardial Infarction


The term ''heart attack'' is a general one that applies to a number of acute abnormalities of cardiac function. The more technical term of myocardial infarction denotes a sudden episode of interruption of blood supply to the muscle of the heart, the myocardium, due to occlusion, hemorrhage, or spasm in the coronary circulation. This event is typically experienced as severe and persistent chest pain, with shortness of breath and weakness, followed by some degree of shock, with blanching of the skin, sweating, and sometimes nausea. The patient may lose consciousness. Because of the reduction in blood supply, the efficiency of the cardiac muscle is reduced, less blood is transported, and some degree of heart failure usually ensues. Rest is clearly of the utmost importance in the acute phase because exercise increases demand for cardiac output, while heart failure means essentially that the pumping power of the heart is reduced (Mann, 1975).

More than half the people experiencing an MI will die before reaching the hospital or within the first two hours of the event. Of those who survive, ultimate longevity is complexly determined. Availability of coronary intensive care plays a role, as do the absolute degree of tissue damage, the presence of other complicating disease, family history, and the patient's age. If the patient survives, the myocardium will repair itself, producing scar tissue to replace dead muscle fibers. The patient rests while this proceeds; then he must recondition himself to maximize the output of the remaining cardiac muscle. Ultimately he must be brought to as close an approximation of his premorbid status as his physiological limits will allow.

Psychological factors play various roles in this process. Before the MI, psychological variables may play a predisposing or even a causal role. A sizable literature has evolved on the role of stress in MI, and the coronary prone, or type A, personality has been widely discussed (Jenkins, 1971). These are controversial issues that will be addressed subsequently, but to anticipate, a case can be made that lifestyle variables are risk factors for MI and they are potentially subject to behavioral manipulation and control.

In the acute phase, psychological variables act in different ways to increase or decrease the chance of survival. One is simply the time it takes to decide to go to the hospital. Gentry defined three categories of factors that determine the patient's behavior after the attack and before hospital admission: demographic characteristics, the patient's perception of his illness, and the social context in which the symptoms occur (1975). Demographic predictors include age (older people are slower to seek admission), history of coronary disease (those with a history seek admission more readily), and sex (men come to hospital sooner than women). As regards perception of illness, the symptoms of MI, especially chest pain, are the usual presenting complaint, the reason the patient seeks help. Yet, a very significant proportion of patients mistake the reason for the symptoms, attributing them to indigestion, heartburn, or whatever.

This situation is aggravated in patients who have gastrointestinal disease such as ulcer (Mann, 1975). Mistaken attribution may keep such patients out of the hospital and taking antacids during the critical early hours after MI. A second perceptual (more accurately, cognitive) factor in recognizing the symptoms of MI is denial of illness (Olin & Hackett, 1964): the patient experiences the symptoms but denies their significance, delaying medical attention and placing life at risk. Social context also plays a big role in post-MI behavior. Tjoe and Luria reported that delay in seeking admission was over twice as long on weekends as on weekdays (1972). Among employed persons, delay was greater during working hours (Goldstein et al., 1972), a finding that fits too well with the description of the work oriented, type A personality. Finally, the presence of another person, usually a spouse, tends to encourage hospital admission.

In discussing such delays, Gentry stressed the importance of patient education: "Patients must be educated to recognize the symptoms of myocardial infarction, those that appear both in the prodromal period and in the acute phase. They must be taught, for example, that chest pain is by far the most common symptom of infarction and thus they should not be falsely reassured by the fact that they have not yet experienced any respiratory symptoms (shortness of breath)" (1975: 61). Certainly, patients with a history of coronary disease deserve special instruction in the critical factor of delay and must be counseled not to be overly confident that they can distinguish angina pectoris from the pain of MI.

For the patient who survives the immediate crisis and arrives at the hospital, a new collection of psychological variables come into play. During the relatively acute period, rest is imperative—both physical immobility and emotional calm (the cardiovascular system is exquisitely sensitive to emotional arousal). The critical variable that must be reduced in the acute phase is demand for cardiac output. Some writers advocate administration of sedatives in the acute phase (Wolf, 1977), but relaxation techniques would seem a useful adjunct. This modality fits well with the generally supportive, optimistic framework advocated for care of the MI patient (Pranulis, 1975), with the behavior therapist offering nonspecific emotional support and concern, as well as a potentially beneficial specific treatment leading to deep muscle relaxation and the sense of well-being described as a usual consequence of relaxation therapy in other settings. Such treatment might have the further beneficial consequence of giving the patient a sense of mastery in a situation characterized by feelings of helplessness. Learning to relax is something the patient can do for himself.

The acute phase of MI fades into the rehabilitation period as physiologic recovery proceeds. After some days in the coronary care unit, the patient will be moved to a general ward, then home. Profound psychological effects are described by almost everyone who has taken the trouble to look at convalescing patients from a psychological perspective. In the first place, MI patients characteristically experience fear of death or anxiety, though individuals differ widely in how they deal with or react to this response. Many deny the seriousness of their condition. Hackett, probably the most prolific contributor to our understanding of the psychological consequences of MI, noted that denial is a regular and expected event in the coronary patient, appearing on about the second day of hospitalization and replacing felt anxiety (Cassem & Hackett, 1971). This response is adaptive to the extent that it affords relief from anxiety and the attendant physiological arousal and ought not to be discouraged early on. Denial becomes problematic, however, if it persists to the point of interfering with treatment. Feelings of depression are common on about the fifth day of hospitalization. Some have argued that these depressive symptoms are an inevitable and a necessary part of the recovery process. Persistent depression, however, is pathological and leads to an attitude on the part of the patient of hopelessness and despair. Wolf argued that the physiologic concomitants of profound depression can lead to cardiac arrest and death (1967). Certainly, ample clinical lore indicates that if the patient really gives up, all is lost. Accordingly, a supportive and optimistic attitude on the part of staff is considered essential in coronary care (Garrity, 1975), and psychological and/or chemotherapeutic efforts to alleviate depression may be warranted.

Once discharged from the hospital, the patient returns to an environment over which the health care system has minimal control, and the best of coronary care may avail very little if the patient fails to pursue the medical and psychological rehabilitation necessary for recovery. Telling patients to do things in no way assures that they will do them, and clinical experience suggests that in even so potentially catastrophic an illness as MI patient compliance is frequently very poor. Compliance is a psychological problem that has a number of complicated facets in the case of MI, one of the most complex being the patient-spouse relationship (Crawshaw, 1974). A number of workers have described group therapy as a useful medium for post-MI patients (for the most part middle-aged men) and their wives (Adsett & Bruhn, 1968). Common areas of patient-wife conflict are control of medications, compliance with rest requirements, and compliance with exercise requirements. Wives may be overly solicitous, reinforcing patient helplessness and impeding recovery. On the other hand, wives tend to be terrified of another heart attack and are thus reluctant to allow the patient to do things for himself. The wives may themselves become symptomatic in response to the stress they experience (Skelton & Dominian, 1973). To make matters worse, many wives feel responsible for the first heart attack and avoid showing any strong emotion for fear of causing another. A major contributing factor to the wife's dilemma may be ignorance about what to expect and the reasons for dietary, exercise, and other recommendations: "Unnecessary problems in the convalescent phase could probably be mitigated if, beginning in the hospital, the physician and nurse would prepare the wife for the usual home difficulties and plan to include the wife in follow-up visits with the physician with the goal of imparting information in a clear, useful form" (Gulledge, 1975: 111–112). Groups for patients and wives or wives alone can serve the very useful function of providing information and reassurance that other people are going through similar events and have similar feelings.

One area that is often fraught with problems is sexuality. Again, ignorance seems to be a major source of the difficulty. In fact, normal sexual behavior is possible for the majority of patients, and some modification will allow sexual satisfaction in many more. This topic should be broached with the couple by the professional staff since many patients are reluctant to bring it up themselves though they may be thinking about almost nothing else.

A final area of general psychological concern is social welfare. The post-MI family may face significant financial worries and problems. They may require home nursing assistance, disability compensation, and a host of other social services. Croog and Levine studied a group of MI patients to find out what sort of information concerning such supports they had been given (1973). Only 1% indicated that their physician had advised them about social services that could help them find a job suitable to their current level of function. One is hard pressed to adduce a more blatant example of failure to care for the whole patient. This statistic shows the medical model at its worst and, given what we know about the essential role of psychological well-being in the survival of post-MI patients, represents shoddy patient care.

Thus far I have reviewed fairly broad psychological variables and mentioned general, nonspecific interventions such as group therapy, social services, and counseling. At a more specific level, a major component of rehabilitation is cardiac reconditioning. Just as anyone who leads a sedentary life gets out of shape, the post-MI patient gets extremely out of shape because of both his cardiac disease and the prolonged recuperative inactivity. Programmed exercise is essential in restoring function and in building up cardiac reserve. Hackett and Cassem advocated as early a beginning of exercise training as possible (1975), even to include simple range of motion exercises in the coronary care unit and this approach is gaining prominence. As exercise training proceeds, programs similar to that of Fordyce (1976) hold great promise for improving compliance and achieving recovery.

## Heartbeat Abnormalities

Abnormalities of the pumping action of the heart figure prominently in clinical cardiology. They take a variety of forms and are diagnosed in part on the basis of EKG findings. Accordingly, EKG is the usual dependent variable in behavioral approaches to correction of beat abnormality.

### BEHAVIORAL ISSUES

Examples of conditioned heart rate increase are commonplace. The visual presentation of frightening events as in horror movies leads in many people to a profound increase in heart rate. Classical, or respondent, conditioning is the presumptive mechanism here and laboratory demonstration of classical conditioning of heart rate increase is easily achieved. The pairing of electrical shock with a light will cause the light to elicit a generalized fear response of which increased heart rate is a component. In such studies, what seems to be occurring is the elicitation of sympathetic discharge by a conditioned stimulus. In recent years, however, a sizable literature has developed demonstrating the apparent success of operant conditioning of autonomic responses, cardiovascular among them and including heart rate acceleration and deceleration. This approach has engendered a good deal of theoretical discussion and controversy.

As we saw in chapter 3, operant conditioning involves the skeletal musculature and is determined by the consequences of behavior, termed reinforcers. Respondent conditioning, on the other hand, involves the autonomic nervous system and is determined by the simultaneous occurrence of neutral or conditioned stimuli with active or unconditioned ones. As research into learning has proceeded, questions have been raised as to how distinct these two models actually are. In the area of cardiac function, problems with operant-respondent differentiation are apparent in the fact that it is possible, employing methods generally considered operant in character, to alter heart rate, a function usually viewed as under autonomic nervous system control.

Kimmel reviewed this issue in historical perspective (1974), noting that opinion has ranged from a fairly dogmatic belief that operant conditioning of autonomic response is impossible (Miller & Konorski, 1928) to an equally dogmatic assertion that there is no biological difference between respondent and operant conditioning (DiCara, 1970). What we may be facing here is the familiar mismatch between phenomena and words, between biological events and verbal and procedural media we must employ in addressing them. Quite likely, neither formulation is an adequate description of the event at issue since the science of behavior is an evolving system. The practical problem is to delineate models that best account for what is observed. The operant-respondent distinction remains useful if for no other reason than the ease of conditioning certain responses under one or the other format.

That autonomic responses can be conditioned using operant procedures has been repeatedly demonstrated in man and lower animals. In any such demonstration, as in all operant conditioning, some stimulus event is made contingent on the occurrence of the response. Biofeedback refers to a procedure in which the consequent event is information about the performance of the organ system being conditioned. The term ''information'' is used here in a technical sense since the subject may or may not be aware that he is being informed about his bodily processes; moreover, it is not clear whether such awareness facilitates, impedes, or is irrelevant to acquisition of control.

As an example of a biofeedback procedure, we might look at an early study by Brener and Hothersall in which subjects learned both to speed and to slow heart rate (1966). The feedback in this study was a tone whose pitch was contingent upon heart rate. The subject was told to keep the pitch high when a green light was on and low when a red light was on. Subjects were not informed of the heart rate–tone contingency. Successful conditioning was achieved in this study and none of the subjects guessed that heart rate was being modified. This study used a typical biofeedback paradigm: an autonomic response, heart rate, was brought under the control of an SD, colored lights, through contingent reinforcement, tone. (This reinforcer, incidentally, highlights the point made earlier regarding the concept of reward and reinforcement. Low or high tones are not rewarding in an obvious way, though in this situation they were clearly reinforcing since they controlled the behavior under study.)

The result of this procedure, speeding or slowing of heart rate with the presentation of variously colored lights, is an empirical fact that cannot be denied. The interpretation of the event, however, is controversial. One camp argues that what is actually being learned is some nonobvious skeletal response, which in turn leads to heart rate change. Alternate tensing and relaxing of the leg muscles might be an example. This position would be held by those who argue on theoretical grounds that operant conditioning of autonomic nervous system responses is impossible. A second interpretation is that the heart response is mediated by some cognitive process such as thinking lascivious thoughts for speeding and visualizing pastoral scenes for slowing. Finally, some suggest that what appears to have happened has, in fact, happened; that is, an autonomic nervous system response has been operantly conditioned. A variety of empirical results have been marshaled by various writers to support these points of view.

Obrist and colleagues argued that there is a general linkage between somatic activity and heart rate in circumstances where sympathetic discharge is minimal (1974). Furthermore, given the subtlety of the somatic-cardiac interaction, it is difficult to demonstrate nonsomatic, behavioral (e.g., ''mental'') effects on heart rate. Even very slight degrees of somatic activation will alter heart rate and evidence suggests that the central nervous system events leading to somatic activity also affect cardiac function; in other words, cardiac effects are not *reactions* to somatic events but are integral parts of them (Obrist et al., 1974). Lacey and Lacey, taking a somewhat different point of view, proposed that cardiac function may reflect psychological processes, such as anticipation, independent of somatic activity (1974). To support this notion, they cited studies in which cardiac deceleration in anticipation of a stimulus occurred even as electromyographic (EMG) signs of gross motor activation were increasing (Eason & Dudley, 1970). Their position is that somatic activation is but one of a number of influences on cardiac rate. Psychological processes like attention to the environment or mental arithmetic also lead to cardiac effects, deceleration in the former case, acceleration in the latter (Lacey & Lacey, 1974).

The cardiac rate conditioning phenomenon brings to the fore an issue that is problematic for behavioral theory generally, namely, response definition. If we take as a simple example the response rate of a rat in a lever-pressing experiment, the response here is arbitrarily defined as a lever-press sufficiently strong to advance the counter. Is that an accurate way to describe the rat's behavior? Yes and no. This procedure is sufficient for demonstrating stimulus control and the effects of reinforcement. Yet, observing the rat, we find that he does a great many things besides pressing the lever during periods when the SD for lever-pressing is present. Furthermore, if we watch the lever-pressing response itself over time, we find that it becomes increasingly efficient in terms of the amount of unneccesssary gross motor activity associated with it. Thus, what we call the response is only part of a complicated, ongoing flow of behavior in the rat, and this part is assessed in only one of its possible dimensions—rate in this case, as opposed to mechanical force or movement fluidity. When these other dimensions are assessed, the curves of acquisition are not all parallel. The basic discrimination, lever-pressing to SD but not in its absence, tends to happen relatively abruptly. The smoothing out of the response from the point of view of its morphology occurs slowly over time. Analogues from human learning to these rather different acquisition patterns are concept formation and motor skill acquisition.

Put another way, the reinforcement strategy offers an explanation for *why* the rat presses the lever but does not address the issue of *how*. Again to use a human analogy Mike Schmidt plays baseball for money. Money is the reinforcement and if it is withdrawn, playing behavior stops. That is *why* he plays. While playing baseball, he engages in a very complex motor behavior called belting them out of the park. At one level, it is fair to say that the reinforcement for this behavior is money—the more frequently Schmidt hits home runs the more he gets paid. Yet, this statement does not explain *how* he does it or how he learned to do it. The usual operant assumption is that the response is shaped by reinforcement of successive approximations, but such an explanation is post hoc and gratuitous and rendered somewhat unconvincing by the fact that a very large number of American males undergo virtually identical contingencies but do not acquire the skill. Thus, motor skill acquisition may follow rules tied closely to physiology and perhaps even genetics. At the macrolevel, exercise of these skills is controlled by the consequences we identify as reinforcers, but to reason that analogues control skill acquisition at the microlevel might be unwise. Proprioceptive feedback, cheering crowds, and money are all consequences of hitting home runs, but they work at very different levels and according to different rules.

What has this example to do with cardiac rate conditioning? Brener argued that the best analogue for this phenomenon currently available is the acquisition of motor skills (1974). From this point of view, the biofeedback procedure, in giving the subject information about internal processes that he normally lacks, operates in a manner analogous to that of a coaching or training device in a motor skills task. Watching videotapes of one's tennis stroke might be an example. The essential difference between controlling heart rate and controlling arm movement lies not in the autonomic-skeletal distinction but in the relative availability of feedback, or response contingent information. Considered this way, the employment of overt muscle contraction in early stages of heart rate training represents a lower level of skill, analogous to the rat's needlessly vigorous lever-presses. As the response comes increasingly under stimulus control, extraneous factors drop out and the subject achieves the heart rate increase or decrease ever more efficiently.

It may be trivial to argue whether the heart rate increase is actually due to motor response and thus not operantly conditioned. Results with curarized animals show clearly that reinforcement contingent heart rate control is not the result of actual muscle movement. However, when such animals are brought out of the curarized state, rats trained to speed heart rate behave differently from those trained to slow: they are much more active (DiCara & Miller, 1969). This finding suggests that some general activation system is being brought under stimulus control. Employing the motor skills analogy, we would expect over time the reinforced response to be differentiated out of the more generalized activation response. The fact that incompatible responses, from a generalized activation point of view, like raising heart rate and lowering blood pressure can be trained simultaneously lends some credence to this notion (Schwartz, 1972, 1974).

To summarize, heart rate control involves complex processes. From a practical point of view, we must proceed with research on technique and allow the theoretical account to follow, realizing, however, that many of the advances in technique are occasioned by attempts to answer hypothetical questions proceeding from one or another theoretical point of view. Ultimately, our understanding of cardiac rate control and of behavior in general rests on resolving these theoretical issues. In the interim, we do what seems to work and operant conditioning of heart rate is one technique that shows promise.

## CLINICAL APPLICATIONS

Abnormalities of heartbeat fall into two general categories, which in individual patients are often combined—abnormalities of beat rate and abnormalities of beat form. The former includes rapid and slow heartbeat, termed tachycardia and bradycardia, respectively. The individual contraction may or may not be normal in form. When the form is normal, the condition is usually viewed as benign from the point of view of cardiac disease. Dysrhythmias, or abnormalities of beat form, have two general causes. One is the presence of an ectopic focus whose depolarizing influence competes with, or is superimposed on, that of the SA node. The second is abnormality in conduction of the SA node wave of depolarization so that the heart does not contract in the normal pattern. Conduction may, for example, be completely absent from atrium to ventricle. In this condition, called total heart block, the two chambers beat in uncoordinated fashion, the atria exhibiting the normal rhythm while the ventricles, following ventricular escape, beat much more slowly at their intrinsic rhythm.

### Tachycardia

There are three general causes for sinus tachycardia, or tachycardia due to increased rate of depolarization of the SA node with normal heartbeat form: elevated body temperature, stimulation of the sympathetic nerves, and toxic conditions that enhance the excitability of cardiac muscle and thus increase depolarization rate at the SA node. The first and last sources of tachycardia require medical attention to attack the causal agents. In the case of sympathetic hyperreactivity, both medical and behavioral approaches have relevance. Blanchard and his co-workers published several studies demonstrating successful reduction in heart rate using operant condition (Blanchard & Young, 1974). Scott and associates reported on normal subjects trained to raise heart rate through a shaping procedure (1973). The reinforcement consisted of providing the video portion of an ongoing commercial television program contingent on meeting heart rate increase criteria; the audio portion was continuously on. In addition, subjects received monetary reinforcement for total time heart rate met the criteria.

On some trials Scott and associates used variable as opposed to constant criteria in training (1973). Typically, experimenters establish some level above baseline and provide reinforcement when this level is exceeded, a practice that has two disadvantages. First, if the subject exceeds the minimum early in training, there is no differential consequence for greater success. Second, if the subject fails to reach criterion or reaches it and then falls below, the application of reinforcement is infrequent and the training is inefficient. Accordingly, the authors devised a complicated collection of rules for shifting the criterion up or down as a function of preceding performance. For example, if heart rate began to slow, the criterion would drop until heart rate began to rise again. If the rate were rising, the criterion moved upward so that ever increasing rates were needed to garner reinforcement. Comparison of constant versus variable criteria contingencies in this study is revealing. One subject increased heart rate 16 beats per minute on the variable condition but only 5 beats per minute on the constant. Another subject made no progress in 24 trials on the constant condition but achieved a 16 beat per minute increase in 9 trials of the variable criterion shaping procedure.

Fig. 4–4 shows heart rate data for a clinical subject trained to lower heart rate via shaping (Scott et al., 1973). As can be seen, his baseline heart rate was 89 beats per minute, well above normal. The patient, a 46-year-old man with a 20-year history of tachycardia, was not working and had been declared partially disabled and eligible for social security compensation. In a constant condition (CC and money) insignificant and irregular change in heart rate was seen; the variable condition (VC and money) led to a dramatic decrease in heart rate, into the normal range. Moreover, the subject's heart rate remained steady, at a normal level, after the experiment, and although the patient had previously described himself as nervous or anxious these complaints decreased along with his heart rate. The man's general functional status improved and he sought employment, decreased his use of tranquilizers, and was working at the 18-month follow-up. A similar outcome was reported for another clinical case. In both these patients, the deceleration response was notably resistant to extinction—in contrast to the usual result with acceleration. In the latter case, once the contingency is removed, subjects move readily (and fortunately) back to a normal rhythm. One might

**Figure 4-4.**    Heart rates in beats per minute for all conditions. Reproduced, with permission, from R.W. Scott, E.B. Blanchard, E.D. Edmunson and L.D. Young, A shaping procedure for heart-rate control in chronic tachycardia. *Perceptual Motor Skills*, 1973, 327-338.

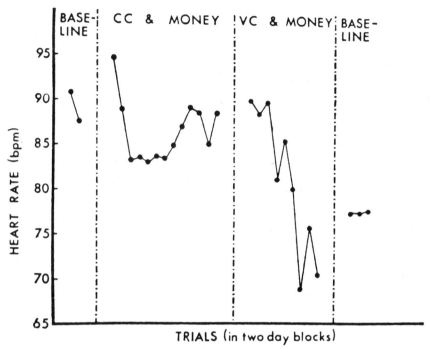

TRIALS (in two day blocks)

hypothesize that the decrease in reported anxiety among deceleration subjects serves to reinforce maintenance of the lowered heart rate; in other words, they are demonstrating an avoidance response.

When the patient's problem is tachycardia with no evidence of cardiac disease, the symptom can be considered essentially behavioral. That is, the response, rapid heart rate, is itself the problem. This problem may well be a part of a more general exaggeration of sympathetic activation, but from the point of view of cardiac function the task is simply to reduce heart rate. Operant conditioning of heart rate deceleration is, as we have seen, possible. How this result is achieved, what the underlying mechanisms are, is currently unknown. Two appealing answers are decreased sympathetic outflow or increased parasympathetic activation, but choosing between these two is not possible on the basis of data reported by Scott and his colleagues (1973) because the response could be caused by either mechanism. Engel and his colleagues, (1971) studying patients with dysrhythmias, have shed some light on possible mechanisms of operant cardiac rate control.

Premature ventricular contractions (PVCs) are a category of cardiac dysrhythmia associated with increased risk of sudden cardiac death (Guyton, 1976). As the name suggests, PVCs are ventricular contractions occurring outside the normal SA node sequence. The physiologic bases of PVCs are various. In many cases, they are benign, reflecting increased irritability of ventricular muscle caused by fatigue, caffeine, or nicotine; mild toxic states; or emotional irritability, the last perhaps mediated by increased sympathetic tone. In other cases, however, regions of diseased cardiac tissue are the source of PVCs. Such contractions are common in patients following myocardial infarction.

Engel and his group have approached the problem of PVCs from the point of view of controlling heart rate (1971). They have trained patients with PVCs in heart rate speeding and slowing, noting the effects of this skill acquisition on PVCs. They also have explored physiological mechanisms by application of autonomically active drugs, which can selectively block or augment parasympathetic and sympathetic effects; in this way, the neural mechanisms through which stimulus control is effected can be teased out. Throughout their extensive studies these workers have relied on a fairly standard training procedure. Accordingly, their training methods will be outlined before surveying the results in some clinical applications.

Feedback, or reinforcement, in Engel's procedure is the illumination of a light. The subject reclines in a hospital bed; before him is an array of three lights—green, red, and yellow. The instruction is to speed heart rate when the green light is on and to slow it when the red light is on. A fixed rate above or below baseline is the criterion. When the criterion is met, the yellow light comes on and remains lit so long as the subject meets the contingency. After a 30-minute adaptation, baseline is established. Contingency sessions of approximately 17 minutes follow. Training sessions run about 80 minutes and subjects receive from one to three daily sessions. Patients are trained both to speed and to slow heart rate. Then they are required to alternate speeding and slowing, a critical test of stimulus control. Finally, subjects are trained in range control. That is, a fixed interval of acceptable rates is established. When the subject is within this range, the yellow light is on. If the subject exceeds the range, the red light comes on and stays on until he is again in the range. If he falls below, the green light is lit until compliance is achieved. A similar procedure in animal studies used shock avoidance as the reinforcer. Fig. 4–5 traces the behavior of monkeys under speeding and slowing conditions. This figure reveals striking stimulus control.

Weiss and Engel described the effect of the training procedure on eight patients with PVCs (1971). The patients, who manifested mild to

**Figure 4-5.** Mean blood pressure and heart rate in monkeys during periods of escape from shock and avoidance of shock in slowing and speeding training. Broken lines represent blood pressure values; solid lines represent heart rates; open circles represent slowing sessions; solid circles represent speeding sessions. Reproduced, with permission, from B.T. Engel, Operant conditioning of cardiac function: A status report. *Psychophysiology*, 1972, 9, 161-177.

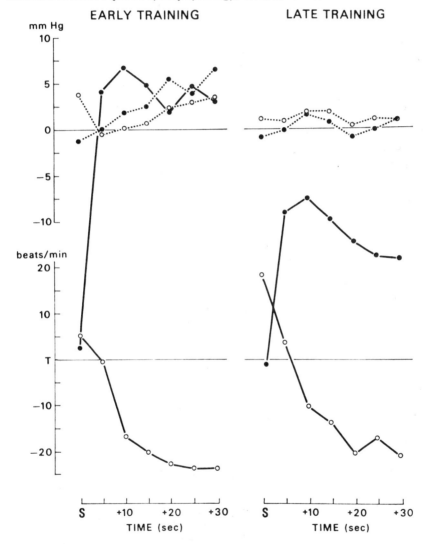

serious cardiac disease, were followed up clinically after the procedure for periods ranging from 1 to 21 months. The training produced stimulus control of heart rate in all eight cases. PVC frequency was reduced in five of the eight patients during training and persisted on follow-up in four. The researchers found marked individual differences in the relationship between days of training and PVC frequency. For example, in some cases speed training was associated with increased PVCs while in others slowing led to heightened PVC incidence. Likewise, telemetry data taken on the ward paralleled training history in some cases but not in others. Finally, patients differed sharply in the degree to which they succeeded in exercising heart rate and PVC control. In three patients with successful PVC control, pharmacologic studies were done in an effort to determine the mechanism of control. In one subject who showed increased PVCs during speeding, administration of atropine led to increased heart rate but no increase in PVCs; administration of isoproterenol, on the other hand, increased both heart rate and PVC frequency. Atropine is an anticholinergic drug that affects heart rate by inhibiting parasympathetic cholinergic activity. Isoproterenol is a sympathomimetic drug similar in structure to epinephrine. Their actions would suggest that in this patient decreased sympathetic tone accounted for decreased PVC rate during slowing. In another patient who showed decreased PVCs during slowing, atropine led to increased heart rate and a marked increase in PVCs, but isoproterenol speeded heart rate and abolished PVCs, which suggests that in this individual PVC control through slowing was mediated by vagal parasympathetic activation.

ATRIAL FIBRILLATION

Atrial fibrillation is a condition in which the normal rhythmic contraction of the atrium in response to depolarization of the SA node is abolished. The SA node originates the heartbeat and causes the atria to contract, forcing blood into the ventricles. The impulse then travels to a second nodal structure, the atrial-ventricular node (AV node), which initiates the wave of depolarization that causes the ventricles to contract. In atrial fibrillation, the muscles of the atria contract in random fashion. In this circumstance, impulses arrive at the AV node at a rate ranging from 300 to 600 per minute and must summate in a random fashion to lead to depolarization. This results in frequent but erratic depolarization of the AV node and ventricular rates of 125 to 150 beats per minute. Such rapid and erratic rates of contraction markedly decrease the efficiency of the heart because it does not fill properly between contractions. This condition is usually treated with digitalis, which has the effect of impeding AV transmission, thus reducing the number of impulses transmitted to the ventricles. However, the heart rate remains more irregular than the normal rate. Since in atrial fibrillation the ventricular rate is not controlled by the SA node, stimulus control of heart rate, if it can be attained, would have to reflect another mechanism.

Bleecker and Engel studied six digitalized patients in atrial fibrillation (1973). Their resting ventricular rates ranged from 50 to 90 beats per minute. All subjects achieved some rate control as evidenced by ability alternately to speed and slow heart rate in response to green and red lights. This finding suggests that the AV node can learn since the normal SA node pacemaker is nonfunctional in atrial fibrillation. Physiologic mechanism was studied by administration of autonomic drugs and Fig. 4-6 shows the results of these studies. As can be seen, only atropine, which raises heart rate through parasympathetic blockade, abolished the conditioning effect. The sympathomimetic isoproterenol increased basal heart rate but had no effect on the subjects' ability differentially to speed and slow heart rate. Propranolol and erdophonium both reduced heart rate, though by different mechanisms. Propranolol is an andrenergic (sympathetic) antagonist, while erodophonium is a parasympathomimetic; neither affected conditioning. These results suggest that conditioning of the AV node is mediated by cholinergic pathways of the parasympathetic autonomic nervous system. Finally, in one patient,

**Figure 4-6.** Effect of various autonomic drugs on voluntary control of heart rate. Solid circles represent baseline conditions; open circles represent speeding; triangles represent slowing. Reproduced, with permission, from E.R. Bleecker and B.T. Engel, Learned control of ventricular rate in patients with atrial fibrillation. *Psychosomatic Medicine*, 1973, 35, 161-175.

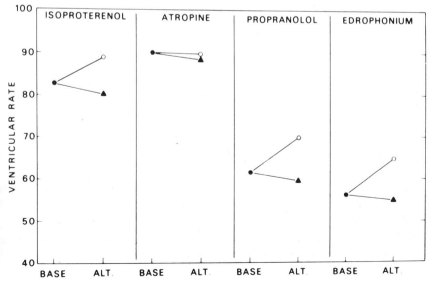

parasympathetic activation during slowing training had the effect of blocking AV conduction leading to ventricular escape. Pointing to a similar effect in digitalis toxicity when AV conduction is impaired, the authors speculated that the conditioning procedure may have unmasked latent toxicity in this case.

From a practical point in view, these studies and others not cited offer evidence that behavioral methods, specifically biofeedback, can benefit patients with heartbeat abnormalities and some of these data shed light on possible mechanisms underlying the effects. Medication does not always control these abnormalities and can have undesirable side effects; hence, continued study of behavioral methods is appropriate.

## Clinical Hypertension

The clinical entity called hypertension refers to chronic elevation of arterial pressure. The usual cutoff points are systolic blood pressure (SBP) greater than 140mm Hg and diastolic blood pressure (DBP) greater than 90 mm Hg. Hypertension is termed essential when there is no identifiable cause, and this condition accounts for the vast majority (over 90%) of hypertensive patients.

Do psychological factors cause hypertension? No simple answer to this question is possible, and the issue is muddied by an equivocal use of the term ''psychological'' in this context. Traditionally the question has been posed within a mentalistic, psychodynamic framework; that is, does hypertension result from psychiatric symptoms like anxiety or in reaction to psychological stress? Asked this way, the question is unanswerable because concepts like stress are imprecise. To the extent that such concepts have been quantified and studied, the results are not clear-cut and it is safe to say that psychological factors do not cause hypertension in any straightforward way (Weiner, 1977). In cases in which such factors do seem to play a role, the critical question concerns mechanism. If hypertension comes on after divorce, how does this effect happen? To say the condition occurs because divorce is stressful simply begs the question. We must understand the mechanisms that translate a social event into visceral responses like increased cardiac output, peripheral resistance, or fluid retention. A behavioral approach has some relevance in this effort.

Behavioral researchers frame questions about the role of psychological factors in hypertension in different terms. Rather than look at stress or personality variables, behavioral models address the learning mechanisms that may play a role in elevating blood pressure. The demonstration of operant visceral learning lies at the center of this formulation.

Summarizing the current status of etiologic theories for essential hypertension, Weiner stated that the mechanisms of sustained high blood pressure seem to change during the course of the disease and that there may be a number of subtypes of essential hypertension, each of which follows a different pathophysiologic route (1977). Good evidence supports a genetic predisposition to the disease, but not all hypertensives have positive family histories and certainly not all offspring of hypertensives manifest the clinical syndrome. Regarding psychological theories specifically, Weiner commented:

> In a general way, animal experiments support the notion that social and psychological factors in human beings may play an etiologic and pathogenetic role in essential hypertension. . . . They support the idea that . . . physiological changes are the consequences of changes in social conditions and behavior. . . . Social injustice, dislocations, and disruption, physical danger, violence, marital discord, separation and poverty promote high blood pressure, fear, and rage. Social stability is conducive to blood pressure levels that remain even throughout a person's life [but] we cannot as yet be certain that in man, social and psychological factors are the antecedents, and not the consequences, of the altered physiological changes in essential hypertension. (Pp. 183–184)

He added that such psychological-environmental factors must interact in complex ways with the familial predisposition, which itself may be socially or genetically mediated, or both. Thus, in the case of essential hypertension, medicine is still at the level of syndromatic diagnosis and symptomatic treatment. It is to treatment that we now turn.

## DRUGS AND DIET

The present treatment of choice in essential hypertension is chemotherapy and dietary control (Freis et al., 1967, 1970). Patients on such a regimen, followed longitudinally and compared to controls, have increased longevity, reduced incidence of the renal, cerebrovascular, and other consequences of high blood pressure, and show decreased systemic arterial pressure. However, hypertensive medications may have negative consequences. In some patients they lead to undesirable side effects, including reduced libido and lethargy. Moreover, in a significant percentage of cases they do not reduce blood pressure. Finally, in some patients, concurrent disease in other systems contraindicates the use of antihypertensive agents.

## BEHAVIORAL TREATMENT

### PSYCHOTHERAPY

Three general categories of behavioral treatment for hypertension exist. First, there is traditional psychotherapy. Here the underlying rationale is that psychological variables in the sense of mental abnormality may give rise to hypertension. Psychodynamic formulations vary with the theoretical predispositions of the therapist. In general, the idea is that personality traits and hypertension are related in a causal way such that changing the personality will alter the symptom of hypertension. If this view were correct, one would expect studies of hypertensive patients and controls to reveal differences in personality variables—to the extent that such variables can be meaningfully operationally defined. Reviewing the corpus of such studies, Weiner concluded that as a group hypertensives are psychologically heterogeneous but that a general relationship seems to exist between emotional reactivity and vascular hyperreactivity, with excessively labile blood pressure more common in hypertensive than in normotensive subjects (1977). A causal inference in either direction cannot be legitimately made on the basis of such correlational findings, but they do suggest that it might be possible to alter hypertension by altering emotional reactivity either directly, assuming an emotionality-hypertension causal link, or indirectly, assuming some naturally occurring confounding between emotionality and other as yet unknown variables that cause hypertension. To take a crude analogy, keeping the floors shiny will reduce the incidence of infection because in making them shiny, one removes microorganisms. It would be incorrect to assume that dull floors cause infections, but the strategy would have a useful effect because of the natural confounding of dull floors and germs. In this light, the psychological question becomes, What is the best way to reduce emotionality? Relying on rather convoluted theoretical considerations, some argue that psychotherapy is the best mechanism.

There is a limited amount of research on the effects of psychotherapy in hypertension. Reiser commented that while much psychoanalytic thought is found in contemporary theories of psychosomatic disease, research on the effects of psychoanalysis as a treatment modality is sparse (1978). Wolf described a psychotherapeutic treatment study of 114 patients with hypertension (1977). A general personality profile, or type, did not emerge from this study, though a tendency toward striving and excessive wariness were described as characteristic of the group. Treatment entailed psychotherapy directed at exploring early life (especially intrafamilial) experiences and included dream analysis and association to explore unconscious material. Expression of emotion and hostility was allowed and the doctor maintained a generally supportive attitude. Of the 114 patients treated, only 14 became normotensive. Titchener and colleagues described group psychotherapy for nine hypertensive patients also receiving medication (1959). Comparison of this group with seven patients receiving only medication found systolic pressure to *increase* significantly, relative to SBP in the controls, even when patients who had dropped out of the therapy group after a session or two were included. Reviewing psychotherapy for psychosomatic disorders in general in 1975, Kellner cited no controlled studies in the area of hypertension save for the Titchener study just described (The review includes, curiously enough, no less than seven citations on the somewhat exotic topic of hypnotic treatment for warts. Results are described as mixed.)

RELAXATION TRAINING

A second category of behavioral treatment for hypertension consists of a variety of relaxation techniques, including Jacobson's (1938) progressive relaxation therapy (PRT), autogenic conditioning (Luthe & Schultz 1969), and meditation exercises derived from Eastern religions, Transcendental Meditation, and yogic practices. These treatments are somewhat more specific than conventional psychotherapy vis-à-vis the presumptive etiology of hypertension. Their use implies that tension, expressed as increased peripheral resistance due to sympathetic overactivity, is a major factor in high blood pressure. Accordingly, any method that causes a patient to relax ought to be useful. While differing widely in their metaphorical and theoretical baggage, all these treatments encourage muscle relaxation, deep breathing, repetitive stimulation, and focusing of attention away from anxiety or distress arousing stimuli and toward the task at hand.

Demonstration that relaxation reduces blood pressure does not mean that tension is the cause of high blood pressure in an etiologic sense. Some animal evidence suggests that extremely aversive environments can generate prolonged hypertension (Benson et al., 1970), but these analogues are at most suggestive. Furthermore, the fact that experimentally induced stress in man raises blood pressure acutely, as has been repeatedly demonstrated, does not in itself imply that chronic elevation of blood pressure is similarly caused. In fact, a great many behavioral events have been shown experimentally to lead to blood pressure elevation; these include strenuous exercise, the anticipation of strenuous exercise, emotionally arousing stimuli, and doing mental arithmetic. No one seriously proposes that mental arithmetic is the cause of hypertension, but it is well to remember that the data supporting a stress etiology for this symptom are very similar in kind and that the great popularity of the stress hypothesis as etiologic rests on its heuristic appeal, not on convincing evidence. Nevertheless, relaxation treatment has led to positive results, which finding is clinically important quite independent of etiologic theories.

Reviewing the literature on relaxation therapies in hypertension, Jacob and associates found numerous methodological flaws: placebo effects were seldom ruled out, control groups were inadequate or absent, potentially relevant confounds such as diet were uncontrolled, and follow-ups to show extra-experimental generalization and persistence of blood pressure reductions were seldom adequate (1977). Granting these limitations, the authors concluded that in hypertensive patients relaxation seems to lead to blood pressure reductions in excess of placebo effects. Their conclusion rested on a comparison of reported effects of placebos in controlled drug studies with effects seen in relaxation studies. They further noted that the effects tend to be greater the higher the initial value. This pattern has important research implications since if results are reported in relative (e.g., percentage of change) rather than absolute (e.g., 160/90 to 120/80) values, interstudy comparisons will be difficult and could lead to spurious conclusions as to relative technique efficacy. That is, if two equally effective (or ineffective) techniques are compared in populations exhibiting different mean initial values, the technique using the group with higher values will appear to be more effective.

Beiman and colleagues reported on successful relaxation treatment of hypertension in two relatively young (37 and 27 years old) male subjects (1978). Modeled on progressive relaxation therapy, this study tailored relaxation instructions and cues to the specific aspects of life the patients identified as stressful. Neither patient received antihypertensive medication during the study. One had taken such agents previously but had ceased to use them; the other refused medication. Basal blood pressure was obtained over a 20-day period both by the patients themselves at home and by the therapist in a clinic setting. The treatment consisted of therapy sessions during which problem areas were identified and relaxation training was performed, along with home practice of relaxation, initially on a twice daily schedule, then whenever the stress cues identified in treatment occurred. Both patients showed decreases in SBP and DBP that were significant statistically and, more important, clinically (the patients fell into the normotensive range). Follow-up at two months in one case and six months in the other suggested that the reduced blood pressure values were sustained after termination of formal treatment. The authors noted that the magnitude of decrease was greater than that in the bulk of relaxation studies reviewed by Jacob and colleagues in 1977 and asserted that at least in these two cases the method represented an alternative to chemotherapy. (The Jacob paper stressed that relaxation treatment should be viewed as an adjunct to, rather than a substitute for, medication. The distinction is moot in patients who refuse to take pills, of course, but in general one would have to agree that

until longitudinal, controlled study demonstrates that relaxation training, or any other psychological method, can achieve stable, long-term
reductions comparable to those seen with drugs, the approach should be
viewed as quasi-experimental or adjunctive and alternative only when,
for whatever reason, drugs are contraindicated.)

A study by Stone and DeLeo is especially interesting in that blood
chemistry analyses were performed in conjunction with relaxation treatment for a group of moderate hypertensives on medication. The researchers wanted to elucidate mechanism (1976). Fourteen patients
underwent a training procedure consisting of five 20-minute sessions
devoted to teaching Buddhist relaxation exercises. An unfortunately
small control group (five patients) was seen for all chemical and blood
pressure evaluations but received no training. Experimental subjects
practiced the exercises twice daily for 10–15 minutes sitting quietly in a
comfortable chair and counting their breaths subvocally while relaxing
their muscles. The results for mean arterial pressure (DBP plus one-third
SBP) showed a drop in supine recording from 110mm Hg to 98mm Hg
and from 112mm Hg to 100mm Hg for standing in the experimental
group. Controls showed no change. A number of blood analyses were
done; the most intriguing finding was a drop in the experimental group
in plasma dopamine-beta-hydroxylase (DBH), an enzyme that breaks
down dopamine to norepinephrine and is discharged during activation of
the sympathetic neurons. Plasma DBH is thus thought to be an index of
sympathetic nervous system function. After treatment, experimentals
showed a statistically significant drop in the level of this enzyme, differing from both control and their own baseline levels. Furthermore, levels
of DBH were correlated positively with mean arterial pressure. This
finding would suggest that a reduction in peripheral sympathetic activity
contributes to the drop in blood pressure occasioned by the relaxation exercises.

In summary, there is accumulating evidence that relaxation treatment can reduce blood pressure in some hypertensive patients. Moreover, this effect is achieved with very simple procedures. In an era of increasing awareness of cost effectiveness, this consideration is important.
The 1976 study by Stone and DeLeo shed some light on the mechanism
possibly underlying the effect, and this style of research, approaching the
problem from more than one vantage point, is extremely promising.

BIOFEEDBACK

The biofeedback treatment of hypertension represents the most
specific of the psychological approaches. Here the application of the reinforcer is made contingent on reduction in blood pressure in the presence
of some SD, a light, for example, or simply the words "lower your blood

pressure.'' The clinical application of this method follows a fairly extensive literature showing successful operant conditioning of blood pressure in animals (DiCara & Miller, 1968) and in normotensive man (Brener & Kleinman, 1970). This approach does not address the problem of whether physiological or psychological factors are mediators of hypertension, though some writers have speculated that essential hypertension is a learned phenomenon entailing either respondent or operant conditioning of the pressor response or a combination of the two (Lachman, 1972). Whatever the ultimate fate of these etiologic speculations, evidence suggests that biofeedback techniques can lead to reduced blood pressure.

In 1971, Benson and his co-workers demonstrated that patients diagnosed as essential hypertensives could, through operant conditioning, lower their blood pressure in laboratory settings. There was, however, no assessment of extralaboratory blood pressure; hence the generality of the effect and its ultimate clinical usefulness were not demonstrated.

Kristt and Engel extended assessment of operant methods to the natural environment (1975). Five patients with hypertension of at least 10 years' duration were trained in a raising-lowering-alternating procedure similar to that described earlier for heart rate control. Before training, however, all patients were taught to take their own blood pressure at home; they obtained readings four times per day and these data served as baseline. Patients were then hospitalized and trained with 14 sessions per week. The first week entailed training to raise SBP; the second, to lower; and the third, to alternate. The contingency shifted over trials depending upon performance; feedback was on a heartbeat-to-heartbeat basis. The patients were then trained to use a stethoscope and cuff to try to lower blood pressure at home by listening for and trying to make Korotkoff sounds beginning at lower and lower cuff pressures. They also recorded blood pressure daily. At one- and three-month follow-up visits, formal conditioning in the alternating procedure was again provided. A number of interesting findings emerged from this study. In the hospital, subjects generally were successful in meeting the contingencies. Furthermore, monitoring of other physiological parameters, including heart rate, EEG, EMG, and respiratory rate, failed to show relationships between blood pressure and these parameters with the exception of an increase in heart rate during the first raising trial. This would suggest that blood pressure was being operantly conditioned specifically and not as part of a general arousal-relaxation response complex. The results for blood pressure reduction maintenance were encouraging: the home recordings after training showed a mean drop of 16mm Hg in SBP; in some cases drops were also seen in DBP. The authors commented that the home training procedure seemed to be important in allowing the patient to see his progress. It also constituted a measure of compliance.

Elder and Eustis described an operant conditioning approach to hypertension that was completely outpatient based (1975). The researchers made no effort to alter the patients' lifestyle in any way—medications were left unchanged and diet and sleep were uncontrolled. Twenty patients, ranging in age from 23 to 80 years, were studied. In half the cases, practice was massed (10 sessions over two weeks); the other subjects had spaced practice (10 sessions at increasing intervals over 80 days). All training took place in a clinical setting. DBP decline was reinforced with a red light signaling increase or no change; a green light signaled decrease. Verbal reinforcement was given once during each half of a training session and there were 20 trials per session. In all cases mean DBPs were lower in the second half than in the first half of each session. As regards the massed versus spaced variable, massed practice seemed slightly superior, with DBP dropping an average of 9% below baseline for massed, 7% for spaced. A small sex difference was noted: women performed better than men. The authors found that the drop in blood pressure in this study was less dramatic than that reported in some other studies, the overall mean decline being less than 10mm Hg. They offered several possible reasons for this result. For one thing, these subjects were outpatients and the outpatient-inpatient status difference might be expected to affect motivation. Hospitalized patients generally feel they are sicker than outpatients because of our popular view that going to the hospital means that one is either having a baby or quite ill. Also, medications were not altered and all patients were taking antihypertensives. Assuming the drugs were having an effect, the amount of additional reduction may have thus been limited. This study is important in highlighting the possibility of outpatient behavioral management of the symptom, and outpatient treatment is far less expensive than inpatient.

Elder and associates evaluated two modes of reinforcement on both DBP and SBP, with reinforcement contingent only on DBP (1973). Eighteen male patients, six per group, were studied in a hospital setting. Two experimental groups were trained to reduce blood pressure with contingent feedback of a light, available every two minutes, if reduction criteria were met. The contingency followed performance so that continuous reduction was required. The experimental groups differed in that one group also received social reinforcement in the form of verbal approval. There were eight training sessions on consecutive days and a follow-up session one week later. Medical management included antidepressants, a salt-free diet, bed rest, but no antihypertensives. The researchers found that the combined praise and light condition led to a greater reduction in DBP than did the light alone. The light-only group began to show the effect by the seventh session, while the praise and light group had a significant effect in the third session. Unfortunately, a significant number of subjects were lost to follow-up, but the means for those who were seen (about half the total group) were near the last session values. Follow-up compliance was also best in the praise group (five of six), followed by the light-only group (four of six) and the controls (two of six). Effects on SBP were nonsignificant though the means for the praise group were lower than those for the other two in all sessions. This study again demonstrates that blood pressure can be reduced in the laboratory and makes a start at finding the differential effects of specific reinforcement parameters.

Perhaps the most dramatic report of successful biofeedback treatment of hypertension is the single case study of Miller (1972). Using daily 45-minute training sessions over ten weeks, Miller found a drop in DBP from 97mm Hg to 76mm Hg, with a concomitant elimination of all antihypertensive medications. Follow-up and continued training kept this patient in the normotensive range. This report is especially impressive because the blood pressure drop was evident during basal measurement, without feedback, which is obviously the outcome of clinical interest.

Reviewing the use of biofeedback training with hypertensives, Blanchard and Young commented that enthusiasm for the technique must be tempered by the general lack of controlled outcome studies (1974). They suggested that single-subject experiments with reversals are an appropriate intermediate step to more expensive group studies. The recommendation seems pertinent but perhaps the time has come for the sort of large-scale effort needed to document conclusively the effectiveness and limits of biofeedback in this area. Given the urgency of the problem and the accumulating positive findings, a sizable investment of clinical research money, perhaps on the model of the VA collaborative study of antihypertensive medication (Freis et al., 1967, 1970), seems now to be warranted.

In a cogent review of the literature on both relaxation and biofeedback treatments, Frumkin and colleagues emphasized the critical point that evaluation of these methods as clinical tools requires documentation of extralaboratory decreases under basal conditions when the control technique, whatever it is, is not being employed (1978). Clearly, patients are not going to spend the bulk of their time meditating or wired to a biofeedback apparatus. Looking at the literature as a whole, Frumkin and his co-workers stated that relaxation methods have been more extensively studied in this way than has biofeedback and would therefore have to be viewed as more promising at this time. Relaxation also has the decided advantage of being easily learned and applied and not requiring complicated electrophysiological equipment. This conclusion must, of course, be tentative. The available data are insufficient to justify unqualified advocacy of either technique. Futhermore, one might speculate that understanding the hypertensive mechanism may be more readily achieved in the biofeedback paradigm if only because more detailed physiological data are accumulated when subjects are wired to the machines. Certainly, relaxation therapies do not preclude simultaneous physiological monitoring, but the very simplicity of these methods, an important clinical advantage, tends to mitigate against the use of expensive and sophisticated equipment when they are being applied.

## Conclusion

In this chapter we looked at the cardiovascular system and three categories of disease, myocardial infarction, beat abnormalities, and hypertension. Behavioral treatments for these disorders were reviewed and promising results identified. Systematic study of long-term effects under these modalities is essential. In the area of post-MI recovery, it seems highly likely that behavioral interventions to control diet and exercise will lead to increased longevity, but this possibility needs to be demonstrated and more specifically tied to characteristics of the disease, as well as to social and psychological characteristics of individual patients. In the area of beat abnormalities also, long-term follow-ups are generally lacking and epidemiologic implications are completely unknown. The same is true of the behavioral treatment of hypertension. In both cases, a fairly massive research effort using large numbers of patients followed for a period of years is needed. The existing literature, however, seems sufficiently promising to justify such an expenditure of effort, time, and dollars.

Two general categories of variable ought to be addressed in future work. First, technical issues such as massed versus spaced practice, type of reinforcers and scheduling, and the interactions of these variables with other modes of treatment, notably drugs and diet, ought to be evaluated. A second major area of interest concerns patient characteristics both in terms of optimal methods of individual management and in terms of isolating mechanisms of action.

Medical opinion is increasingly moving in the direction of viewing hypertension as a spectrum of disorders rather than a single entity. It seems probable that psychological methods will be variably effective depending on the type of disorder being treated. For example, it may well be that emotional factors mediated sympathetically are more important in the early stages of labile hypertension, at which time the relaxation method could be of special utility. In the later stages of fixed hypertension, the motor skills model implicit in the operant approach seems heuristically more pertinent. In any case, as more information comes from the physiologic study of the symptom, permitting empirical classification of patients other than by symptom magnitude, behaviorally oriented workers ought to be increasingly specific in defining physiologic type when forming clinical research samples. Clearly, medical and psychological professional collaboration is of the utmost importance in this regard.

# 5

# Medicine II: Renal Disease

The kidneys remove toxins from the blood and must function for life to be maintained. If the kidneys fail, uremic poisoning results, leading to death. As recently as 20 years ago, this was the scenario for almost all patients with diseases leading to loss of kidney function, or end stage renal disease (Friedman, 1978). In the 1950s, experimentation in transplantation began; efforts at artificial purification of the blood by machine (dialysis) began even earlier. It was not until 1960 and Scribner's invention of a workable external shunt, however, that wide application of chronic dialysis became a possibility. With this innovation, life expectancy for persons with end stage kidney disease rose dramatically. In the years since, continued technical advance has led to greater availability of artificial kidneys, more reliable and compact machines, and consequent increasing life expectancy for this patient population.

The modes of treatment for end stage renal disease fall into four categories: transplantation, dialysis in hospital (center dialysis), dialysis at home, and conservative management. Transplantation may be either donor or cadaveric; that is, the patient may receive a kidney from a relative or an accident victim.

Dialysis refers to the use of a machine to remove from the blood a variety of toxic chemicals that normally would be removed by the kidney and secreted in the urine. In hemodialysis, blood is passed through channels bounded by membranes that are permeable to the toxic compounds normally removed by the kidney (Guyton, 1976). On the other side of these membranes is a fluid called the dialysate. The toxins diffuse across the membrane from the region of high concentration, the blood, to a

93

region of low concentration, the dialysate. The cleansed blood returns to the body via the shunt, or fistula. Hemodialysis must be done periodically, on alternate days, for example, and requires from a couple to many hours depending on the type of machine, the status of the patient, and other considerations. In the early days of hemodialysis the procedure was always done in hospital, but in recent years simpler machines have allowed a growing number of persons to dialyze at home. The choice of center versus home dialysis, as we shall see, is a major decision in which psychological factors play a prominent role.

Conservative treatment means doing nothing therapeutic to halt the progression of renal failure. The patient is made as comfortable as possible and given emotional support up to the end, but is not dialyzed or transplanted. A number of writers (Reichsman and McKegney, 1978) have emphasized that this choice should be available to patients for whom dialysis does not offer a quality of life they find acceptable, or who, for a variety of reasons, do not comply with the complex dietary, medical and technical requisites of the procedure. The choice not to continue dialysis is but one example of the complex ethical and personal dilemma generated by a technology which can sustain vital signs and thus life as many doctors define it, but which may not sustain life as particular patients define it. The effort to come to terms with these different perspectives by both the staff and patients is a psychological and philosophical task of some magnitude.

The importance of psychological factors in the management of patients in end stage renal disease was acknowledged early in the development of the support technology. Gombos and colleagues described the psychological problems of patients in a dialysis program (1964), and De Nour and Czaczkes addressed the emotional reactions of dialysis team members to their task (1968). Mental health workers figured prominently in the early days of dialysis, in which a very limited resource had to be apportioned. Accordingly, much attention was paid to psychological predictors of successful adjustment to the procedure and to factors associated with high risk of failure (Sand et al., 1966; Shae et al., 1965). Wright and associates described the stress that patients face during dialysis (1966), as did De Nour and associates (1968).

With the advent of home dialysis, the task of patient training became critical and was subjected to psychological analysis by Blagg and his co-workers (see Stinson et al., 1972). While dialysis presents significant problems to the renal patient, the family also is deeply involved and mental health workers have devoted considerable attention to the family as the unit of study. In the area of transplantation, donor selection and donor-patient relationships have been discussed (Adler, 1972) and the complex interactions that surround home dialysis have also been seen as potential areas of psychological conflict and stress (Shambaugh &

Kanter, 1969). Finally, the psychology of rehabilitation has been given insufficient attention here, as in other areas of medicine. Blagg has written eloquently on this topic, stressing the critical·role of staff attitude and expectation in rehabilitation outcome (1978).

This chapter reviews several of these areas. The literature on hemodialysis has exploded during the last decade, mandating a gross truncation and selection of material for discussion. While the general orientation of this book is behavioral, the psychological literature on chronic renal disease is psychodynamic in character. Accordingly, the language and concepts used in the following sections are different from what has gone before. The behavioral perspective is discussed where it has something special to offer, but behaviorists as a group have not been prominent in the area of renal disease.

## Patient Characteristics

Scribner, who invented the shunt essential for mass use of dialysis, associated five attributes with a good prognosis (1963). The patient should be a self-supporting adult under 45 years of age, be stable and mature in personality, have no associated heart or circulatory disease, show a willingness to cooperate, and be in stable renal failure or showing a slow decline in function.

Foster and colleagues examined retrospectively a sample of 21 patients who had begun dialysis two years previously (1973). Of these, seven had died. The study identified several variables that discriminated survivors from the deceased. Data were available on a wide range of factors, including demographics, medical status, neuropsychiatric status and history, psychological tests, and physiological parameters such as weight gain and blood chemistry. The neuropsychiatric data addressed level of adaptive function at the beginning of dialysis, history of psychological problems, and level of previous adjustment. Psychological tests included the Cornell Medical Index, Rotter's Locus of Control measure, an adjective checklist assessing mood, a self-report of degree of disability, and a series of measures designed to tap body image and fusion-boundary orthogonal dimensions (this refers to the tendency to see oneself as distinct from others versus a tendency to feel part of a community or group).

A number of predictor variables emerged from this study, but equally interesting are some of the nonpredictors. Level of social adjustment prior to illness was not predictive of survival, nor was previous psychiatric history. These findings are at variance with a widespread belief that any history of psychiatric disorder is a poor prognostic sign.

Although a number of studies have reported a higher incidence of failure among patients with preexisting emotional problems, the Foster study raised questions as to the universality of this phenomenon (1973). Psychosocial factors predicting success were the presence of one living parent and a strong religious affiliation, in this case Roman Catholic. Survivors had less evidence of neurological dysfunction, or uremic encephalopathy. Self-description of degree of disability also correlated with survival, suggesting a link between patients' subjective sense of well-being and ultimate outcome. Cause and effect are not clear, but the patients in this study ''predicted'' their course with some accuracy. The psychological tests yielded complicated results: they were not predictive alone but interacted with other variables in a range of ways. The authors concluded that a patient's sense of boundary, a sense of separation from the patient group, leads to longer survival, perhaps because he thereby avoids repeated grief reactions when other patients die.

In dialysis, survival is intimately connected to compliance with the dietary regimen. De Nour and Czaczkes studied prediction of dietary compliance in a group of 43 patients at six dialysis centers (1972). Compliance with diet was assessed at six-month intervals and rated on a five-point scale based on criteria of body weight, serum potassium, and blood urea nitrogen (BUN), all of which measures rise if patients do not eat properly. In the group as a whole, dietary compliance was relatively poor, with only 5 patients rated excellent and 20 showing either some or great abuse (i.e., binge eating). Psychological factors were clinically assessed and several were associated with poor compliance. Low frustration tolerance by history, a tendency to act out, and apparent secondary gain from the sick role all predicted noncompliance. Likewise, extreme reactions of denial of illness or suicidal ideation were associated with abuse, the latter being predictive of severe overeating, which may, in fact, have been suicidal in intent at a conscious or unconscious level. As in the Foster study, nonpredictors are revealing. Here, however, evidence of organic brain syndrome was not predictive.

Greenberg and colleagues evaluated seven patients with end stage renal disease to assess their adjustment to dialysis (1975). In this group, the presence of a supportive family member was critical to successful adaptation. Personal psychological stability and willingness to cooperate also were associated with good outcome. However, age did not operate as a significant predictor of success, a finding at variance with the generally held opinion that older (over 45) patients are poor risks.

Taylor and associates reported a most interesting study of physician behavior in making dialysis decisions (1975). Whatever the predictors, they are applied to individual cases by physicians and selection committees, particularly in the event of resource limitations. To explore which factors influence these decisions, Taylor and co-workers had eight physicians make disposition decisions on 100 cases, some real and some created, on the basis of 18 variables that all raters agreed were relevant. Each item was ranked on a severity dimension. For example, renal disease was classed end stage, stable; active progressive; or associated with other diseases. Each physician rated the cases' prospect for dialysis on a seven-point scale ranging from excellent to unequivocal rejection. The researchers then retrospectively determined which of the 18 items were most important to each physician.

The Taylor study found considerable variation in the absolute number of persons placed in each of the seven categories (1975). The excellent rating was used only once by one physician and seven times by another; others fell in between. Likewise, the worst category showed extreme variation, frequencies ranging from 14 to 58 cases. There also was considerable variability in how individual cases were rated: only six cases received unanimous ratings and these were all in the worst category. Dividing the ratings in half on the positive-negative dimension, 32 cases fell on the same side of the midpoint in all physician ratings. The analysis of items used in making decisions also revealed interesting differences. Though all raters agreed that the 18 items were relevant, the actual number statistically significantly associated with decisions ranged from 3 to 9 among the physicians. However, the relative importance of the items was rather consistent. Advanced age, history of psychiatric disorder, presence of cardiovascular disease, and presence of other diseases were all associated with decisions against dialysis.

This is an instructive paper, suggesting that unanimity is the exception rather than the rule when professionals assess cases independently. Taylor and co-workers concluded that independent rather than group decision making was preferable, in order to avoid interpersonal influence. The study also found consensus as to what variables are important. Systematic prospective study of these factors seems indicated since, as noted earlier, the predictive power of at least two, psychiatric history and age, is not completely clear.

## Stress of Dialysis

### SOURCES OF STRESS

Reichsman and McKegney identified eight sources of stress in dialysis (1978). The patient must adjust to these factors if he is to succeed. The first major stress is physical disability. Renal disease brings a variety of physical symptoms and complaints that dialysis does not completely alleviate. Furthermore, the dialysis process may introduce new sources of disability such as infection, malfunction of the shunt, and a progressive brain syndrome. A very frequent complaint is chronic weakness and malaise, which often is not helped by dialysis; indeed, a more acute weakness follows each dialysis run. Understandably, the patient experiences considerable disappointment when the rather arduous hemodialysis regimen does not lead to subjective feelings of well-being.

Fear of death is a feature of all chronic debilitating diseases and dialysis seems to encourage this fear since the process itself brings to awareness the tenuousness of the patient's grip on life. Beard described the dialysis patient as impaled on the horns of a dilemma: ''The fear of dying and the fear of living [are] an integral part of the whole problem of renal failure and its treatment . . . To these patients . . . working out some solution to this dilemma was their primary task'' (1969: 380).

Related to the fear of death is the patient's feeling about the dialysis machine. Reichsman and McKegney remarked: ''The visible circulation of the blood outside the body is a very unusual feature that makes the facts of treatment (and disease) unavoidably apparent, compared to the less obvious actions of medication, radiation therapy or even cardiac pacemakers and surgery, with its anesthesia and post operative bandaging'' (1978:442–443). Abram, working in a psychoanalytic paradigm, described several patients' reactions to the machine and their dependent relationship upon it (1977). There is confusion about body boundaries and image, with the machine viewed as in some sense a part of the person yet obviously at the same time distinct. Strong feelings of ambivalence toward the device and fantasies about it are often reported.

For many patients, hemodialysis is an interim measure as they await a cadaveric kidney for transplantation. This is inevitably an indeterminate period of time and waiting is a fourth stressor in Reichsman and McKegney's list (1978). After transplantation, the recipient must adapt to the idea of a foreign organ in the body and there are reports of elaborate patient fantasies concerning the identity and circumstances of death of the donor (Cramond, 1971). One patient wrote: ''I received my new kidney from a cadaver donor. The hardest things for me to deal with were the idea that someone had to die so that I might live, and the fact that the donor would be kept biologically alive until the doctors were ready to remove his kidneys, at which time the machines would be turned off'' (Barger, 1978: 69).

A related problem arises in donor transplantation in that the relationship between donor and recipient is potentially complicated by feelings of overwhelming indebtedness. Adler described the case of one female patient who received a kidney from her brother and detailed a variety of psychological mechanisms that operated to solidify the relationship between the two of them (1972). The literature on donor-recipient relationships and on the psychology of the decision to donate an organ is sizable and interesting. Fellner observed that the decision to donate a kidney seems often to occur with great speed, in contrast to the prolonged deliberation that physicians deem an essential part of the donor selection process (1971). On the other hand, Simmons and co-workers described families thrown into agonizing turmoil by the selection process (1971). Fortunately, with increasing success of cadaveric transplantation, the issue of live donors may soon be mainly of historical interest.

Conflicts over dependence are mentioned by virtually every writer on the topic of dialysis. The patient is obviously dependent on the machine for life, and this dependence is made dramatically evident at each dialysis session. Furthermore, the patient is dependent on the staff in center dialysis and to a greater or lesser degree on spouse-helpers in home dialysis. Medical complications and attendant disease additionally reduce the patient's competence. Resolution of these feelings of dependence, of ambivalence toward helpers and staff, and of bitterness about declining function and decreasing competence are major tasks and represent a fifth important source of stress in hemodialysis.

A sixth stressor is the rigorous dietary regimen necessary to dialysis. Fluid, electrolyte, and protein consumption must be controlled and serious dissatisfaction may arise from restrictions on eating.

Interpersonal relationships are the seventh source of stress listed by Reichsman and McKegney (1978). Specific problems are seen in sexual relations since dialysis reduces libido. Interestingly, sexual activity has been seen to decrease with the onset of dialysis, though the uremic state and thus the biological cause of sexual dysfunction is lessened by the process (Levy, 1974). This would suggest that an important role is played by the overt manifestation of dependence on the machine. Dialysis also entails profound adjustment in family relationships. The former breadwinner becomes dependent on his wife and children; the active housekeeper can no longer perform her accustomed role; all must live with a constant awareness of a potentially fatal disease. As Reichsman and McKegney eloquently put it: ''The family and patient engaged in hemodialysis live the multiple problems twenty four hours a day, seven days a week, until transplantation or death intervenes. There is no vacation, time off, or other escape from the realities of maintenance hemodialysis as they impinge on interpersonal relationships'' (p. 446).

The final sources of stress are financial and occupational (Reichsman & McKegney, 1978). First, huge medical bills may go hand in hand with partial coverage. Medicare supports the much more expensive center dialysis to a greater degree than home dialysis, rendering the latter actually more expensive for the patient. Furthermore, ceasing to work entails a drop in income in most cases, and for relatively affluent persons the drop may be profound. Downward adjustments in standard of living are difficult in any case and are complicated by feelings of self-blame in the patient.


PATTERNS OF COPING

The literature describes a variety of coping methods and patterns of adjustment for the stresses hemodialysis patients and their families face. Reichsman and Levy studied 25 patients and identified a three-stage adaptation during which a variety of coping mechanisms were brought into play (1972). The reported pattern did not occur in all patients but is nevertheless a clinically useful portrait of the modal trend.

The beginning of dialysis is a honeymoon period characterized by marked improvement in both physical and psychological function. This stage usually begins during the first three weeks of dialysis and lasts for six weeks to six months. The patient accepts his dependence on the machine and shows a grateful, positive attitude toward staff. Intense anxiety was seen in most patients and these feelings manifested themselves in many of the males by unconcealed masturbation while on the machine. When asked about this behavior, patients said it helped them forget about the danger of the procedure.

The honeymoon is followed by a period of disenchantment, characterized by feelings of helplessness and sadness, that lasts from 3 to 12 months. This period was preceded by a stressor in many cases, frequently impending return to work or housekeeping. Clotting of the shunt and other physical complications followed onset of the disenchantment period and in 12 patients a clear sequence of stress, negative affective shift, and complication at the shunt site was seen. Dietary noncompliance increased during this period, bringing feelings of guilt. Hostility toward staff increased in both frequency and intensity.

Long-term adaptation is the third stage and entails varying degrees of acceptance of personal limitations and of the difficulties and shortcomings of chronic hemodialysis. Patients experience alternate periods of contentment and depression. The major coping strategy is denial, and this tendency to employ denial is described with great frequency in the literature on dialysis. Complications decreased in frequency during this period, and patients seem resigned to their dependence on the machine and the staff. Anger was most frequently directed at obtaining more support from staff. Rehabilitation during this period followed an all-or-none pattern: 11 patients spent less than 25% of their available time at gainful work; 14 patients spent 75–100% so employed; no patients fell in the 25–75% midrange.

The literature on psychological function in hemodialysis patients shows nearly universal reliance on the mechanism of denial. Reichsman and Levy commented: "We have not seen denial used as massively as by this group of patients, as a whole, in any other patient population with physical illness" (1972:862). Abram noted: "As with the dependency conflicts associated with dialysis, denial is a universal finding in psychological studies of chronic dialysis" (1977: 303). Short and Wilson added: "The capacity for denial in these patients is phenomenal. [They] accept their condition and the inevitability of their outcome. What is denied is that it is happening now" (1969:434). To the extent that denial is adaptive, minimizing distress and maximizing optimism, this strategy is helpful and ought not to be interfered with (Reichsman & McKegney, 1978). On the other hand, denial may be so complete as to interfere with treatment and to put the patient's life at risk. Staff must be sensitive to these two possibilities and respond appropriately. Psychologists can work directly with patients and indirectly though staff in-service programs to resolve such problems. Reichsman and McKegney listed four criteria for adaptive coping that are applicable to denial. (1978). Coping reactions are adaptive if they help the patient or family member

1. to maintain a sense of reasonable personal psychological comfort;
2. to remain in communication with professional staff and family members about a wide range of topics and feelings;
3. to comply appropriately with the prescribed medical regimen;
4. to take actions and to make life decisions that are appropriate to the seriousness of the illness situation. (P. 449)

These general principles can guide staff in deciding when denial should be supported or confronted. Typically, patients use denial appropriately; only the exceptional case requires psychotherapeutic intervention.

Dependence is a common source of stress in hemodialysis and subjective conflict over enforced dependence is aversive to many patients. On the other hand, the ability to accept this constraint and to use it as a coping mechanism is important in patients whose physical reality mandates a degree of dependence. Like denial, dependence is a topic of universal discussion among writers on hemodialysis and a number of interesting observations have been made. Abram, for example, pointed out that the dialysis patient is inevitably given double messages regarding dependence (1977). On the one hand, he must comply with dietary and medical requirements and he must depend on the machine, staff, and helpers. On the other hand, when he is not being dialyzed, he is urged to be independent—to lead a normal life.

Adjustment to these conflicting demands is difficult for many patients. Abram described two modes of maladaptation to dependence (1977). Some patients become excessively dependent and are unable to give up the sick role. Such patients are described by staff as demanding and compulsive about all aspects of treatment. The opposite reaction is rebellion. The patient who completely rejects the sick role, denying illness, may do so because he is unable to accept the amount of dependence dialysis requires. Patients of this type take poor care of the shunt, come late to treatment, and show very poor dietary compliance. Strong feelings of anger, boiling just below the surface, are commonly expressed in outbursts at staff.

Blagg, discussing dependence in the context of rehabilitation of the dialysis patient, observed that staff expectations and attitudes play a major role in fostering or discouraging dependent behavior in patients (1978). The highly technical nature of the treatment poses the danger that human needs will become obscured in an effort to achieve technical goals. The goal of treatment in renal disease or any other illness is to maximize life function. To the extent that patients grow dependent upon staff, adopt the sick role, and resign themselves to invalidism, this goal is not achieved, no matter how successful the treatment is from a technical point of view. Accordingly, Blagg and his colleagues would orient the treatment program around the goal of independence, reinforcing independent behaviors, offering structured learning experiences to increase them, and emphasizing home as opposed to center dialysis as the treatment of choice. Blagg pointed to the role of behavioral theory and approaches in a dialysis enterprise so directed, an area to be explored shortly. The message here is that dependence can be addressed behaviorally in a program designed to reinforce responses that are incompatible with dependent ones and to teach the skills necessary to maximize independence, thereby offsetting the potentially reinforcing consequences of the sick role.

Denial and dependence are two methods of coping with renal disease and dialysis. A third one mentioned by Reichsman and McKegney is death (1978). At some point in the course of protracted treatment the patient may cease to feel that the quality of life he is able to achieve is sufficient to make life worth living. When that point is reached, the patient may decide to cease treatment. Such a decision is not easily accepted by staff, working to maintain life and dedicated to the maintenance of life as an absolute value. They may feel rejected or betrayed and experience hostility toward the patient, for whom they have done so much. In such cases, the staff's personal values and tendency to deny failure may interfere with their ability objectively to assess the quality of life the patient on chronic dialysis has achieved and thus to understand his, to them unacceptable, decision: "It seems imperative that hemodialysis programs—indeed, perhaps all of medicine and society—eventually arrive at the position that the decision not to accept or to discontinue prolonged, heroic treatment is not equivalent to 'suicide' in the common parlance" (Reichsman & McKegney, 1978:453). Reichsman and McKegney, citing studies by Holcomb and McDonald (1973) and Levy and

Wybrandt (1975) that found widespread depression or dissatisfaction among hemodialysis patients, stressed that staff and patient may view the success of dialysis quite differently (1978). What the patient considers a minimally acceptable level of function may not coincide either with what the staff deems minimally acceptable or with what is possible to achieve. In this event, the choice to die may be "a coping reaction, albeit the extreme and final one" (Reichsman & McKegney, 1978:450).

## Home versus Center Dialysis

With advances in technology, it has become possible for patients to perform dialysis at home. This procedure is in the long run much less expensive than center dialysis and shows survival outcome comparable to that of center dialysis or donor transplantation and superior to that of cadaveric transplantation (Delano, 1978). Blagg reported that almost all nonpsychotic, normally intelligent, medically uncomplicated patients can be dialyzed at home (1972). However, Shupack argued that less than 40% of dialysis patients are suitable for home dialysis (1973). At present in the United States, only 27% of all dialysis patients are on home dialysis.

Personality variables linked to both good and bad response to home dialysis are familiar. Overly dependent patients who rely heavily on denial do poorly in home dialysis, as they do in center dialysis. Also, home dialysis places additional stress on the family, particularly when the spouse serves as a helper. Some argue that home dialysis may have the negative consequence of making the illness an even more central part of life than does center dialysis. From this point of view, going to the center for treatment allows a degree of compartmentalization of the illness so that it intrudes less on normal family life. Robinson, on the other hand, suggested that the sense of mastery and control resulting from doing for oneself and the relative independence from the hospital help the patient adjust to the disease (1971).

Obviously, the choice between center and home dialysis is complicated, involving factors ranging from patient personality and family status to such mundane but critical variables as geography, reliability of electrical power, and space. Delano reported that 64% of the patients in her sample who began training for home dialysis were successfully dialyzing at home when the study ended (1978). The current national figure of only 27% suggests that insufficient attention has been paid to this cost effective treatment modality. Furthermore, home dialysis plays a central role in rehabilitation, the next and final topic.

## Rehabilitation

Rehabilitation in renal, as in all, patients refers to bringing the patient to his maximal level of function. As an outcome variable, rehabilitation is inherently multifaceted, entailing physical, psychological, and social dimensions. In practice, however, gainful employment or successful homemaking has tended to be the major criterion of rehabilitation. In the early days of dialysis there was a general expectation that full return to work was possible. However, reports on rehabilitation outcome from various centers have shown that return to full employment occurs with widely divergent frequency and is the exception rather than the rule. The most common outcome seems to be partial employment.

In discussing the rehabilitation process, Blagg observed that research on dialysis patients has failed to address this variable systematically:

> Review of the literature reveals a paucity of articles on dialysis and transplantation containing the word "rehabilitation" in their titles. This is in contrast to the growing list of articles on the psychiatric, psychological and psychosocial aspects of these treatments, particularly dialysis. . . . [M]ost patients treated by dialysis and transplantation and in whom physical and vocational rehabilitation is encouraged can make a reasonable adjustment to their lives and do not necessarily require specific psychiatric or psychological help and counseling. Rather, vocational advice and training and the services of a good practical-minded social worker in assisting the patient to return to work, household duties or school, and the usual family and other interests are the most important necessities for rehabilitation. (1978:145)

This passage reflects a very optimistic expectation for rehabilitation in the renal patient, which is supported by the data in Table 5–1. Percentages in the table show the rehabilitation status of 105 hemodialysis patients aged 50 or less; only 25% were retired or unemployed, and almost half of the latter category were seeking employment.

An interesting comparison was made between patients in dialysis at a VA medical center and those at a university hospital (Blagg, 1978). Only 14% of VA patients as opposed to 38% of the other group had returned to work; 44% of the VA patients compared to 13% in the university setting were not seeking employment at the time of assessment. This outcome suggested to the researchers that staff and system expectations affect rehabilitation outcome. The VA patients were regarded by the VA system as totally disabled. No expectation for rehabilitation existed and rehabilitation was minimal. By contrast, patients in the university setting (who were older than the VA patients) were not viewed as disabled, were encouraged to return to work, and did so to a much greater degree

## TABLE 5.1

|  | DIALYSIS | TRANSPLANT |
|---|---|---|
| *Working*  *full-time* | 29% | 30% |
|           *part-time* | 7% | 7% |
| *Unemployed* |  |  |
|   *looking for work* | 10% | 13% |
|   *not looking for work* | 12% | 10% |
| *Retired* | 2% | 3% |
| *Homemaker* | 29% | 21% |
| *School* | 11% | 16% |
| *Number of patients* | 105 | 61 |
| *Average age* | 33.6 | 32.0 |

*Source:* Reproduced, with permission, from C. R. Blagg, "Objective Quantification of Rehabilitation in Dialysis," in E. A. Friedman (ed.), *Strategy in Renal Failure* (New York: Wiley, 1978), p. 426.

than did their VA counterparts. Both groups were on home dialysis, suggesting that their medical conditions were similar.

Blagg's program stresses home dialysis and places great emphasis on the patient's assuming primary responsibility for the treatment process. Earlier efforts in which spouses were trained to play a critical role in the procedure generated inordinate amounts of familial conflict and the program now teaches family members to handle emergencies but otherwise to be minimally involved (Blagg et al., 1970). In this way, independence is encouraged and reinforced and dependence on staff and center is minimized. A key element in the program is the training patients receive in the procedure: "Our program, developed in conjunction with an educator who had experience with both dialysis and behavioral psychology, makes use of video tapes and correlated written material and is adjusted to individual equipment needs and the intelligence of the patient" (Blagg et al., 1970:149). A psychological analysis of patient and family precedes and determines the course of training. All staff—nurses, doctors, and technicians—participate in the training procedure.

Stinson and associates described a home dialysis training procedure that requires only 15 days of actual training (1972). This self-paced program is delivered via videotape and workbook. Each unit is evaluated in turn, and the patient must show 95% correct responses in one unit before going on to the next. There are three major sections: identification, which concerns mechanical aspects of the machine; procedure, addressing use of the machine; and information about diet, medical aspects of dialysis, and the principles of the procedure. This demystification of dialysis undoubtedly goes a long way toward giving the patient a sense of mastery over the disease and control of the treatment—feelings that have therapeutic value. Assessment of the program finds patients to be satisfied with it, to show no increase in complications or mechanical problems, and, in fact, to have a better knowledge of emergency procedures that do patients trained under other approaches. This format represents a creative collaboration between behavioral psychology and medicine.

## Conclusion

In this Chapter we have looked at psychological factors in the treatment of chronic renal disease with special emphasis on dialysis. The problems these patients and their families face and the coping styles they employ to meet them have been outlined. Perhaps the most striking thing to observe is the variability in rehabilitation outcome in this patient group, and the widely differing expectations for rehabilitation that characterize different workers in the field. One gets the impression that treatment philosophy varies considerably among dialysis centers and psychologists who would work in this area need to be conscious of that fact. A mismatch between the psychologist's goals and those of the medical staff will lead to serious problems. These can be avoided if goals and methods are made clear at the outset.

# 6

# Surgery

Perhaps the most dramatic category of medical event is the surgical procedure. Having an operation is for most of us a signal occurrence eliciting powerful emotions. Similarly, the people who perform operations, surgeons, are viewed with strong feelings, positive and negative, by their patients and colleagues. The surgical event is thus a psychologically potent one to which both psychologists and psychiatrists have addressed themselves. To put the case simply, there is much more going on in the surgical situation than cutting and sewing. This chapter explores some of what has been learned about psychological variables associated with surgical procedures from the point of view of preparation for surgery, outcome of surgery, and rehabilitation.

## Personality Variables in Surgical Outcome

Two patients undergoing the same operative procedure may react quite differently. These differences may be physiological, psychological, or a combination thereof. Some patients tolerate surgery well while others find it extremely upsetting, causing acute terror in a few cases. A time-honored practice among surgeons, in fact, is to operate as early in the day as possible on more anxious patients, thus minimizing pre-operative turmoil. The role of personality variables, defined in terms of psychoanalytic or other theories, in reactions to surgery has been explored formally by a number of investigators, but Janis's 1958 study bears special notice because of its widespread impact.

In simplest terms, Janis argued that a curvilinear relationship exists between anticipatory fear and surgical outcome viewed from the perspective of psychological adjustment. Patients showing either very little anticipatory fear or extremely high levels are more likely to experience high degrees of postoperative distress than are patients showing moderate degrees of anticipatory fear. The reason for this better outcome is that moderate fear leads to a realistic anticipation of the negative aspects of surgery and a working through of associated feelings, the so-called work of worry. With low anticipatory fear, these impending realities are simply denied and are therefore experienced as a most unpleasant surprise. A somewhat similar mechanism operates with high fear, but the denial takes different forms. High-fear patients tend to place great emphasis on the good results to which the surgery will lead and turn frequently to authority figures for reassurance. In both cases the patient enters the postoperative phase ill prepared psychologically to deal with the inevitable unpleasant aspects.

Janis's model parallels observations of the general relationship between motivation and performance. Curvilinear relationships between criterion measures and motivating events have appeared in a wide variety of experimental contexts in psychology, beginning perhaps in 1908 with Yerkes and Dodson's demonstration that avoidance motivated discrimination learning in species ranging from mice to men reflects an interaction between aversive stimulation and task difficulty. In this situation, learning is not linearly related to motivation but rather tends to be best at moderate levels of aversive stimulus intensity.

Janis's work was anecdotal in character but led to a number of attempts objectively to assess the curvilinear hypothesis. Some of these were descriptive in intent; others included an intervention designed to improve psychological readiness for surgery. Overall, research results have not consistently supported Janis's point of view. Wolfner and Davis, for example, assessed a wide range of preoperative and postoperative variables in 146 patients but found no relationship between preoperative fear and anxiety and postoperative outcome; this was true even when only the high and low preoperative extremes were examined. On the other hand, Auerbach found that preoperative anxiety was related in a curvilinear way with one postoperative measure of patient satisfaction, with both highly and mildly anxious patients expressing dissatisfaction with the surgical experience (1973). Johnson and associates reported a linear and positive relationship between preoperative and postoperative fear, a result at odds with Janis's expectation (1970).

It is hardly surprising that clear confirmation or refutation of Janis's thesis has not been forthcoming. The model is stated in rather general terms, so specification of both dependent and independent variables is complex and differently achieved in different studies. Furthermore, the application of the model to surgery as a general situation or variable ignores what are undoubtedly extremely important differences among procedures. In his original paper, for example, Janis noted that the relationship between low fear and negative postoperative course was confined to procedures classified as major from the physician's perspective. Thus, if postoperative events are, in fact, minimally aversive, the failure to prepare for them will have fewer debilitating effects.

In Janis's model, fear is seen as a motivating force that leads to adaptive coping through the mechanism of worrying. Leventhal and his colleagues offered an alternative formulation of the relationship among fear, coping , and outcome (1970). Termed the parallel process theory, Leventhal's idea is that coping and fear are somewhat independent, a view based on observations that fear provoking messages do not reliably lead to appropriate protective action although informational messages do, provided some degree of fear is present (Leventhal et al., 1966). Thus, the degree of preoperative fear would not be expected to lead to protective action (worry) unless informational stimuli were present to guide this activity.

A study by Vernon and Bigelow cast some light on this distinction (1974). Two groups of surgical patients were observed preoperatively and postoperatively. One group was given detailed information about the procedure; the other was not. Preoperatively, there was no difference in fear between the two groups, though there were differences in the degree of knowledge the two groups had and in the degree of confidence they had in the staff (informed patients had more confidence). Postoperatively, the groups differed in hostility, with informed patients showing less hostility. These data suggest that information does lead to adaptive coping, but they do not support the idea that fear is the motive force behind such coping. This would seem to be more in line with the parallel process point of view.

Whatever the specifics of the preoperative anxiety–postoperative course function, abundant anecdotal and objective evidence shows that high degrees of preoperative anxiety are associated with postoperative difficulties. The debate centers first on whether an optimal level of anxiety can be defined and second on whether anxiety is necessary as a motivator for coping.

Another personality dimension that has been examined as a possible predictor of surgical outcome is vigilance versus avoidance. Cohen and Lazarus reported an extensive descriptive study of 61 surgical patients who were evaluated preoperatively in terms of the use of vigilant or avoidant coping patterns, as well as other psychological variables (1973). Postoperatively, four recovery variables were assessed: days in hospital, amount of pain medication, medical complications, and psychological symptoms such as depression or anxiety. Using preoperative measures, Cohen and Lazarus divided the group into subsamples in terms of the degree to which they showed vigilance or avoidance, the amount of anxiety present, and the number of recent stressful events in the patient's life. The Holmes-Rahe Schedule of Recent Events was used to assess the last dimension; anxiety was rated objectively by interview and subjectively by the patient; finally, several measures of vigilance-avoidance were employed and one instrument, a sentence completion test, assessed an avoidance-coping dimension.

This study yielded a number of interesting results. First, comparison of the subject protocols with historical controls showed no differences in the dependent variables supporting the observational purpose of the study; the interviews and rating procedures did not have a placebo effect. As regards vigilance-avoidance, patients rated as avoiders went home earlier and showed fewer postoperative complications than did the vigilants. Anxiety as rated by the patient was positively related to the incidence of postoperative psychological distress, but interviewer rated anxiety was unrelated to the dependent variables. Recent life stress had no effect on recovery variables. Use of pain medication was associated with high coping scores on the avoidance-coping dimension but not with high vigilance scores. This would suggest that coping and vigilance are functionally different. While one would expect on heuristic grounds that vigilance would lead to extensive use of medication, the authors speculated that a feeling of helplessness following surgery may overwhelm the hypervigilant patient so that he ceases to try to control his circumstances and assumes a passive role, not requesting medication. The coper who is not vigilant, by contrast, is not overwhelmed and continues to act on the environment, demanding medication when he wants it. Perhaps the most important overall conclusion to be drawn from the Cohen and Lazarus study is that measures of psychological traits and dispositions, with all their inherent limitations, were predictive to some degree of variables usually considered essentially physical in character—days until discharge and incidence of complications. Such findings argue in favor of attempts to intervene at a behavioral level in order to facilitate recovery from surgery.

## Psychological Preparation for Surgery

Typically, psychological preparation for surgery has included information about the procedure and/or instruction in specific techniques for dealing with difficulties. Egbert and co-workers described an intervention by the anesthesiologist designed to reduce preoperative anxiety and to improve postoperative coping (1964). Fifty-one control patients were given standard anesthetist's instructions, which consisted of a visit the night before surgery during which the anesthetic procedure was described though postoperative pain was not discussed. These patients were compared with 46 experimentals, who got detailed information about post-operative pain, including an explanation that muscle spasm is a major cause of such pain and that relaxation and deep breathing methods can relieve distress. These patients were also told that pain medication would be available if they needed it. The instructions were reiterated by the anesthetist postoperatively.

The results from this rather simple intervention were striking. Experimental patients were discharged from the hospital two to seven days earlier than controls, they took less pain medication, and they were rated by observers blind to the experimental conditions as showing less pain. The authors concluded with a plea to their colleagues to take a more active role in the surgical enterprise: "Since the sole purpose of the anesthetist in administering anesthesia is to reduce pain associated with operations, it appears reasonable for him to consider the whole job. The anesthetist who understands his patient and who believes that each patient is 'his' patient ceases to be merely a clever technician in the operating room" (Egbert et al., 1964:827).

Healy described a similar intervention, but in this case the nurse was the behavioral agent (1968). One hundred eighty-one surgical patients were given specific instructions in deep breathing, turning in bed, and coughing in a manner less likely to elicit pain, as well as more general information about operative procedures. Postsurgery follow-up visits reinforced the instructions. One hundred thirty-five of the instructed patients were discharged early from the hospital. In contrast, only 3 of 140 controls were released early. Pain medication had been ceased by the fourth to sixth day in 160 of the experimentals, while 120 of the controls did not cease until the period running from the sixth day to discharge. Complications were infrequent in both groups but less frequent in the experimentals. Family estimates of postoperative recovery were positive in 176 of the 181 experimentals but in only 45 of the 140 controls.

The most detailed analyses of the consequences of preparation for surgery have been conducted with children. As a group, children are more overtly fearful of, and upset by, doctors, hospitals, and operations than are adults; accordingly, acknowledgment of the importance of psychological preparation is more readily forthcoming. Research in this area generally has assumed that anxiety is a source of postoperative problems and is at least in part a result of lack of knowledge. Preparation studies have thus addressed the task of familiarizing the child with what is to come. Some investigations have tried to teach coping skills and two variables, information and training, often have been confounded. Finally, research on children has relied heavily on modeling as a teaching strategy, an approach extensively documented in the behavioral literature (Bandura, 1969).

Melamed and her colleagues' work on the effects of modeling in children's reactions to surgery exemplifies the trend toward more fine-grained analysis of relevant variables. The medium of preparation used in these studies was a film entitled *Ethan Has an Operation,* which shows a seven-year-old white boy going through the admission and preoperative procedures, induction of anesthesia, recovery room events, and preparation to go home (Melamed, 1977). The film is intended to be realistic in that the actor shows appropriate degrees of fear and pain, but he also is seen to master these feelings. Identification with the character, Ethan, is encouraged by his ongoing narrative, by the use of other children (multiple models) in the film who describe their experiences, and by Ethan's demographic characteristics (research has shown that white boys are more readily modeled by children than are white girls or black children). Modeling is also facilitated by the fact that Ethan is frequently rewarded during the course of the film and emerges from the hospital in the same condition he entered. Specific information rather than general reassurance is emphasized in the film on the basis of Leventhal's parallel process model (Johnson & Leventhal, 1974).

An initial study compared children who viewed the preparation film with a control group who saw a film called *Living Things Are Everywhere* (Melamed, 1977). This film was a suitable control because the main character is a young white male engaging in a mastery experience in an unfamiliar setting, but having nothing to do with hospitals or illness. Both groups received the standard hospital preoperative preparation, consisting of a talk with the doctor, description of procedures, including photos of other patients, and a visit to the ward playroom. Various state anxiety scales were administered before showing the film, after showing the film, immediately before surgery, and after surgery. Rating scales assessed anxiety and hospital fears, as did a physiological measure, palmar sweat index. Measures of trait anxiety were given on only the first and last evaluations. The researchers rated physiological indices of recovery globally on the basis of time to first liquids, nausea, pain medication, and the like.

Results from this carefully designed study generally supported the idea that film modeling preparation leads to better adjustment to the surgical experience in children aged 4 to 12 years. Ratings of fear and anxiety consistently favored the experimental group after the films were viewed, although the groups were equal before. The measures of palmar sweat showed an interesting pattern. Experimental subjects had a rise after viewing the film; controls, a drop. At the preoperative testing, this situation reversed and remains reversed at the postoperative testing.

This would suggest that the Ethan film elicited an immediate rise in anxiety, which declined in the actual operative situation—supporting Janis's notion that moderate anxiety may facilitate coping. The global estimate of physiological recovery showed a trend in the direction of better results for the experimentals ($p < .10$). The trait anxiety measure revealed the usual stability across the study period. A four-week follow-up found parents of controls reporting many more behavioral problems than parents of experimentals. This striking result suggests a rather long-lasting effect of the intervention.

A second study evaluated the effect of time of viewing the preparatory film and related outcome to patient's age (Melamed, 1977). In addition, preparation independent of the film was manipulated so that half the subjects received the standard hospital routine while the other half were denied this source of information and support. All subjects viewed the film, half of them a week before entering the hospital and the other half on the day of admission. Results of the study were somewhat complicated but suggest that preparation a week before surgery is helpful in children older than seven but not in those younger. No difference as a function of degree of preparation independent of the film emerged, which suggests that the modeling technique may be sufficiently powerful to obviate the need for extensive one-to-one preparation. Such a conclusion must, however, be tempered with the awareness that routine hospital preparation and no preparation may imply vastly different procedures in different settings.

Though the Melamed studies of modeling as a preparation technique indicated that preoperative psychological maneuvers have positive effects on postoperative course, "the questions asked need to be more clearly specified. There is a need for better research designs which allow for comparison across studies. . . . A greater concern with the reliability and validity of the measurement tools needs to be forthcoming" (Melamed, 1977:70).

Before leaving the issue of preparation, something should be said regarding more extreme types of patient preoperative reactions. The discussion thus far has addressed what might be termed normal variation around the population mean on such dimensions as anxiety, denial, and vigilance. In a fraction of cases, however, patients show gross psychiatric disturbance in response to the stress of surgery. These reactions can take a wide range of forms, from profound depression to acute excitement. The patient may refuse lifesaving procedures or in other ways show grossly impaired judgment. In such circumstances a psychiatrist must be consulted and a decision made regarding the advisability of surgery and the proper treatment for the psychological symptoms. Hackett and Weisman described some of these reactions and the treatments indicated (1960a,b). These difficulties fall at the borderland of medical psychology as defined in this text and fade into clinical psychology and psychiatry. Clearly, one ought not to attempt to manage such problems unless one is specifically trained in this area.

## Psychological Factors in Postoperative Recovery

During the immediate postoperative period, physical recovery is the essential interest and psychological factors play a minor role. As the patient grows stronger and stronger, however, the focus shifts so that psychological variables increasingly account for outcome variance. As recovery fades into rehabilitation, behavioral factors assume an ever more prominent role in determining outcome. It seems likely, therefore, that behavioral intervention during this period should have at least as much yield as the preoperative preparation methods just described. Indeed, postoperative follow-up plays a role in some of these interventions. Unfortunately, the literature includes relatively few studies on behavioral methods in postoperative recovery.

One exception to this general lack of explicit psychological interest is obstetrical surgery, an unusual category in that there is usually no illness. Recovery is thus psychologically different in obstetrical as opposed to other types of surgery. If things go normally, the recovery period will pass quickly, characterized by intense joy and excitement. Maternity wards are typically the happiest places in any hospital because their focus is so strongly on health rather than sickness. The exceptions to this rule are the stillbirth or the seriously ill newborn. In these cases, psychological distress may be profound and support after the event may be required.

Moos defined four problem areas for parents following birth of a seriously ill child (1977). First there is the loss of the perfect baby who fills the fantasy life of expectant parents. This is followed by the necessary acceptance of the actual infant and the anxiety of waiting if the child's condition is life threatening. If the child does not survive, normal grieving takes place but is complicated by feelings of emptiness and exhaustion attendant on the long period of anticipation during pregancy and the stress of the birth process itself. If the child lives, the family must adjust to the care requirements of the child, which will differ with the illness or handicap. Feelings of inadequacy and incompetence in the face of the handicapped child are common and the parents must deal with their own ambivalence concerning the survival of the severely handicapped infant. Should they or should they not permit heroic surgery, for example, on a seriously deformed child, who, if he survives the surgery, faces a life of extreme mental and/or physical handicap and whose care may come to dominate the lives of both parents and other siblings? This question has no simple answer, and surgeons ought to avoid urging such efforts on parents; the option of letting nature take its course is a reasonable one that ought not to be ruled out simply because it is technically feasible to intervene (Paton, 1971).

In dealing with these issues, parents need psychological support. Often this comes from family and friends, but professional help may also be required. Certainly the primary physician must be involved, but unless he is willing to spend protracted periods of time with these parents, the supporting role is better shifted to a psychologist, social worker, or nurse trained to provide the requisite help and information. Sensitive and skillful supportive psychotherapy may facilitate the process of grieving and/or adjustment. Golden and Davis described a counseling intervention with parents of a child with Down's syndrome, a form of mental retardation formerly known as mongolism (1977). The therapist provides accurate information about the lifelong, incurable nature of the condition but stresses the important similarities in needs between the Down's infant and the normal child. Questions from the parents are encouraged. Families given such information typically react in one of two ways. Some will accept the reality, grieve, then begin making plans for home care. Other families will ask about institutional placement. Here it is absolutely essential that the options be explained. Many public hospitals will not accept infants and private facilities are costly. Furthermore, the early care of the Down's infant does not cause any particular hardship at home and placement can be made later if parents find they cannot cope. "Doctors often suggest institutionalization as an alternative to home care without having any knowledge of the availability, quality or cost of such care" (Golden & Davis, 1977:51). Such advice can lead to a serious breakdown in confidence between family and doctor at a time when the support of professional staff is vital. Families must be reassured that help in home care will be available to them as they go through the profoundly difficult process of accepting and adjusting to the realities of caring for a mentally retarded child. The fact is that at birth it is impossible to predict what the child will be like—what his limitations will be and what care he will ultimately require.

Guilt is common among parents of handicapped or stillborn children. Mothers will wonder about medications they may have taken during pregnancy, for example:

> Parents . . . need a great deal of help, especially during the initial phases of shock and disbelief and developing awareness. Because of their feelings of guilt and failure, they need continual reassurance that they were not responsible for what happened. They need to express their feelings of guilt over and over again and receive assurance that these feelings are acceptable and normal. (Jackson, 1977:33)

The last point deserves emphasis: hearing and accepting something are not the same. The adjustment process in these special circumstances will proceed in convoluted ways and parents may need to approach the reality many times and from many directions before acceptance occurs. A sense of being overwhelmed is prominent in many cases. Caring for the child may facilitate the parents' psychological recovery, reestablishing their sense of mastery and thereby counteracting feelings of helplessness and despair.

Birth, then, is one surgical event in which psychological factors play a significant role. What of other types of surgery? Hesse described a comprehensive program that has reduced the incidence of postoperative adjustment problems in patients receiving a cardiac pacemaker (1975). The pacemaker corrects irregularities in cardiac function arising from failure in beat generation or propagation. When successful, the procedure allows essentially normal existence provided the patient is able to adjust to the device. Hesse's program is designed to handle psychosocial probelms that compromise successful adjustment. Becker and associates found significant psychological problems in about 30% of patients undergoing the procedure (1967). Hence, intervention seems indicated. A major source of difficulty appears to be the patient's lack of understanding of the procedure and the things he must do (Blacker & Basch, 1970); lack of adequate social support is another (Green & Moss, 1969). Hesse's program addresses both these sources of difficulty.

The education phase begins as early as possible and includes family members. The heart's pumping function is described and the role of the pacemaker is explained. The specific indications for the technique in the particular patient are described so that if the patient has heart block, for example, the nature of that dysfunction is explained, as is the pacemaker's corrective action. The patient is taught the terms doctors and nurses use and the reasons for follow-up care are clarified. Patients who have working pacemakers are introduced to give the new recipient appropriate models. These interactions are tailored to meet the learning abilities of individual patients and frequent repetition and checking for understanding are employed.

Patients have many misconceptions about medicine in general and about their own diseases in particular. This lack of knowledge offers fertile ground for maladaptive fantasies to develop. Hesse cited erroneous beliefs patients and families held about the pacemaker (1975). One wife, for example, did not want her husband to operate the television set on the assumption that the TV would in some way interfere with his pacemaker. The follow-up routine, if not understood, also offers many opportunities for fantasies that the device is malfunctioning in some way. Correct information can preclude such misconceptions and resulting maladaptive behaviors. The recurrent theme of mastery also seems relevant here. If the patient is ignorant of the procedure, he is likely to assume a dependent posture in relation to staff and not to assume responsibility for his own recovery. Information allows for a more cooperative approach, with the patient becoming an active participant.

The support phase of Hesse's program begins before the operation and is a permanent postoperative feature. Counseling is provided to foster independence and social function; improved compliance seems a likely by-product. The service is offered to all patient, with the clear understanding that a particular patient is not being singled out as needing psychological help. Through interview, the patient's psychological and social resources are assessed and the patient gets the opportunity to explore his fears and concerns. Educational material is reiterated during postoperative counseling sessions, and patients who miss appointments are contacted for follow-up.

Counseling can help patients deal with their anxiety and depression and foster both a vital interest in present activities and a future orientation, both of which are associated with better long-term prognosis (Kimball, 1969). Group sessions can provide strong social support.


## Conclusion

In this Chapter, psychological factors in surgery were discussed. In both preoperative and postoperative periods, intervention at a behavioral level has been found to be useful. These efforts take several forms including delivery of factual information, training in particular recovery maneuvers, and emotional support. In several studies, reduced hospital stay has followed such interventions, a finding of considerable importance given the presently escalating costs of inpatient care. Continued development of psychological interventions in surgical situations thus seems timely and appropriate.

# 7

# Pain

Pain is a common nonspecific symptom for a vast array of conditions. Its subjective importance is not proportional to its objective importance as a sign of morbidity—one has only to contrast the excruciating agony of torn ligaments with the painlessness of most degenerative diseases of the brain. While pain is generally viewed as a negative attribute, it also serves an adaptive purpose. At the most obvious level, it signals one to stop doing whatever one is doing. The child learns not to burn himself by experiencing the pain associated with touching fire and individuals born with a lack of pain sensitivity are subject to all manner of accidentally inflicted mayhem because they lack this biological warning system. The angina of cardiac disease likewise serves a purpose: the patient learns not to exert himself to the point of pain or to stop if he feels pain. A distinction might be drawn between adaptive pain and morbid pain—the former serving as a signal and leading to health enhancing behavior, the latter being only a symptom of underlying pathology and leading to no adaptive behavior. Pain management is directed to the latter category.

Pain management takes either an etiologic or a symptomatic approach. Consistent with the disease model, elimination of the underlying cause should lead to the end of symptoms and in many cases it does. This is etiologic treatment. The symptomatic approach typically involves the use of analgesics to reduce the subjective experience of pain. Aspirin for the nonspecific headache is surely the most common analgesic. In extreme cases when other avenues of control have been exhausted, neurosurgical procedures may be used that either sever the connection to peripheral organs giving rise to pain or alter perceptual processes at their brain site. Behavioral treatment is an additional tool in pain management, particularly beneficial to the chronic sufferer. This chapter reviews the current theory of the physiology of pain and examines the nature of the pain experience. Behavioral research into pain management is addressed in some detail.


## Theories of Pain

The stimuli that give rise to pain are various: pressure, electricity, temperature, and chemical substances all may elicit pain, but these same stimuli also elicit other responses such as hot or cold, tingling, or itchiness. The sites from which pain can be elicited are scattered throughout the body but are neither universal nor homogeneous. The skin and cornea are sensitive to pain stimuli; the viscera are less responsive and vary among themselves; the central nervous system is largely insensitive to pain stimuli. Pain elicited from different locations also differs qualitatively with surface or skin pain tending to be sharp or fleeting and deep muscle or visceral pain long-lasting and aching.

In 1826 Müller enunciated the doctrine of specific nerve energies, which has served sensory physiologists well in the area of vision, audition, taste, and smell. Müller observed that a given nerve fiber leads to a certain class of sensory experience whenever and however the nerve is aroused. In the area of cutaneous sensitivity, however, Müller's doctrine has been difficult to confirm; that is, the various sensory receptors in the skin seem to show relative rather than absolute specificity as regards the experiences their stimulation elicits.

Problems with specificity prompted a number of alternative formulations, collectively referred to as pattern theories, which hold that there is no specific pain receptor. Rather, pain stimuli lead to specific patterns of response among the various cutaneous receptors, which in turn lead to the perception of pain centrally. Stimulus intensity and a central process of summation are deemed key factors in the process. Several writers have further proposed that there are two cutaneous systems, one fast acting, the other slow; the latter mediates pain on the basis of summation. Under normal circumstances the fast system inhibits the slow; in pathology the reverse obtains, leading to pain events.

The specific model and the pattern theories of pain run afoul of several empirical observations. Both approaches rely ultimately on peripheral stimuli as necessary for pain sensation and differ as to how such peripheral events are encoded and transmitted upstream to the brain, the presumptive site of pain experience. The phenomena of phantom limb pain and of pain after total transection of the spinal cord are difficult to explain within any model that considers peripheral stimuli essential to pain experience. Melzack and Loeser described several cases in which phantom pain in the lower extremities persisted after cordectomy (removal of a portion of the spinal cord) and isolation of the sympathetic ganglia, which events interrupted all known neural connections between the brain and the lower half of the body (1978). In such cases, pain is inexplicable on the basis of any sort of peripheral receptor–cord–brain formulation.

In 1965 Melzack and Wall offered an alternative model. Melzack and Wall's gate control theory suggests that the stimulus for pain is a summation of incoming events in particular lamina of the spinal cord, which are inhibited until they reach a critical level, both by mechanisms intrinsic to the cord and by influences moving centripetally from the brain downward. Details of the gate control theory are speculative and complex. The important point is that Melzack and Wall identified a downstream influence, and by incorporating a quasi-independent generating mechanism for pain perception in the cord this theory can be made to fit the phenomena of pain below cord section:

> Instead of considering pain primarily as a projection system from the periphery to the brain, it may be more profitable to look closely at centrally modulating mechanisms. Our assumption, which derives from the gate control theory, is that pain occurs when the number of nerve impulses per unit time from somatic projection systems to the brain area that subserve pain exceeds a critical level. Injury or noxious stimulation may produce such a level. We propose . . . that a similar suprathreshold level may occur either directly or secondarily as a result of loss of input. (Melzack & Loeser, 1978: 203)

To summarize this point of view, the spinal cord contains pattern generating mechanisms that are normally under the inhibitory control of both afferent and efferent stimulation. After cord section, the afferent impulses are eliminated, allowing the pattern generator to run free and thus to elicit pain, referred to the region that would normally excite that generator. Such a model suggests that this referred pain could be elicited, worsened, or lessened by a wide variety of factors operating upstream by either increasing or decreasing the inhibitory influence on the pattern generator. It follows that with activation of the pattern generator, inhibition of generators for locations above the cord section should be increased and, in fact, it has been shown that paraplegics with referred pain do have heightened pain threshold (Hazouri & Mueller, 1950). According to this model, cordotomy fails to relieve pain because deafferentiation may decrease inhibition and thereby worsen pain through release of pattern generators.

The nature of pain stimuli and receptor mechanisms continues to be an area of controversy and research. Current thinking emphasizes the interactive relationship between upstream and downstream structures in pain phenomena and this conceptualization is consistent with current thinking in other areas of perceptual research. The notion that visual perception is a passive process, analogous to the camera's projecting on to a photographic plate, was abandoned long ago. Seeing is an active process. Likewise, pain is coming to be viewed not wholly as a passive reception of impulses from pain receptors but as a created event, a behavior involving a complex interaction of stimulus and response throughout the neuraxis. Stoicism may not be a personality characteristic divorced from physiology. On the contrary, it may well involve processes of inhibition far away from the brain and the implications of this possibility for pain control are considerable.

Pain is a subjective experience and, as I just noted, there are significant individual differences in what people acknowledge as painful. This problem is not unique to pain, of course: visual perception is equally private. However, the vocabulary for pain events is not elaborate, as is the language we use for vision, reflecting the ultimately internal nature of pain phenomena and our adaptive efforts to avoid painful experiences. Pain researchers face an added problem in defining pain: reactions to pain may be radically altered by the symbolic meaning of the event. In 1956 Beecher observed that surgical patients requested morphine in four out of five cases, whereas soldiers wounded in battle asked for morphine to control pain associated with similar incisions in only one out of three cases. Less drastic circumstances also have been shown significantly to modify the subjective estimate of pain intensity. The simple device of allowing subjects to control the time of delivery of a painful stimulus, for example, leads to a reduction in subjective intensity of pain. (Hill et al., 1952).

Recent work in neurochemistry offers other conceptual and theoretical insights into pain phenomena. Looking at the mechanism of analgesics, Snyder summarized current thinking on this subject (1977). Specific receptors in the nervous system have been identified that are selectively affected by morphine and related drugs. Interestingly, these systems are located in the limbic system and substantia gelitinosa of the spinal cord, one of the lamina identified in the gate control theory as mediating spinal modulation of pain. This discovery led researchers to probe the usual role of these receptors since morphine is not normally found in the body. As it turns out, specific substances, the enkephalins and endorphins, act as neurotransmitters in neuronal systems modulating pain and emotion. Accordingly, the analgesic and euphoric effects of morphine may lie in their augmentation of the actions of these naturally occurring transmitters. Thus, the body appears to have biochemical mechanisms for pain reduction, which are overcome in disease. Understanding this mechanism may lead ultimately to more effective and nonaddicting analgesics.

To sum up, the physiology of pain is incompletely understood, a circumstance complicated by problems in defining the pain response, particularly in situations of clinical relevance. It is clear that numerous situational factors play a role in the pain experience, which includes both a sensory and a cognitive, or evaluative, aspect, what Beecher (1957) denotes the primary and secondary components. Before turning to strategies of pain management, let us survey some of the variables that determine the pain experience. While it may be more theoretically tidy to think of pain as a simple quantitative response to a stimulus, the data overwhelmingly reveal the inadequacy of this notion and any strategy of pain management that ignores this fact is unlikely to be maximally effective.

## Pain Research

Research has shown that differential reactivity to pain is not randomly distributed in the population and that a number of variables seem to be implicated. Before examining these factors, I want to point out, first, that pain stimuli in experiments and pain in illness are not the same thing and, second, that pain is not directly observable and can be measured only indirectly through verbal reports, physiological reactions, requests for analgesics, and the like. Thus, there is simply no way of knowing whether the stoic person experiences less pain than, or reacts to the same amount of pain differently from, the more demonstrative person. Pain management aims to reduce the patient's discomfort and whether this goal is brought about by reducing the pain itself, changing the patient's reaction, or both is of more theoretical than practical import.

### DEMOGRAPHICS

Pain reactivity has been found to differ as a function of race, national origin, sex, age, and even family size. Inducing pain in over 40,000 subjects by progressively increasing pressure on the Achilles tendon, Woodrow and colleagues found that males tolerated more pain than females, younger subjects more than older, and whites more than blacks, who in turn withstood pain better than Orientals (1972). Both age and race effects were more marked in men than in women. Interested in the influence of family size, Sweeney and Fine compared groups of army recruits, who made ratings of pain severity on a seven-point scale in response to immersion of the hand in cold (4°C) water (1970). Recruits from large families gave lower pain ratings than did recruits from smaller families (one to three children). Although family size was confounded with birth order in this study, Schachter found firstborn and only children had lower pain tolerance (1959).

In a fascinating series of studies, Sternbach and his co-workers examined pain reactions in housewives from Yankee, (white, Anglo-Saxon, Protestant), Irish, Jewish, and Italian ethnic groups (Tursky and Sternbach, 1967). They found, first, that the groups differed in their attitudes toward pain in general and, second, that physiological indices of reactivity to shock induced pain corroborated the impressions derived from a study of attitudinal differences. In general, the Yankees tended to be more matter-of-fact in their view of pain; the Jews were apprehensive about its implications; the Italians had a present orientation and wanted immediate relief; the Irish were stoic, inhibiting expression of any feeling about pain. The physiological indices, the details of which need not concern us here, suggested that peripheral responses occasioned by the pain stimuli differed among the groups, for the most part in expected directions; for example, heart rate and skin potential tended to be higher in the Italians while skin resistance was lowest in the Irish.

Zborowski studied Yankees, Italians, and Jews in hospital settings where pain was part of illness (1952). Here, Italians again showed a present orientation, wanting immediate relief by whatever means and being satisfied when this goal was achieved. The Jewish patients, while also seeking relief, tended to be skeptical and remained concerned about pain even after treatment. The Yankees tended less to seek relief and to be more optimistic about pain's implications. When in pain the groups also showed differences in social behavior—the Jews and Italians seeking contact, the Yankees withdrawing. In another clinically pertinent study, Winsberg and Greenlick evaluated nurses' ratings of patient pain in normal childbirth, comparing black and white women (1967). No differences were found. These workers also compared ratings by various staff to see whether any differences would emerge as a function of status of the raters; again, no differences were seen.


PSYCHOLOGICAL FACTORS

Various perceptual, cognitive, and personality characteristics also have been related to differences in pain response. The augmentation-reduction continuum first studied by Petrie in 1967 has been related to pain in a number of studies. Briefly, people can be classified as augmenters or reducers on the basis of a size estimation task. Augmenters tend to overestimate a comparison stimulus; reducers, to underestimate it. As might be predicted, reducers have a much greater tolerance for painful stimuli than do augmenters. Also as might be expected, people best able to tolerate pain, reducers, are least able to tolerate sensory deprivation. Thus, the augmentation-reduction variable seems to affect a wide variety of experiences of which pain is only one.

Another perceptual variable that has been related to pain is that of field dependence versus field independence (Witkin et al., 1954). Again as might be expected, subjects most independent of the field were most reactive to pain, while the field-dependent were least reactive. In an interesting physiological study, Heinz, Cohen, and Shmavonian found that field-independent subjects responded to pain stimuli first with cardiac acceleration, then with deceleration, while the field-dependent showed only deceleration (1966). This suggests that both sympathetic and parasympathetic autonomic nervous system activities characterize the field-independent subjects, while the field dependent are parasympathetic dominated. Translating these physiological events to psychological metaphors, the field-independent are ready to do something about the pain while the field-dependent simply accept it and take mainly restorative rather than defensive action.

The personality trait of anxiety has been widely studied in relation to pain. These phenomena frequently occur together and clinicians generally believe that anxiety worsens or potentiates pain. The experimental, as well as the clinical, literature seems to support this view. Schalling and Levander compared pain tolerance in two groups of delinquents, one rated as tense and anxious, the other as minimally anxious or psychopathic (1964). Results with shock stimuli supported the prediction of better pain tolerance in the psychopaths, reflected in less rapid and smaller sweating responses.

Summarizing the clinical significance of anxiety and other personality variables, Sternbach observed: "It would seem that the quiet brooding anxious and resentful individual is the one who is most likely to have symptoms of pain and is least able to tolerate them" (1968: 72). Taken in toto, the literature strongly suggests that pain experience is modified in systematic ways by broader personality, cognitive, and perceptual characteristics and reinforces the impression that pain must be conceptualized as a complex interaction between stimulus events and organismic variables.


SITUATIONAL FACTORS

Beecher's classic report on civilian and military wounded (1956), cited earlier, pointed toward the symbolic meaning of pain as having a very direct effect on how pain is experienced. Another way of demonstrating the role of situational variables in pain experience is the use of placebos.

A placebo is a substance given for a purpose for which it has no phar-macologic effect; the result of placebo administration is termed the placebo effect. Shapiro defined placebo effects as "the psychological, physiological, or psychopharmacological effect of any medication or pro-cedure given with therapeutic intent, which is independent of or minimally related to pharmacological effects of the medication or to the specific effects of the procedure and which operates through a psycholog-ical mechanism" (1960: 110). To the extent that placebo effects can be seen in pain responses, such responses are under the control of psycho-logical factors independent of pain stimuli. Again, placebo effects argue against a peripheral model of pain.

In discussing placebos, Shapiro suggested that in spite of scientific medicine the physician himself is the major cause of therapeutic change (1960). In illustration he recounts two stories from nineteenth century French medicine. It seems that one physician at Salpatriere favored suspending patients by their feet to allow blood to flow to the head, while a physician at Nancy suspended them head up. Frequency of success was equal for the two and obviously due to something other than the treat-ment. One suspects that escape from the doctor's ministrations was a major motivation for recovery. Beecher, looking at placebo effects in pain reduction, estimated that 35% of clinically significant pain is re-lieved by placebos and that placebo effectiveness is proportional to the amount of anxiety attendant upon the pain (1959). Perhaps the classic paper on this topic was written by Evans and Hoyle, who reported that placebos and active agents were about equal in reducing angina pectoris (1933).

It should be remembered that in clinical practice, placebo and real drug effects are completely confounded. That is, when a physician gives a drug, he expects it to be effective; this expectation is communicated to the patient either implicitly or explicitly. This being the case, it is im-possible to demonstrate a pharmacologic effect on the basis of conven-tional clinical practice, particularly in light of research that shows how communicated expectations can profoundly affect response. Two studies report giving placebos, stimulants, and tranquilizing medications to subjects with instructions as to the drugs' effects that were sometimes the opposite of their pharmacologic action (Krugman et al., 1964; Lyerly et al., 1964). Subjects' responses to the medications correlated with the in-structions regardless of the drug taken. For this reason the double-blind procedure is now deemed essential in the evaluation of analgesic agents (Nash, 1962).

Although the placebo effect is a prime example of the modification of pain experience by psychological factors, studies on experimentally in-duced pain have not found the striking degree of placebo relief that is con-sistently seen in clinical pain. Averaging across studies, Beecher stated that the effectiveness of placebos in clinical pain is about 35% while in experimental pain it is about 3% (1959). That is, the placebo is 10 times more effective in clinical than in laboratory induced pain. Beecher interpreted this finding as evidence supporting his distinction between primary and secondary factors in pain experience. It is not unreasonable to assume that the reactive components of dread and anxiety are higher in clinical than in experimentally induced pain, and it would seem that the placebo is operating on these secondary factors, accounting for the huge difference in effect when experimental and clinical studies of analgesic agents are compared. This reinforces the point made earlier that pain management can be more fruitfully approached from a model that is not tied to peripheral mechanisms.

In experimental settings, a number of other situational factors have been shown to alter the pain experience in predictable ways. Buss and Portnoy demonstrated that delivery of a seemingly irrelevant bit of information—that Russians could tolerate more pain than Americans—increased the pain tolerance of male American college students (1967). Being told that women could stand more pain than men also raised their tolerance, but not as much as did the information about Russians. This experiment makes clear that the level of pain perceived as intolerable is not absolute and can be modified by manipulating, through verbal instructions, the reference group. The role of pain tolerance in fortifying group identification has, of course, long been recognized in fraternity initiation rituals, football practice, and so on.

Modifying the pain experience by focusing attention elsewhere has also long been known informally. Blitz and Dinnerstein demonstrated this effect experimentally (1971). Subjects immersed their hands in cold water (5°C) and were asked to state when they felt what they would call pain, then to keep the hand in "as long as you possibly can." On subsequent trials, instructions were given, first, to focus on the temperature rather than on the pain and, second, to imagine a hot day, that the water is refreshing, etc. These instructions significantly raised the pain threshold but did not affect the quitting point. A possible relevance of this study to the gate control theory comes to mind: at fairly low levels of stimulation, suppressor activities initiated at a very high level, both psychologically and neurologically, override the painful stimuli. At higher intensities this mechanism gives way and pain is experienced. A clinical corollary might be that simple distraction methods are most likely to be effective for pain that is near threshold, the routine pains of everyday living.

Modeling provides another means of situationally modifying the pain experience. Craig and Weiss administered shock at a level below that usually associated with pain (1972). For one group of subjects, a model made stimulus intensity judgments ranging from undetectable to painful, progressing upward as the experiment went on. Subjects also made judgments. The intesity of stimulation was constant. For another group, the model did nothing. In the nonmodeling group, "painful" was selected only once out of 50 opportunities, while the modeling group selected this judgment 37 times. As in the placebo studies, suggestion seems to alter significantly the perception of pain, even to the point of causing pain to be experienced in response to a stimulus that is not perceived as painful in the absence of suggestion.

## Behavioral Treatment of Pain

In addition to the traditional methods of drug induced analgesia, surgery, and hypnosis, a variety of procedures derived from behavioral theory have recently figured both in the literature and in the clinic. Interest from the behavioral point of view has focused on problems of chronic or episodic pain that are not treatable etiologically.

### PAIN AS LEARNED BEHAVIOR

Pain is a subjective experience that is, by definition, not observable to an outsider. In approaching the pain problem, then, we must deal with something other than the pain itself. One of the things we can deal with is behavior related to the pain. Such behaviors include operants and respondents and the two may fade into one another as the history of pain proceeds. Operants include complaining, grimacing, taking medications, and lying down; respondents, the range of physiological reactions of arousal, muscle spasm, and so forth.

Imagine a football player who takes a severe blow to the shoulder, causing pain to be experienced. The pain itself may be thought of as a respondent event, elicited by the contusion and displacement of shoulder ligaments, tendons, and muscle; in addition, there will be a sudden inspiration of breath, a facial grimace, a reflex muscular contraction, and general arousal (Pavlov's orienting reflex), with sympathetic discharge and parasympathetic rebound. The player will also emit a great variety of operant behaviors, taking himself out of the game and favoring the shoulder, making the arm immobile, and collapsing on the bench. A range of verbal behaviors from exclamations to directions to his helpers will occur as he struggles out of his equipment. When at last the ice packs are in place and the extremity of pain begins to subside, a new range of operants emerges—reorienting toward the game, walking the injury off, denying its severity, or whatever. At night, when the excitement of the game is past, respondent pain recurs with severity and analgesics are taken. With each subsequent day, pain lessens and pain motivated operants also begin to decrease in frequency. By the following Saturday, the player returns to the field.

This chain of events includes a number of opportunities for conditioning. In the first place, the respondents elicited by the blow may be conditioned to other stimuli. This effect may be evidenced in an unusual amount of nervous flutters in the first few plays of the next week's game. Operants are also reinforced, the various tactics of pain alleviation being strengthened to the extent they are successful. In fact, their occurrence in the first place reflects a reinforcement history from childhood through high school athletics in the player. Walking it off is a tried and true remedy among football coaches. To the extent that grimaces and statements of pain are responded to sympathetically, they, too, are reinforced. Finally, the analgesic effects of pills reinforces pill taking in the presence of the SD, pain.

In the case of the student athlete, reinforcements for playing football are overwhelming—admiration of peers and girls, the pleasures of the game itself, scholarship support, and so forth. This being the case, the pain behaviors that keep the player out of the game are opposed by powerful reinforcements to keep him in it. It has been frequently observed that athletes continue to function with injuries that would incapacitate most of us. However, when respondent pain reaches sufficiently high levels, the reinforcing consequences of pain behavior outweigh those of continued play; when respondent pain subsides through biological healing, the contingencies reverse and playing resumes. From a behavioral point of view, courage may be defined as a relatively low level of reinforcement for pain behaviors and a relatively high level of reinforcement for playing, behavior that is incompatible with pain behavior.

### CHRONIC PAIN

An operant approach to pain is described in *Behavioral Methods for Chronic Pain and Illness* (Fordyce, 1976). Fordyce's formulation stresses the importance of environmental events in maintaining pain behavior and eschews psychogenic notions. The patient is told that he may be experiencing more pain than he needs to. The rationale for and methods of behavioral intervention are explained to the patient, as well as to the spouse. Inclusion of the spouse or some significant other is deemed essential to the program, a feature that proceeds inevitably from the reinforcement model.

Fordyce's progam is remarkably straightfoward. There is a generally held view that if people know the contingencies, they will not work. The success of the Fordyce program suggests otherwise. Furthermore, whether or not one spells out the contingencies, patients usually figure out what is going on and may conclude that an attempt has been made to trick them. This realization in turn engenders resistance. Behavior modification programs benefit from a mature, contractual sort of relationship between therapist and patient and between patient and environment; the Fordyce program exemplifies this approach.

A second notable feature of Fordyce's model is that it emphasizes what is lacking, well behavior, as much as current responses, pain behavior or illness behavior. Well behavior does not occur automatically. Most of us receive adequate environmental reinforcement to maintain such behavior when illness does not preclude it. Fordyce's program focuses on the fact that well behavior, like sick behavior, must have environmental support if it is to occur. Because the two modes are incompatible, reinforcing the one discourages the other. This phenomenon works to the patient's detriment when pain behavior is reinforced and to his advantage when well behavior is reinforced.

A third significant element of the Fordyce program is the dissociation of pain medication from pain behavior. In the normal course, drugs are given in such a way that they become major reinforcers for pain behavior. PRN (*pro re nata,* or as needed) means, in effect, contingent on pain behavior. In this circumstance, the behavior is reinforced both by the chemotherapeutic effect of the drug and by the staff attention with which the medication is inevitably associated. In many hospitals, in fact, about the only way a patient can get attention is to request pain killing medication—it is hard to imagine a more effective way to teach people to complain about pain and ill health. Pain medication is given in a noncontingent manner in the Fordyce program. In addition, medication is faded slowly and replaced by placebo in order that the lowest possible amount is used. This procedure eliminates the operant component of medication taking, leaving only the dosage necessary to cover respondent pain.

Finally, Fordyce's explicit inclusion of spouse in the treatment plan is essential. In introducing the program to the patient the importance of this provision is spelled out in a way that avoids issues of blame and encourages a cooperative effort to resolve a problem that is mutually troublesome. The importance of the spouse's role can hardly be overemphasized. Fordyce cited the example of a woman with back pain whose husband was extremely solicitous and concerned, discouraging any type of activity. As it turned out, the husband was impotent and his wife's disability served to free him from aversive attempts at sexual intercourse. (In this case, treatment of the sexual problem proceeded along with treatment of the pain problem, with successful outcome in both areas)

The core of the Fordyce program is exercise, tailored to the individual case and maintained by carefully controlled contingencies. Progressing in systematic steps, the patient approaches normal or optimal levels. His performance is useful in itself from the general health vantage point, but in addition these responses are incompatible with illness behavior. One cannot hike and recline simultaneously and to the extent that hiking increases, illness behavior decreases. Exercise is thus encouraged both by positive reinforcement and by withdrawal or avoidance of any negative reinforcement previously associated with such activity. The latter issue bears a few words of explanation. Chronic pain patients often experience two sources of negative reinforcement for exercise: respondent pain and spouse disapproval. By ceasing to exercise, these negative reinforcers stop; hence, not exercising (or illness behavior) is reinforced. Exercise in the Fordyce program is structured so that the patient does not work to tolerance, thereby bringing on pain, and increases are kept small to insure a high probability of success. Quota achievement is followed by various positive reinforcements.

## MIGRAINE

Presently, two varieties of migraine are recognized: classic, or typical, and common, or atypical, the latter being far more prevalent. The classical variety begins with an aura, or prodroma, consisting of unilateral neurologic symptoms such as visual field abnormalities, body sensations and weakness, or aphasia. These are followed after a few minutes by hemicranial headache, first throbbing, then constant, and by nausea and vomiting lasting several hours or longer. In common migraine, there is no aura and gastrointestinal disturbance may be absent, but headache is similar and follows a similar course. The pain of migraine varies from case to case and attack to attack, but it can be devastating, forcing the patient to lie down for many hours and rendering him exquisitely sensitive to noise or bright light.

It is now generally accepted that the syndrome has a vascular origin. A genetic predisposition is evidenced by the much greater frequency of migraine among first-degree relatives of sufferers relative to population expectations (60–80% versus 5–10%). The course of events in classic migraine seems to entail an intracranial vasoconstriction giving rise to the prodroma, followed by an extracranial vasodilatation yielding the headache. This view has evolved over the years, based initially on clinical observation and simple manipulation: "As long ago as 1792, Perry reported that pressure on the homolateral carotid artery in the neck reduced the intensity of headache in migraine, an observation that has been many times confirmed" (Marshall, 1978: 131). Most recently, techniques for studying quantitatively regional cerebral blood flow (CBF) have in general confirmed this formulation. Summarizing the current understanding of the hemodynamics of migraine, Marshall noted: "Perhaps we can now draw the various strands of evidence together and try to determine the implications. It can now be considered as established that CBF in the prodromal phase of migraine is reduced. . . . The headache phase is accompanied by extracranial vasodilatation which the cerebral circulation shares" (137).

In the past, migraine generally was considered a benign disorder in the technical sense that it does not lead to tissue damage. Recent studies using the computerized axial tomogram, a very advanced X-ray technique that allows visualization of the cerebral contents, however, have raised question as to just how benign is migraine. Hungerford and associates studied 40 patients who had suffered from very severe migraine over periods averaging 20 years (1976). Of these, 22 were normal, but 18 showed a variety of abnormalities including focal and diffuse atrophy and infarction. Findings such as these suggest that migraine attacks may have long-term negative consequences that render control of this condition all the more pressing.

Some authorities suggest that personality variables play a key role in migraine. Wolff observed that "personality features characteristic of individuals with migraine are feelings of insecurity and tension manifested as inflexibility, conscientiousness, meticulousness, perfectionism, and resentment. These temperamental features lead to frustration, to dissatisfaction about family financial and personal status, and to intolerance to periods of low energy in themselves or of relaxed standards in themselves and others" (Dalessio, 1972: 399). He went on to hypothesize intrapunitive mechanisms: "This reaction of resentment and inability to forgive was often turned on the subject himself, so that personal deviations from set standards resulted in devastating self accusation and flagellation" (p. 377). In sum then, Wolff, while admitting exceptions, argued that migraine sufferers exhibit a characteristic personality pattern. He based this conclusion on his protracted clinical experience and not on psychometric or other methods of blind assessment. However, others have also identified a neurotic personality style characteristic of migraineurs. Gough described MMPI profiles in a group of military referrals with migraine: "The pattern was the basic neurotic one, . . . both HS (Hypochondriasis) and HY (Hysteria) were higher than D (Depression) in most of the cases" (1956: 345). Gough argued that the psychoneurosis is superimposed on the organic defect rather than causative of it in the conversion sense. It should be noted that Gough's sample were men referred to a neuropsychiatric hospital. Modlin looked at MMPIs in another group of servicemen with migraine and found normal MMPIs in 41%, but "fifty-seven percent had a high anxiety score, illustrating the diverse features of this syndrome" (1956: 397).

A fundamental methodologic problem runs through most of the literature on personality and migraine. The persons described are patients; that is, they are self-selected for special attention. In an epidemiologic study, Waters and O'Connor found that almost half of the female migraineurs did not consult a physician about the problem (1971). One wonders whether the addition of this large group to the clinical population would alter the so-called migraine personality. Some evidence of this possibility came from Phillips, who employed psychometric instruments in groups surveyed by postal questionnaire and selected as migraineurs (1976). These subjects had normal N (neuroticism) scores while a group of clinical mirgraineurs had elevated N scores. Henryk-Gutt and Reese found that survey selected migraineurs fell between clinical and control samples in N scores (1973). Phillips reached the following conclusion on the question of the migrainous personality:

> The prevailing view of headache sufferers as neurotic may well have evolved from clinical experiences of the minority of headache sufferers who complain to their doctors about headache. They are more neurotic and they suffer more pain. The population of headache sufferers in a community sample—independent of complaint behavior—is indistinguishable from the rest of the normal population in any of the four personality dimensions assessed. (1976: 359)

Psychological treatment of migraine, proceeding on the assumption of underlying personality disturbance, has tended to be psychodynamic in approach. The success of such endeavors is variously reported. Although one neurology textbook stated that "a long term psychological study of the patients in an attempt to give them understanding of the basis of their tensions and assistance in the resolution of their conflicts has proven of value in decreasing the frequency of attacks" (Merritt, 1973: 738), Adams and Victor noted that "in general long and costly psychotherapy has not been helpful, or at least one can say there is no substantial data as to its value" (1977: 107).

In summary, the role of personality characteristics in migraine is not clear. To the extent that they are accurate, the attributes described in clinical samples may be as explicable in terms of illness behavior and a propensity to seek medical help as in terms of migraine itself. Successful psychodynamically oriented treatment may act on this latter mechanism, freeing the patient of whatever it is that causes him to complain about head pain. In any case, the success of such efforts has not been overwhelming. Alternative methods, behaviorally derived, sidestep the personality question altogether and have had some good results. We turn to two studies that used operant techniques on vasomotor responses.

Reasoning that migraine pain is due to vasodilatation, Friar and Beatty used biofeedback to train subjects to reduce peripheral pulse volume (vasoconstriction) (1976). In order to control placebo effects, they assigned subjects to two training conditions. One group (experimental) was trained in vasoconstriction at the site of pain, the forehead on the most frequently involved side. The other group (control) received the same training, but in the hand. The training procedure entailed computer delivered auditory feedback that was contingent on progressive decreases in pulse volume. The training took three weeks with three sessions per week. During the study, the month before, and the month after, subjects kept detailed records of headache phenomena. On the last training trial, no feedback was given in order to assess the degree to which subjects could control pulse volume without external cues.

Results as regards measures of pulse volume on the last training trial were impressive. Control subjects reduced finger pulse volume to .67 of the pretraining baseline but showed no significant reduction of forehead pulse volume. Experimental subjects showed significant reduction of pulse volume at both sites; head .80, finger .69. The mean number of headaches dropped from 57 to 31 in the experimental group but did not change significantly in the control group (51 to 44). The measures of compliance with the regimen showed both groups to be equally highly compliant. Interestingly, both groups showed decreases in medication taking, though experimentals exceeded controls in this regard. This suggests that factors other than head pain are involved in medication taking since control patients showed no significant drop in pain symptoms.

Friar and Beatty's elegant study demonstrated that an operant technique can significantly decrease migraine frequency and that the effect is specific to the site of training. Placebo effects were effectively ruled out by the control group. The results also make sense in light of what is known about the mechanism of migraine—the dilatation is a local and not a generalized phenomenon. One would expect, therefore, that training in vasoconstriction should be effective only if it is done at the site and this is what occurred. The fact that the experimental group showed as much finger vasoconstriction as the control group is unexplained; one might hypothesize that cerebral vasoconstriction has generalized effects, while vasoconstriction elsewhere does not. In any case, the important point from a therapeutic point of view is that training of the cerebral vasoconstriction response is possible and useful in migraine.

Sargent and associates took another approach to the behavioral treatment of migraine (1973). Their rationale can be outlined as follows: migraine is a stress related event; sympathetic nervous system activity is part of stress reaction; reducing sympathetic activity through conditioning ought to reduce migraine. Sargent and co-workers trained subjects in peripheral vasodilatation, a response incompatible with sympathetic outflow since the latter leads to vasoconstriction. They relied essentially on relaxation training, emphasizing a generalized state of equilibrium, in contrast to Friar and Beatty's local model.

Results were reported in clinical ratings derived from records the subjects kept for a month preceding training, during training, and for a year afterward. Improvement ratings ranged from none to very good. A very good outcome entailed almost total absence of medication and only slight to moderate symptoms. In a series of 75 patients, 81% showed some improvement; the remainder were unaffected by the training procedure. Those who improved to a "good level" demonstrated relatively consistent detection behavior of preheadache symptoms and voluntary relaxation to avoid migraine attacks.

Relating the Sargent procedure to the Friar and Beatty approach is not easy since they apparently took opposite routes but got similar results. Sargent trained vasodilatation; Friar and Beatty, vasoconstriction. Since migraine is caused by vasodilatation, one might have expected relaxation training, to the extent that it engenders vasodilatation, to worsen, not relieve, headache. On the other hand, since the technique is to be used during the prodromal phase, it may be that relaxation reduces the prodromal vasoconstriction, in turn reducing the rebound vasodilatation and headache. Obviously, these vasomotor responses are complex and inadequately understood at present. What is perhaps most important is that both these procedures taught subjects to exert control over vasomotor responses of some kind, a skill they previously lacked. Once that ability is acquired, subjects may do a variety of things to control headache pain, the various things being reinforced by pain avoidance.

As a final example of behavioral treatment of migraine, we will look at Mitchell and Mitchell's 1971 work. These researchers used behavioral psychotherapy, derived more from respondent than from operant conditioning models, in an attempt to reduce tension and anxiety, the idea being that these states are migraine precipitators and characterize the migraineur's personality. This series of studies applied various combinations of behavioral treatment methods, following Kanfer and Phillip's argument that conditioning methods are more likely to succeed if they are combined with a total approach to lifestyle (1969). In the case of migraine, then, simple relaxation therapy was contrasted with a combination of relaxation therapy, desensitization to patient constructed hierarchies, and assertiveness training. A control group received no treatment. In one study, the combined treatment method significantly reduced both frequency and severity of migraine as compared to control levels while the simple relaxation therapy did not. In another study, the combined procedure, which included assertiveness training, was compared with a relaxation-desensitization format. The procedure that included assertiveness training showed significant effects on both frequency and severity; the other modality was indistinguishable from the control condition of no treatment.

Here, as in the Friar and Beatty study (1976), we see a sophisticated evaluation of a behavioral method that had useful effects on migraine. The approaches differed conceptually, one proceeding from physiological constructs, the other from psychological ones, but both generated testable hypotheses that the workers pursued rigorously. To what extent psychotherapeutic methods yield the same sorts of physiological effects that more direct biofeedback approaches generate is not known, but it would be most interesting to look at pulse volume values before and after combined desensitization therapy.

## Conclusion

In this chapter we saw that pain is not a simple matter of stimulus and response. Our understanding of this phenomenon is still very primitive. I suggested that an operant-respondent conceptualization of pain events is more useful than the traditional physical-mental dichotomy.

Psychologically derived modalities have sizable contributions to make in this area. Techniques and supporting data already exist and are being applied, but there is ample room for additional experimentation and development. Learning theory undoubtedly will contribute to a unified theory of pain that brings together physiological and psychological paradigms.

# 8

# Compliance

The medical control of hypertension has been possible for years and requires only that patients take their medicine faithfully. Dilantin can reduce the occurrence of seizures in most epileptics, often to zero, but they must take the drug on schedule. Why, then, do epileptics still have fits and hypertensives still have strokes? No matter how efficacious a medication, it can do no good in the bottle. Getting medicine into the patient is a behavioral event, subject to behavioral principles.

This chapter reviews studies on compliance and identifies pertinent principles. The general conclusion that will be reached might be summarized at the outset: simply telling patients to do things does not guarantee that they will do them. Fortunately, research has identified variables that can encourage compliance with medical advice.

## Traditional and Behavioral Views of Compliance

In general, compliance refers to a circumstance in which the behavior of the patient is controlled by the physician, at least as regards a finite range of health related activities. The particular behaviors to be controlled differ widely in complexity, and they upset or change the patient's life to varying degrees. A seemingly simple behavior might be taking a pill each morning. Following dietary regulations in diabetes or moving to a dry climate may profoundly disrupt the patient's life. Compliance may be an all-or-none affair or a matter of degree: if the behavior to be controlled is that of submitting to gall bladder surgery, it either happens or it does not; dietary compliance, on the other hand, is notoriously a matter of more or less.

Traditionally, verbal communication from the doctor to the patient is relied upon to induce patients to do what is indicated. Oral communication is perhaps the most frequent method, with printed material or occasionally film used as adjuncts. Methods of monitoring compliance most frequently entail questioning the patient and relying on his verbal report. Laboratory studies or other objective indices are employed when possible. Blood levels of a prescribed medication may be measured to see whether medication is being taken as prescribed. Weight may be monitored as a measure of dietary compliance. Responses to non-compliance usually take the form of exhortation ("You've *got* to stop smoking!"), threat ("If you don't stay on the low sugar diet, you'll go blind,") or threat of service withdrawal ("I cannot continue to work with you if you will not take the medication.").

Compliance is a problem with consequences extending beyond the health and welfare of the particular patient. To the extent that treatment is effective, failure to comply predisposes the patient to illness and illness translates directly to health costs and indirectly to decreased general productivity. Both categories of costs are borne by society at large via insurance premiums, taxes, and, arguably, through inflation if the gross national product is depressed by illness related absenteeism. Furthermore, failure to comply with treatment for infectious diseases like tuberculosis increases the risk for all who come into contact with the defaulter, and all who come in contact with those who come in contact, and so on. Finally, drugs are evaluated for use through clinical trials. When subjects in such studies are noncompliant, they seriously compromise inferences concerning drug effects. Soutter and Kennedy reviewed 768 such studies and found objective assessment of compliance in only 19% (1974). With estimates of noncompliance generally running in 30–50% range, this is a sobering observation.

To cast the compliance situation in behavioral terms, what the doctor seeks to do is to modify the patient's behavior by bringing certain aspects of it under the control of specific stimuli. He seeks to create SDs for the behavior to be learned and SDs for the behaviors to be avoided. For example, if the patient is to take a pill at 9:00 A.M., that time must acquire SD properties in relation to pill taking. Likewise, for the diabetic chocolate must become an SD for avoidance rather than approach. Identifying or altering reinforcers is the crucial task here: one need not look very far to see what the reinforcer is for approaching chocolate; to find a reinforcer for avoiding it is a challenge.

Traditionally, the issue of reinforcement has not been specifically addressed, but from an examination of doctor-patient behavior one can infer what sorts of reinforcement mechanisms must be assumed to be operative. Three general categories of presumed reinforcers for compliance are evident: feeling better, doctor praise, and what might be termed a sense of virtue.

At the most obvious level, a behavior that leads to alleviation of whatever brought the patient to the doctor is reinforced through the negative reinforcement mechanism. The prescription of analgesics for pain is the paradigm example here, but any successful modality that changes the subjective state in a positive direction, that relieves illness, is being reinforced. It should be pointed out that relief of illness, not of disease, lies at the root of this mechanism and accounts for the wide utilization of biologically useless remedies. Moreover, in addition to reinforcing pill taking, relief from illness also reinforces both going to the physician and compliance with his directives. On this basis, one would predict that persons experiencing relief on one occasion would be more likely to comply on subsequent occasions than persons not experiencing relief; this, in fact, appears to be the case although the reverse is also true. Most of the time, sick people recover with or without treatment. This generally happy circumstance may have a perverse effect on compliance, however, since when one recovers without treatment, doing nothing is reinforced.

Many physicians use positive reinforcement in the form of praise, signs of approval, and the like when the patient on follow-up visits seems to be complying with the regimen. This mechanism is especially important when relief from symptoms cannot occur. Hypertension, for example, usually lacks symptoms and the patient may experience no illness. Compliance in this case cannot yield negative reinforcement except as mediated by the physician. He may in such cases state that the patient's blood pressure has dropped, providing negative reinforcement. In addition, he may praise the patient, thus adding positive reinforcement for compliance. Doctors differ drastically in the way they use reinforcement and in their acknowledgment of it as a mechanism. Such differences may reflect various types of reinforcement events in the physician's own life. Some doctors feel that praise for compliance is demeaning to the patient, the doctor, or both. In transactions with physicians of this sort, the third general category of reinforcement is important.

The word "should" lies at the heart of virtue as a reinforcer. The patient takes the medication because he "should." He "should" stay on his diet and he "should" return to the clinic at the time appointed. Doing as one "should" is deemed to lead to feelings of self-worth, which "should" maintain the complying behavior—virtue, they say, being its own reward. A related idea is "doing something for one's own good." This view implies strong approval of self-maintained compliance and disapproval of its absence. Patients lacking these traits are deemed overly dependent and low in self-control. Physicians who subscribe to this view do not, of course, think in reinforcement terms since the value system itself suggests that behavior is not controlled by the environment but by internal qualities like will power or self-reliance. Yet behavior so described can be conceptualized within a behavioral framework: for people who *do* comply in this type of doctor-patient transaction, compliance itself has reinforcing properties.

The literature on compliance suggests that on the whole traditional reinforcers do not work very well. Patients are not notably compliant with medical prescription. This observation has led to a number of interesting efforts to identify the variables that affect compliance rates. These studies have yielded more or less specific recommendations to improve compliance.

## Studies of Compliance

### RATES

The bulk of the research on compliance has addressed two classes of patient behavior: taking medication and adherence to diet. The latter topic is addressed in detail in part three of this volume. Here the focus is compliance with prescription of medication.

The usual way of studying this problem is to monitor the response of outpatients to prescriptions given in a clinic or office setting. In addition, some studies have looked at compliance with medication regimens after discharge from hospital. Response measures include interviews with patients after some passage of time; stool, urine, or blood analyses to detemine presence and/or level of prescribed medication; pill counts to see whether the amount of medication left in the bottle tallies with what should be left if the prescription has been followed; and failure to get filled a prescription within some specified time (Blackwell, 1972).

All these methods have problems. Patients may lie or innocently report compliance when, in fact, they are not complying. Pill counts are unreliable: finding that the pills are not in the bottle is no guarantee that they are in the patient. They may well be in the toilet or in a neighbor. Laboratory studies are expensive, variably accurate, and inapplicable to some medications. Failure to dispense is reliable in itself, but its relation to ultimate compliance is unknown. Moreover, the incidence of this event is low, 3% in one study (Hammel & Williams, 1964), far below the usual noncompliance figures. It should further be noted that some of these sources of error tend to inflate estimates of compliance (e.g., patient report) so that the situation may be even worse than it appears.

The literature on compliance has been reviewed several times. Stimson listed 19 studies carried out mostly in the United States and the United Kingdom (1974). His survey revealed that noncompliance rates ranged from 19% to 72%, with the great majority of studies finding 30% or more of patients noncompliant with the prescribed drug regimen. Stewart and Cluff reported that up to 35% of patients in some studies were found to be misusing medication in ways dangerous to health (1972). It must be borne in mind that the criteria for noncompliance differ across studies and this may account in part for the wide range of variability. For example, some researchers distinguish between errors and noncompliance (Stewart & Cluff, 1972); clearly, inclusion of the former response class in the noncompliance category will inflate the latter estimate. Whatever the methodological pitfalls, all studies have found huge numbers of people failing to follow medical advice on the use of medication.

Bergman and Werner studied a group of patients prescribed antibiotics for 10 days following streptococcal infection: 58% had stopped taking the drug by the third day, 71% by the 6th, and 82% by the 9th day (1963). Thus, only 18% were fully compliant with the regimen. Watkins and associates reported that 58% of diabetics in their sample made errors in the use of insulin (1967), and Wilcox and co-workers found noncompliance in 33–58% of psychiatric patients prescribed major tranquilizers or antidepressants (1965). Sackett, summarizing 185 studies related to the problem, concluded that only about half the patients on long-term medication take it as directed, while compliance with short-term regimens drops rapidly after a day or two: "This stark summary emphasizes the serious nature of the problem of compliance, and its brevity also serves to underscore a vast inattention to this problem" (1976:22).

## PATIENT CHARACTERISTICS

Attempts to explain noncompliance have focused on several classes of variables. Patient characteristics have been a favorite class. Some doctors think they can predict who will and who will not follow a drug regimen. The literature on this subject suggests that, in fact, doctors predict compliance at about chance levels (Caron & Roth, 1968). In the traditional mentalistic paradigm, noncompliance has been viewed as a manifestation of some underlying variable residing in the patient and a good deal of effort has been expended in trying to define these patient attributes. The most notable product of these efforts has been the dearth of patient characteristics found to be related to noncompliance. At best, one could say that these efforts have met with mixed success (Ley, 1977). A variety of demographic characteristics have been studied but show inconsistent or no relationship with compliance. And, aside from the observation that psychiatric patients are less compliant than others, no predictions regarding compliance can be made on the basis of diagnosis (Haynes, 1976a).

Several more subtle patient characteristics have been investigated and seem to bear a relation to compliance. In general, compliance is better to the extent that patients believe their health problem is serious, that they are susceptible to the problem, and that therapy is likely to be effective. These factors have been conceptualized in a value-expectancy framework termed the health belief model, reviewed by Becker (1976). The model suggests that compliance is a predictable consequence of the interaction between patient and provider, modified by a group of patient expectations and beliefs. A central feature of this approach is the emphasis on *perceived* severity, susceptibility, etc., as opposed to objective indices of these variables. A number of reports have supported the utility of this way of viewing compliance. For example, while *objective* indices of disease severity are not consistently related to compliance, *patient estimates* of severity affect compliance in the predicted direction—the more serious the disease is believed to be, the greater is compliance (Becker, 1976).

In summary, patient demographic and personality characteristics are not consistently related to compliance, but patient beliefs do seem to be. A major challenge facing this field is the creation and standardization of techniques to measure these beliefs and an intervention strategy to modify them if the evidence continues to suggest that they are important determinants of compliance.

REGIMEN

Several studies found factors intrinsic to the drug regimen to affect compliance. In general, the more complicated the regimen, the worse is compliance. Francis and associates reported that compliance decreased significantly if more than two medications were employed or if two different treatment methods, such as diet and medication, were employed (1969). The patients in this study were children. Schwartz and co-workers found in geriatric patients that compliance decreased as the number of medications increased to three but did not continue to decline thereafter (1962). Malahy reported similar results and cautioned that increasing instructions or adding a more informative label to medication bottles did not improve compliance (1966). It seems clear that multiple medications are taken less reliably than single ones. Furthermore, multiple dosages of even one medication cause compliance to decline. Gatley found that noncompliance rates doubled when the dosage regimen was changed from once per day to four times daily (1968).

The implication of these findings is obvious: the drug regimen should be as simple as possible. In practice, this means that the physician must calculate the relative *biological* advantage of a complex regimen with the *psychological* risk factors of noncompliance. Thus, while it might be in some sense optimal to take a low-dose preparation every four hours as opposed to a higher dose once in the morning and once at night, the former regimen is far less likely to be followed. Also, if a patient has several problems, each requiring a different medication, the possibility of special pharmacologic preparation of several medications in one pill should be explored. Alternatively, the physician must consider the absolute gravity of various secondary problems relative to the fact that treating them—adding medicines to the regimen—increases the risk of noncompliance and thus puts treatment of the primary problem at hazard.

Four other factors intrinsic to the drug regimen have been related to compliance. There is some evidence that duration of the regimen is negatively related to compliance; that is, the longer the regimen goes on, the more poorly it is followed (Luntz & Austin, 1960). From a behavioral perspective, this sounds rather like extinction. It might also be expected that unpleasant side effects would have a decidedly negative effect on compliance. Michaux found this to be true of psychiatric patients (1961), and Wynn-Williams and Arris confirmed this effect with tuberculosis patients (1958). Other studies, however, have reported weak or no effect of side effects on compliance (Wilcox et al., 1965). In fact, Sackett and Haynes, after reviewing the literature, concluded that "it is probably safe to say that side effects do not have an important effect on compliance" (1976:33). Only a few studies have examined the effect of drug cost on compliance (Donabedian & Rosenfeld, 1964). As might be expected, the two variables are negatively correlated. Finally, Lane and associates looked at the effect of the new so-called child-proof medication bottle and found that compliance among adults was negatively affected by the use of these bottles (1971).

Practical implications of these factors can be suggested. First, extremely protracted treatments will require frequent evaluation in some cases. It is hazardous to assume that over a long period patients will continue to take medication as directed. As regards side effects, though the data are inconsistent, it seems prudent to attempt to determine their presence and intensity in particular cases in order better to calculate risks of noncompliance; this precaution may be especially important in psychiatric patients. In patients with significant unpleasant side effects, the addition of covering medication complicates the regimen and increases noncompliance risks. This factor must be weighed against the possible risk of default because of side effects. To the extent that side effects can be managed by changing medication dosage or delivery time, such a course seems preferable to complicating the regimen. At any rate, the patient with side effects may be a default risk and this possibility needs to be considered by the physician. As regards the child-proof bottle, we are faced with a trade-off here between safety and compliance. Such trade-offs seem to be the rule rather than the exception in medicine and the decision to use or not to use this sort of container must be made on the basis of factors specific to a given case. In an older patient living alone, for example, the safety factor may be largely irrelevant and the conventional bottle would be preferable.

Finally, several studies have addressed the form of drug administration as it relates to compliance. Pills have been compared to liquids, and injection to oral administration. While no satisfactory generalization can be made, in specific patient samples form of administration does seem to affect compliance. Freeman found the dropout rate to decline from around 45% to 16% when chronic schizophrenics were shifted from oral to injected neuroleptics (1973). Dixon reported a similar result in tuberculosis patients (1957). It should be noted, however, that more than the form of the drug is altered when injections are substituted for pills. An injection must be actively refused to yield noncompliance, while a pill can be merely forgotten. The former will likely elicit reproof from the doctor or nurse; in this circumstance, compliance can be seen as an avoidance response, reinforced by the absence of the nurse's harangue.

## DOCTOR-PATIENT TRANSACTION

A sizable literature addresses variables in the doctor-patient transaction as they relate to compliance rates. Charney and colleagues reported the not surprising finding that patients were more compliant with instructions from a familiar than from an unfamiliar practitioner (1967). Another study found that compliance increased as the doctor's enthusiasm for the particular regimen increased (Reynolds et al., 1965). This is an important finding that appears in a variety of forms in the literature on placebo effects. To address this variable experimentally requires ingenuity, but the doctor's attitude about the patient's regimen should prove a fruitful area of investigation.

Analyses of doctor-patient transactions have employed a variety of techniques to define relevant dimensions of this complex behavior. In 1968 Davis, analyzed doctor-patient interactions employing Bales's Interaction Process Analysis (1950). Using factor analysis, Davis identified 10 factors reflecting different patterns of doctor-patient transaction, such as active patient–passive doctor (patient talks, doctor listens), nondirective antagonism (doctor is antagonistic and opinionated, giving little information), and tension release (jokes and laughter). Low but significant relationships between five factors and compliance were reported. Freemon and colleagues evaluated doctor-patient transactions in a pediatric setting and found that longer transactions, those including a higher proportion of doctor inquiries, and those with a relatively high proportion of non–problem centered statements were all associated with better compliance (1971).

In a cogent review of the whole area of doctor-patient communication, Ley discussed compliance in relation to the patient's expressed satisfaction with the transaction (1977). On heuristic grounds, it would seem that compliance is likely to be related to degree of satisfaction and this has been found by Korsch and co-workers studying visits at a pediatric clinic (1968). Francis and associates found that compliance percentages decreased systematically as the degree of satisfaction with the visit decreased—from a high of 53.4% with high satisfaction to a low of 16.7% with high dissatisfaction (1969). Korsch and co-workers analyzed the data from this study to define the correlates of degree of satisfaction, finding four general classes of doctor behavior related to patient satisfaction (1968). Doctors who were rated friendly, who gave the impression they understood the mother's concerns, and who were seen as effective communicators tended to generate expressions of satisfaction in patients. In addition, patient expectations were important in individual cases. Some mothers, for example, expected to hear a diagnosis or to be given medication. When expectations were present and fulfilled, satisfaction resulted; otherwise, the patient left unsatisfied. Satisfaction, then, seems related to compliance. Nevertheless, in this series of studies, nearly half the patients rated highly satisfied were still noncompliant with medical advice (Francis, *et al*, 1969).

To the extent that patients do not comprehend and recall what they are supposed to do, they are not likely to do it. A number of studies have looked at patients' comprehension and forgetting of medical advice. As regards memory, the results are singularly disquieting. The usual finding is that immediately upon leaving the consulting room patients forget one-third to one-half of what they have been told (Joyce et al., 1969; Ley & Spelman, 1965, 1967; Ley et al., 1973). Some consolation might be taken from the fact that there seems to be relatively little further forgetting. Joyce and associates found 48% recall immediately after consulting the doctor and 46% recall at four weeks (1969). Ley and Spelman reported that patients are particularly prone to forget advice and instructions (1967). In an attempt to explain this unfortunate tendency, Ley hypothesized that the usual delivery of advice at the end of the consultation might contribute to its rapid evaporation (1972). He further speculated that patients may consider advice less important than other sorts of information. Accordingly, he compared the usual consultation format with one in which advice was presented first and one in which the importance of advice was stressed by the doctor. Both these strategies improved recall of advice from 50.3% in the usual procedure to 87.3% and 68.8% for the placement and stress formats, respectively. Interestingly, total quantity recalled was the same for the three methods; hence, the effect was specific.

In reviewing the problem of comprehension, Ley listed three potential sources of incomprehension (1977). In the first place, the material may simply exceed the patient's ability by being too complicated. Second, there may be a professional assumption that the patient possesses a higher level of technical knowledge than he in fact has. Finally, the patient may bring to the situation active misconceptions that must be overcome if he is to comprehend what is being said to him. Research suggests that all these factors are operative in the usual medical practice.

A number of studies on British patients' medical knowledge have yielded astonishing findings. Fifty-four percent of Boyle's 1970 sample, for example, did not know the location of the kidneys and 48% could not locate the heart. Active misconceptions are equally surprising. Spelman and Ley found that nearly a third of their sample of laymen thought that cancer of the lung is a relatively minor condition that can be cured with ease (1966). In the face of that belief, exhortations to stop smoking might be expected to have little effect. Generalization from these studies to other populations is hazardous since educational experiences, both formal and informal, vary regionally and nationally. However, the data suggest that knowledge may be rather limited and incorrect in individual cases. In fact, a survey of a representative sample of patients in any particular setting might have considerable practical importance. Medical psychologists are the natural persons to undertake this task and they might design educational programs to correct identified deficiencies.

The practical consequences of patient knowledge on compliance have been the subject of debate. On heuristic grounds, one might expect greater understanding to lead to better compliance, but the literature does not consistently support this assumption (Haynes, 1976b). For one thing, there need be no relationship between the objective accuracy of the patient's understanding of his disease and the subjective intensity of his belief in the treatment. Faith healers demonstrate that patients will comply with all sorts of bizarre treatments. The critical variable may be a higher order interaction such that compliance is a function of the degree to which the patient's understanding, whatever its accuracy, leads him to believe in the treatment. To the extent that patient education is helpful, the mechanism may be of this sort, with the teaching process leading to increased belief in the health care deliverer, relatively independent of any objective increase in medical knowledge. This hypothesis is open to empirical test: existing findings suggest little relation between objective knowledge and compliance but at least some increased complaince following educational efforts (Haynes, 1976b).

## Improving Compliance

As we have seen, patient satisfaction is related to compliance and satisfaction is in turn partly a function of degree of patient understanding. Memory and comprehension are also implicated in the problem of noncompliance. Hence, strategies to improve compliance have focused on improving comprehension, satisfaction, and recall, realizing that these are in no sense independent of one another.

Korsch offered several recommendations for improving satisfaction, and thus compliance, that deserve systematic study (Korsch et al., 1968). In the first place, the patient brings to the situation expectations and worries and will leave dissatisfied if these are not addressed. The assumption by the doctor of a businesslike, information gathering posture, to the exclusion of meeting the patient's often unstated needs, leads to dissatisfaction. The simple strategy of spending some time in nonproblem centered conversation offers promise of some compliance yield. As regards the medical problem itself, patients seem often to want a diagnosis and an explanation of cause presented in language they can understand. Thus, avoiding jargon is recommended and explicit efforts to convey information and answer questions also may be useful. Research in this area could be done by contrasting business as usual clinic contacts with contacts structured around these variables. Should results support the hypothesized utility of these strategies, structured teaching of these skills to physicians, nurses, and others imparting health information would follow.

Efforts to improve comprehension of medical advice have taken several forms. Ley, Jain, and Skilbeck compared leaflets given to groups of psychiatric patients (1976). The leaflets, which contained information about prescribed medication, differed in complexity. The number of inferred medication errors (determined by a pill count) was lowest in the easy leaflet group, higher in the moderate leaflet group, and equal and highest for those receiving a complicated leaflet and no leaflet. The last type of leaflet was no different from those usually employed. In a study on oral communication, Bradshaw, Kincey and Atherton looked at patient satisfaction as a function of special efforts to increase understanding (1976). Subjects were inpatients. Members of one group were visited by the doctor for five extra minutes daily, during which time the doctor specifically assessed the patient's understanding of things he had been told and provided an opportunity for patient questions. The transaction was limited to information already given and no new topics were introduced. To control for the effects of simply receiving extra attention, a second group was visited, but only general matters like food and hospital comfort were discussed. A third group received no special attention. Satisfaction with hospitalization was expressed by 80% of the information group, 41% of the second group, and 48% of the controls. This study strongly suggests that information, and not just attention, is important in patient satisfaction with hospitalization.

Reviewing the compliance issue, Stewart and Cluff observed: "In our society, better instructions are provided when purchasing a new camera or automobile than when the patient receives a life-saving antibiotic or cardiac drug" (1972:467). In their view, inadequate information is a major cause of compliance failure in patients discharged from hospital on a medicine regimen and they recommended a procedure of training patients in self-medication in hospital. Stewart and Cluff's program allows for reinforcement of appropriate drug taking behavior and for protracted patient-staff interaction around drug related information. This approach merits systematic study.

Studies on memory have focused on various strategies of message delivery in the interview setting. Earlier I cited the Ley study on advice placement and stress (1972). Explicit categorization of information also has been shown to increase recall. Ley reported increases in recall when categorized versus ordinary, free-flowing communication was employed (1973). Interestingly, advice was particularly affected, while diagnosis was not. Patients, it seems, really want a diagnosis and remember it if given. On the other hand, advice needs to be strengthened by techniques such as categorization.

Following a discovery by Ley that the perceived importance of a medical statement varies as a function of its specificity (1969), Bradshaw and co-workers demonstrated truly remarkable differences in recall of general versus specific statements (1975). Student volunteer subjects were given both general and specific medical statements to remember. Of the general statements, 10.25% were recalled compared with 45% of the specific. Likewise, obese women given general or specific recommendations for dieting recalled 51% of the specific and only 16% of the general. These differences suggest that much of physician speech, addressing general topics and pronouncing general principles, is a waste of time since patients either forget or never comprehend 80–90% of it.

Pulling these data together to form practical recommendations, Ley describes a study comparing recall of medical information presented to patients by four general practitioners (1977). A leaflet was prepared for the physician outlining the various relevant studies and making a series of explicit recommendations for increasing patient recall. Recommendations included giving advice at the beginning of the consultation and stressing it, using simple words and sentences, employing categorization and repetition, and employing specific as opposed to general recommendations (e.g., "Don't eat chocolate" versus "Watch your diet"). Patients seen before the doctors had read the leaflet were compared to patients seen after the leaflet had been read. Increases in recall of 9–21% were seen among patients of the four doctors. While these increases were not huge, to modify patient recall behavior *at all* through a maneuver as simple as having doctors read a leaflet is little short of amazing and bears testimony to the importance of the identified variables. One would expect rather dramatic effects through more careful training of these skills in physicians.

## Operant Conditioning and Compliance

The focus of attention in research reviewed thus far has been patient characteristics or doctor-patient interaction at the time of prescription. Both these are antecedent variables relative to the behavior of interest, compliance. What of the consequences of compliance or non-compliance? Studies on the effects of reinforcement of compliance are notable mainly for their absence. As I noted earlier, three general categories of reinforcement can be inferred theoretically, but there has been little systematic attempt to study their effects. A number of reasons can be offered for this lack.

First, compliance is in essence a problem of patient behavior physically outside the health care system. For this reason, observation of reinforcement for compliance, let alone manipulation of it, is technically difficult. The tendency has been to address variables over which the doctor has control, say, his own speech. Second, many physicians do not think in terms of reinforcement controlling behavior. Given this orientation, exhortation, warnings, and speeches—all antecedent variables—are about all one would expect the doctor to employ and this is in general what occurs. Ley and others have presented compelling evidence that manipulation of some antecedent variables does affect compliance. One wonders to what extent additional improvement might be realized by focussing on consequent events as well.

Arguing from an operant point of view, one could say that these antecedent manipulations are effective because they *do* alter consequences by changing the significance patients attach to compliant behavior. For example, the moderate decline in cigarette smoking during the decade following the first surgeon general's report might be interpreted behavioristically by saying that the information (antecedent variable) altered the experience of smoking cigarettes by making the act itself a conditioned stimulus for fear. Not smoking, which for a smoker is an operant response, is thus reinforced negatively. This behavior avoids the aversive experience of fear. The study showing that specific recommendations are better than general advice also can be interpreted in this framework: it is easier to condition avoidance responses to a specific stimulus like chocolate than to a general one like fattening foods.

Epstein and Masek did approach the issue of compliance from an operant point of view (1978). Their format included several reinforcement strategies. In a technique called response-cost, the subject deposits a sum of money and forfeits fixed amounts for failure to do some agreed upon behavior. In another method, self-monitoring, the subject simply records his own behavior, the accumulating checkmarks functioning as reinforcers. Following a suggestion by Zifferblatt (1975), Epstein and Masek also included taste of medication as a variable on the assumption that any stimulus characteristic that increases the salience of a medication might increase compliance.

The regimen to be followed in this study was the taking of vitamin C four times per day as a prophylactic for colds. Subjects were student volunteers. Baseline measurements identified a subgroup of noncompliant subjects with compliance rates around 30–40%. Introduction of self-monitoring raised compliance to 49%. The introduction of self-monitoring and taste yielded a 67% compliance rate. Rates for control and taste-only subjects were 24% and 31%, respectively. Introduction of response-cost raised compliance considerably, independent of other treatments. That is, controls put on a response-cost program did about as well as self-control plus taste subjects on the response-cost regimen. The mean compliance for all subjects given response-cost was 78%, which was good in absolute terms and particularly striking since the subjects in this study were preselected for being very noncompliant during the baseline procedure.

Epstein and Masek's results suggest that the response-cost method can significantly improve compliance. The authors noted that the particular regimen studied, vitamin C four times per day, is a fairly good analogue for medication that does not have a dramatic effect on the illness experience, such as chronic maintenance medications. Both hypertension and tuberculosis are treated on such protracted regimens and the medications do not in general make the patient feel better. In fact, side effects may make him feel worse. In this circumstance, inventive engineering of reinforcement to maintain compliance is especially necessary and response-cost is a promising possibility.

## Conclusion

Several conclusions can be drawn from this review of compliance with prescription regimens. First, the problem is huge in proportion and serious in effects. Many people are needlessly ill because of non-compliance and everyone pays, one way or another, for the fact that about half of us fail to take our medicine. Second, prediction of non-compliance on the basis of readily identifiable patient characteristics is impossible. On the other hand, patient beliefs about health care seem to be related to compliance and this connection has been usefully explored through the health belief model. Third, several parameters of the doctor-patient interaction have been related to compliance. These factors can be manipulated by the doctor himself and should be addressed in medical schools. Finally, we lack research on the consequence of compliance, reinforcement. Given the power of this approach in other types of behavior, innovative efforts to bring the operant model to bear on the compliance problem can be expected to have good cost-benefit effects.

# 9

# Psychiatry

The history of psychology and of medicine shows clearly that the most extensive and sustained interaction between the two disciplines has occurred in the area of mental health, the province of the psychiatrist and the clinical psychologist. Both these practitioners have been viewed by colleagues in their parent fields as slightly odd or out of touch. Psychiatrists have long been among the lowest in the specialty pecking order and clinical psychology has been denigrated by experimentalists and others because it is applied and thus somehow impure and because the subject matter is seen as bizarre. It is almost as though psychiatry and clinical psychology together formed a separate discipline, distinct from both medicine and psychology—distinct from medicine in tending to be non-biologic in paradigm and from psychology in being treatment rather than knowledge oriented.

The shift away from biological thinking about mental illness came originally from within medicine, not from without. Freud, a neurologist by training, played a major role in this development by affixing a medically legitimizing stamp on psychological theories, and on treatment derived from them. Although Freud's followers, Adler and Jung, differed from him on important questions, neo-Freudians, egotheorists, and orthodox Freudians have all come down squarely on the psychological side of fundamental issues, for example, the relative emphasis of psychological as opposed to biological explanations for deviant behavior. This distinction was critical to the development of both clinical psychology and psychiatry in the United States, paving the way for psychologists to enter medicine's traditional domain, the care of the patient.

Clinical psychology as we presently know it was born in the wake of the Freudian revolution. Freud himself favored the practice of psychoanalysis by non-physicians, supporting that view unequivocally in his book originally published in 1926, *The Question of Lay Analysis* (1950). Orthodox Freudians in the AMA have been somewhat less enthusiastic in their orthodoxy on this point than on some others, but the principle seems largely to have won out. In no other area of medicine is there such a massive sharing of the treatment role and this sharing follows logically from the adoption by psychiatry of a psychosocial model for mental illness and behavior deviance. Yet, psychiatry remains a medical specialty and controversy continues, centering on issues of the definition of "illness," on the appropriateness of various treatment modalities to those conditions, and on the criteria of expertness in diagnosis and treatment.

If from Freud onward American psychiatry has tended to stress psychosocial factors as causative of mental illness, the field also has steadily expanded the range of behaviors classified as mental illness. Madness ceased to be the primary concern of psychiatrists decades ago. The APA's *Diagnostic and Statistical Manual* includes an astonishing array of events conceptualized as requiring medical, that is, psychiatric, intervention (American Psychiatric Association, 1968, 1980). Yet other authorities argue that many such disorders are psychosocial, not biological, in origin and therefore not uniquely within the purview of medicine.

This circumstance has led to no end of confusion and debate as to who is qualified to do what to whom and who ought to pay for treatment. If an individual enters a hospital because of tension headache and is treated with wholly behavioral techniques by a psychologist, should his medical insurance pay for that hospitalization and treatment? When this question is answered in the affirmative, medical supervision is invoked, but since many physicians have little knowledge of behavioral techniques the term "supervision" is being stretched to its limits. When outpatient treatment is provided for tension headache, these already murky waters become opaque and many third-party carriers refuse to pay for outpatient psychotherapy no matter who provides it. The issue here turns on the definition of medical illness, since that is what insurance covers, and on who is qualified to treat such conditions. Insurance companies often argue that a condition is medical if a physician treats it, but in psychopathology physicians and psychologists may do precisely the same things with the same sorts of patients. If, on the other hand, the insurer were to follow the APA's diagnostic manual, virtually every type of problem would be covered as a medical illness. Finally, if we define as medical only those conditions serious enough to require hospitalization, it is still unclear who should be paid for providing the care.

Perhaps in response to this perplexing state of affairs, some psychiatrists have advocated redefining the field along more traditional, medical lines. The Washington University approach, taken in Woodruff, Goodwin, and Guze's *Psychiatric Diagnosis*, is an example of this trend (1979); a series of artic s by Ludwig made a similar point (Ludwig, 1975, 1976; Ludwig & Othmer, 1977). The argument is that the psychiatric disease category ought to include only those mental, affective, or behavioral disturbances that have a known or presumed biological basis and that the psychiatrist ought to be skilled both in the differential diagnosis of these conditions and in somatic treatment modalities (e.g., psychoactive drugs and electroconvulsive therapy). It is further argued that the treatment of other sorts of conditions, designated problems in living, is the proper purview of nonphysicians such as psychologists, social workers, and ministers of religion.

This reformulation has shortcomings, not the least of which is that many American psychiatrists would be unemployed if they gave up treating so-called problems in living. This scenario may in part explain the hostility with which this view has been greeted in some quarters. Other problems with a medical reformulation of psychiatry work at a more conceptual level and have to do, first, with categorizing disorders on the basis of presumptive etiology; second, with categorizing treatments on the basis of their biological or nonbiological nature and classifying those providing treatment as competent to do so; and third, with interfacing the treatment category with a disease category.

Reconceptualization of the field of psychiatry on the basis of etiology is problematic because the causes of psychiatric disorders are almost totally unknown. The applicability of the traditional medical model of etiologic diagnosis leading to treatment of choice is, in psychiatry, completely theoretical. Psychiatric treatment is syndromatic, symptomatic, or palliative (in some cases, of course, patients experience spontaneous remission). Why such treatments are effective is not known, and to reparcel disorders as properly psychiatric and not properly psychiatric on the basis of etiology is infeasible. Ludwig and Othmer suggested classification by "known, suggestive, or presumed biological abnormalities or dysfunctions" (1977: 1088), but "suggestive" and "presumed" are not helpful guidelines.

The categorization of treatments seems simple enough at first glance. Closer study raises questions. The difficulty lies in establishing a dichotomy between the biological and the psychosocial, as if these were ontologically distinct. Several centuries of the mind-body debate should have made clear that the distinction is more apparent than real, a philosophical convenience rather than a fact of nature. If the modalities being considered are drugs and marital counseling, one can be fairly comfortable with calling the former biological and the latter psychosocial and with Ludwig's contention that psychiatrists ought to be concerned with the former but not necessarily the latter. When we look at a modality like biofeedback, however, the biological-psychosocial distinction entirely breaks down. Biofeedback training proceeds from psychological learning theory and is thus psychosocial in origin; yet the dependent variables in such applications—heart rate, EMG, blood pressure—are conventionally considered biological not psychosocial, phenomena. As for who should take care of psychosocial problems, Ludwig rather cavalierly includes clinical psychologists, social workers, nurses, and ministers without explicit attention to necessary levels of training, supervision, etc. (1976).

Finally, the reformulation gets into difficulty in relating biological treatment to biological disease and psychosocial treatment to problems in living because current practice finds a disconcerting amount of crossover. Conditions that do not meet Ludwig's weakest criterion for biological etiology (presumed) are treated biologically while other conditions for which a strong case can be made for biological causality are sometimes effectively treated using psychosocial methods. Legions of unhappy housewives are given Valium for problems for which a unique biological cause is not even suggested. On the other hand, chronic schizophrenics have been shown to respond to token economies in numerous studies, Ludwig's among them (1971). Deciding just who the expert is here is not always easy. With regard to the unhappy housewife, the law states clearly that only the physician can prescribe, but one could certainly argue that the practice is a poor one and that her problems could be better addressed on psychological grounds. As for the schizophrenic, to comply with the requirement that psychiatrists alone can care for the biologically ill, and assuming schizophrenia is a biological illness, a great many token economies are going to have to be dismantled or their originators replaced by psychiatrists, many of whom know little about how such systems work.

If clinical psychology approaches psychiatric patients from the psychosocial perspective and shares this orientation with much of psychiatry, what, then, is the role of medical psychology in relation to psychiatry? There is a school of psychiatry that emphasizes medical, biological points of view, and psychology as the study of behavior has contributions to make to such an approach. I said earlier that recent efforts to recast psychiatry in medical model terms are suspect. Yet there are also both conceptual and practical problems with psychosocial and other formulations since mental illness and behavior deviance are poorly understood phenomena. For practical purposes, one can meaningfully divide the psychiatric patient population into persons with disorders for which there is a plausible assumption of biological abnormality and persons about whom such an assumption is improbable. Clinical psychology concerns the latter; medical psychology, the former. Thus, medical psychology interfaces with those aspects of psychiatry that address the major psychoses, the psychophysiologic disorders, problems of addiction, and organic brain syndromes—conditions in which physiological factors can be defended as playing a unique role either as causes, concomitants, or effects of the conditions.

This subdivision based on diagnostic categories is admittedly arbitrary. Obviously, physiology plays a role even in variations among normal people. The four categories just identified differ from the problems of living group in that there is at least some evidence that people having these conditions differ physiologically from people who do not have them. The data are more compelling in some instances than others, but the possibility that a physiologically oriented paradigm may lead to unique treatments for these conditions seems greater for them as a group than it does for the problems of the living as a group. Yet one should not press this distinction too far. Anxiety neurosis has physiological concomitants; there is also evidence that it runs in families (Slater & Shields, 1969). Does anxiety neurosis represent a problem in living or a physiologically based disorder? I am obviously not going to resolve this issue here, but I think the division can be defended as a useful way currently to divide up a murky field.

That said, what is the role of medical psychology in relation to psychiatry? Medical psychologists have several specific types of skills to offer medically oriented psychiatrists and some of these skills overlap with those of clinical psychologists. The differentiation is based on the sort of patient seen and on the inclination toward biological as opposed to psychosocial etiologic theories. Whatever the cause of psychiatric disorder, the symptoms are behavioral or are revealed through behavior. Medical psychology's first contribution, then, is in the area of assessment. This activity entails developing and applying more sensitive methods for observing and quantifying behavior for both descriptive and diagnostic purposes. Second, psychologists often are better versed in research methods, design, and statistics than are psychiatrists and can therefore provide essential service in this area. Finally, treatment methods proceeding from learning theory have utility in a number of psychiatric conditions and can thus be applied either in addition to or instead of somatic therapies. The biofeedback management of tension headache is an example and the use of contingency contracting to improve compliance with medication in affective disorder is another. The rest of this chapter reviews examples of such applications.

## Interfaces between Medical Psychology and Psychiatry

### STUDIES OF SCHIZOPHRENIA

One disorder for which a medical model seems especially suitable is schizophrenia. There is extensive evidence that the disease is at least in part determined by genetic factors and a number of physiological parameters have been shown to differentiate schizophrenics both from normal persons and from patients with other diagnoses. Rosenthal, reviewing studies on twins, reported consistently much higher concordance for the diagnosis of schizophrenia between monozygotic than dyzygotic twins; he also noted that family risk of schizophrenia is greatly increased when there is a schizophrenic blood relative (1970). The issue of family environment was answered by adoptee studies in which the incidence of schizophrenia reflected the biological parents' status rather than that of the adoptive parents (Heston, 1966; Wender et al., 1974). Such data argue forcefully that there is a biological factor operative in schizophrenia.

Research on the psychophysiology of schizophrenia has been extensive and the literature is choked with conflicting results. The overall impression is that at least a subsample of the heterogeneous group called schizophrenics shows physiologic peculiarities not attributable to the effects of drug treatment, but diagnostic ambiguity confounds many such studies. Parameters addressed have included autonomic reactivity (Shagass, 1969; Sternbach et al., 1969), neurologic soft signs (Cox & Ludwig, 1979), and a plethora of biochemical factors in blood, cerebrospinal fluid, and urine (Kety, 1978). Summarizing the biochemical studies of schizophrenia and the theories proceeding from them, Davison and Neale commented: "The history of research on whether biochemicals figure in schizophrenia has been one of discovery followed by failure to replicate. Methodological problems plague this research, and many confounds, unrelated to whether or not a subject is schizophrenic, can produce biochemical differences" (1978: 379). The same might be said of psychophysiological studies of schizophrenia. One of the major difficulties lies in the fact that by the time the patient is studied, he has a history of being diagnosed schizophrenic. This may imply protracted hospitalization, drug treatment, and schizophrenic behavior, which might itself induce physiological change. A possible solution to such difficulties is to study schizophrenics before they have clinical manifestations of the disease. The problem here, of course, is deciding whom to study.

Reasoning that children of schizophrenic parents are at exaggerated risk for developing the disorder, Mednick and Schulsinger put together samples of 207 children of process schizophrenic mothers and 104 children of normal mothers matched on socioeconomic status, age, sex, and other relevant or potentially relevant variables (1968). The criteria for a diagnosis of schizophrenia in the mother were rigid: "The intent in the selection of the mothers was to choose only cases that would be readily agreed upon in Europe or the United States as being severe and typical schizophrenics" (p. 271). The mothers were diagnosed on the basis of their clinical record, which had to include hospitalization of five years' duration or at least three separate hospitalizations of at least three months' duration with no evidence of intercurrent improvement. Each case had to manifest at least two types of schizophrenic symptoms to a severe degree.

Raters blind to the risk category of the subjects assessed a wide range of parameters, including psychophysiological studies, intelligence tests (Wechsler Intelligence Scale for Children), MMPI (modified for use with children), two word association tasks, an adjective checklist of self-descriptors, a psychiatric interview, a structured interview with the parent, a questionnaire on school behavior filled out by the teacher, and a report of birth events by the attending midwife.

Mednick and Schulsinger evaluated autonomic conditionability in their high- and low-risk samples. A neutral buzz stimulus was paired with an annoying noise in a classical conditioning paradigm; heart rate, electromyographic (EMG) response, and galvanic skin response (GSR) were measured. Once conditioning had taken place to the neutral stimulus, generalization trials were run. Taken together, several findings from this study suggested a pattern of autonomic hyperreactivity in the high-risk group. The high-risk children showed stronger GSRs to the UCS and stronger conditioned response to the CS. The GSR also failed to habituate in the high-risk group, growing stronger as trials proceeded and returning more quickly to baseline after each trial. This physiological finding in high-risk children bears a heuristic similarity to the observation that adult schizophrenics respond to all stimuli as if they were new and unfamiliar (Salzinger, 1973).

Thought disorder is a primary characteristic of clinical schizophrenia. This symptom is described in terms of loosening of associations: things that usually go together, so that if one is presented as a stimulus the other will occur as a response, become dissociated. Tangentiality is another descriptive term for the schizophrenic's tendency in speech to wander off the point. Salzinger's immediacy hypothesis is a way of bringing such observations together (1973). He argued that the schizophrenic is responsive to an exaggerated degree to the most temporally recent stimulus event. In the case of loosening of associations, the conventional pairing is remote relative to whatever the patient happens to be thinking at the time. The result is an idiosyncratic response. As for tangentiality, the patient's own words as he responds to a question are immediate relative to the original question, which is remote. The result here is the wandering discourse characteristic of schizophrenic speech.

Cognitive processes have been studied in high- and low-risk children to identify possible characteristic differences antedating overt symptoms. Didericksen used a continuous association task requiring the subject to offer associations to a stimulus word in a continuous fashion (1967). The stimulus word thus is given but once and is to be associated to serially. "House," for example, might be expected to elicit a string such as "home, roof, dwelling, door, window, chimney, yard, bricks, and garage." Comparing the responses of high- and low-risk children, Didericksen reported that the former were more likely to drift away from the original stimulus word and to offer associations to their own responses. "House," for example, might elicit "home, warm, summer, sun, yellow, lemon, and sour." Such a result fits with the immediacy hypothesis and may be evidence that very early in development there are harbingers of the schizophrenic thought disorder.

The longitudinal character of their research gave Mednick and Schulsinger (1968) a unique opportunity to look back at earlier data once patients manifested the clinical syndrome and thus to see to what extent those who developed the disorder could be distinguished from other high-risk individuals. They noted, for instance, that on the continuous association task the earlier performance of those who subsequently became ill was worse than that of the high-risk subjects who were still well. Likewise, the psychophysiological parameters showed more overreactivity in the sick than in the well high-risk subjects. Subjects who subsequently became ill also had had greater difficulty in school, having been teacher rated as more disruptive in a number of ways. Examination of the degree of maternal psychopathology revealed that 75% of the mothers of the sick group were rated as very severely ill versus only 33% of the well group mothers.

A very interesting question arises from these data: what factors lead some high-risk children to subsequent illness? One possibility is that the abnormalities seen early on are themselves causative; in other words, they impair social learning in such a way that a schizophrenic decompensation results in adulthood. Another possibility is that the high-risk group consists of two subgroups, those who have inherited the disorder and those who have not. A third possibility might be that while the groups are genetically equivalent with regard to potential for schizophrenia, other factors either experiential or biologic in character differentiate those who grow ill from those who do not. A later report by Mednick cast some light on this question (1970).

When the high-risk ill and well groups were retrospectively evaluated for any birth complications noted in the medical record, the rate of such events in the former group was 70% versus 15% in the latter. For the control (low-risk) population it was 33%. This is a striking finding, suggesting that perinatal insult may dramatically increase the risk of schizophrenia in an infant genetically vulnerable to the disorder. A subsequent reevaluation of the psychophysiological data revealed that only those high-risk children who had sustained a birth trauma showed a pattern of response deviating from that in the low-risk control group. Birth trauma does not seem to be the whole story, however, since 30% of the ill subjects had no such event recorded. Nevertheless, in a multi-causal illness, a variable that differentiates as well as birth trauma appears to in this highly select group deserves very careful study. The high-risk studies already conducted exemplify a useful collaboration between a medically based psychiatric formulation of schizophrenia (genetic transmission) and a combination of psychophysiological and psychological methods to yield a better understanding of this major health problem, which afflicts roughly 1% of the population.

## THE PDI AND THE MMPI

Another example of collaboration between physicians and psychologists in psychiatry is the Psychiatric Diagnostic Interview (PDI) (Othmer, et al., 1982; Othmer & Penick, 1980). The interview uses a behavioral assessment of patients in the context of medical model psychiatry; that is, the PDI attempts to assign people to categories of disease on the basis of a systematic assessment of their verbal behavior in response to structured interview items. The interview follows a branching logic with diagnoses hierarchically arranged, beginning with organic psychosyndrome (organic mental syndrome) and ending with sexual deviations. Within each diagnostic category, moreover, symptoms are hierarchically ordered, beginning with cardinal symptoms and ending with an evaluation of the temporal characteristics of symptoms such as age of onset and duration. The interview is recommended for both clinical and research purposes and offers exceptional advantages in the latter regard. Since the PDI is based on a well-established collection of diagnostic criteria (Feighner et al., 1972), patient characteristics across studies can be described with a minimum of ambiguity. The importance of this feature in evaluating intervention effects can hardly be overemphasized.

The PDI addresses 15 basic psychiatric syndromes and 3 that are derived from combinations of basic ones. Table 9–1 lists the syndromes. For each basic syndrome a series of questions is asked stratified into four levels. First come the cardinal symptoms, which are experiences or behaviors essential to the diagnosis. If they are absent, by definition the patient does not have that disorder. For example, the cardinal items for depression are (1) feelings of sadness, hopelessness, and emptiness; (2) irritability and tiredness; (3) duration of these problems for a month or more or hospitalization for these problems; and (4) independence of these moods from life-threatening physical illness. For the cardinal symptoms of depression to be considered positive, the patient must affirm both (3) and (4) and either (1) or (2).

If the cardinal symptom evaluation is positive, the social interference questions are then asked. These are essentially the same for all conditions except organic psychosyndrome and mental retardation (the presence of these conditions precludes reliable responses). The social interference

**TABLE 9–1    Basic and Derived Syndromes Identified by the Psychiatric Diagnostic Interview**

*Basic*
>    Organic psychosyndrome
>    Alcoholism
>    Drug abuse
>    Mania
>    Depression
>    Schizophrenia
>    Antisocial personality
>    Hysteria (Briquet syndrome)
>    Anorexia nervosa
>    Obsessive-compulsive neurosis
>    Phobic neurosis
>    Anxiety neurosis
>    Mental retardation
>    Homosexuality
>    Transsexuality

*Derived*
>    Polydrug abuse
>    Schizoaffective disorder
>    Manic-depressive disorder

*Source:* Reproduced, with permission, from E. O. Othmer, E. C. Penick, and B. J. Powell, *Psychiatric Diagnostic Interview,* 8th rev. ed. (Los Angeles: Western Psychological Services, 1982).

category assesses conflict with family, friends, and authorities, addresses interference with work or school, ties the syndrome to a point in time when the problem was most severe, and asks whether treatment has ever been sought for the problem. If any one of the social interference items is affirmed, the time question is asked; then the auxiliary questions are begun.

The auxiliary questions concern a range of symptoms that are associated with the diagnosis to varying degrees. These questions serve to broaden the description in individual cases. The scoring of the interview requires that various combinations of auxiliary symptoms be affirmed for the syndrome to be positive. This pattern differs from syndrome to syndrome. For example, hysteria has 60 auxiliary symptoms broken into 10 groups. The patient must affirm at least 1 item in 9 of the 10 groups and affirm a total of at least 25.

After completion of the auxiliary questions, a determination is made as to whether or not the syndrome is positive. If so, four questions covering age of onset and most recent experience of symptoms are asked. Table 9-2 shows the questions and criteria for a diagnosis of anorexia nervosa.

In its present form, the PDI correctly diagnoses approximately 97% of patients vis-à-vis the diagnoses given patients by a psychiatrist trained in use of the Feighner diagnostic criteria (Feighner et al., 1972). This is a gratifying but not surprising outcome since the psychiatrist is presumably looking for the same bits of data that the interview assesses though he uses different methods (unstructured or less structured interview, review of the medical record, staff conference transactions, response to medication, and so forth). Other evidence for the validity of the instrument comes from comparing medical inpatients with psychiatric inpatients and outpatients. One would predict the highest incidence of syndrome identification for psychiatric inpatients; next, psychiatric outpatients; and last, medical inpatients. In fact, this pattern emerged (Othmer & Penick, 1980). In another study, 20 patients on lithium were given the PDI. In such a group one would expect a high incidence of positive syndrome identification for mania and depression, with other identifications quite low. The PDI yielded a mania syndrome identification in 95% of the cases, depression in 60%, and 20% each for obsessive-compulsive neurosis and phobic neurosis. Reliability data, also indicate little interobserver disagreement. In short, the PDI appears to do what it proposes to do.

Certainly the single most widely used psychological instrument in psychiatric diagnosis is the Minnesota Multiphasic Personality Inventory (MMPI) (Hathaway & McKinley, 1951), a questionnaire designed using diagnosed psychiatric patients and hospital visitor controls. Items that distinguished these groups were collected and assembled by diag-

**TABLE 9-2  Questions and Criteria for Anorexia Nervosa**

*Cardinal Questions*

1. Have you ever *deliberately* lost so much weight that people started to seriously worry about your health?
2. (If yes) Did this first happen before you were 25 years old?

1
2  Both "yes"

*Social Significance*

1. Did this weight loss ever cause you problems in your life?
2. Did it ever interfere with your school, your work, or your job?
3. Did it ever cause you any problems with your family or cause your family to worry about you?
4. Did this weight loss ever interfere with your social activities or friendships?
5. Did you ever need treatment or medication because you *deliberately* lost so much weight?

1
2  Any one
3  "yes"
4
5

6. How old were you when your weight loss caused you the most trouble in your life?

6

*Auxiliary Questions*

I want to find out more about the time when you lost so much weight

1. What was the most you weighed before you lost so much weight? What was the least you weighed after you began to lose weight? How long did it take you to lose weight? (Positive if the patient lost at least one quarter of the original body weight during a period of not more than one year)

1  "Yes"

2. Did a doctor rule out or eliminate the following medical problems as a cause for the weight loss?
   A serious infection?
3. A growing tumor?
4. A severe hormone problem?
5. Any other major physical illness?

2
3  Any one
4  "yes"
5

162

6. Did you lose weight deliberately even though people said you might die from it?  6
7. Did you stop eating because you felt there was something nasty or bad about food?  7
8. Did people have to beg you to eat?  8
9. Did you want to prove that you could live with almost no food?  9
10. Did people threaten to force you to eat?  10
11. Did it make you feel sort of good to refuse to eat?  11
12. Did you want to be thinner than almost everyone else?  12
13. Did you hide or store up food without anyone knowing about it?  13

Any one "yes"

14. Did you try to get rid of the food in your body by taking laxatives or forcing yourself to vomit?  14
15. Did you at times eat so much food, so fast, that it made you sick?  15
16. Did the hair on your body become very fine and thin like a baby's?  16
17. (For women only) While you were losing so much weight, did you tend to skip your menstrual periods?  17
18. Were there times when you felt very excited and restless?  18
19. Did your heart slow down a lot? (Persistent resting pulse of 60 or less if measurement is known)  19

Two of six "yes"

*Time Profile*

1. How old were you when you first lost this much weight?  1
2. How old were you when you last lost this much weight?  2
3. Have you experienced this problem in the past month?  3
4. Have you experienced this problem in the last two years?  4

*Source:* Reproduced, with permission, from E. O. Othmer, E. C. Penick, and B. J. Powell, *Psychiatric Diagnostic Interview*, 8th rev. ed. (Los Angeles: Western Psychological Services, 1982).

nostic category to yield a 10-subtest format plus 3 validity scales designed to identify aberrant response sets, lack of comprehension, or faking. Over the years a staggering volume of material has accumulated on this test. Contemporary practice favors profile analysis as a diagnostic strategy and a number of actuarial methods have been developed for MMPI diagnosis (Finney, 1966; Gilberstadt & Duker, 1965; Marks & Seeman, 1963). It might be instructive at this point to contrast the PDI with this more traditional psychological instrument.

The same philosophy regarding the nature of psychiatric disorders underlies these two instruments. Though the MMPI has been used in a variety of ways, its development proceeded from a model viewing psychiatric disorder as analogous to physical disorder. That is, the MMPI's original goal was to expedite the identification of disease states that are revealed in behavior but nevertheless enjoy an existential status independent of those behaviors.

Formally, the PDI and the MMPI are quite different. Though both employ yes/no (or true/false) questions, one is an interview, the other a questionnaire. One involves a personal transaction between the patient and the interviewer while the other, after brief instructions, is quite impersonal. Furthermore, the questions are structured in an entirely different matter. The MMPI consists of over 500 items, which are totally discrete from the respondent's point of view. The PDI has an apparent logical structure and, in fact, which questions are asked is in part dependent on responses to preceding items. In terms of time frame, the PDI is explicitly longitudinal. The patient is asked whether he ever experienced the symptoms; dates and durations are requested. The MMPI items are a mix, some addressing present feelings ("I believe I am being plotted against"), some addressing the remote past ("I was a slow learner in school"), and others addressing a vague period including the present but extending back in time over an unspecified period ("Sometimes I feel that I must injure either myself or someone else").

Finally, the PDI assumes veridical response. If the patient says he has no troubles associated with drinking, it is assumed that, in fact, he does not have trouble associated with drinking. The MMPI, by contrast, is mixed with regard to face validity, and veridicality of responses is essentially irrelevant. Some items refer to obvious aspects of psychopathology ("There is something wrong with my mind"); others do not ("I hardly ever feel pain in the back of my neck"). With regard to veridicality, the MMPI was empirically derived so that the central issue in scoring is not what the person experiences but what he says he experiences: "The test subject is instructed to describe himself as accurately as he can . . ., but the test scorer and interpreter does not assume that the subject has in fact provided a veridical account" (Dahlstrom et al., 1972: 6). The instruments thus differ in the degree of subtlety among item content, subject response, and diagnostic inference.

The relative utility of the two methods is, of course, an empirical question. Answering that question introduces a number of complexities. Perhaps the most fundamental is the issue of criteria. Psychiatric diagnoses are notoriously unreliable and both these methods have been validated against such diagnoses. In the case of the PDI, the criterion was fairly explicit: the diagnoses were reached by experienced clinicians employing the Feighner system. With regard to the MMPI, the criteria are much more difficult to specify. The initial reference groups were hospitalized patients carrying the particular diagnoses that generated the original scales. Subsequent work has used a vast array of criteria to generate the actuarial profile interpretations and diagnoses. Reported hit rates for particular diagnoses are lower than with the PDI, but this difference is inevitable since the nature of what is being assessed is much more variable. If one agrees that the Feighner criteria identify, for example, schizophrenia, then one would conclude that the PDI is vastly superior to the MMPI in identifying schizophrenics. On the other hand, if one believes that the term "schizophrenia" includes a broader range of patient attributes than the Feighner criteria allow, the issue is not nearly so clear. One would expect the PDI to miss a great number of such schizophrenics. As for the MMPI, its performance would depend on which diagnostic system one used, with better results likely the more closely the system originator's notion of schizophrenia coincided with one's own.

The purpose of the PDI is psychiatric diagnosis. This instrument does not address personologic descriptors beyond what is implied by the diagnosis. While the MMPI began as a diagnostic instrument, the years following its introduction have seen a vast number of other uses, with subscales created to assess ego strength, anxiety, dissimulation, and rigidity of defense (Dahlstrom et al., 1972). The actuarial systems also provide varying amounts of descriptive data beyond the diagnosis. There is debate as to the value of such descriptive material from both the concurrent and the predictive point of view, but the fact remains that the MMPI does provide such descriptors, whatever their value, while the PDI does not.

Finally, the cross-sectional versus the longitudinal character of the instruments bears emphasis. The PDI is longitudinal in orientation, reflecting the assumptions of the school of descriptive psychiatry that spawned it. The MMPI is mixed in terms of content but certainly is used in an essentially cross-sectional manner. Changes in MMPI profile configurations, for example, are employed clinically as evidence for improvement or deterioration in function. Given the nature of the content and the logic of the PDI, reevaluation with the instrument is inherently nonsensical, except for the purpose of filling in events that occurred since the last interview.

In summary, then, these two instruments, while proceeding from similar paradigms, approach the problems of diagnosis differently. Attempts to decide which of them is better are probably vain because so much depends on what particular task the clinician wishes to accomplish. For reaching diagnosis based on the Feighner system, the PDI is certainly preferable. The MMPI, on the other hand, by virtue of its long history and prodigious literature, offers a wealth of information beyond diagnosis that may be of interest. Moreover, its cross-sectional character lends it to longitudinal assessment of change, for example, in response to treatment, an application for which the PDI is totally unsuited. What the tools share is a focus on diagnosis as part of adequate psychiatric care and exemplify contributions psychologists can make to the diagnostic enterprise.

## Conclusion

This chapter looked at the role of psychology in relation to psychiatry, with particular reference to medically oriented psychiatric theory and practice. Clinical psychology sits on the same side of the fence as psychiatry oriented along psychosocial lines. Medical psychology is not likely to supplant clinical psychology in the field of psychiatry, nor should it. Yet it does offer an alternative point of view shared by a portion of psychiatrists. Development of medical psychology can thus broaden the role of psychologists in relation to psychiatric patients.

# 10

# Terminal Illness

The inevitability of death has played a changing role in relation to medicine over the centuries and is differently viewed across cultures. In the West, death tends to be seen as the enemy, with the physician cast in the role of a warrior against death. As the weapons have grown more sophisticated, the attractiveness and plausibility of this conception of medicine has grown.

But technical advance plays a paradoxical role in relation to this aspect of medicine. Before efficacious treatment for life-threatening illness existed, that is, for most of human history, the physician provided comfort to the dying and support to the grieving—partly because he had nothing else to offer but also and most important because he thereby met real needs. As effective treatment for life-threatening disease became increasingly available, physicians began to make good on their commitment to the preservation of life. This technology began with antibiotics and now includes an arsenal of life support systems, resuscitation methods, and powerful drugs. The war against death is no longer fought and lost in the first skirmish but goes on for a very long time. The physician thus becomes, to continue the military analogy, a general directing an army of technicians and formulating technological strategies to stave off the enemy. Herein lies part of the paradox. As the doctor has grown more adept at fighting the battle, he has gotten further away from the battlefield itself, the patient. The lasting, personal relationship between patient and doctor is gone.

Technology has also altered our posture of resignation toward and acceptance of death, a sensible attitude when medicine proceeded haphazardly. Today, however, doctors can take action to forestall death, but to win such battles they must assume a stance that implicitly equates resignation with defeat.

Social expectations also color the present medical posture in relation to death. Commitment to the preservation of life, even in the face of fatal disease, brings with it an inevitable experience of failure. It has been frequently observed that in contemporary hospitals staff members tend to avoid the dying patient. One sometimes hears the fact decried as an example of the lack of humanity among doctors, nurses and others, or as evidence of a profound callousness, but is this judgment not too harsh? This avoidance reflects the value system that promotes life as an absolute value. Cast as a warrior against death, the doctor (and other health professionals) must react with a degree of avoidance and denial when death occurs for, given his role, death is coextensive with failure. If dying in Western society has become a sadly dehumanized process, as it has, and if doctors and hospitals have contributed to this dehumanization, as they have, this circumstance must be understood in a broad social context.

This chapter looks at the evolution of treatment of the dying patient, with particular emphasis on recent innovations in humanistic care following the lead especially of Saunders and the hospice movement. The role of psychology—broadly construed to include family dynamics, religious feelings, and so on—in the care of the dying patient is central and psychologists have contributed to this field and to the literature on it. The essential attribute of recent developments in terminal care is an emphasis on the psychological aspects of both life and death as opposed to the prevailing preoccupation with definitions of life and death in biological terms. The chapter concludes with a discussion of innovative treatment modalities for the dying patient.

## Contemporary Models of the Dying Process

### KÜBLER-ROSS'S STAGE THEORY

*On Death and Dying* is deservedly viewed as a landmark in the recent history of medicine (Kübler-Ross, 1969). This book brought to widespread attention not only the plight of the dying patient and his family but also the attitudes of the profession toward these patients. Kübler-Ross called for a searching reevaluation of the meaning of death in our culture as a whole and for the helping professions in particular, a reevaluation presently under way.

*On Death and Dying* presents a stage model for the dying process derived from interviews with about 200 patients with life-threatening disease. It describes a seminar on death and dying begun for student chaplains, but which grew into a multi-disciplinary conference on the subject attended by up to 50 people per session. The format includes an interview with a dying patient which is observed, then discussed. In addition to focusing on the patient, participants are encouraged to express their own reactions to the event in an effort to understand their own attitudes toward death. The model has been criticized on both empirical and conceptual grounds but remains influential and therefore merits discussion. The stages are (1) denial and isolation, (2) anger, (3) bargaining, (4) depression, and (5) acceptance.

Denial is the person's initial reaction to the knowledge that he is dying, though the denial defense may appear at various times during the dying process. Behaviors characteristic of the denial phase are doctor shopping, leaving the hospital against medical advice, engaging in inappropriate long-range plans, and refusal to discuss, or gross misinterpretation of, obvious symptoms. Characteristically, denial dissipates as the patient moves on to subsequent stages. This response is not seen as pathologic early in the course and ought not to be discouraged. Even late in the course, episodic denial is considered adaptive: "What I am trying to emphasize is that the need for denial exists in every patient at times, in the very beginning of a serious illness more so than towards the end of life. Later on the need comes and goes, and the sensitive and perceptive listener will acknowledge this and allow the patient his defenses without making him aware of the contradictions" (p. 37).

Denial operates differently in different interpersonal contexts. For example, denial is often seen in patients when they deal with staff who also use this mechanism in avoiding the dying patient and thus, by inference, their own mortality. It is as though the patient strikes an unconscious bargain with staff, discussing his coming death only with staff who are comfortable working at that level. The danger, of course, is that if there is universal denial among staff and family, the dying person may have no one with whom to share his feelings about death. Thus, the key to working well with patients in this stage is to be sensitive to the need to deny but to avoid entering a conspiracy of silence. The therapist must be available to the patient so that he can share his emerging awareness of the finality ahead when he is ready.

Anger and rage follow the period of denial. Envy of the healthy also is seen. While denial may be relatively easy for both staff and family to live with, in the period of anger the patient may lash out at those closest to him and express hostility and dissatisfaction with people trying to help. Behaviors characteristic of this period include frequent complaints about all aspects of care—plans for discharge are interpreted as showing a lack of interest; continued hospitalization is seen as an infringement on privacy; and family may be chastised for not visiting often enough, only to be told the patient does not want to see them when they come.

Kübler-Ross identified all five stages of dying as natural rather than pathologic. To deal with the period of anger, the staff must understand the source of the angry behavior and avoid taking hostility personally: "The problem here is that few people place themselves in the patient's position and wonder where this anger might come from. Maybe we too would be angry if all our life activities were interrupted so prematurely. . . . [W]hat else would we do with our anger but let it out on the people who are most likely to enjoy [the things we are denied]?" (p. 45). In dealing with patient anger and hostility, the staff must realize that the putative issues are frequently irrelevant. When the patient says, "My dinner is late," he means, "I am still alive. Pay attention to me!" One danger is that the patient's angry responses may feed into staff and family tendencies to deny terminal illness, offering a rationalization for avoiding such patients when the therapeutic response should be approach. If the anger is understood as a necessary part of coming to terms with death, if staff are available to the patient at a personal as well as a biological level, the anger will dissipate as this stage passes.

The third stage involves bargaining. In this period, the patient attempts to enter into an agreement, usually with God, to gain more time. This stage has the quality of a recapitulation of childhood behaviors in which something is obtained from the parent for good behavior. Extension of life and avoidance of pain are the goals sought and the patient tacitly promises that this is all he seeks. The promise is not usually kept as the patient tries to effect another bargain. Kübler-Ross hypothesized that guilt lies at the root of many of these bargains. For example, the patient may feel that he has not attended church with sufficient regularity. From this perspective the bargaining is a symptom of something else, guilt, and this strategy may be usefully employed as a way of initiating help for the patient in dealing with unresolved conflicts.

Depression, the fourth stage of terminal illness, is characterized by a sense of profound loss. Loss has many aspects and they vary as a function of the disease's course and treatment, the patient's financial and social circumstances, and a host of highly individual determinants. Kübler-Ross identified two categories of depression in terminal illness. The first encompasses the areas just listed and is reactive in character. The second type is part of the patient's preparation to separate finally from this world and is termed preparatory as opposed to reactive depression. The mode of help is different in these two conditions and staff must distinguish them to be maximally useful to patients during this fourth stage.

Reactive depression is addressed directly and is easily understood by staff. The response is to help the patient deal with realistic concerns, such as financial difficulties, and to bolster self-esteem through affection and support. For example, following mastectomy a woman may show reactive depression to this perceived loss of femininity. She can be helped by emphasizing other aspects of her femininity, by breast prosthesis, and by sensitive listening. Depression frequently lifts when the patient sees that his concern for his family's financial well-being is shared and attended to by a competent social worker. Thus, practically oriented intervention, augmented by psychological support, is the appropriate response to reactive depression in terminal illness. The goal is to help the patient see the brighter side of things and to emphasize the positive.

Preparatory depression is different in character and should be handled differently. Here it is not appropriate to encourage a happier outlook because the depression is appropriate and analogous in many ways to the normal grieving response. We do not tell the grieving person not to be sad for sadness is normal and necessary in this circumstance. The dying person with preparatory depression is grieving the loss of all his object relations and all contact with his loved ones. His grief is thus necessary and inevitable and the appropriate staff response is silent support. Staff ought not to try to cheer him up but rather should make clear their willingness to share his grief: "In the preparatory grief there is no or little need for words. It is much more a feeling that can be mutually expressed and is often done better with a touch of a hand, a stroking of the hair, or just a silent sitting together" (p. 77).

The final stage of dying is acceptance:

> If a patient has had enough time . . . has been given some help in working through the previously described stages, he will reach a stage during which he is neither depressed nor angry about his "fate." He will have been able to express his previous feelings, his envy for the living and the healthy, his anger at those who do not have to face their end so soon. He will have mourned the impending loss of so many meaningful people and places and will contemplate his coming end with a certain degree of quiet expectation. (p. 99)

This stage is neither happy nor sad but rather lacks strong emotion. The patient is ready to die and simply waits. The appropriate therapeutic posture may be only to wait with him.

Kübler-Ross drew a distinction between this stage of readiness and that of withdrawal in depression. Staff must learn to distinguish when a patient has given up too early as opposed to when a patient has made his peace with the world and is ready to leave it. She described a dramatic episode to illustrate that failure to see acceptance for what it is can have very negative consequences for the patient. An elderly woman had reached this stage and was ready to die. She had refused any further drastic procedures to prolong her life. Her husband, on the other hand, was unable to accept this decision and agreed to a surgical procedure without her knowledge. When informed of the impending surgery, the woman weakened rapidly and ultimately became psychotic in the operating room. The procedure had to be postponed. Back in her room, she asked to see Kübler-Ross and said in the presence of her husband, "Talk to this man and make him understand" (p. 104). Her psychosis cleared as soon as the operation was permanently abandoned. She and her husband were then able to share her remaining days. Kübler-Ross interpreted the patient's psychosis as a defense against prolongation of her life. The husband misinterpreted his wife's acceptance of death as rejection of him and of their life together and this misinterpretation was reinforced by the physician who wanted to go ahead with surgery. The patient was unable to refuse the surgery in the face of her husband's pleas; the psychosis was a way to avoid this event without overtly refusing. What is critical here is the accurate identification of the final phase and willingness to honor the patient's right to withdraw from this world when he feels the time has come.

There is implicit in *On Death and Dying* the idea that these stages are natural and in some sense good. Many critics have questioned the universality of the stages and the definition in general terms of a good as opposed to a bad death. Kalish raised several pertinent questions regarding Kübler-Ross's stage theory (1978), noting that her international fame and charismatic persona have tended to discourage critical analysis of her model. A proper evaluation of the stage theory must address four issues. First, do the stages occur in everyone in the stated order; if not, do they occur in anyone and, if so, in whom and under what conditions? Moreover, to what extent does their wide currency render them self-fulfilling prophesies? Kalish then questioned the suitability or adaptiveness of the stages. Is acceptance the appropriate state for all dying patients? The issue leads to a third, the meaning of failure of the stages to appear. Does this imply a problem in either the health care system or the family, or does it represent individual or subcultural variability? Finally, is the model universal?

Kastenbaum pointed out that Kübler-Ross's book pays almost no attention to sex, age, and ethnic differences (1975). The model is psychoanalytically oriented and one of the problems frequently noted with psychoanalytic theory is that it presumes a cross-cultural, quasi-biologically based universality, which may not be justified. Kastenbaum described the literature on stage theories that followed publication of Kübler-Ross's work. Though not extensive, the literature tends not to support the idea that dying is a staged process in the sense of showing predictable sequences across individuals. The most one can say at present is that Kübler-Ross presented a provocative model that needs careful study. Kalish suggested that empirical research might be directed toward each of the four issues he raised in connection with the stage theory (1978).

Pattison also reviewed the literature and found no evidence to support specific stages (1976). However, he stated that he does not read Kübler-Ross to mean that the stages are inevitable and suggested that the concretization of stage theory proceeds from the enthusiasm of others for her work. This seems to me a rather selective reading of *On Death and Dying*: the various stages are not presented in the least bit tentative terms. A more important consideration turns on the consequences of the formulation. For example, Pattison noted that with the advent of stage theory "it was no longer acceptable to respond to the dying person in terms of his or her individual dying experience. Rather, the dying were being pushed and forced into a Procrustean process of dying that had been scientifically established" (1978:140). Of course, this model was not scientifically established but is presented as if it had been, leading professionals to insist on its application in individual cases as a necessary component of healthy as opposed to neurotic dying.

## PATTISON'S PHASE MODEL

Pattison's formulation proceeds from Weisman's three-phase model (1974). In the acute phase, the patient is maximally anxious and the task at this point is to resolve the crisis presented by awareness of impending death. This crisis is seen as having five key characteristics. First, the situation is stressful because it is by definition unsolvable. Second, it stretches one's coping ability since it is by definition unique in one's experience. Third, death threatens one's goals and is anxiety arousing for that reason. Fourth, the crisis usually follows a pattern of rising intensity, then decline as defensive maneuvers begin to take effect. Finally, the crisis awakens unresolved conflicts so that one is faced not only with the present crisis but also with a need to resolve old conflicts and concerns. Pattison stated that during this acute phase the patient typically employs a variety of relatively primitive defenses, which ought not to be too vigorously attacked. Rather, in a supportive environment that provides a reality orientation to help the patient deal with the issues he faces, this acute phase will naturally fade into the chronic.

The chronic living-dying phase is, as the name suggests, a more protracted state, lasting from the awareness of impending death to the event itself. A variety of problems confront the patient during this period and must be dealt with seriatum. As each problem is dealt with, the patient comes to feel he is succeeding in separating from this life and this is the meaning for Pattison of a healthy death. The specific tasks, however, differ from case to case. The common element is the need to overcome specific fears so that a sense of self-esteem can emerge that allows the patient to enter the terminal phase feeling peaceful.

Whereas the acute phase is by nature abrupt in onset, the terminal stage begins less precisely. Pattison suggested that we define its beginning when the patient starts to withdraw within himself and thus to conserve his energy. The similarity between this period and Kübler-Ross's stage of acceptance is clear, and most writers on death and dying have been impressed with the frequency with which death seems to be experienced as a peaceful event.

In discussing the terminal phase, Pattison developed a very useful model of death as having four aspects: sociological, psychic, biologic, and physiologic. The good death is one in which these four aspects are in appropriate temporal relationship to one another, and good, caring treatment of the dying patient is the process of helping the person coordinate these different but related events. Sociological death refers to withdrawal of the patient from those around him and is usually the first form of death to occur. Psychic is synonymous with the regression described earlier; the person accepts death and withdraws into himself to await the event. Psychic death is followed by biologic death, which refers to the dissolution of the body's life support system. Cessation of heartbeat is the classical definition of this type of death, but permanent loss of consciousness is also an acceptable definition. Physiological death refers to the final ceasing of all bodily functions. Thomas commented rather drolly on the processes of biological and physiological death: ''Death is not a sudden-all-at-once affair; cells go down in sequence one by one. You can, if you like, recover great numbers of them many hours after the lights have gone out and grow them in cultures. It takes hours, even days, before the irreversible word finally gets around to all the provinces'' (1972:826).

Fig. 10-1 diagrams five possible relationships among these four aspects of death. The first is the ideal circumstance: after a period of readying himself, the patient accepts that he is going to die, withdraws from the world into himself, surrenders the self to death, and bodily functions cease. The second pattern characterizes the patient who is abandoned in a nursing home or who dies slowly in an acute hospital, ignored by staff and family. He is socially dead before he is ready to die. This is certainly the saddest scenario and seems unfortunately characteristic of death in Western culture. The third pattern reflects massive use of denial in which the patient, family, and staff conspire in a pretense that death is not imminent. Protracted denial renders the death event especially traumatic since neither the patient nor the family has accomplished the practical and psychological tasks of parting. In the fourth pattern, the patient shows readiness for and acceptance of death before those around him do. This might be the case in the dialysis patient who rejects further treatment. Finally, there is the case of rejecting a death that is both psychic and biological and keeping the patient physiologically alive through the action of machines; such a death can be completed only

**Figure 10-1.** Types of death sequences. Reproduced, with permission, from E.M. Pattison, The living-dying process. In C.A. Garfield (editor), *Psychosocial Care of the Dying Patient.* New York: McGraw-Hill, 1978.

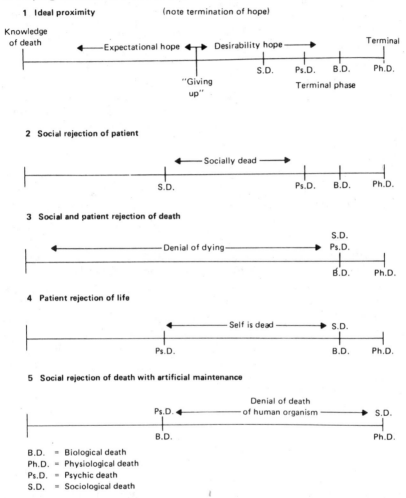

when the machine fails or the social group accepts that death has oc-curred and withdraws the artificial support.

## Contemporary Care of the Dying Patient

The majority of people in the Western world die in institutions, most fre-quently hospitals or nursing homes. Mount reported that in Canada the figure is approximately 70% (1976). In the United States and in

England, well over half of the annual deaths occur in general hospitals (Cartwright et al., 1973; Lerner, 1970). It seems logical to ask whether this is where people prefer to die and, if not, why this situation exists.

Kalish and Reynolds offered fairly compelling evidence that most people would prefer to die at home (1976). What explains the discrepancy between preference and actuality? First, the person may have an illness that requires hospital treatment whether or not death is expected. Others die in hospitals so quickly that there is no option to be explored. The postcoronary patient might exemplify the first case; the motor vehicle accident victim, the second. A second reason has to do with practical concerns. There may be no one at home to provide care. Alternatively, financial factors may preclude home care for many insurance companies cover only inpatient care and will not pay for home nursing even if it is less expensive. A third group of patients might be cared for at home but are not either because the hospital staff fails to present home care as a possibility or because community agencies do not provide the sometimes minimal amount of supplemental help that would render this option workable (Kalish, 1978).

Kalish and Reynolds also identified patients who prefer to die in an institution (1976). The middle-aged are more likely to choose hospital than are the young or the old. The reasons for this interesting finding are not known, but one might speculate that the currently middle-aged have a more positive attitude toward medicine in general and hospitals in particular because they have lived through a period of major advances in health care. Furthermore, this group, as compared with the old, has had less contact with hospitals and doctors because they have been ill less frequently. The young, on the other hand, are generally suspicious of the establishment and are most likely to be aware of recent criticisms of the health care professions.

Thus far the discussion has hinted at problems in staff-patient transactions. Garfield discussed the reaction of the physician to the dying patient, noting that in the growing literature on death and dying relatively little systematic attention has been paid to this central issue (1978). He outlined three general categories of typical reaction—anger, denial, and depression/resignation—and pointed out that there currently exists no vehicle through which the physician can share his feelings about a dying patient or about dying in general. Kübler-Ross (1969) and many others have called this lack of exploration of subjective response a major stumbling block to increasing our understanding of the dying patient and improving his care.

Denial takes many forms, from avoidance of the patient because of "other responsibilities" to a redefinition of the doctor-patient relationship once curative action is no longer possible. Garfield described an extreme example of denial in an oncologist who stated that he had never had a patient who died (1978). Further exploration revealed that the physician used one of two rather pathetic methods to avoid the dying patient: he either transferred the patient to another doctor's care or had him moved to a different facility.

Depression in physicians as a consequence of contact with dying patients is a poorly understood event that seems to occur with some frequency. This response happens when the mechanisms of displacement and denial cease to operate and the physician experiences overwhelming feelings of failure. Several factors conspire in generating this reaction. A major one is our value system, which places death in a wholly negative light and sees the physician as the person responsible for preventing it. Another is the traditional Western view of emotional expression as a sign of weakness and femininity: the male physician is thus encouraged not to express strong emotions, whereas female physicians face even greater pressure to act in this ''strong'' and ''masculine'' way in order to legitimize their position in a traditionally masculine profession. For some physicians, particularly those who deal constantly with the dying, this control may finally give way and a clinical depression result.

Mount and associates presented interesting empirical data on staff attitudes toward the dying and on mismatches between what patients want and feel they need and the attitudes and beliefs of those who care for them (1974). For example, patients expressed a desire for open and frank communication about the illness and its prognosis while physicians expressed reluctance to discuss such matters. Interestingly, this reluctance was related to the physician's attitude toward his own death. Of those who said they would want to know their prognosis, 84% expressed willingness to talk frankly with patients. Of those who preferred not to know, only 45% were willing to be open with the patient. Other studies found that a variety of changes in staff behavior occur when the patient is defined as terminal and these changes seem plausibly related to the attitudes here being discussed. For example, Bowers and colleagues found that it takes nurses longer to respond to the call of a dying patient than to one of a patient expected to recover (1964); likewise, the amount of nursing care provided generally declines (Mervyn, 1971). Physicians pay fewer and fewer visits to the dying patient (Anonymous, 1972), and many nurses admit discomfort in talking to dying patients (Quint, 1966).

In sum, staff tend to deny the reality of death. This translates into avoidance of the dying patient and/or a preoccupation with wholly biological aspects of his condition. Physicians, like the rest of us, are not comfortable with death and several writers have commented on the historical absence of discussion of this topic in the medical school curriculum (Kerstein, 1973). Clearly a major task in improving care of the dying patient involves changing these staff attitudes. Cassell suggested the relatively simple procedure of setting time aside for house staff and attending physicians to discuss their terminal patients not only from the point of view of their disease but also from a broader perspective (1972).

## THE HOSPICE

Saunders, the leader of the hospice movement in Great Britain, noted the tendency to define the beginning of terminal illness as the moment when a doctor opines that nothing more can be done (1975). This is a revealing comment contrasting the traditional (curing) view of the terminally ill with emerging approaches to these patients. The fundamental goal of hospice care is the maintenance of the dying patient without pain, alert and comfortable (Woodson, 1978). The care system that achieves this goal conceptualizes pain as having four components—physical, psychological, social, and spiritual—each of which requires unique attention and strategies.

Physical pain may be treated by administering chemotherapy or by alleviating underlying causal factors that may be independent of the terminal illness (infection, for example). Saunders stressed the importance of avoiding pain, rather than relieving it once it occurs, because the experience of pain leads to fear, which acts to potentiate pain: ''Terminal pain *can* be controlled and there is no excuse for inept medication. Pain and relief of pain are both self-perpetuating. Patients with the constant pain that is so typical of terminal cancer require their analgesics regularly and should neither suffer pain nor have to ask for relief'' (1975:567). Saunder's approach routinizes medication so that the patient can be confident that his pain will be covered and he therefore need not worry about it. Saunders also noted the value of alcohol as both an analgesic and a means to achieve conviviality. The now famous Brompton's cocktail, a mixture of alcohol, narcotic analgesic, and phenothiazine, was developed to facilitate pain relief and social interaction (Mount et al., 1976; Woodson, 1978).

Psychological pain is addressed both chemotherapeutically and psychologically. The term refers to feelings of anxiety, depression, and agitation that arise as the patient attempts to ready himself for death. These feelings are viewed as a normal part of the dying process and psychological support is seen as part of human caring rather than as psychiatric intervention in the usual sense. Antianxiety agents and other psychoactive drugs are employed in the hospice approach but are seen as only part of the solution to psychological pain in the dying: ''Thirty minutes of catharctic grieving with a family member, nurse or skilled therapist can have profound effects on a dying patient's depression and concomitant anxiety. Five milligrams of diazepam or fifty of phenothiazine may do little more than add one additional order the attending pharmacist has to fill and the nurse has to administer'' (Woodson, 1978:371).

The concept of social pain revolves around the idea that the dying person usually feels the need to share his grief with important people in his life and to come to a sense of closure about his life by settling interpersonal conflicts and putting more mundane affairs in order. Social pain is seen as the result of failure to provide the opportunity for the dying patient to accomplish these tasks. The hospice approach insures that necessary social contact is provided with either family or surrogate family, the staff. It is important that social pain not be misconstrued as psychological pain (depression) for treatment differs in the two cases. Medication does not address the issue of shared grief and may only serve further to separate the grieving person from those whose contact he seeks and needs.

Spiritual pain encompasses the range of religious and philosophical concerns patients experience as they face death. The content and quality of this pain vary with the patient's belief system and the vehicles of alleviation his religion provides. The central person in relieving this category of pain is the clergyman acting as a consultant to the staff, working directly with the patient, or both. Saunders pointed out that hospice staff must not attempt to force contact with clergy on a patient who shows no interest but must be sensitive at the same time to the patient's possible needs in this regard, particularly if there is religious disharmony in the family (1975). People who work with the dying often note that a sustained relationship with a clergyman seems to be of tremendous help to dying patients, and the occasion of death has led to sometimes profound changes in belief or to a deepening of religious conviction.

Woodson listed seven other attributes that are central to hospice as opposed to other models of terminal care (1978). As we look at them, it should be clear that the system is designed to address the fourfold problem of pain through the work of a variety of staff in several settings but with the consistent goal of preventing pain and keeping the patient as functional as he can and cares to be. Furthermore, explicit attention is given to the family as a unit, with care provided when the patient has died, particularly by clergy but also by social service and other personnel.

The first and foremost attribute is that terminal care must be a team effort and this means more than simply multidisciplinary care. In the hospice, the multiple disciplines form a coordinated whole whose efforts are complementary and directed toward the common goal of caring for the dying patient. What this means in practice is that the team regularly talks over what is going on with each patient. Furthermore, the dying patient and his family are seen as part of the team, which includes as well physicians, nurses, social workers, voluntary workers, and clergymen where appropriate.

Around-the-clock service for patients both in and out of hospital is the second attribute of hospice care. Visiting nurses and homemakers make it possible for many patients to spend their last days at home. Recent changes in Medicare regulations allow compensation for home care for patients participating in designated hospice programs in the United States.

An intimate connection between inpatient and outpatient facilities is a related and third aspect of the hospice approach. Most authorities think that hospices are best separated from acute hospitals; this arrangement allows for a fuller commitment to the caring role in the absence of a preoccupation with curing illness (Saunders, 1975). Moreover, physical independence fosters a sense of professional identity among hospice workers and seems generally to encourage morale and administrative efficiency. The development of such facilities is in its infancy in the United States, though they are fairly common in Europe. In the interim, the establishment of hospice units within general hospitals is a possibility (Mount, 1976), as is pursuing home based care coordinated with a general hospital as the backup facility (Malkin, 1976). In any event, successful hospice care requires that inpatient and homebased services be tightly coordinated by an overlapping staff and explicit organizational arrangements. The arrival of a terminal patient at the hospital ought never to come as a surprise, nor should he be sent home unless the nature of that home is well understood.

The fourth attribute described by Woodson is the special attention hospice workers pay to the family. Separation from family is one of the major tragedies of the American way of death in institutional settings. Hospice care focuses on this problem directly by striving to keep the family unit together until the end and after.

The fifth attribute, care for the bereaved, concerns follow-up services for the family. Risk of serious illness rises precipitously after the death of a family member, particularly a spouse (Holmes & Rahe, 1967), and research by Parkes suggested that regular visits by trained staff during the year following death can lessen the risk of psychiatric complications (1970).

Sixth, volunteers play a central role in hospice care. This emphasis on community participation represents a change in health care philosophy since volunteers have played little or no role in care of dying patients in American hospitals. The volunteers are professionally trained and provide two categories of help. First, they are available for housekeeping, transportation, babysitting, and other home needs that, if not met, place unnecessary hardships on the dying patient and may eventuate in hospital admission. Second, volunteers provide friendship and support to the patient and his family on a continuing basis and in a way professionals cannot do because of time constraints. Woodson commented, "Volunteers are indeed the vital thread that ties the whole hospice program together and extensive use of them is absolutely essential" (1978:380).

Woodson's seventh attribute is that all aspects of the hospice—volunteers, visiting nurses, inpatients, outpatients, physicians, clergy, and so on—must fall under a single organizational umbrella. Well-intentioned amalgamations of distinct service entities generally will fail to cover the needs of the dying patient because of difficulties in information flow, competing responsibilities, and other seemingly inevitable consequences of efforts to coordinate separate agencies. The hospice requires a free-standing administrative structure responsible for all aspects of care for the dying patient.

## THE PALLIATIVE CARE UNIT AND THE SHANTI PROJECT

While many advocate the creation of a free-standing, physically separate hospice unit, this goal cannot always be achieved. Other approaches to terminal care include the palliative care unit (PCU) within a general hospital (Mount, 1976).

The PCU is a 12-bed unit that provides care for patients who have malignant disease for which only symptom alleviation is possible. The multidisciplinary staff operates on a philosophy much like that described for hospices. The family is given explicit attention as the unit of care and support services are offered to them. Hospital regulations are modified to meet the needs of patients and family so that visiting hours are less rigid, and certain routine procedures are not performed. This may seem a minor and obvious response for health care providers to make, but one has only to read the accounts of surviving family members to learn how rigid hospital staff usually are in matters of routine procedures and adherence to rules (Driver, 1972). The PCU also includes a domiciliary service that provides care for patients at home. The service coordinates efforts in pain control and psychological support, employing visiting nurses and volunteers in addition to PCU staff. Finally, a consultation service evaluates hospitalized patients in other wards to determine their eligibility for the PCU and counsels terminal patients who, for whatever reason, remain on their original service.

The SHANTI project represents quite a different approach to care of the dying (Garfield & Clark, 1978). This project is organized outside the medical profession and interfaces with the health care system only at the request of the client. It began operation in 1975 as a telephone answering machine: callers were contacted, their needs were evaluated, and a SHANTI volunteer went to see them. Clients include any person who is struggling with life-threatening illness—a patient; a relative of a dying patient or of one who has recently died; or a person who works with the dying outside institutional settings, private duty nurses or clergymen, for example. All clients are self-referred. In cases of a patient who is too ill to call, a family member or friend may act as the referral source provided the patient clearly desires the contact.

The SHANTI volunteer acts as the client's advocate, helping him in whatever way he needs—lending an ear, assisting family members, or providing transportation. If the client enters the hospital, the volunteer maintains contact, facilitating communication between the patient and the medical staff. One can imagine situations in which the volunteer would be viewed as an impediment by hospital staff, but given the way dying patients are treated in American hospitals this challenge is appropriate. While SHANTI volunteers do not function as psychotherapists, they are trained to be sensitive to psychological nuance and may refer to psychotherapists or other care providers if the client agrees. The fundamental principle, however, is the advocacy relationship, giving the patient someone he can rely upon throughout the terminal crisis.

SHANTI volunteers are carefully selected on the basis of attitudes that experience has shown to be important in their role. For example, persons whose religious convictions encourage proselytizing are excluded, as are those who view helping the dying as another in a series of personal growth experiences. Volunteers must be compassionate, tolerant of ambiguity, self-confident, and aware that assisting the dying is a learning and helping process that goes both ways.

## Conclusion

In *Illness as Metaphor* Sontag suggested that the plight of the gravely ill is rendered more difficult by the fact that both in literary and vernacular language, disease names are used metaphorically to convey ideas and images (1978). She contrasted the tubercular patient of the last century, around whom a vast romantic literature developed, to the contemporary cancer patient, the name of whose disease finds widespread metaphoric use that is wholly pejorative. Sontag argued that the patient's phenomenal world is altered by these metaphors as they tend to reflect popular lore about the diseases and the people who have them. Tubercular patients were seen as sensitive, artistic, and heroic; cancer patients are regarded as repressed and pathetic. In both cases, susceptibility to the disorder is in some way related to the patient's personality or temperament.

Sontag dismissed the idea that personality and disease are related, although the possible role of personality in the genesis of particular diseases is an open question on present evidence. Whatever the fate of this issue, however, her more important point is well taken and germane to the present discussion. Our metaphoric use of the word "cancer" to refer to insidious and destructive forces in economic, political, and interpersonal contexts tends to generalize to the cancer patient in particular and to the terminally ill in general. If nothing else emerges from a reading of the literature on death and dying, one cannot escape the impression that once a patient is seen as terminal professionals think about him and relate to him in new ways. If the dying are to be treated humanely, this attitude must change and abandonment of the metaphoric use of disease terms, as Sontag advocated, would be a helpful step.

# PART III

# Preventive Medicine

This concluding section reviews topics in preventive medicine. We have seen in the preceding chapters that psychological factors and strategies play an important role in the treatment of disease. In disease prevention, however, psychological factors may be even more critical because prevention is behavior—the patient must do particular things and not do other things if disease is to be avoided. Mass inoculation is the paradigm case. If people do not show up at the clinic to take the shots, it matters very little how effective is the vaccine. Getting people to come to the clinic is a behavioral problem. Alteration of lifestyle is a more general and subtle behavioral problem that is being ever more clearly implicated in disease prevention. Choosing and avoiding foods, smoking or ceasing to smoke cigarettes, and exercising appropriately—these are behavioral variables whose effects on health status and longevity grow more compelling with each passing year. Modification of these variables is a psychological problem. Finally, social variables at the system level are believed to play a part in health and disease. Stress has a central place in this view. Modification of the social system is a problem with economic, political, and psychological dimensions.

# 11

# Geriatric Health Care

This chapter looks at the health problems of the aged from a psychological point of view. First, environmental and personal factors affecting health maintenance are discussed with particular emphasis on institutionalization. Factors leading to such placement and factors which mitigate against it are examined. Second, the topic of age and intelligence is examined. This is a major focus in recent research in gerontology, particularly with regard to contrasting findings in cross-sectional and longitudinal studies. Maintenance of intellectual functions into old age deserves a high priority in future efforts at improving the health status of the aged. Efforts along these lines, however, are in their infancy.

## Prevention of Illness

Prevention, or health maintenance, appears to be a relatively simple matter in the young and vigorous. This appearance is misleading, but the epidemiologic fact is that young people usually interact with the health care system either because something is wrong that requires intervention or because nothing is wrong and the patient is appearing for an annual checkup. Aged persons very frequently suffer from a variety of chronic illnesses that must be managed in one way or another. This management can be viewed as preventive in that if the conditions are not carefully controlled acute illness may result, requiring intervention.

Since prevention is an essentially behavioral problem, the role of psychological factors increases with advancing age. First, issues of compliance become increasingly pertinent because greater numbers of long-term treatments are prescribed. Likewise, as age increases the connection between psychological well-being and physical health becomes ever more intimate. Decreasing biological resilience of the older organism plays a part here, as does the decreasing behavioral latitude available to the aging person. A physical illness that is merely troublesome to a 30 year old may be a disaster to an aged person and every clinician who treats older patients can recall individuals who, following a broken hip, went into a general and precipitous decline leading to death, this outcome bearing no obvious relation to the orthopedic problem. Causal factors in these cases seem to be social and psychological. Third, the living circumstances of older persons may compromise health. In the worst case, older persons may find themselves in nursing homes, a grotesque misnomer in many instances, which provide unsanitary living conditions, inadequate diet, and depressing surroundings. In other cases, financial limitations may make it hard to meet the costs of medication, proper diet, or safe and pleasant living facilities. Finally, many aged live alone, usually following the death of a spouse. Characteristically an older women, this patient may find it difficult to keep up with the required medication without the presence of another person to reinforce these useful behaviors. Someone who has had a life partner for 40 years or so may find it impossible to adjust to solitary existence and depression may result, with loss of appetite, sleep disturbance, and listlessness, all of which jeopardize health.

A sizable literature has evolved in the last decade addressing the effect of the environment on the behavior of aging persons. In the present context, health maintenance is one category of behavior of special interest. Environments differ in several dimensions that may affect health maintenance behavior and ultimately longevity. A major variable is resource accessibility—are doctor, nurse, pharmacy, grocery store, and fresh air available? A second dimension is social—is the person in contact with relevant others? Is there a network of social support and stimulation available to help maintain his psychological well-being? Third, are living quarters clean and properly heated or cooled? Are food preparation facilities adequate? A fourth dimension, environmental consistency, also has been found to be related to health. The aged person's environment may change because of complex social factors such as outmigration or because the person himself relocates. In turn, relocation may be voluntary (moving to Florida), quasi-voluntary (moving because the rent has been raised), or forced (being put in a nursing home).

Many data on aging and health come from the United Kingdom, where the establishment of a national health service (NHS) has led to a somewhat more systematic approach to geriatric medicine than is evidenced in the largely entrepreneurial American system. In most cases, however, empirical findings on health related social and psychological variables are comparable across industrialized societies, and it is probably safe to assume that what is true of older persons in Britain is also true of the American aged. In one study of aged persons in industrialized societies, for example, the proportion of aged in U.S. and U.K. institutions was comparable (Shanas et al., 1968). Likewise, the reasons for institutionalization are remarkably constant across industrial societies, and these determinants are often psychosocial as opposed to biological in origin; that is, except at the extremity of disability, whether or not older persons reside in the community or in institutions seems to reflect the availability of social support rather than the degree of biological impairment. Institutionalization then will serve as a good starting place for examining behavioral factors in geriatric health.

Institutionalization means the placement of a person in a facility for chronic care with little or no prospect of discharge. The character of such facilities varies widely. In the United States ability to pay is a major factor in institutional choice, both in terms of whether or not one will be placed in such a setting at all and in terms of the institution. In Great Britain, the cradle-to-grave welfare philosophy mandates provision of care to all citizens. Whatever else this philosophy may have caused, it has led to a more rational development of aging services than has occurred in the United States. For example, a geriatric ward is customary in NHS hospitals, whereas the aged usually appear on general medical wards in the United States. Likewise, day hospitals, where discharged and semi-independent elderly can receive continuing treatment, are characteristic of the British system, while in the United States such services are provided in a haphazard fashion, with drastic regional differences and with ability to pay a prominent determinant of service availability. Furthermore, the nursing home so typical of American geriatric care is essentially nonexistent in Great Britain—old patients are either in hospital, at home, or in a sheltered home setting, attended by visiting nurses on a regular basis. "The overriding philosophy animating all British geriatric care is that old people should be kept at home and as nearly independent as possible, except under extraordinary circumstances where constant medical and nursing services are needed. Irreversible terminal illness is not considered one of these extraordinary circumstances" (Somers, 1977: 383). While most American physicians would undoubtedly agree with this goal, the American health care dollar has not been spent on the support services essential to realizing such a system.

On both sides of the Atlantic a number of social and psychological variables often render older patients less able to care for themselves and thus more likely to be institutionalized. The presence of family is one variable; financial status is another.

The marital status of an aged person seems to play an important role in his likelihood of being institutionalized. Using British census figures, Jefferey reported that "the single, divorced and widowed of both sexes in descending order of frequency are more likely than currently married people to be enumerated in institutions in the 1971 census" (1978: 769-770). A related variable is surviving children. Obviously, people who have had many children are most likely to have family support, both financial and psychological. The presence of children has been repeatedly shown to increase the well-being of elderly persons and most evidence suggests that in general children are supportive of their aging parents, often at considerable personal sacrifice (Sanford, 1975). The mediators of this care are usually daughters rather than sons, even with the increasingly frequent case of gainful employment for women.

Financial solvency is another factor that plays a role in decisions regarding placement of older persons in institutional settings, and it has repeatedly been demonstrated that by and large institutions for the elderly tend to be populated by the economically disadvantaged. In cases of extreme disability or acute medical illness, there is often no choice but to institutionalize. There is, however, a gray zone of partial disability. In the United States, if such persons are unable to pay for home nursing care, are unable to prepare meals and cannot afford domestic help, and/or do not have access to day hospital facilities, they are much more likely to be sent to rest homes or domiciliaries than are the more solvent. This financial variable relates to the former, kinship ties, in that children may help support their aged parents either by providing services that would otherwise have to be paid for or by giving them money.

Granting the necessity in some cases to institutionalize, the environmental variables making up that milieu ought to have some effect on longevity and quality of life. At the most fundamental level it ought to be possible to demonstrate that being in the institution is in some ways better than not being in it, at least for some persons. Yet, "it is nothing short of astonishing that to date no complete longitudinal control group study allowing a critical test of the effects of institutionalization has been reported" (Lawton, 1977: 293). Tobin compared a group of persons awaiting admission to a group already admitted (1971). He found differences in the affective area, with feelings of abandonment characterizing the waiters and bodily preoccupations and death fantasy characterizing the inmates. Obviously, considerable research on the fundamental utility of institutions needs to be undertaken. A sizable body of literature already exists on within-institution variables, however.

Study of the quality of institutional care presents a more difficult problem than it might at first appear. Since such places are usually one-way streets, survival is the most obvious criterion. But to compare survival rates in various institutions and to attribute outcome differences to differences in institutional quality assumes comparability of patients, which assumption can almost never legitimately be made. Another approach is to relate patients' expressed satisfaction with different environmental variables. Kahana found that an important determinant of patient satisfaction was a high degree of congruence between patient and staff views of patient needs (1975). Studying the effects of transfer to a different institution, Marlowe found that environmental variables were reasonable predictors of patients' well-being and degree of autonomy granted patients was a major factor in satisfaction (1973).

The phenomenon of transfer has itself been a topic of study. Marlowe compared relocated and nonrelocated institutionalized elderly, finding that the effect of transfer differed considerably with the initial health status of the patient (1973). Those most fit initially showed the greatest degree of change, either improving significantly or deteriorating such that relocation was a "make or break affair" (Lawton, 1977: 291). The upsetting effects of relocation can be ameliorated by preliminary exposure to the new setting and counseling (Bourestom & Pastalan, undated). Lawton concluded that "there is such a thing as favorable stimulation consequent to a change of scene" (1977: 292). The critical issues in relocation thus seem to be matching the new environment to felt patient needs and adequately preparing persons for transfer.

The concept of institutionalization has generated considerable emotion, particularly in response to media exposés of gross neglect in some settings. There has been a consequent movement in the direction of reducing the number of persons in institutions in favor of community based treatment, a tendency evident in both the United States and Britain (Brody et al., 1976; Jefferey, 1977). However, this shift may have at least one negative consequence:

> While one obviously does not wish to discourage the development of . . . community-based service programmes for the elderly, the prevalent motivating cast of mind behind their development . . . has tended to inhibit efforts to develop a more positive stance toward institutions and institutional care, as well as constructive advocacy to improve institutional life, especially in relation to social and psychological quality of life supports for the residents. Realistically, both community-based services and insitutional care services are needed, now and in the future. (Bigot & Munnichs, 1978: 397)

This is an important point because some role for institutional management is inevitable and is, in fact, likely to increase as biological life maintenance technology, for better or worse, continues to advance. However, the community based and institutional care systems must function as a whole to maximize independence for as long as possible. When independence ceases to be possible, the role of the institution is one of maintenance not only of life but also of maximum dignity and freedom of choice at the end of the life span.

At present approximately 5% of the population over 65 is institutionalized. The rest are living at home independently or in quasi-independent settings. A major concern obviously is to identify the social factors that maintain this level of adaptation and health. Some of these factors are implicit in what has been said regarding institutionalization: family support, adequate financial resources, and access to social and other resources all mitigate in favor of health maintenance.

While it is generally true, horror stories notwithstanding, that most people respond to the needs of aging parents in responsible and sympathetic ways, the continual care of an infirm, sometimes confused, and belligerent person can tax a family's emotional as well as financial resources. Geriatricians in Britain acknowledge this problem explicitly and relief for the family is seen as a legitimate reason for admission to hospital. At some hosptials, homebound geriatric patients periodically check in: "The primary purpose is to enable severely disabled patients to be maintained at home by assuring them of periodic assessment stays in hospital, at the same time relieving their families or caretakers on a periodic basis" (Somers, 1977: 387). This seems a fairly widespread practice in Britain. Isaacs (1971) reported that over 30% of geriatric admissions were undertaken to relieve the strain on families of older patients living at home.

Regarding solvency there is little one can say after pointing out the not very surprising fact that rich elderly do better than poor. Societies differ in their philosophy about the distribution of wealth and, in this context specifically, redistribution of wealth from the young and earning to the old and dependent. Britain has minimized the effect of wealth on care by providing adequate pensions and a truly astonishing array of social services. American society has moved in that direction in recent years but is still far from a commitment to providing all of the care needed by aged persons. It is noteworthy that in the United States the focus has been on acute intervention rather than on prevention, on the one hand, or chronic care, on the other. Medicare, like private insurance, will pay for operations but not for improved diets, social services, and the other things that are important in health maintenance. Where as a society we will go on this issue is more a political than a medical or psychological question, but there is some evidence that a national policy toward home care for the aging similar to that in Great Britain began to emerge in the 1970s (U.S. Senate, 1974). The fate of such proposals given the present conservative tide is unknown, but some sort of policy along these lines seems inevitable since there are going to be more and more elderly people living longer and longer, receiving fixed incomes of shrinking dollars.

In addition to family and financial support, a major factor in maintaining the independence of the aged is the availability of resources, both essential such as medical facilities and life enhancing such as entertainment. Lawton conceptualized the resource environment on several dimensions (1977). The physical resource environment consists of all the resources within some defined geographic area. The functional resource environment includes those facilities actually used by any particular aged person. The perceived resource environment refers to what the individual sees as the neighborhood, an admittedly vague concept with physical, social, and symbolic aspects. Finally, the salient resource environment consists of those resources the individual values highly.

This framework allows analysis of the way individuals interact with the environment. Such analysis shows consistently that a major determinant of resource utilization is physical proximity, especially in the case of inessential resources. Elderly persons will travel great distances to see relatives or doctors. Persons who drive perceive the neighborhood as larger than do nondrivers (Regnier et al., 1973), showing that functional proximity of resources affects how persons define their social space. Transportation, public or private, is a critical resource since it is the medium through which persons contact the environment. Transportation interruption has been shown to increase hospital admissions among the elderly (Prinsley, 1971) and it is obvious that if one is unable to reach essential services, health will deteriorate, possibly leading to institutionalization.

In the United States there has been some activity in recent years in the area of planned housing for aged persons. These efforts have occurred in both the private and the public sector, the former type often in semirural areas and in pleasant climates, the latter in the inner city. Retirement communities are designed for affluent persons in stable health, while public facilities run the gamut of cost and health expectations. Given what has been said about resource availability, a major consideration in such planned housing must be access to services. Newcomer studied access to resources in a variety of planned units (1973). Looking at distance-use interactions, he identified four resources for which distance seemed irrelevant to use: church, doctor, library, and restaurant. The last probably reflects economic restrictions while the first three are strongly colored by personal choice. Newcomer suggested that adequate public transit is probably more important than actual physical distance in rendering resources functionally available.

In addition to physical location, service provision is a debated subject in planned housing. Some argue that health services, meals, and recreational facilities ought to be part of the plan; others protest that this arrangement encourages dependency and may, in fact, lead to withdrawal from contact with the larger community. Several studies have suggested that provision of on-site medical service is much approved by residents and eclipses other sorts of services in attractiveness (Lawton, 1977). Perhaps the range of services ought to differ across sites, allowing some freedom of choice. One might additionally argue that such choice ought to extend throughout the income strata.

Prevention is the critical variable in older patients because they are more vulnerable than others to disease, they tend already to be afflicted with a variety of chronic conditions, and the effects of contracted disease are especially devastating in this age group. Unfortunately however, the thrust of health technology in the United States is interventionist, with social factors viewed as only tangentially related to health. Accordingly, elderly persons are forced into ill health for want of adequate food or into institutions for want of home nursing care. Broadly conceived preventionist strategies for the elderly can prevent these untoward results of current policy.

## INTELLIGENCE AND AGING

A topic of major research interest in the area of aging is intelligence. Does IQ decline with age and, if so, what does that mean practically? Some understanding of intellectual processes in the aged is of importance in health care since limitations in intelligence may place constraints on what can be achieved in terms of independence in health maintenance. In the following pages the research on the effect of age on intelligence will be discussed. The question has been addressed both cross-sectionally and longitudinally. That is, people of various ages have been compared with one another and individuals have been followed and compared with their own performance at earlier ages. Different conclusions proceed from these alternative methods. One notable lack in research on age and intelligence is a focus on practical application.

Summarizing the relationship between intelligence and aging, Botwinick states, "After reviewing the available literature, both recent and old, the conclusion . . . is that decline in intellectual ability is clearly part of the aging picture. The more recent literature, however, is bringing attention to what has been underemphasized in the older literature, viz., these declines may start later in life than heretofore thought and they may be smaller in magnitude; they also may include fewer functions (1977, pg. 580)." We will look at some examples of studies leading to this conclusion, focusing first on cross-sectional data.

The standardization study in constructing the WAIS (Wechsler, 1958) and extension of the method to include samples up to age 80 (Doppelt and Wallace, 1955) are often cited as suggesting that intelligence declines with advancing age. In these studies, the downward trend for Performance items was steeper and evident at younger ages than the

Verbal. This is a frequently replicated finding when the WAIS is applied to aging samples. Looking at Full Scale score, the rate of decline was slow up to about age 70, then becoming more precipitous. It is not until quite late in life that mean Full Scale scores fell a full standard deviation below the best performance of younger samples. Shaie (1959) reported a similar result in studying the 20- to 70-year age range cross-sectionally with the Primary Mental Abilities (PMA) test. No decline at all was seen until age 50, after which it was continuous but reached a level one standard deviation below the peak value in youth only at age 60. Data generated clinically with the WAIS also showed Performance score drops, but no change in Verbal score in the age range under 30 to over 60, provided educational level is used as a co-variate. All of the Performance subtests except for Picture Completion showed an age decline (Norton, 1979).

A question frequently raised about the decline in Performance score concerns the role of speed on these tasks. Many of the measures are timed, hence to the extent older persons work slowly, their scores will decline. Several studies have looked at the effect of removing the speeded aspect of the Performance measures and found minimal change in result. Doppelt and Wallace (1955) found that the elimination of time constraints had almost no effect on inter-age comparisons. A more recent study (Klodin, 1975) did report reduction in age differences when subtests were untimed, but the older subjects still did significantly less well than the young. Shaie *et al* (1953) did a similar study using the P.M.A. subtests and found that, on this measure, eliminating time constraints actually exaggerated age differences.

With regard to verbal functions, Botwinick and Storandt (1974) gave WAIS Vocabulary items to young and old subjects, but refined the scoring methods. "Each response to a test word was scored on the basis of six levels of correct response. The highest level was that of an excellent synonym; the lowest level, but still correct, response was that of an illustration, a demonstration by hands or body, or by correct repitition of the word in sentences. One of the mid-level responses was a relatively poor explanation" (Botwinick, 1977, pg. 588). The subjects were then matched on their quantitative scoring. The results showed that frequency of the best response class declined systematically with age, suggesting that verbal functions also may show a decline when evaluated cross-sectionally.

The Verbal-Performance organization of the WAIS, is only one of the several ways to organize the concept, intelligence. Factor analytic studies have yielded others, but that of Cattell (1968) has special relevance to the study of aging. Cattell and his colleagues defined two broad categories of intellectual function, fluid and crystallized. By fluid intelligence is meant the ability of the organism to learn and to adapt to its environment. Crystallized intelligence, on the other hand, is seen as a result of learning, a cultural product, especially educational. Horn (1970) summarized cross-sectional study of these two factors across the age span. Crystallized functions increased over the life-span, at least until 61, while fluid intelligence declined from adolescence onward. An omnibus measure combines the two and reflects in a general way what the subject can do, i.e. general intelligence. This factor remained relatively constant over the adult years. If we think of the WAIS Performance measures as being more fluid and the Verbal as being more crystallized, the Cattell scheme fits with what we have already described and examination of the tests making up these four categories reveals that Performance and fluid measures are fairly similar as are Verbal and crystallized.

In summary then, the cross-sectional studies are fairly consistent in showing a differential decline in intellectual functions with advancing age, non-verbal, spatial or fluid abilities declining in excess of verbal ones. Furthermore, in absolute terms, the declines occur relatively late in the life-span and are not great in magnitude. Finally, their practical significance in terms of daily living is not known and this is a very serious omission. As Botwinick observed, ''How crucial even these test abilities are in the daily business of carrying out life's responsibilities is an important questions not answered by the investigations carried out to date'' (1977, pg. 589).

In recent years, longitudinal study at the upper end of the life-span has begun and among the many results emerging from these studies are reports of less decline in intelligence in aged persons than had been seen in cross-sectional study. Some writers have gone so far as to say there is virtually no decline in intelligence as a function of age, at least until very late in life (Greene, 1969). Certainly taken at face value, a number of longitudinal studies do show measures of intelligence to increase or at least to hold steady for longer than cross-sectional studies would indicate. As Botwinick noted, however, interpretation of these findings has often failed to acknowledge the very significant fact of selective attrition of longitudinal samples, a confounding factor of as great importance as that of cohort differences in cross-sectional study (1977).

A study of Eisdorfer & Wilkie (1973) illustrated this point. Here subjects aged 60–69 were followed longitudinally for 10 years. The study continued for another five years and the subjects remaining were retested an additional three times. The scores on the first five testings for those subjects who remained in the study for 15 years were higher than those of the subjects seen only the first five times, and showed no decline in WAIS Full Scale Score. Thus inclusion of only those subjects remaining in the study obscured a mean decline in score for the sample (and presumably the population) as a whole. After age 76, the mean score for those remaining did show a decline. A second important point seen in these data is that those subjects who do survive did not show a decline. This illustrates the point that averaged data obscure important individual variation. Thus many individual aging persons do not reflect the general downward trend and show rather complete maintenance of their level of intellectual function into extreme old age. Other data from this same study, for example, showed a group of older survivors to show no decline until after age 84 and even then the drop was small in absolute terms. From a practical point of view the implication is clear. Individual aged persons must be viewed in terms of their own performance in making judgments of ability level as assumptions based even on the best studies of average age trends will apply to individuals only marginally. Thus, if one wishes to use psychological function as part of the planning process for care of aged patients, these functions must be assessed and not assumed. This point is so obvious that one hesitates to make it, but the stereotypic expectation of decline in intelligence with age is so prevalent that the point is worth stressing. No doctor would use normative age expectations to estimate a patient's blood pressure, but he might make assumptions about psychological functions on a similar basis.

With regard to the pattern of inter-ability relationships, Botwinick concluded in general that the longitudinal data parallel the cross-sectional in suggesting a greater decline in non-verbal than in verbal abilities (1977). Owens (1966), for example, used the army Alpha and studied subjects aged 49 and again at age 61. He analyzed that data according to a factor analytically derived structure, such that the test scores could be used as measures of a verbal, reasoning, and numerical factor. Over the period, only the numerical factor declined. Jarvik *et al* (1962) employed the WAIS over a seven year span with subjects whose mean age at the first testing was about 68 years. Decline was seen only in the Digit Symbol sub-test. When some of these subjects were again tested at twenty years after the first testing (mean age 84.3), statistically reliable declines were seen on all sub-tests (Blum *et al*, 1972).

What can we conclude from these studies of intelligence and age? First, there does seem to be a relationship between advancing age and decline in intelligence, insofar as it can be measured using conventional tests, but this relationship is confined to the latest life period, after 65 or so, and is greater for non-verbal or fluid than for crystallized intelligence. Second, in terms of practical application, rather little is known about the predictive and/or concurrent validity of these measures vis-a-vis issues of daily living in general or health maintenance in particular. It seems heuristically plausible, for example, to argue that decline in intelligence ought to compromise compliance with medical advice, but there are no systematic data on this point except at the most extreme levels of deterioration—there is abundant clinical evidence that demented persons do not reliably take medication or even feed themselves. The practical importance of a 10 point drop in I.Q., however, is obscure. This circumstance stands in contrast to the situation at the other end of the life-span, where there is ample evidence of the predictive power of intelligence tests against school achievement criteria, and a major source of the difficulty in the aged population is the absence of an easily quantifiable validation criterion like grades. What is required is a greater amount of correlational data between I.Q. and performance in normal day to day life so that these measures can begin to see practical utilization at advanced age commensurate with their use in children and young adults.

One further issue concerning intelligence and age must be addressed and concerns the degree to which intellectual abilities are modifiable. While it is quite evident that such abilities develop during childhood and adulthood as a function of environmental transaction, there is a tendency to view them as fixed once they are acquired. Furthermore, little systematic attention has been paid to specification of the particular aspects of organism-environment transaction critical to development of intellectual functions. This is clearly due in part to the fact that, traditionally, learning research and study of the nature of intelligence have been quite divorced from one another. Learning theorists and researchers have focused on the determinants of response acquisition, with the response itself being of secondary concern. Theorists and researchers in intelligence have focused on the response, devoting only minor effort at describing the learning mechanisms giving rise to the response.

Once intellectual functions are acquired, their exercise or performance is dependent upon environmental factors, yet almost nothing is currently known about the particular environmental parameters which support intellectual behavior. It seems likely that the typical aged person's environment is not conducive to maintaining flexible cognitive skills and Lindsley (1964) has stressed the point that an analysis of the environment is necessary if we are to identify factors which may cause the apparent decline in age of intellectual functions. "From an operant perspective . . ., deficient intellectual performance does not necessarily imply a biological condition. In contrast, deficiencies in intellectual performance may either reflect poor acquisition due to inadequate programming of reinforcement and discriminative stimuli, or they may result from poor maintenance conditions associated with loss of stimulus control, extinction, random reinforcement and similar contingencies" (Baltes and Labouvie, 1973, pg. 193).

Thus, the modifiability of intelligence throughout the life-span, but particularly in advanced age, is an open question. To answer it, experimental strategies employing complex environmental manipulations and multivariate behavioral assessment at various points in the life-span are needed. In this effort cross-linkage between theories of intelligence

and theories of learning is essential. Certainly a logical place for these interests to come together is education. ''Unprecedented amounts of
money and effort have been invested in designing educational and social
intervention programs for the young aimed at accelerating the rate of ontogeny; however, similar investments in modifying or monitoring intellectual ontogeny of the aged are at best miniken'' (Baltes and Labouvie, 1973, pg. 202). The decline seen in intellectual function with
advancing age may well reflect in part the fact that programmed instruction ends so early in life, while the phenomena learned at that time grow
out of data at an ever accelerating rate. The greater cohort than age effects reflected in cross-sectional versus longitudinal data comparisons
support this idea and argue strongly for the importance of programmed
research in this area.

# 12

# Stress

In recent years the concept of stress has figured prominently in conceptualizations of the relationship between behavior and disease. In simplest terms, the stress notion posits that the body reacts to threatening environmental events in a more or less stereotyped way and that this response can have negative health consequences. The response is termed stress; the events giving rise to it are stressors. It follows that if stress leads to disease, methods of modifying the response or removing the stimuli giving rise to stress would have useful health consequences.

The concept of stress has a long history, harkening back to Hippocratic ideas of harmony between the person and his environment. Use of the word dates to the seventeenth century, but in this century the term "stress" took on a more technical meaning with the work of Cannon (1935), Bernard (1927), and Selye (1936). Selye described a pattern of adjustment in animals placed in a variety of aversive environments. He called this pattern the general adaptation syndrome (GAS) dividing it into three stages: the initial alarm reaction is followed by a period of resistance to the aversive stimulus; if the stimulus is not removed, exhaustion ensues and finally death (1936). For Selye, the striking finding was the relative constancy of the organism's response, no matter what the stressor (heat, immobilization, toxic substance), and he identified this response as mediated by the anterior pituitary and the adrenal cortex.

The sequence of events is roughly as follows. The pituitary releases adrenal cortical stimulating hormone (ACTH). This causes the adrenal cortex to release the corticosteroids, which act on a wide range of body sites to generate defensive reactions. If the condition persists long enough, involution of the thymus (pituitary) and lymph nodes, enlargement of the adrenal gland, and ulceration of the stomach results. "These observations lead to the current definition of stress as the 'non-specific response of the body to any demand'" (Tache & Selye, 1978:5).

Working in the 1940s and early 1950s Wolff began to relate particular diseases to stress: "I have used the word [stress] in biology to indicate that state within a living creature which results from the interaction of the organism with noxious stimuli or circumstances, i.e. it is a dynamic state within the organism; it is not a stimulus, assault, load, symbol, burden, or any aspect of the environment, internal, external, social or otherwise" (Hinkle, 1975:31). In a general way, Wolff related stress to external events, but he saw this relationship as nonlinear, the external events acting like a trigger leading to an internal elaboration of the stress response.

Since publication of these early works by Selye, Wolff, and others, the literature on the relationship between stress and disease has grown at an astonishing rate. Reviewing the field in 1977, Selye stated that he had collected over 110,000 publications dealing with the stress concept in biology, medicine, and social science. With the possible exception of Darwin's theory of evolution, one is hard pressed to find another theoretical position in biological science that has been so productive of research and speculation in a multidisciplinary context.

## Contemporary Stress Theory

Stress theory has contributed tremendously to the reemergence of a multicausative notion of disease. Furthermore, it has led to an appreciation of the intimate connection between physiological and psychological responses to environmental events. This latter idea is central to psychosomatic medicine as a discipline and offers a rationale for a psychological approach to disease. Let us examine the theory in more detail. First, stress theory holds that stressors, external forces giving rise to the stress response, may be biological (toxins) or psychological (divorce) in character. Second, the response itself has biological (ACTH secretions) and psychological (subjective feelings of tension, overt behavior of flight) aspects. Third, and perhaps most important, the stress theory implies that the traditional biology-psychology, body-mind distinction is arbitrary, having more to do with the history of science than with the ontological character of the subject matter. The stress response is, in fact, a total response of the organism, which can be described in biological or psychological language and studied with the observational tools of those two disciplines but remains a unity. Stress theory reminds us that scientific analysis may obscure the functional unity of the stress response in particular and of the organism in general.

The stress theory as enunciated by Selye emphasizes that the response is stereotyped and relatively independent of the stressor. His term "general adaptation syndrome" suggests this transituational constancy. In reaction to any particular stressor, for example, a local infection, there is a specific response, local inflammation, superimposed on the more general response of the anterior pituitary–adrenal cortex axis. Selye called the specific response the local adaptation syndrome (LAS). If the local stimulus is relatively mild, the GAS may not evolve as the LAS is sufficient to restore homeostasis. For the GAS to evolve, either the local stressor must be sufficiently severe as to affect the whole body or the stimulus must by its nature affect the system as a whole. Such conditions directly elicit the GAS.

One criticism of the stress theory centers on the notion of generality:

> In the 1940's concepts of "stress" and of "life-stress" were applied to biological and social systems because they appeared to provide an explanation for the apparently "non-specific" effects of biological agents, and for the occurrence of certain pathological phenomena, and of certain illnesses, as a part of the response of people to their social environment. At the present time, the "stress" explanation is no longer necessary. It is evident that any disease process, and in fact any process within the living organism, might be influenced by the reaction of the individual to his social environment or to other people.
>
> It is clear that there are a variety of physiological mechanisms which might occur. These mechanisms might involve not simply the anterior pituitary and the adrenal cortex, but any combination of neuro or hormonal effector systems of the organism. . . . These mechanisms are either understood or potentially understandable on a straight-forward physiological basis. It is not necessary to invoke a special variable called a "stress" in order to understand their occurrence; in fact, it seems illogical to do so. It is hard to think of a single general state of the living organism which could evoke such a wide variety of internal reaction patterns that are so closely attuned to coping with the internal and external disturbances which initiate them. (Hinkle, 1975:42)

From Hinkle's perspective, stress, an intervening variable, cannot account for biological adaptation. The GAS, Hinkle would argue, consists simply of those aspects of adaptive response that play a role in a great many different adaptations. Hinkle underlined the exquisite specificity of the adaptation response:

> It is true, for example, that the response of the organism to mechanical damage, to thermal damage, to bacterial invasion and to rupture of interpersonal relations, may all have elements in common; but a fracture of an

ankle, a burn of the skin, pneumonia of the lung and a reaction of suppressed rage and grief are very different reactions. An animal which responded to a bacterial invasion of its lung by creating inflammation and new bone in its left ankle would not survive very long. (p. 43)

From the point of view of physiological adaptation, then, the concept of stress as a transituational response may be superfluous.

In the stress theory as enunciated by Selye, the GAS is a response to physiological stressors primarily and to psychological stressors secondarily via conditioning. While he admitted that a limited range of psychological stimuli may be innate stressors in some species, certainly in the human case the bulk of what is referred to as stressful acquires this property via learning and thus is essentially psychologically mediated. For Selye, however, this mediation is secondary in that it develops on a pattern of response to physical stressors like cold or toxins. Several writers have questioned the view that the GAS is physiologically elicited, Mason (1971) and Lazarus (1975) among them.

Mason observed that in the usual stress experiment the physical stressor and the psychological reaction to it are inevitably confounded (1971). In Mason's view the GAS is, in fact, psychologically caused; it is not a direct consequence of the physical stressor. Evaluation of the stressor, a central nervous system event, gives rise to the GAS, presumably via the hypothalamus-pituitary connection. In support of this contention, Lazarus cited a study (Symington et al., 1955) in which it was found that an unconscious animal can sustain bodily injury without elicitation of the endocrine responses of the GAS (1975). Symington and associates also noted that patients dying of disease but comatose during the terminal stages showed normal adrenal glands at autopsy. Patients conscious during the fatal disease showed the changes in the adrenal cortex described by Selye: "Such studies support the possibility that it is the *psychological significance* of the injury rather than the injury itself that produces the adrenal cortical changes associated with the GAS" (Lazarus, 1975:18).

Research on correlation among indices of stress also has raised question about the generality of the response. One frequently cited study showed that heart rate is bidirectional, rising when the subject is oriented to the environment, falling when his attention is directed inward (Lacey, 1967). This suggests that the arousal response is not a monotonic and generalized activation of an organism but has some situational specificity. Similarly, it is difficult to relate physiological indices to emotional states in a direct way across subjects. Physiological response seems to show considerable individual variation and to be only marginally related to subjective states identified introspectively (Lang et al., 1972). These findings challenge the view that the stress response is fairly constant across both organisms and situations. Lazarus summarized his view on the generality-specificity issue:

> It seems unnecessary to adopt an either/or position with regard to the generality-specificity question. They are not mutually exclusive, and it seems wise to entertain the likelihood of a degree of generality as well as specificity in the sequence starting with disturbed commerce with the environment and eventuating in somatic illness. (1975:21).

In light of current data, this seems a most sensible position, but it runs counter to traditional stress theory. What, then, is the meaning of stress? The accumulating data on response specificity render the traditional view of stress untenable and at this point in time the term is vague. Is there any place in science and medicine for vague terms? There most certainly is, provided their vagueness is admitted. The concept of stress, like that of intelligence in psychology or fever in medicine, serves to bring issues to the fore, to orient research, and to stimulate debate. For the present purpose, the following working definition of stress is offered. Stress refers to organismic responses to environmental events that give rise to disease through mechanisms apparently involving the organism as a whole. Stress has psychological aspects, which are behavioral at both the micro- and the macrolevel, as well as subjective. The term likewise includes physiological aspects, particularly neuroendocrinological.

## Basic Research on Stress

Research on the relationship between environmental stressors and disease states is both extensive and unusually varied, ranging from epidemiologic studies of coronary disease to carefully controlled animal experiments. This section describes some representative studies that examined basic questions of mechanism. Later, applied research will be described.

### EPIDEMIOLOGICALLY ORIENTED STUDIES

#### Urbanization

To most people, stress connotes the subjective feelings of frustration, tension, fear, and irritation that seem so frequent a consequence of urban living in the twentieth century. The romantic appeal of a simpler time is evident in everything from popular music to advertising. The relationship between environment in general, and particularly urbanization, and the incidence of cardiovascular disease has been studied in a variety of contexts. For example, Tyroler and Cassel reported studies of death rates from coronary and other heart disease in stable groups surrounded by different degrees of social change (1964). In white males aged 45–54 years, a regular increase in death from all heart disease accompanied increasing urbanization.

### CROSS-CULTURAL COMPARISON

Cross-cultural studies have provided interesting data on the relationship between bodily respone and changing social conditions. Scotch studied hypertension among urban and rural Zulus in South Africa and found a number of social variables that were related to the incidence and degree of hypertension (1963). In both the urban and the rural sample, females had more hypertension than males and advancing age, obesity, and widowhood or separation all were risk factors. In the rural group, postmenopausal women had more hypertension, while this was not true of urban Zulus. For urban Zulu women, having five or more children was associated with hypertension as was low family income, a belief in sorcery, and living in a traditional extended family as opposed to the Western style nuclear family. Among males, hypertension was more frequent among urban dwellers and worsened the longer they stayed.

Moss interpreted these differences in terms of a disparity between social beliefs and expectations and enviornmental realities (1975). The traditional, rural Zulu culture provides its members with a clear-cut value system, status hierarchy, and role expectations. Transition from the rural to the urban environment calls many of these values into question and requires changes in behavior, some of them drastic. For example, the traditional emphasis on large familes implies higher status to fertile women. In the Western oriented city, large families are maladaptive and a value conflict results. Likewise, belief in sorcery is traditional, but in the city Christianity is prevalent and sorcery is devalued; hence women who continued to believe in sorcery while living in the city were more likely to be hypertensive than were those who adopted Christianity.

Social change, then, is associated in some studies with incidence of disease, as Scotch found among Zulus in the throes of urbanization. For Zulus continuing to live in rural areas, "change was more or less absorbed within the traditional social structure . . . while tribal traditions are completely distorted and engulfed in the city" (Scotch, 1963:1205).

### OCCUPATION

Aspects of the work environment, particularly the level of responsibility and the necessity for making decisions, also may play a role in the genesis of disease. Russek and Zolman studied 100 coronary patients under 40 years old and found that job related emotional stress preceded heart attack in 91% of the cases (1958). A quarter of the group had been holding down two jobs and another 46%, while working at only one occupation, spent 60 or more hours per week on the job. Buell and Breslow found that the risk of death from coronary disease among men under age 45 increased dramatically as hours per week spent working exceeded 48 (1960).

Physicians show an interesting maldistribution of coronary disease. Russek had independent judges rank various specialities as being relatively high or relatively low in stress (1960). Dermatology, for example, was viewed as minimally stressful while general practice was viewed as maximally stressful. Prevalence of coronary disease tended to rise up to age 69 among all physicians, as would be expected. However, the relative prevalence by specialty was striking, with general practitioners more than three times as likely as dermatologists to have heart disease (11.9% versus 3.2% over the age range 40–69). At the youngest age, GPs outnumbered dermatologists by a factor of six.

In a 1962 study Russek found similar links between perceived stress and coronary disease in other professions. Like physicians, air traffic controllers work under considerable pressure. This occupation is, in fact, almost the paradigm case of the pressure cooker environment, with instantaneous responses demanded by perpetually changing circumstances. Not surprisingly, air traffic controllers are at risk for a number of disorders, including peptic ulcer and hypertension (Cobb & Rose, 1973).

LIFE CHANGE

One of the most widely cited studies on the relationship between environmental events and disease was conducted by Holmes and Rahe (1967). They described a scale developed to assess recent life change events, the underlying hypothesis being that if stress is a cause of disease and if change in life circumstance is stressful, there ought to be a relationship between disease incidence and life change events. Such a relationship has been repeatedly documented. The Schedule of Recent Events (SRE) is scored according to an empirically derived scaling of life change units (LCU) that reflects the relative seriousness of particular events. Receiving a traffic ticket, for example, would have a low LCU rating while death of a spouse would have a high score. The result is a ratio scale for operationalizing the concept of stressfulness of recent events occurring in the subject's life.

A retrospective study evaluated men discharged from the marines for psychiatric difficulties (Rahe et al., 1967). On the basis of service records, LCU scores were attached to each man for each year of service.

It was then possible to relate these scores to illness events in medical records. Illnesses were classified as major or minor and the health raters were blind as to the LCU scores. The mean LCU score for the year prior to minor illness was 130, while for major illness it was 164, and both exceeded the mean for all years combined, 72, to a statistically significant degree. Thus, this study suggested a relationship between life change events and illness.

In a prospective study, highly selected naval personnel being trained for hazardous duty were given the SRE to assess life change units during the year preceding entry to the training program (Rahe et al., 1972). The men were followed up through reports of medical illnesses during training that were sufficiently severe to prevent completion of the training. The correlation between life change events and number of dispensary visits before discharge from the program was .50 and significant.

Studies using the SRE in Scandinavia have addressed the incidence of myocardial infarction and sudden death from coronary artery disease retrospectively. LCU scores for the six months before the event were 50–100% higher than those for the preceding six-month interval (Rahe, 1975).

FAMILY DYNAMICS

Perhaps because asthma occurs mainly in children, this condition has been frequently studied in relation to family dynamics. Apparently, disturbed family relations play a role in the incidence of the disease at least in some cases. Rees rated parents of hospitalized asthmatic and control children as to their suitability as parents (1963). Only 44% of the parents of the asthmatic children were rated satisfactory, promoting feelings of security with affection and acceptance. Eighty-two percent of the control parents were so rated. Removal of an asthmatic child from the home often alleviates symptoms (Long et al., 1958), but such an outcome is difficult to interpret. It may be that separation from the family is critical, but in removing the child from the home family and physical environment are confounded. The relevant variable may be separation of the child from allergens in the home. Purcell and colleagues submitted this question to a critical test (1969). They identified 13 children in whom emotional factors seemed to play a role in attacks; instead of removing the child, they had the family move to a hotel while a substitute mother cared for the child. Twelve children whose asthma did not seem emotionally triggered were similarly treated. Dependent variables were expiration rate and flow, rated wheezing, amount of medication required, and daily frequency of attacks. For the emotionally triggered children all these parameters dropped during separation; for the control group, only daily frequency changed though less than for the experimentals.

## STUDIES OF MECHANISM

Two approaches to elucidating mechanism can be discerned in the literature. One looks at the psychological characteristics of the patient in an attempt to identify personality variables that mediate the environmental event–physical disease association, such as Friedman and Rosenman's work on the type A personality (1974). A second approach assesses physiological variables in order to define dimensions that differentiate the person who develops illness from those who do not. In related research, animal analogues are employed to assess the effects of environmental stress. Selective breeding permits some control of genetic factors and tissue analysis can yield detailed information on pathology in response to stress. We shall consider examples of both approaches.

### TYPE A PERSONALITY AND BEHAVIOR

The concept of the type A personality evolved over many years in response to experimental findings, clinical observations and hunches, theory formulation, and prospective validation (Jenkins, 1975). Friedman and Rosenman, both cardiologists, observed a pattern of behavior particularly in the young coronary patient that apparently differentiated him from the run of people. It occurred to Friedman and Rosenman that this behavior set might belong on the list of risk factors for MI.

Friedman defined type A people as "those individuals who are engaged in a relatively chronic struggle to obtain an unlimited number of poorly defined things from their environment in the shortest period of time, and, if necessary, against the opposing efforts of other things or persons in this same environment" (1969). Jenkins added other descriptors, including extreme competitiveness, achievement motivation, impatience, restlessness, and time sense urgency (1971). In type A's, identification with vocation is extremely high and personal worth is defined in terms of occupational success. It should be noted that these attributes can be operationalized, which contributes to the power of the construct in epidemiologic and other studies.

Reviewing their clinical observations, Friedman and Rosenman set about designing instruments for assessing type A behavior. As part of a large-scale collaborative study, a structured interview was designed to tap both the content of the subject's utterances and his style of response on a four-point scale from strong to mild type A behavior and strong to mild type B (Rosenman et al., 1964), the latter being in essence the opposite of the type A. Type B's, described as easygoing and relaxed, are relatively rare in cardiology clinics. Reliability studies using this interview showed it to be psychometrically acceptable (Jenkins et al., 1968).

In addition, a self-administered scale for identifying the type A personality has been developed, the Jenkins Activity Survey, which was validated against clinical judgments of the type A pattern. The Jenkins survey yields a continuously distributed score for type A behavior and for three factor analytically derived dimensions of the syndrome—speed and impatience, job involvement, and hard-driving conscientiousness (Jenkins et al., 1967).

The first major prospective study of the relationship between type A behavior and cardiovascular disease was the Western Collaborative Group Study (Rosenman et al., 1964). Using the interview technique to assess type A behavior, researchers followed well men for periods ranging from 4.5 to 8.5 years; subjects were independently evaluated for coronary disease. The incidence of cardiovascular disease for type A as opposed to type B men was 1.7–4.5 times as high and the relationship was stronger the younger the patient. A similar prospective result was found using the Jenkins Activity Survey (Jenkins et al., 1974). The predictive power of these personality assessment methods is largely independent of other risk factors.

Groen conceptualized the psychological factors in myocardial infarction as having three critical aspects (1976). The first is a pattern of personality, the description of which is similar to that of the type A. Second, the event usually follows an episode of personal difficulty, ranging from the death of a spouse to a slow accumulation of problems. Frustration is considered a key aspect of the precipitator. Finally, the patient reacts to this event in a characteristic way–increasing involvement in work and suppressing emotion. This three-part typology, originally developed through retrospective analysis of 24 patients with acute MI, has been pursued by Groen and his colleagues in both retrospective and prospective cross-validations in several countries.

One study assessed the prevalence of coronary disease among some 700 Israeli workers (Groen et al., 1968). Subjects were asked about a range of psychosomatic symptoms such as insomnia, fatigue, dizziness, and headache. Persons with coronary disease scored higher on these symptoms than did normals. However, a subsequent survey of relatives of the probands showed that coronary patients complained to family of these difficulties less than did the normals. This intriguing finding supports the notion that coronary prone persons do not express their fears and concerns as openly as do others, at least within the family (Groen & Drory, 1967).

These studies taken together present a fairly compelling picture of a relationship between the type A behavior pattern, variously defined, and incidence of coronary disease, angina, and myocardial infarction. However, the relationship is complex and the critical questions of mechanism remain to be answered. If Type A behavior led directly to heart disease, the prospective incidence figures should be much higher than they are. Selye himself commented that the type A pattern does not invariably lead to early disease and death for at age 70 it describes him perfectly:

> From the time I became addicted to medical research, at the age of 20, to the present (age 70 and still actively directing our Institute), I have been the very prototype of this personality. Yet I have never had a coronary heart attack or any other manifestation of stress induced illness. . . . [I]f I should die of a coronary accident before this book appears in print, it will not be "untimely." Besides, if I could be assured of survival until age 150 by turning into a "Type B," I would not do it! (1977:7)

Likewise, Type B's do sometimes appear in coronary care units. Obviously, the outcome variable is complexly determined and a complete understanding of the relationship between personality and cardiovascular disease requires both improved specificity in personality description and detailed analysis of the mechanism translating personality variables or behavioral styles into myocardial infarction. Work to elucidate these problems is under way and we turn now to a discussion of several such efforts.

CARDIOVASCULAR DISEASE

It is becoming increasingly clear that the endocrine system and its controlling structure in the central nervous system, the hypothalamus, play a critical role in illness. If worrying leads to atheromatous plaques, the likely process involves the hypothalamus, the pituitary, and the endocrine system. Taggart and Carruthers reviewed one hypothesis along these lines and described data pertinent to it (1977).

Carruther's original hypothesis, presented in 1969, stated that the mechanisms relating life stress to coronary disease entail increased sympathetic nervous system activity, which leads to mobilization from adipose tissue of free fatty acids into the bloodstream. If these fatty acids are not utilized via metabolic activity, they are converted to triglycerides by the liver and are then available for formation of atheroma. Hypertriglyceradermia, is statistically associated with increased incidence of coronary artery disease (Lewis et al., 1974). Release of the catecholamines, particularly norepinephrine, in emotion thus is the precipitating event. In an attempt to elucidate the relationship among emotion, exertion, and blood triglyceride, Taggart and Carruthers studied racing car drivers on the ground that they work in a highly emotionally arousing stimulus situation that entails relatively little physical exertion—a possible analogy to the occupational stress in less romantic circumstances, for example, the air traffic control tower.

In one study plasma samples were taken at various times during the three hours following a race (Taggart & Carruthers, 1971). Analysis showed a linear relationship between circulating catecholamines and free fatty acids and a dramatic rise in each at the end of the race. Triglycerides rose as free fatty acids fell during the following hours, lending support to the conversion hypothesis. In another study, Taggart and associates assessed catecholamine and free fatty acid levels before and after public speaking (1973). Norepinephrine rose while epinephrine held constant. Free fatty acid also rose, supporting the idea that norepinephrine is the critical catecholamine in the arousal–fat release phenomenon.

An interesting variation on this study used a drug-placebo trial. Oxprenolol, the active drug, is a beta andrenergic blocking agent that selectively suppresses norepinephrine rise. Free fatty acid levels actually fell after public speaking in persons given oxprenolol. Beta andrenergic blocking drugs such as oxprenolol have the general effect of blocking sympathetic activation. They lower pulse, for example, and can relieve anxiety, especially when somatic factors play a major role in the the patient's complaints (Tryer & Lader, 1973). This would suggest, then, that emotional arousal leads to increased free fatty acid level and that this effect can be modified by blocking the activity of the sympathetic nervous system. A possible role of the sympathetic nervous system in atherosclerosis might therefore be hypothesized.

Wolff and his colleagues examined the relationship between a person's way of coping with a stressful environment and measures of 17-OHCS, a secretion of the adrenal cortex (1964). The parents of children dying of leukemia were studied to determine both their method of coping with the tragic situation and the concentrations of 17-OHCS in urine. Parents who used denial, minimizing fear and dread and expressing hope, had lower levels of 17-OHCS than did parents who showed overt despair. Those parents most upset showed the highest 17-OHCS elevations. "Thus, even extreme environmental press or involvement can be countermanded at least temporarily by the individual's defenses" (Moos, 1975:87).

The same dependent variable was employed to look at the effect of the experience of responsibility among training pilots during aircraft carrier landings (Miller et al., 1970). The planes had two-man crews but only the pilot had control of the aircraft; the radioman remained passive. Although 17-OHCS levels were found to be higher in the men controlling the plane, greater subjective experiences of fear were reported by the radiomen. Similar results were reported by Bourne and associates, who compared officers and enlisted men in Vietnam during a period of expected enemy attack (1968). The officers showed higher 17-OHCS levels. In a similar vein, several studies reported dramatic increases in resting heart rate among executives given increased responsibility (Moos, 1975).

The data suggest that stressful environments interact with personality attributes like denial and with specifics of the subject's role in the situation to yield different neuroendocrinological effects and, presumably, different degrees of disease risk. The relevance of such observations to the hypothesized role of type A behavior in coronary disease is obvious. Type A behavior involves sympathetic discharge, and this method of dealing with environmental events, in turn, has a variety of effects, some of which may be atherogenic. Animal studies have pursued these questions in detail. The use of tricyclic antidepressants in depression is widespread, but there are reports of sudden cardiac death and of sublethal cardiac disease in patients so treated. Kristiansen concluded some years ago that these drugs may increase the risk of cardiac disease in patients with preexisting circulatory abnormalities or possibly even in well persons who do strenuous work (1961). Davidson studied the effect of these drugs on rats submitted to procedures leading to cardiomyopathy (1977). Sudden death was not seen in these animals until they were placed under environmental stress of sudden, extremely loud noise. This led to no deaths in rats without cardiomyopathy and treated with tricyclics, to death in 2-6% of the animals with cardiomyopathy but not receiving tricyclics, and to sudden death in 70-90% of animals with cardiomyopathy and treated with tricyclics. The cause of death was ventricular fibrillation.

Since the effects of the sympathetic nervous system are potentiated by tricyclics, it seems possible that a profound overreaction of the system operating on a diseased heart is the cause of the observed dramatic increase in mortality under stress. This possibility was tested by administering a beta andrenergic blockade, propranolol, in a repeat of the experiment. Death rates dropped to 2–10% in the tricyclic treated cardiomyopathic rats receiving this drug, offering support to the idea that sympathetic discharge is causative. Davidson pointed out a possible relationship between these data and a retrospective study by Engel of 107 sudden deaths (1971). An emotionally arousing event could be identified in the recent past in all these cases, interpreted as causing activation of the autonomic nervous system. Fox and associates reported that long-term administration of beta andrenergic blocking drugs may prevent myocardial infarction (1975).

It is generally agreed that organisms of the same species show individual variation in physiologic response to environmental events. These differences may be inherited and are quite persistent (Thomas et al., 1968). In a beautifully designed series of studies, Friedman and his associates looked at the relationship between inherited and environmental factors in the genesis of hypertension in the rat.

Friedman used as subjects two strains of rats developed from the Sprague-Dawley line, one of which is exceedingly susceptible to hypertension ($s$), the other being quite resistant ($r$). Among the factors that can induce hypertension in the $s$ group are salt in the diet, administration of hormones from the adrenal cortex, and renal artery occlusion (Dahl et al., 1963, 1965). The $r$ strain is strikingly resistant to these risk factors. The strains also show some interesting behavioral differences, the $s$ strain being less adept at learning both passive and active avoidance, showing less exploratory behavior, and being less aggressive (Ben-Ishay & Welner, 1969; Friedman & Weiss, 1974; Welner et al., 1968).

Initial studies of these two strains had no success in inducing hypertension via either a stressful environment (overcrowding) or aversive conditioning of the Pavlovian type (shock intermittently paired with a tone stimulus) (Dahl, 1970). However, suggestive evidence emerged that hypertension induced by increased sodium intake was worsened by use of aversive stimuli. These data suggest that stress may be an aggravating but not a causative factor even among organisms predisposed genetically to hypertension.

In a later study, Friedman and Dahl used a different category of stressor and reached different conclusions (1975, 1977). Here the stressful event entailed placing the subject in a situation of unavoidable conflict for periods of six hours per day for 13 weeks. The subject was initially trained to lever-press for food following a period of food deprivation; this response was thinned to a VI51.2 sec schedule. In addition, electric shock was made contingent on lever-pressing on a VR 8 schedule. While water was freely available throughout the experiment, food was available only in the conflict situation; in order to live, the rat had to self-induce shock on apparently random trials. The metaphorical similarity of this regimen to many human work environments cannot pass without notice. Control rats were fed ad lib throughout the experiment. All subjects were on a low-salt diet.

Weight gain data for the four groups showed controls to gain throughout the experiment, with no strain differences. Experimentals manifested initial loss of weight then very slow gain; again, there were no differences between the strains. The conflict situation thus had a drastic and expected effect in limiting weight gain. The similarity in effect between the strains suggested very similar overt responses to the experimental conditions among the $s$ and $r$ rats.

Data on the incidence of hypertension dramatically differentiated the groups: only $s$ subjects showed rises. However, as fig. 12–1 reveals, the specific type of stressor employed, conflict, had a large effect on blood pressure only in vulnerable individuals. The stressor had no effect on blood pressure in the resistant subjects. At the end of the 13 weeks, several of the $s$ experimentals were removed from the conflict situation. By the twenty-sixth week, their weight had risen to control levels and

**Figure 12-1.** Reproduced, with permission, from R. Friedman and L.K. Dahl, Psychic and genetic factors in the etiology of hypertension. In D. Wheatley (editor), *Stress and the Heart.* New York: Raven Press, 1977.

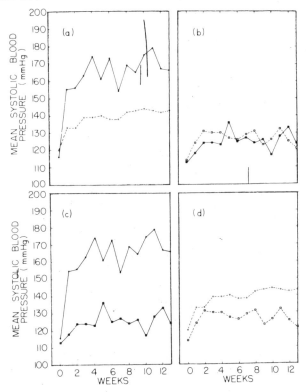

**(a)** Mean systolic blood pressure of S-strain conflict subjects (—●—●—●—) and S-strain control subjects (-○--○--○-) during the base-line|week and first 13 experimental weeks. **(b)** Mean systolic blood pressure of R-strain conflict subjects (—■—■—■—) and R-strain control subjects (-□--□--□-) during the base-line week and first 13 experimental weeks. **(c)** Mean systolic blood pressure of S-strain conflict subjects (—●—●—●—) and R-strain conflict subjects (—■—■—■—) during the base-line week and first 13 experimental weeks. **(d)** Mean systolic blood pressure of S-strain control subjects (-○--○--○-) and R-strain control subjects (-□--□--□-) during the base-line week and first 13 experimental weeks.

blood pressure had dropped somewhat below the level of *s* strain controls. *S* rats remaining on the aversive schedule showed a mild decline in blood pressure, suggesting some degree of habituation.

This very interesting work indicates that psychological factors may play a role in hypertension. Nevertheless, the simple application of random shock alone did not lead to hypertension in the *s* strain, which points to the specific conflict situation as having the etiologic role. It is also very important to note that a genetic predisposition is the necessary setting event for the disease, and a similar mechanism may account for some of the outcome variability seen when genetic factors vary randomly, as in much animal and almost all human studies of hypertension-environment relationships. Finally, in this study, removal from the conflict environment led to normalization of blood pressure. Whether or not longer exposure to the conflict situation would have produced chronic hypertension remains to be seen.

### CROWDING

As noted earlier epidemiologic evidence shows that a variety of illnesses increase in frequency as human populations become increasingly dense through urbanization. Deaths from coronary disease were reported as being higher in urban than rural U.S. populations as long ago as 1960 (Enterline et al., 1960), and a comparison of prison inmates found those housed in dormitory groups to have higher blood pressure than inmates housed alone (Ostfeld & D'Atri, 1975). Harburg and co-workers compared urban geographic districts differing in population density and found blood pressure to be higher in the denser, more stressful living conditions (1970).

A voluminous animal literature has evolved on the behavioral and physiological effects of crowding. The overall impression is that crowding leads to a wide range of negative consequences. Overactivity and hypertrophy of the adrenal medulla have been found in mice and other animals enduring crowded conditions (Bullough, 1952; Christian, 1960), and rats living in overcrowded conditions are hyperglycemic (Barnett et al., 1960). Zoo animals have been reported to show a tenfold increase in coronary disease over a decade of increasing density (Ratcliffe et al., 1960).

Crowding as a source of stress is a complicated variable that can be conceptualized in different ways. First, of course, there is simply the number of organisms per unit area. The relevance of this dimension to human health is not completely clear. Cassel reviewed the evidence and found no linear relationship between humans per unit space and disease incidence (1971). This suggests that other ways of conceptualizing the crowding variable may be necessary. In a later publication, Cassel elaborated four hypotheses that might allow one to relate the animal and human data (1974). His view entails a reformulation of the critical dimension of crowding as a stimulus.

Cassel suggested that it is not crowding per se that is critical in disease genesis but rather disorder in interindividual relationships, which is an inevitable consequence of crowding in animals but perhaps not in man. As a result of this social disorganization a variety of behaviors emerge, including repetitive behavior, withdrawal, and the formation of deviant groupings of animals. He argued that a critical aspect of this social

216    PREVENTIVE MEDICINE

disorganization is the fact that behaviors cease to have their usual consequences and a process of relearning is necessary for the animal to adapt to the crowded circumstance. Analogues to the human condition can be drawn: as a population adapts to new circumstances, there is an initial rise, then a decline, in illness events in some studies. Cassel and Tyroler found that second-generation moutaineers working in industrial settings showed significantly less illness absenteeism and had lower Cornell Medical Index scores than did a group from the same milieu whose fathers had not worked in the industrial setting (1961).

All studies of the relationship between stress and disease show individual variation. Christian found that the animal's position in the social hierarchy had an effect on disease incidence in conditions of crowding, with those at the top of the hierarchy least affected (1968). Variability in outcome mandates that factors besides crowding itself must be identified to account for results. Behavioral and physiologic attributes that the organism brings to the situation may play the critical role.

Cassel pointed to a collection of factors that modify the effects of crowding. These factors buffer the effects of the independent variable and thereby alter outcome. For example, there is much less crowding induced illness among animals raised in crowded conditions than in animals introduced to the situation in adult life (Kessler, 1966). A possible analogue is the higher incidence of lung cancer in farm-born persons who migrate to cities than in the city-born even when the major known risk factor, cigarette smoking, is controlled (Haenzel et al., 1962). Such data suggest that a chronologically evolving biological adaptation plays a role in modulating the effects of stressors. Social factors also have been identified and chief among them is degree of group affiliation and familiarity. Shock induced stomach ulcers in rats, for example, are strongly affected by group membership: rats shocked in the company of litter mates show lower ulcer rates than do rats shocked in isolation (Conger et al., 1958). Human analogues can again be suggested but are complicated by confounds. The incidence of tuberculosis, for example, is higher in the socially isolated (Brett & Benjamin, 1957).

Cassel concluded:

A more adequate formulation would hold that risk consequences will be dependent on 1) The importance or salience of the interpersonal relationships that become disordered; 2) The position of the individuals experiencing such disordered relationships in the status hierarchy; 3) The degree to which the population under study has been unprepared by previous experience for this particular situation (i.e. has had sufficient time to adapt); and 4) The nature and strength of the available group supports. (1974:294)

This formulation is representative of recent efforts to refine the meaning of stress as it relates to disease, suggesting as it does that the variable, crowding, conceptualized simply in terms of density is too gross to have predictive value.


### DEVELOPMENTAL EVENTS

The effect of early life experience on later manifestation of disease has been studied using a variety of animal species, stressors, and dependent variables. Differential disease incidence in apparently similar organisms placed in the same experimental conditions may reflect developmental differences, as well as genetic variability. As Ader noted, given the concept of multicausation, a search for developmental risk factors seems a logical undertaking and might serve to specify in more explicit terms the innate differences sometimes invoked to explain outcome variability (1975).

An early study by Wolf serves as a paradigm for this type of research (1943). Rat pups were submitted to either temporary blindness or temporary deafness for the developmental period 15–25 days. Subsequently, they were compared with each other and with controls in two learning tasks, one sight cued, the other sound cued. All animals were able to learn the discrimination. Subsequently, they were paired in a competitive task. In this situation, the effect of early deprivation clearly emerged: the sight deprived did better in the auditory task and the hearing deprived did better in the visual task. Thus, though both groups of animals were able to master the task in isolation, their early experience put them at a competitive disadvantage, impairing their ability to cope with a specific class of environmental demands. Deprivation later in development did not have this effect.

This study illustrates several important points. First, different types of stress cannot be viewed as equivalent. Second, the effect of stressors in later life is dependent upon the way the dependent variable is assessed. Finally, the point during development at which the stressor is applied determines its subsequent effects. In looking at the literature on developmental stress and subsequent disease incidence, these three points must be borne in mind for there is a distinct tendency to view stress as a single response and stressors as equivalent. Apparently conflicting results thus may simply reflect the fact that different conditions have been employed though similar words are used to interpret the results.

A sizable literature addresses the relationship between early stress and subsequent development of gastric lesions in the rat. As Ader noted, this is an especially interesting animal model because the lesions are similar to ulcerous lesions in man, they occur fairly readily in the rat, and they are demonstrably affected by a complex of variables—psychological, social, and physiological (1975).

Two studies found an interaction between early life stress and subsequent social living circumstances in determining the incidence of gastric lesions in the face of subsequent stress. In the first study stress in the form of handling or electric shocks was applied between birth and weaning (Ader, 1965). Controls received no stress. Subsequently, the rats were housed individually or in groups. Physical immobilization, a stressor used by Selye and many others, was applied for a period of 18 hours once the rats were mature. They were sacrificed. The group housed animals tended to have more lesions than the individually housed. In addition, however, the effect of early stress showed an interaction with housing in that early handling led to fewer lesions relative to both shocked rats and controls, but only among rats housed individually. A second study found a similar result in the offspring of female rats manipulated or not manipulated during pregnancy. Offspring of the handled females were more susceptible to lesions, but there was an interaction with housing (Ader & Plaut, 1969).

NOISE

The idea that environmental noise is stressful has enjoyed wide popular support for some years. Federal programs addressed to the problem of noise pollution are in place and a conference concerning the topic was convened by the American Speech and Hearing Association in 1969 (Ward & Frick, 1969). A number of American cities have noise abatement programs in effect (Anderson, 1970) and there is a flourishing legal commerce in noise complaint suits, particularly around airports (Hildebrand, 1970). Among researchers, however, there is far from universal agreement that noise per se is either stressful or deleterious to health, aside from causing deafness at very high levels. The usual explanation offered for this lack of effect is the adaptability of the human organism: "Man should be able, according to this concept, to adapt physiologically to his noise environment, with only transitory interference effects on pyschological and mental and motor behavior activities during this period of adaptation" (Kryter, 1970:287). Yet the conviction that noise is bad for people persists, and it is worth looking at some research on the subject.

Glass and Singer reported on an extensive series of studies examining the effects of noise on psychological function (1972). While health status was not specifically addressed in this work, the results have some relevance if one takes the point of view that stress is both a consequence of noise and a factor in disease. The studies used volunteers who performed a variety of tasks in a controlled environment, with the independent variable of noise manipulated as to intensity, frequency, and predictability. A number of interesting results emerged, some of which go against conventional ideas on the relationship between noise and performance.

In general, Glass and Singer did not find noise per se to interfere with performance on motor or cognitive tasks among college students as well as older subjects. The study did not address the issue of chronic exposure to noise, but the finding that subjects readily adapted to acute noise levels makes the assumption that chronic noise impairs psychological functioning quite suspect. On the other hand, by changing task characteristics or by altering the cognitive context in which noise is experienced, deleterious effects on performance can be demonstrated. Continuous vigilance tracking tasks, for example, show this effect, and unpredictability or lack of control over the noise contributes to its negative effects. "These findings underscore the importance of cognitive factors in mediating the effects of noise on behavior, for unpredictability and uncontrollability are extrastimulus variables" (Glass & Singer, 1972:156). As we found earlier, stressors and their effects are dependent upon context and subjective evaluation to a significant degree. The variable of uncontrollability is especially interesting. In addition to playing a role in task degradation, this variable also had negative effects on posttrail performance. By manipulating the subject's sense of control, poststimulus effects could be modified even when the noise was actually uncontrolled. The critical variable thus appears to be the subject's belief that he has control. Glass and Singer also presented evidence suggesting that physiological arousal to noise is reduced by the control experience and that this arousal habituates more readily under these circumstances. The issue of mastery versus helplessness, arises. Glass and Singer commented that their findings, while obtained in the context of noise research, may be simply one instance of a general attribute of stressors—the sense of helplessness in the face of changing environmental events is inherently stressful.

Glass and Singer examined only the acute effects of noise on psychological performance in humans. Studies of chronic effects in both humans and animals are difficult to interpret. The human studies are epidemiologic in character and subject to numerous confounds. In the case of animal work, we must reason by analogy and these analogues are sometimes forced. Be that as it may, several studies on the chronic effects of noise are revealing.

In the 1940s two studies appeared that related long-term exposure to noise to chronic disease in the Norwegian rat. Farris and associates employed blasts of air as the stimulus and obtained hypertension in 10 of 12 subjects, with no hypertension in controls (1945). Yeakel obtained a similar result with rats subjected to air blasts five minutes per day for a year (1948). In the last two months mean systolic blood pressure was

154mm Hg, as compared to 113mm Hg at the outset, and in some of the rats significant elevations were also seen in diastolic blood pressure. Blood pressure of control rats was virtually unchanged over the year.

Studying a human industrial population, Jansen found increased circulatory, cardiac, and equilibrium problems in workers in noisier environments, but numerous confounding variables can be identified that also differentiated the high- and low-noise groups (1961). Cohen reported increased autonomic reactivity, irritability, and social dysfunction in noisy conditions (1969). In a more recent study, Cohen compared workers in more or less noisy working conditions in two different plants (1973). He looked at the number of diagnosed medical problems and the number of on-the-job accidents over five years. In one plant, high noise was associated with significant increases in both dependent variables, but not in the other plant. The plants differed in their production activities and Cohen suggested that association with risk of injury, rather than noise itself, may be the critical factor.

A study by Carlestam and associates (1973) bears some relation to Glass and Singer's finding in their 1972 study that annoyance and performance effects are not precisely covariate. Looking at the effect of noise in the workplace, Carlestam and colleagues reported that feelings of distress and fatigue increased as noise increased from 76 to 94 db. However, simultaneous evaluation of urinary epinephrine and norepinephrine failed to show a relationship with noise level, suggesting that autonomic activation was not correlated with the subjective report of distress and fatigue.

In 1976 Kryter summarized the data on health and noise:

> The question of the existence of extraauditory health problems in industry because of noise must, I believe, remain open until studies are completed in which personnel selection procedures, socioeconomic status and other factors (such as differential bodily injury hazards in different quiet versus noisy work situations) related to the general health conditions of the workers before and during employment are more fully understood and controlled. (P. 543)

Tarnopolsky and McLean also reviewed the relationship between noise and health defined both medically and psychiatrically (1976). They reached the same general conclusions as the other writers cited: "Deafness apart, there is no common illness that has yet been shown to be caused by noise" (p. 98–99). They pointed out, however, the interesting possibility that a subsample of the population may be particularly sensitive to noise. Hypertensives, for example, do not show the ready adaptation of the cardiovascular system to noise characteristic of nonhypertensives (Arguelles et al., 1970). Thus, while in most people there is an initial vasoconstriction and rise in blood pressure with noise presentation, this response habituates and therefore has no likely pathological significance. Among hypertensives, however, this adaptation does not seem to occur and hence noise may put these people at risk.

Is it possible now to reach any general conclusion on the relationship among environmental events, stress, and disease? Beyond the acknowledgment of some sort of relationship, all one can say is that we are now in a position to ask better questions since we know some of the variables that are likely to be relevant. This is no small achievement and major credit for it must lie with Selye, Wolff, and other writers who pointed to a relationship between the subject's general adaptive capacities and the genesis of disease at a time when the field generally favored specific etiologic models couched in wholly physiological terms.

## Applied Research on Stress

Granted the present understanding of the genesis of any stress related disease is incomplete, preventive and therapeutic intervention has been elaborated relying usually on analogous reasoning. I discussed the behavioral treatment of hypertension in chapter 4. Here a strategy to modify type A behavior is described.

Roskies and associates published the first study on a community recruited sample of well type A men (1978). In this study, 25 men were randomly assigned to either psychotherapy or behavior therapy conditions. The subjects were recruited through newspaper and radio advertisements and were screened on the basis of demographic characteristics associated with the type A pattern. The subjects were between the ages of 39 and 59, were employed full-time in a professional or executive capacity, and were earning more than $25,000 per year. In addition, potential subjects were given the Rosenman interview and had to show a strong type A pattern (Type $A_1$) to be included in the study. A commitment to at least 12 of the 14 treatment sessions was required and a deposit of $100 was used to substantiate this commitment. Finally, inclusion in the program was contingent on no evidence of coronary disease on the basis of clinical examination and stress EKG. Comparison of this sample with a preexisting type A sample (Howard et al., 1976) showed the present subjects to be somewhat more health conscious and in somewhat better physical condition, a not surprising fact since they were self-referred and hence presumably interested in the problem of behavior and heart disease. Their serum cholesterol and triglyceride levels, for example, were somewhat lower and a very small percentage (4%) were cigarette smokers as compared with 41% of the comparison sample. Regular exercise was more frequent in the experimental sample.

The psychotherapy condition (13 subjects) was conducted along traditional lines. The therapists worked from a psychodynamic paradigm and formulated their treatment hypotheses and goals on the basis of psychological tests (Rorschach, MMPI) and observation of the patient in therapy. The therapists stressed family dynamics during the patients' childhood as central to their exhibiting the type A pattern. The treatment goal "was to provide both a corrective emotional experience—using a male and female therapist as role models—and an awareness in the men that their current behavior was the replaying of an out-dated family script" (Roskies et al., 1978:210).

The behavior treatment group (12 subjects) was more casual in atmosphere and was oriented along skill learning lines. Jacobsonian relaxation and record keeping were the major modalities. During sessions, the men were trained in muscle relaxation and were assigned homework consisting of two 15-minute daily sessions. Record keeping was used to make the men more aware of their tension level during the day and better at discriminating high from low tension and identifying precipitating events. The relaxation response was to be used to reduce tension in a variety of circumstances.

At the end of the treatment program, all clinical studies were repeated. These included physiological parameters, a survey of life activities, and a series of psychological tests. Of the psychological measures, the measures of general health (Goldberg, 1972), of sense of life satisfaction, and of time pressure all showed changes in the healthier direction as a function of treatment; the treatments were equal in effect. Of the physiological variables, serum cholesterol is of particular interest. Nineteen patients showed drops in serum cholesterol. Eight behavioral therapy cases were initially in the intermediate- or high-risk range (220mg/100ml or higher); six had decreased to the lowest category after treatment. Seven men in the psychotherapy group initially fell in the high-risk category but only two dropped to low risk. Interestingly, overt behavior as assessed by interview showed no significant changes in either group. Body weight rose slightly in the psychotherapy group but dropped slightly in the behavior therapy group; the interaction was significant.

This study is interesting and important in a number of respects. First, it represents primary prevention in a topic that has tended mainly to be approached either from an interventionist point of view or from the vantage point of secondary prevention. Vast sums of money and effort are expended on the heart attack patient. Ultimately, however, resolution of the current epidemic of coronary disease must be preventive, addressing the entire range of identified risk factors. The Roskies study represents a promising beginning at primary prevention. Second, overt behavior, as assessed by the survey of life, health, and recreation habits, and serum cholesterol, were apparently dissociated in this study. The psychological intervention lowered serum cholesterol presumably by modifying subjects' mode of reacting to events, yet their surface behavior remained constant. Earlier studies on the relationship between emotion and serum cholesterol have relevance here. Friedman and co-workers found that serum cholesterol was related to variations in stress at the workplace (1958). It may be that in the Roskies study new modes of dealing with stressful events explicitly taught in the behavioral group altered the subjective response to stressors and thereby reduced serum cholesterol level. This finding, if replicated, has the utmost importance because modification of the work environment is impossible to achieve in many cases. Thus, altering the subject's response to the environment may be the only way to reduce a risk factor for coronary disease, in this instance, serum cholesterol.

Obviously, much work needs to be done in this area. The Roskies study is flawed by a lack of nontreated controls and long-term follow-up, small sample size, and population homogeneity. Moreover, two different treatment methods, proceeding from contrasting paradigms, had only slightly different effects. Analysis of technique efficacy in relation to patient characteristics is critical.

## Conclusion

In this Chapter, the concept of stress as it relates to physical illness was reviewed. The most significant point to be made is that the mechanisms relating environmental events termed stressors to disease states are exceedingly complex. Basic research with both animal and human subjects is beginning to elucidate these mechanisms, but wholly successful preventive strategies will not emerge until this process is further along. In the interim, some useful and promising innovations have occurred and it seems reasonable to expect that a growing awareness of stress as a risk factor in disease will lead to healthier life styles.

# 13

# Substance Abuse

## Alcohol

Alcohol abuse is a health problem of truly monumental proportions. Over 100 million Americans consume alcohol. The estimated number having problems associated with drinking varies: the National Institute of Alcohol Abuse and Alcoholism (NIAAA) estimated that there were 9 million alcohol abusers in the United States in 1972; the present figure is probably near 12 million, with 200,000 new cases identified annually (Davison & Neale, 1978). The problem is much more common in men than in women, though estimates of drinking problems in women are undoubtedly low—the relative privacy of the home allowing the problem to be more effectively hidden among female homemakers (as women enter the work force, greater numbers of female alcoholics are being identified).

Adolescent problem drinking has dramatically increased in recent years. The NIAAA reported that the proportion of high school aged people who have been drunk at least once rose from 19% before 1966 to 45% in 1975 (Noble, 1978). The proportion of adolescents intoxicated at least once a month increased from 10% to 19% in the same period. Among college students the figures are analogous but higher. These statistics augur ill for the future since problem drinking in late adolescence and young adulthood presages alcohol problems in later life (Cahalan & Room, 1974).

The costs of the disorder to society are staggering by any calculation. Lost work days, highway fatalities and accident related disability, family disruption and resultant juvenile problems, and the direct medical complications of alcohol abuse add up to an annual figure in the tens of billions of dollars. Current estimates of the total expenditure for mental health services alone run to $15 billion annually for patients with alcohol problems (Bowers, 1977). Total costs of alcohol related problems were estimated by the NIAAA at $43 billion in 1975 (Noble, 1978). Finally, almost a third of all arrests made in the United States are for public drunkenness and alcohol is implicated in over half of all violent crimes.

Alcohol is potentially addicting. That is, most persons who regularly use alcohol in large quantities will experience tolerance, or decreasing effectiveness of a given dosage, and withdrawal when ingestion is stopped. Withdrawal refers to a pattern of physiologic response to the lack of a substance to which the metabolic processes of the body have become adjusted. In alcohol, the syndrome includes tremors involving the limbs, head, and tongue, subjective feelings of agitation, and motor hyperactivity. The reaction ranges in severity from a hangover to the syndrome known as delirium tremens (DTs), a very serious condition with a mortality rate of about 20%. As the condition's name suggests, the patient has extreme tremulousness and delirium, with delusions and hallucinations of the most frightening variety. The syndrome, which may last from a couple of days to as long as a week, is followed by profound sleep. Seizures sometimes occur as part of the withdrawal syndrome and about a third of those who have seizures will go on to manifest the full delirium tremens sequence.

The issue of addiction to alcohol and the definition of the term "addiction" are complicated and controversial issues. There is debate, for example, as to whether addiction is necessary for a diagnosis of alcoholism. Likewise, the two physiological attributes of addiction, tolerance and withdrawal, occur in less severe form among persons whom no one would call addicts by any definition of that term. The point is that addiction seems to be a continuum: one is tolerant to varying degrees.

The acute effects of alcohol on behavior have been frequently described and are known to most people from personal experience. Alcohol is readily absorbed from the gut and circulates in the blood to all parts of the body. Alcohol has caloric value but contains no other essential dietary substances and does not require digestion—it enters the bloodstream in pretty much the same form it enters the mouth. The conventional method of describing the amount of alcohol a person has consumed is to evaluate the concentration of alcohol in the blood or the blood alcohol level (BAL), a figure often expressed as milligrams per milliliter (mg/ml) of blood. A BAL of .10 means that the subject has a one-tenth of a milligram of alcohol for each milliliter of blood. BAL values cannot reliably be related to psychological and behavioral effects, however, because there are large individual differences. Among tolerant alcoholics, apparently normal psychological functions can be maintained with considerable increments of BAL.

Alcohol is a depressant drug, inhibiting central nervous system activity. The phylogenetically newest centers are affected first, causing disinhibition as the frontal lobes shut down. The cerebellum is also particularly susceptible to alcoholic depression, as motor and speech difficulties demonstrate. High dosages of alcohol can cause death by depression of the respiratory center.

Chronic use of alcohol has deleterious effects on almost every body system. Alcoholics are at increased risk for cardiomyopathy, gastrointestinal bleeding, hepatitis and pancreatitis, anemia, impotence, and a variety of dementias and neuropathies. To what extent these various conditions are produced directly by the toxic effects of alcohol or indirectly by the dietary irregularities that almost invariably accompany chronic alcoholism differs from disease to disease and is not known in every case. In any event, chronic alcoholism is a major risk factor for other diseases and a medical approach to alcoholics is essential for this reason alone, even if one favors other models to account for the drinking problem per se (Norton et al., 1977).

Many definitions for alcoholism have been offered. Each definition makes assumptions about the cause of the disorder and implies a consonant course of treatment. The following discussion describes existing models and definitions of alcoholism and the matter of definition is not trivial. What we view as the attributes of alcoholism determine what will be studied in trying to understand it, and what will be done in trying to treat it. For example, if one views alcoholism as a specific physiological vulnerability to alcohol, one will study the tissue response to alcohol and will advocate abstinence as the only goal of treatment. On the other hand, if alcoholism is viewed as a psychological consequence of childhood experiences, psychotherapy will be advocated as treatment and family transactions will be scrutinized and researched. Finally, if a definition focuses only on current descriptions of behavior, little guidance is given for etiological research, while treatment may be behavioristic in character, focussing in the particular case on the descriptors making up the definition.

## MODELS AND DEFINITIONS

### Moral Model

The moral model, probably the oldest view, holds that drinking is due either to failure of the will in the individual or to the influence of an external evil force, either a spirit (as in possession models) or alcohol itself (demon rum). The contemporary manifestation of this point of view usually stresses personal failure or willful sin as opposed to possession. The alcoholic is viewed as personally responsible for the problem; hence, punitive social response, say, a drunk tank, is considered legitimate, even necessary. We generally think that the moral model has been supplanted in Western culture by the medical. However, this is only partially true: excessive drinking among the middle class and the affluent is treated as a medical problem, but the poor and disenfranchised, those charged with public intoxication, tend to be regarded as reprobates. Even so, the medical point of view is increasingly espoused.

MEDICAL MODEL

Taking a variety of more or less specific forms, the medical model holds that alcoholism is a disease, runs a fairly predictable course, and has a biological origin; that is, the alcoholic is in some way physiologically different from the nonalcoholic, either from birth or from his drinking history, and continued drinking will be fatal to him. At the core of this formulation is the view that alcoholism is a unitary phenomenon and is, for that reason, predictable in course. Jellinek is the single most important advocate of this view, and his *Disease Concept of Alcoholism* has profoundly influenced the field (1960). Although Jellinek saw his model as a working hypothesis, other writers consider the disease concept the final word.

Jellinek described five varieties of alcoholism. The first two constitute diseases: the gamma alcoholic is addicted to alcohol and shows tolerance, withdrawal, episodic abstinence leading to craving for alcohol, and loss of control; the delta alcoholic is similar but, unlike the gamma, drinks continuously. The alpha alcoholic uses alcohol continuously to relieve physical or emotional pain but is not addicted and shows no physical consequences. Beta alcoholism leads to physical complications but not addiction. Epsilon alcoholism is a poorly defined entity characterized by episodic drinking to excess.

Jellinek also outlined a typical course of the disease, broken down into prealcoholic, prodromal, crucial, and chronic phases. The prealcoholic phase entails increasing frequency of relief (alpha) drinking. The prodromal phase includes a variety of symptoms including blackouts. Loss of control marks the crucial phase and chronic alcoholism follows with bender drinking. The person is addicted to alcohol and there is a rather gross and generalized deterioration of function leading to death. This scenario was derived from retrospective reports of Alcoholics Anonymous (AA) members and seems to describe the development of gamma and delta alcoholism, the two varieties Jellinek called diseases.

In arguing for a disease model, Jellinek apparently hoped to counteract moralistic points of view and to earn for the alcoholic the right to treatment as opposed to incarceration. Pattison and associates pointed out that legislative and medical response was a major goal; hence, opting for the term "disease" may have been at least in part a tactical move (1977). Certainly the subtleties of Jellinek's distinctions have been lost in more dogmatic statements of the medical model (Mann, 1968).

Under the general framework of the disease model, specific theories have been formulated. Findings of consanguinous incidence of alcoholism in excess of population expectations spawned genetic theories differing as to the inherited variable but usually implying a specific proneness to alcohol addiction due, for example, to metabolic defect (Williams, 1959) or special autonomic responsivity (Wolff, 1972). Theories positing brain dysfunction as causative may include the notion that the neurologic abnormality is inherited (Tarter & Schneider, 1976). To date there is little convincing evidence for a biological factor distinguishing alcoholics from nonalcoholics that cannot be attributed to alcohol use itself. On the other hand, the genetic data strongly support the view that an inherited factor plays a role in at least some alcoholics (Cadoret, 1976). In sum, one would have to conclude that there is a physiological element of some sort operative, though its nature remains obscure.

### PSYCHOLOGICAL MODELS

Psychological models of alcoholism reflect psychodynamic or behavioristic points of view but share a deemphasis on biological factors. Social learning phenomena are seen as causal factors in both these models, though the psychodynamic involves emotional-mental states as explanations for drinking behavior while the behavioristic looks to contemporary environmental contingencies. Etiologic speculations particularly around childhood experiences and the symbolic meaning of drinking are characteristic of psychoanalytic thinking, while the history of reinforcement and the role of alcohol in avoiding negative emotional reactions, notably anxiety, figure in behavioristic models. Treatment methods differ in predictable ways.

The data in support of psychological theories of alcoholism are no more convincing than those supporting a biological hypothesis. Studies of personality find a plethora of abnormalities in alcoholic samples using the MMPI, but within-group variance is unusually large. Alcoholics differ from normals, from other psychiatric patients, and from each other so extensively that Keller remarked: "Alcoholics are different in so many ways that it makes no difference" (1972: 1147). Although a specific alcoholic personality has not been defined, a variety of provocative hypotheses have been generated and may be relevant to particular subsamples.

SOCIAL MODELS

One of the more striking facts about alcoholism is its maldistribution across societies and, within the United States, across demographic groups. Jews, for example, have very low rates of alcoholism; Irish, relatively high. Alcoholism has been more prevalent in France than in Italy, though recent evidence suggests increasing frequency among Italians. Furthermore, the judgment that someone is an alcoholic is made against some prevailing social norm—the American social drinker might be deemed an alcoholic by standards used elsewhere in the world. A number of writers have discussed the role of specific social expectations as contributing factors to the genesis of alcoholism. Cultures differ, for example, in the uses of alcohol that are sanctioned (ritual, convivial, nutritional, medicinal, or utilitarian). According to Bales, a society that supports utilitarian use of alcohol—that is, for personal reasons like feeling relaxed—and also generates high degrees of tension will have a higher rate of alcoholism than will an equally tense society that limits alcohol largely to ritual purposes (1946). Irish and Jewish Americans may exemplify these differing expectations and outcomes.

The social models have produced a great deal of descriptive literature contrasting groups and cultures and identifying risk factors. For instance, Cahalan's survey studies generated important data that previous research methods failed to yield. The usual approach to studying alcoholics had been to examine the inmates of jails, asylums, or hospitals or to elicit retrospective accounts from AA members—in all cases, people who were in trouble because of drinking. This approach produced a portrait of the alcoholic such as Jellinek's (1960). Cahalan, by contrast, surveyed random samples of persons on their drinking habits and experiences. He found that a number of the symptoms thought to be unique to alcoholics were present in the population at large at very high levels of incidence (1970). Moreover, when he resurveyed years later, some of the people no longer had the problem or had additional ones. This research dealt a serious blow to the view that alcoholism follows a predictable course. Cahalan also identified groups at especially high risk for developing alcohol problems, giving quantitative expression to patterns that had previously existed in science only at the level of clinical anecdote.

DEFINITIONS

More recent formulations on alcoholism acknowledge that the condition is probably not monolithic. Jellinek asserted as much in his writing, but the traditional approach that followed his lead lost sight of this point, tending to think of alcoholism as a unitary phenomenon. So viewed, the definition of alcoholism must either be very general or limited to a highly specific subsample of people who get into difficulty with drink. Some authorities have proposed to limit the term "alcoholic" to individuals who show physical signs of addiction, calling others problem drinkers or alcohol abusers (APA, 1980). The alcoholic thus defined manifests a biological problem, addiction, which might or might not reflect an underlying inherited vulnerability.

Davies offered a definition that includes dependence as one criterion: "Alcoholism is intermittent or continual use of alcohol associated with dependency (psychological or physical) or harm in the sphere of mental, physical or social activity" (1976: 72). Note that neither dependence nor harm is essential, but one or the other must be associated with frequent consumption.

Straus elaborated on the problem drinker–alcoholic distinction and provided a useful framework, more specific than Davies's, for thinking about the issue (1973). According to Straus, the population includes three general categories of people classified on the basis of their relationship to alcohol: abstainers; social drinkers; and problem drinkers—social, psychological, or physical harm being the criterion of problem drinking. Problem drinkers are subdivided into those whose drinking is situationally determined or responsive to psychological distress and those who are addicted to alcohol. This latter group have the disease of alcoholism, approximating Jellinek's gamma or delta alcoholic. Over time, particular individuals may manifest different behavior in relation to alcohol, the social drinker becoming addicted or abstinent, for example.

The value of Straus's formulation is that it points out the dynamic nature of the man-alcohol relationship and highlights the need for tailoring therapeutic approaches to the particular relationship. The addicted problem drinker obviously requires a different type of treatment from that of the nonaddicted problem drinker. For the social drinker, primary prevention is an issue since shifts to problem drinking frequently occur. One might be tempted to assume that no problem exists among abstainers, yet Cahalan's data suggest that abstainers are at particularly high risk for developing problem drinking if they begin to drink (1970). The question in this group pertains to factors likely to shift them in the problem drinking direction and to preventive strategies suited to their particular needs and values. Straus emphasized that our understanding of person-alcohol relationships must be highly individualized, that too much alcohol is a relative, not an absolute, amount, and that the determinants of what is too much entail biological, social, and psychological variables operating in a matrix at the center of which sits the individual (1979).

BEHAVIORAL STUDY

Recent studies of drinking behavior under laboratory conditions have shed considerable light on the specifics of response morphology and temporal pattern and their relations to environmental and social factors. Nathan and Lisman reviewed these studies (1976).

In 1964, Mendelson published a report of his work with Mello, the first lengthy, controlled study of drinking behavior in alcoholic men. Ten skid row alcoholics were observed over a 24-day period in a correctional institution. They were provided with straight 86 proof alcohol every four hours, with gradually increasing amounts available, reaching a maximum of 40 ounces per day on the nineteenth day. "Most of their subjects did in fact consume most of or all of the . . . alcohol offered them, confirming clinical lore as to the prodigious capacity of such alcoholics" (Nathan & Lisman, 1976: 481).

Sobell and associates studied the morphology of the drinking response in alcoholics as compared to nonalcoholics in an experimental environment arranged to look like a bar (1972). Three differences emerged between the alcoholic and the social drinker: alcoholics more frequently drink straight as opposed to mixed drinks; alcoholics gulp their drinks while social drinkers sip; and alcoholics more frequently drink to the point of obvious intoxication. Other researchers making observations in the natural environment have reported different patterns of consummatory behavior (Kessler & Gomberg, 1974), and Nathan and Lisman commented that it may be necessary to take a very broad range of environmental (geography, social setting) and subject (socioeconomic status, age) variables into account in analyzing consummatory behavior among alcoholic and social drinking subjects (1976).

Several studies examined alcoholic drinking patterns over time in relation to schedules of reinforcement in a free operant setting. Opportunity to drink was contingent on operant work in a token economy framework. In general results showed that drinking behavior has the same relationship to changing contingencies as do other classes of behavior and, in fact, amount consumed can be rather exquisitely fine-tuned by changing the reinforcement schedule. Furthermore, the availability of essentially unlimited quantities of alcohol did not lead to uncontrolled consumption and oblivion. Rather, subjects exhibited cyclic patterns of working and drinking (Mello & Mendelson, 1970, 1972).

In an interesting variation on this type of study, Nathan and O'Brien put nonalcoholic heavy drinkers in a similar contingency circumstance and found a continuous rather than a cyclical pattern of work and drink (1971). Subjects maintained moderate but continuous levels of alcohol consumption, a pattern "presumed to reflect a drinking behavior outside the laboratory which permitted these men to support themselves by working even while they continued to drink" (Nathan & Lisman, 1976: 484). The cyclic spree pattern of alcoholics precludes regular employment. Nathan and Lisman also described a study of alcoholic women who showed a pattern very like that of the nonalcoholic men—steady, continuous work and drink (1976). This pattern would allow the female alcoholic to maintain a household while continuing to drink.

A series of studies by Nathan and his co-workers examined the relationship between socialization and drinking in alcoholics (1970, 1971). Offering socialization opportunity as an alternative reinforcer to alcohol for operant work, they found that skid row alcoholics almost always chose to drink rather than escape a situation of enforced isolation and even chose increasingly to drink alone when they were not forced to do so as the period of drinking wore on. By way of contrast, skid row nonalcoholics consistently chose to spend a substantial portion of their earned tokens on socialization rather than alcohol (Nathan & O'Brien, 1971). The same was true of the four women alcoholics described by Nathan and Lisman (1976). The alcoholic's preference for isolated drinking is not, however, a universal phenomenon. Bigelow and his co-workers found alcoholics to be consistently more sociable when drinking (1974). Furthermore, contingent isolation following drinking reduced consumption to half of baseline levels in their group. Removal of the contingency caused consumption to return to baseline levels. Possible factors accounting for differences in socialization preference are individual patterns of preexperimental drinking and absolute amount consumed. Socialization seems to decrease as a prolonged drinking bout progresses.

The other side of the socialization coin is social influence: to what extent is alcoholic drinking behavior affected by the behavior of others in the environment? Goldman and colleagues demonstrated a significant effect of group processes on the drinking behavior of four chronic alcoholics (1973). The experiment required the men to make decisions about whether or not to drink every 2 hours for 16 hours per day. Five of these decisions were binding on the group, while three were individual decisions. Consumption was lower during periods governed by group decisionmaking. Other studies also have found very significant degrees of social influence on drinking in alcoholics, arguing against a model of alcoholism based solely on internal processes be they conceptualized as psychological or physiological (Griffiths, et al, 1974).

Caudill and Marlatt employed an ingenious experimental design to study social influence in consummatory behavior of nonalcoholics (1975). Subjects were invited to participate in a taste study. In making taste judgments subjects could consume as much or as little of the substance as they liked. One study evaluated modeling, with subjects observing a model consuming heavily (700ml) or lightly (100ml) or no model at all. The results showed highly significant increases in consumption when the heavy drinking model was employed (Caudill & Marlatt, 1975). Nathan and Lisman commented that this study offers tentative support for the view that parental modeling may play a role in the genesis of alcoholism (1976). Further research on this possibility is necessary, especially to identify the characteristics of the model that facilitate drinking in particular observers.

Several studies have challenged the widely held belief that drinking decreases anxiety and depression in alcoholics. Nathan and his co-workers reported studies showing that anxiety and depression increased as alcoholics drank (Nathan & O'Brien, 1971). Interestingly, however, this pattern did not obtain in women alcoholics (Tracey & Nathan, 1976). Vannicelli found that drinking led to two distinct patterns of emotional response in her sample of 30 male alcoholics, some growing increasingly anxious, some decreasingly so (1972).

In summary, experimental studies on drinking behavior in alcoholics and social drinkers have used innovative methodology to generate objective data on both consummatory response morphology and temporal patterning. The findings point to morphologic differences between alcoholic and nonalcoholic drinking, but such differences are not universal. The research also has demonstrated conclusively that all drinking is to some degree under environmental control and this control can be mediated by social influence or token reinforcement. Comparisons of male and female alcoholics show the latter to behave rather like nonalcoholic men, suggesting that sex is significant in this disorder. Among male subjects, two different relationships between anxiety and alcohol consumption have been identified, possibly another significant subdivision. Finally, in situations of virtually unlimited access to alcohol, drinking to oblivion is not consistently seen, even among skid row alcoholics.

TREATMENT

Alcoholism has been treated with a vast array of techniques that fall into three general categories: drugs, psychotherapy, and behavioral methods. The first two will be only briefly described.

A recent review of drug treatment for alcoholism listed more than 40 preparations (Cole & Ryback, 1976). Some drugs are used to alleviate the symptoms of withdrawal. Disulfiram (Antabuse) and similar agents are used to maintain sobriety by causing a toxic reaction should alcohol be ingested. Finally, drugs are used to complement psychotherapy or to maintain mood where drinking is viewed as a symptom of underlying psychological distress amenable to chemical modification. Neither conventional agents (Valium) nor more experimental ones (LSD) are effective in modifying the long-term pattern of drinking in alcoholics, although recent evidence suggests that lithium carbonate is useful in decreasing alcohol consumption in patients who also show depressive symptoms (Kline et al., 1974).

Alcoholics have enjoyed the benefits (or lack thereof) of every variety of psychotherapy yet conceived. Convincing evidence of effectiveness has not been produced and the literature suggests that outcome is best predicted by premorbid status. That is, alcoholics who are physically healthier, richer, smarter, and more happily married do better than the sicker, poorer, duller, and less socially stable. There is little evidence of differential outcome as a function of type of psychotherapy, though there is some indication that the longer the patient is in treatment the better the outcome. Whether this means that people who stay in treatment drink less because of the treatment or because of personal attributes that in addition to keeping them in treatment also lead to better drinking outcomes is difficult to ascertain.

### OUTCOME EVALUATION

Conceptualizing alcoholism in the traditional manner, as a disease characterized by craving and loss of control and leading inevitably to death, implies only one useful treatment outcome—abstinence. Accordingly, evaluation of treatment methods has tended to view nonabstinent patients as treatment failures.

Pattison and others have criticized this criterion (Pattison, 1977; Pattison, et al., 1977). First, abstinence may not be necessary for all alcoholics. In addition, the emphasis on abstinence may discourage some problem drinkers from seeking treatment. In many programs drinking is ground for dismissal from treatment. As Ludwig remarked, there is a fundamental absurdity to such strictures in that they mandate refusal of treatment to people who show symptoms of their illness (1980). A third consequence of the abstinence criterion is the tendency to view alcohol consumption as the only problem needing attention. Yet the achievement of abstinence may not mean significant improvement in function more broadly viewed (Pattison et al., 1968). The so-called cured alcoholic may cease drinking yet remain unemployed, grossly dependent on the treatment facility or an AA, and cut off from family and friends. This myopic view of treatment outcome proceeds from the traditional model, which equates drinking with deterioration and pays insufficient attention to other aspects of the patient's life; this model also tends to ascribe all the alcoholic's problems to drinking.

Sobell and Sobell designed a comprehensive model of multiple outcome measures, which they used to evaluate their behaviorally oriented

3

5

Substance Abuse 235

treatment program (discussed shortly) (1976). Ten measures are included, allowing an exceptionally fine-grained analysis of relevant variables. Models like these promise better understanding both of the effects of treatment and of the nature of the problems alcoholics present by operationalizing man-alcohol relationships in a multivariate domain.

## BEHAVIORAL APPROACHES

Behavioral treatment of alcoholism has progressed over the years from methods addressed simply at suppressing drinking behavior to broad approaches that include intervention in a variety of problem areas. There has likewise been a shift from classical conditioning models to operant ones, though many of the most recent programs use both approaches. Finally, behavioral methods in recent years have paid careful attention to outcome evaluation and follow-up, again stressing the entire range of problems.

The earliest behavioral treatments used aversive techniques, either electrical or chemical in nature, through which the consummatory response was paired with unconditioned aversive stimuli, the goal being the elicitation of a conditioned aversion response to the stimulus, alcohol. Such methods have a very long history. Benjamin Rush wrote in the nineteenth century as follows:

> The association of the idea of ardent spirits, with a painful or disagreeable impression upon some part of the body, has sometimes cured the love of strong drink. I onced tempted a Negro man who was habitually fond of ardent spirits, to drink some rum (which I had placed in his way) and in which I had placed a few grains of tartar emetic—the tartar sickened puked him to such a degree, that he supposed himself poisoned. I was much gratified by observing he could not bear the sight or smell of spirits for two years afterwards [1943].

More recent work has systematically evaluated aversive methods comparing, for example, shock and emetics or covert sensitization employing imaginal rather than real aversive stimuli. Summarizing the research on aversive techniques, Nietzel and associates commented that "aversion techniques have at best a limited impact on uncontrolled drinking. Therapy-instigated aversions appear to extinguish rapidly, resulting in large decrements of generalization and maintenance of improvements observed or reported at treatment end" (1977: 199). The authors also noted that these methods do not address the other areas in which alcoholics are so frequently deficient—vocational skills, marital adjustment, etc.

Operant approaches proceed logically from observations made in controlled settings that drinking behavior is responsive to environmental contingencies. Accordingly, programs designed to modify the consequences of drinking in the natural environment have been devised and show some success in reducing alcohol consumption. Miller used a contracting strategy to reduce drinking behavior in a 44-year-old man (1972). The program involved reciprocal reinforcing contingencies between the subject and his wife: (1) the husband would drink no more than three drinks per day and in the presence of his wife and would pay $20.00 to his wife if he broke the drinking rule; (2) the wife agreed not to criticize his drinking and to pay $20.00 if she broke the rule; and (3) the couple agreed to show attention and affection toward one another for desired behavior. As a result of this intervention the husband's consumption dropped from a baseline level of seven or eight drinks per day to the contracted level. Follow-up at six months showed continued controlled drinking and marital improvement.

The study by Miller is representative of a number of demonstrations that operant strategies, working in the natural environment, can modify drinking among alcoholics. Significantly, in many of these interventions abstinence is not the treatment goal. Rather, continued consumption at reduced levels, without intoxication, and only in appropriate settings is the treatment objective. This emphasis on controlled drinking is one of the more important contributions of the behavioral approach and reflects the behavioristic focus on response morphology and on environmental as opposed to indwelling factors as determinants of behavior.

The multimodal treatment program of the Sobells exemplifies the behavioral approach (Schaefer et al, 1971; Sobell & Sobell, 1973, 1976; Sobell et al, 1972). Their program offers the patient a choice between abstinence and controlled drinking as the treatment goal. Initial consummatory behavior is studied in an experimental bar setting and extensive historical data are collected. Treatments include aversive conditioning, videotaped feedback of the effects of overindulgence, training in specific behavioral alternatives to drinking, and identification of stimulus situations that lead to excessive drinking in individual patients. Follow-up in this program is extremely diversified, assessing drinking behavior in terms of number of days of excessive consumption, abstinent days, controlled drinking days, and incarcerations. Vocational status is assessed, along with use of other treatment facilities such as AA. Data are corroborated by designated significant others—spouses, employers, or friends. Residential stability is evaluated, as is the patient's status vis-à-vis the motor vehicle department. Finally, physical health is evaluted from the patient's perspective. Research subjects have been followed for periods up to two years and the program has generated promising results when compared to controls treated in the same setting using conventional methods. For example, at two-year follow-up, experimental subjects choosing controlled drinking had spent an average of 12% of the posthospital days drunk, while control subjects had spent 49% of these days inebriated. Experimental subjects choosing abstinence were drunk

20% of the time while controls were drunk 39% of the time. Sixty percent of the controlled drinking subjects possessed a valid driver's license at the end of two years, compared to only 37% of the controls; analogous figures for abstinence subjects were 50% and 29%.

A project reported by Hunt and Azrin also indicated that environmental manipulation can reduce the incidence of abusive drinking in alcoholics (1973). The treatment goal, abstinence, was achieved by 80% of the experimental subjects at the six-month follow-up compared to 20% of the controls. The program included development of vocational, family, and social forces as agents of reinforcement for sobriety, and patients were trained in skills relevant to these areas. For patients lacking families, synthetic families consisting of employers, ministers, or friends were engineered to provide support for abstinent behavior. One particularly interesting innovation was the conversion of a former tavern into a social club where drinking was prohibited, but in which appropriate social behavior was mutually maintained by patients and which allowed the development of friendship relationships outside a drinking context. Counselors regularly visited discharged patients both to provide reinforcement for continued abstinence and to collect follow-up data. This ambitious program had very useful results: in addition to drinking less, experimental subjects were earning more money per month ($255 versus $190), were more socially active, and were functioning more effectively in their marriages.

These two projects exemplify the new look in behavioral approaches to alcoholism. They include a broad range of services and assess effects in a multidimensional way. They employ a variety of treatments for alcohol consumption behavior and do not rely on one-shot methods like aversive conditioning. The Sobell and Sobell format is flexible as regards treatment goals, allowing controlled drinking as an alternative to abstinence. Finally, both approaches are meticulous in specifying outcome variables, often employing sources of information besides the patient. Summarizing the status of behavioral treatment, Miller made these same observations and added:

> Eventually, specific behavioral treatment packages for different sub-groups of alcoholics must be developed . . . the eventual goal would be to match up patient characteristics with specific treatment strategies to predict the most parsimonious (in terms of time, money, and personnel) and most efficacious treatment for each individual alcoholic. (1976: 681)


PREVENTION

A more fundamental issue than treatment is the prevention of problem drinking. One heuristically pertinent tactic is education. People are profoundly ignorant about the facts of alcohol use and the dangers of abuse. Programs of alcohol education in the public schools and in the workplace promise a preventive yield, particularly if resources are made available to individuals who are concerned about their drinking. A number of major corporations have taken enlightened steps along these lines, providing diagnostic and treatment services to employees so that drinking problems can be addressed before they so impair performance as to mandate dismissal. The U.S. armed forces also have made strides along preventive lines, yet, as Straus pointed out, little attention has been paid to the possible role of the workplace in generating alcohol problems:

> In contemporary industrial society, there are many jobs that demand more skills, or impose greater responsibilities, than most human beings can comfortably or healthfully maintain on a continuing basis. When men and women are promoted to positions beyond their level of competence or beyond a level of human endurance, they often suffer great physical and emotional discomfort and stress because of the very jobs that symbolize their success. Alcohol provides a convenient, quickly effective, temporary, and often dangerous antidote for their discomfort.
>
> A much larger segment of the working force includes men and women who find themselves at a plateau in their jobs beyond which they can never advance. They may be victims of rapid technological change, corporate policy, or their own incompetence, but they work in a society that places strong moral value on job promotion and advancement as symbols of success. In the face of these prevailing values, many workers experience a kind of anomie. Their jobs become empty, meaningless, and intrinsically unsatisfying; they often feel little identification with the purpose or product of the work, no loyalty, and no sense of pride. For those whose jobs become hateful necessities, alcohol offers a chemical antidote. Still other aspects of work that can contribute to problem drinking are job associated situations that are perceived to require drinking—such as selling, attending conventions or demonstrating appropriate conviviality. (1976: 211)

These are cogent observations and bring to attention the fact that the current epidemic of problem drinking may reflect fundamental social problems and dislocations, the solution of which goes beyond the ken of medicine or psychology and to the core of the social and political realities of contemporary life.

A group of Canadian alcohol researchers addressed the macrosocial issues of problem drinking and advocated social engineering approaches as a method of curbing the incidence of this problem (Popham et al., 1975). According to their unimodal approach to alcoholism, per capita alcohol consumption is continuously rather than discontinuously distributed; that is, if we look at populations, we see not a bimodal pattern with an alcoholic and a social drinking mode but a continuous rise in amount consumed from none to two fifths a day. This observation raises some problems for the view that alcoholics represent a discrete group, different from the normal population. If that were true, we would see a bimodal rather than a unimodal distribution, an abrupt change in consumption rate in alcoholics as compared to everyone else. The Popham thesis also argues that if alcoholic drinking represents simply the extreme of a continuous distribution, the way to reduce the frequency of alcoholism is to shift the whole curve in a downward direction. Research by Popham and his colleagues has suggested a possible mechanism through which to effect this shift.

Although profound social change may be necessary optimally to resolve the drinking epidemic (Straus, 1976), actions short of gross social change but operative at the social system level might have useful effects in the short run. Popham and co-workers analyzed the effects on the incidence of alcoholism of various government measures in societies around the world. They used cirrhosis of the liver as an index of problem drinking. Laws concerning number of liquor outlets, hours of sale, state versus private dispensary ownership, and variety of types of drinking establishments were found to have surprisingly little effect on the prevalence of alcoholism. One variable, however, affected incidence systematically: relative price. Put simply, as the cost of alcohol rises, the quantity consumed and the incidence of alcoholism decline. Fig. 13-1 shows this relationship for the province of Ontario in the period 1928-1966. The implication is obvious. By manipulating through taxation the price structure of beverage alcohol, government can shift consumption and resultant problems up or down.

It might at first appear that this cost-consumption relationship does not obtain in the United States. The cost of liquor has risen over the past 20 years, but so has consumption. If one considers relative cost, however, a different conclusion emerges. The cost of alcohol has risen, but at a rate far below that of other consumer goods. The six-pack of beer, which cost $1.25 or so 10 years ago, now costs around $2.25. Hamburger, on the other hand, has risen from something like 40¢ a pound to $2.00. Hence, the American experience does seem to fit the cost-consumption inverse relationship.

Popham and associates concluded:

> In the manipulation of the relative price of alcohol, governments theoretically have at their disposal a powerful instrument to control the prevalence of hazardous drinking and alcoholism. However, at the present time there are apt to be formidable political and emotional obstacles to the use of this instrument. The most practical approach to their removal would appear to be a vigorous educational program designed to generate public recognition of the hazards of heavy consumption, and the preventive value of this mode of control. Price increases would have to be seen as having a protective function and not as just another device of government to increase its revenue. (1975: 142).

**Figure 13-1.** Alcohol price and consumption and liver cirrhosis death rates for Ontario, 1928-1967. Reproduced, with permission, from R.E. Popham, W. Schmidt and J. deLint, The prevention of alcoholism: Epidemiologic studies of the efforts of government control measures. *British Journal of Addictions*, 1975, 70, 125-144.

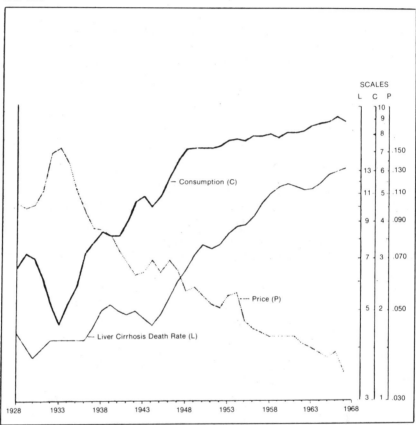

This approach to control, manipulation of relative price, is an action at the level of the social system to control consumption. As such, it must interact with other factors currently in place, for example, laws concerning liquor sales. Also, variations in state and local laws will modify the effect of social system efforts designed to operate through the system as a whole. The phenomenon of local option, for example, introduces complexities into the cost-consumption relationship. Patterns of consumption in dry areas differ from those in wet areas in that dry counties have fewer people who drink alcohol but more people with drinking problems. In general, cost of contraband alcohol is higher or money must be spent in the effort to go get it. This would suggest that relative availability and cost have paradoxical effects on some segments of the population under conditions of absolute prohibition. How changes in relative price in wet areas would affect consumption in dry areas is difficult to say, but the point is that local jurisdictional conditions introduce complexities into the operation of what appears to be a generally valid principle.

The drinking response is complexly determined and it should not surprise us that social mores and legal restrictions affect this behavior in convoluted ways. In research done some years ago, greater numbers of students at colleges with liberal policies toward drinking drank, but fewer of them drank excessively relative to students at conservative institutions, again suggesting that control strategies may have paradoxical consequences (Straus, 1970).

## Conclusion

This section has introduced the rather complex topic of alcoholism. Over recent years, a trend toward multivariate models of this problem, such as that of Straus, have supplanted the traditional unitary point of view in large measure. Likewise, alternative treatment goals have emerged, such as controlled drinking, which appear to be useful in some cases. Work at the macro level in which broad social policy decisions affect drinking patterns have recently been explored and deserve serious attention, admitting that political forces will be a major factor in implementation of such programs.

## Smoking

The history of alcohol appears to be about as long as the history of man. In contrast, the use of tobacco originated with the Indians of the New World and did not appear in Western Europe until after Columbus made his voyage. "Columbus' sailors . . . went on a search for the great Chinese Khan only to find Indian men and women smoking cigars [Van Lancker, 1977, p. 230]." The habit spread quickly through Western Europe as the various colonial powers made contact with the Americas and thence across the world.

### TREATMENT

Smoking has at least two components. First, there is addiction to nicotine. Smoking is an extraordinarily efficient method of maintaining blood nicotine levels. In addition, however, smoking is a complex motor behavior occasioned by a broad range of SDs and maintained by a built-in reinforcing mechanism—the rise in blood nicotine levels, puff after puff. Furthermore, given the short half-life of nicotine in the body, the beginnings of withdrawal are frequently experienced and just as frequently alleviated by smoking behavior, a chain of events exquisitely designed to maintain smoking behavior at a high frequency and to render it very difficult to eliminate even if the addiction can be overcome. Smoking also takes up a great amount of the smoker's time, and if this behavior ceases something must fill the void. Weight gain upon smoking cessation is commonplace. Psychoanalysts interpret this event in terms of orality but perhaps a more general and simple mechanism is involved. If an organism is deprived of one source of reinforcement, it is likely to offer a range of operants in search of another. Since for smokers the denied category of reinforcer followed sticking cigarettes in the mouth, a generalization to sticking food in the mouth seems likely, particularly given the universal history of reinforcement inherent in eating. When one consummatory response is thwarted, another readily emerges.

Viewed in this way, treatment for smoking might profitably address the addiction and the habit aspects as at least partially distinct phenomena. Smokers may well have developed physiological dependence on smoking via addiction, but one suspects that the behavior to some degree takes on a life of its own and this may be what is expressed by the reforming smoker's complaint of having nothing to do with his hands. Habitual nail biters are certainly not addicted to their fingernails, but the behavior apparently has reinforcing properties whose loss is experienced as profoundly disturbing. Something analogous may occur with smokers and might in part account for relapse after years of abstinence, when withdrawal phenomena are clearly absent. One certainly hears of the relapse of ex-smokers during periods of stress—a new job, a move, a divorce—and this pattern is also common in compulsive overeaters. In both cases, the stressor can be viewed as a deprivation of reinforcement, which rekindles an old habitual source of reinforcement, say, smoking, eating, or nail biting. In the case of smoking, however, re-addiction occurs, with all its physiological complications.

Russell pointed out that getting people to stop smoking has at least two aspects, which are sometimes confused (1977). On the one hand, there is the problem of motivation. People may or may not say that they would like to stop smoking. Obviously the first goal of treatment is to instill the wish to give up cigarettes. Assuming that the patient is motivated to stop, the problem is to overcome his dependence on cigarettes. Russell commented that confusion of these two problems may result in inappropriate patient-treatment combinations. For example, people who go to the trouble of coming to smoking clinics are obviously motivated, yet the treatment they often get is aimed to develop motivation—which these patients presumably already have. Experimental techniques directed at altering dependence are characteristic of research studies applied to college students, yet many of these students do not feel a strong motive to stop and, given their youth, may be minimally dependent; for them, motivational variables probably do need to be addressed.

Raw reviewed the treatment modalities applied to help people cease smoking (1977). These include a variety of drug treatments and the range of behavioral methods from aversive conditioning to hypnosis.

Drug based approaches fall into two general categories, nicotine substitution or tranquilization. The former approach entails giving a nicotine congener or nicotine itself via some route other than smoking. Such methods have had only modest success. Tranquilizers seem quite useless as a treatment for smoking. Psychotherapy of every kind has been tried with smokers and a number of self-help groups have formed more or less outside the official medical-psychological chain of command, rather like AA. The literature on the treatment of smoking seems to show little differential effect as a function of type of treatment; that is, no technique has been reliably demonstrated to exceed attention-placebo controls in reducing smoking behavior. On the other hand, most treatments including attention-placebo are superior to no treatment.

The failure of nicotine substitution seems relevant to the distinction made earlier between addiction and habit. Substitution addresses the addiction but does nothing for the habit. The negative results have also been interpreted pharmacologically by suggesting that nicotine interacts with tar to yield addiction; hence, nicotine substitution alone would be expected to have no success on pharmacological as well as psychological grounds. Oral administration without smoking of both tar and nicotine as a treatment for smoking would seem a critical test of the pharmacological hypothesis. If smokers on such a regimen persisted in smoking, the role of habit over and above addiction would be supported. Tranquilizers would not be expected to affect addiction except to cross-tolerant drugs, of which nicotine is not one.

Behavioral approaches to smoking cessation have been heavily weighed in the direction of aversive techniques. Shock has been especially popular; the most common approach is a pairing model that generates aversion to smoking related stimuli. A number of studies have shown high rates of abstinence following treatment (Pope & Mount, 1975), but control studies have found that the shock need not be contingent to achieve the same result, which puts a classical conditioning interpretation in considerable doubt. The use of imaginal rather than real shocks seems to work about as well, and neither method is superior to supportive placebo treatments (Sipich et al., 1974).

Two widely publicized aversive methods deserve discussion. Wilde (1964), Franks and co-workers (1966), and Lublin and Joslyn (1968) have all employed blowing hot, smoky air in the subject's face as an aversive stimulus to counteract smoking. Some promising results were reported but they seem not to be specific to the technique. Grimaldi and Lichtenstein, working initially with hot, smoky air, went on to develop rapid smoking (1969). As the name suggests, the subject is required to smoke extremely rapidly, say, inhaling every six seconds. This leads to nausea, which leads to a break, then to more rapid smoking. Abstinence rates with rapid smoking initially were higher than those in support control groups (Lichtenstein et al., 1973), but Raw stated that as the technique is replicated the apparent specificity of treatment is shrinking such that support controls do as well as rapid smokers vis-à-vis abstinence (1977). Danaher reviewed the rapid smoking literature and argued that procedural deviations may account for the failure of some replications to achieve results comparable to the initial findings (1977). Pechacek and McAlister stressed the importance of a warm therapist-client relationship, persistence, and treatment flexibility in attaining success with techniques of this type (1979).

Hypnosis has been employed to reduce smoking with varying results. West reviewed the topic and concluded that there are a sufficient number of positive outcomes to justify hypnosis in treating smoking (1977). However, not all people can be hypnotized and the method requires the availability of suitable professionals and may therefore be costly. Hypnosis seems most useful as an adjunct to other forms of treatment, though some studies of single-session hypnosis have reported significant reductions in smoking (Spiegel, 1970). Raw concluded that firm inferences vis-à-vis hypnosis for smoking cannot be drawn because of methodologic problems with the various studies (1977), and Pechacek reached a similar conclusion (1979).

A number of self-control procedures have been developed more or less from operant ideas of controlling behavior by manipulating its consequences. Azrin and Powell designed a cigarette case that delivered shock when it was opened, but subjects tended to abandon the case (1968). Another method is to smoke on a random schedule determined by a mechanical timer; the rationale here is to break up the various SD-smoking response bonds that normally occasion smoking behavior and thus to reduce its frequency (Shapiro et al., 1971). Raw described success with these methods as modest leading only to a reduction in frequency, and concluded that the literature lacks definitive evidence for or against a self-control technique (1977). Pechacek also describes the self-control literature as discouraging (1979).

In most of the work on smoking, the goal of treatment has been abstinence. Another possibility is reduced smoking. Several studies have addressed reducing frequency of smoking, depth of inhalation, or puffs per cigarette in the hope of lessening the health hazard even as patients continue to smoke. Getting cigarette smokers to shift to a pipe has been advocated since pipe smokers do not usually inhale.

Frederickson and Simon described an operant approach to training smokers to puff less frequently, to puff more briefly, and to alter the amount smoked per cigarette (1978). Using single-subject designs, the authors reported significant change in smoking behavior generalizing to the natural environment. These changes were documented in reduced carbon monoxide concentrations, a significant health parameter. The authors concluded that given the apparent unwillingness or inability of many people to stop smoking, techniques that reduce the health hazard deserve continued study.

Studies of this type address the habit dimension. Addiction goes on unabated. Hence, one would not expect abstinence to result and it does not. However, adjustment downward may be possible; in other words, smokers may be able to adjust to lower blood levels of nicotine. This expectation seems to violate the concept of tolerance, but for nicotine tolerance seems empirically to be a matter of more or less. That is, smokers do not, in fact, continually increase the dose. Rather, use rises during the initial period of smoking, then settles to a constant intake of a pack or two a day. Thus, it may be possible at least to modify smoking behavior, while not eliminating the addiction, by addressing the habit aspect of the problem.

Another approach to reducing the health hazard in smoking is the production of a cigarette that delivers less carcinogenic tar and less nicotine. Some progress on that score has been made (Wynder, 1977). Figure 13-2 shows the U.S. average consumption of tar and nicotine per person over age 15 from 1950 to 1975. A clear downward trend is evident and is also reflected in an increasing market share for the low tar and nicotine brands. This conclusion is based on sales patterns, however, and may tend to exaggerate the actual reduction of tar and nicotine people consume. That is, people may inhale more deeply and smoke to shorter butt lengths cigarettes with lower tar and nicotine and there is some evidence that this does occur (Jarvik, 1977).

Evidence suggests that nicotine is the addictive substance in tobacco smoke, while tar contains the worst carcinogens. Accordingly, Russell proposed a safer cigarette with drastically reduced tar and middle-level nicotine (1977). Most low-tar cigarettes are also low in nicotine so that the addict tends to reject these brands in favor of brands with higher levels of both nicotine and tar. Empirically, smokers seem unable to go below a per cigarette nicotine yield of 1-1.5mg. Russell therefore argued for a cigarette with much reduced tar but nicotine levels around 1.3 or 1.4mg. If smokers could be induced to switch to cigarettes of this type, the cancer risk should be significantly reduced though the damaging effects of nicotine would, of course, remain. This seems an eminently rea-

**Figure 13-2.**   Changes in tar and nicotine exposure in the U.S. population over a twenty-five year span. Reproduced from E.L. Wynder, Interrelationships of smoking to other variables and preventive approaches. In M.E. Jarvik, J.W. Cullen, E.R. Gritz, T.M. Vogt and L.J. West (editors), *Research on Smoking Behavior: NIDA Research Monograph 17*. Washington, D.C., 1977.

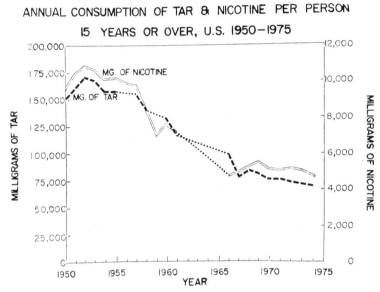

ANNUAL CONSUMPTION OF TAR & NICOTINE PER PERSON
15 YEARS OR OVER, U.S. 1950-1975

sonable approach given the disappointing results achieved thus far in the quest for abstinence.

Certainly every effort should be made to motivate smokers to stop and to help them quit. However, many years of experience in smoking research centers and treatment clinics, as well as massive media campaigns and epidemiologic outcome surveys, reveal that it is exceedingly difficult for smokers to remain off cigarettes. In one report about 80% of ex-smokers were smoking again four years after treatment, and the data include only those who successfully completed the treatment, ignoring a large number of smokers who dropped out along the way (Hunt & Matarazzo, 1970). Given this high relapse rate, specific attention needs to be directed at maintaining abstinence once it has been achieved, yet there is a dearth of studies addressed to this critical problem. Behavioral treatment has generally addressed addiction without addressing alternative behaviors to fill the void when smoking ceases. Curing addiction, even to heroin, while subjectively quite unpleasant is easily achieved by preventing the patient from taking the drug. After withdrawal the person is no longer physiologically dependent. Yet both smokers and heroin addicts characteristically relapse and the reason may well be that the behaviors of smoking or drug taking have not been extinguished and have not been

**Figure 13-3.** Relationships between corrected price and consumption of cigarettes by males in Britain, 1946 to 1971. Solid circles represent number of cigarettes smoked per year; open circles represent price in old pence. Reproduced, with permission, from M.A.H. Russell, Changes in cigarette price and consumption in Britain, 1946-1971, A preliminary analysis, *British Journal of Preventive and Social Medicine*, 1973, 27, 1-7.

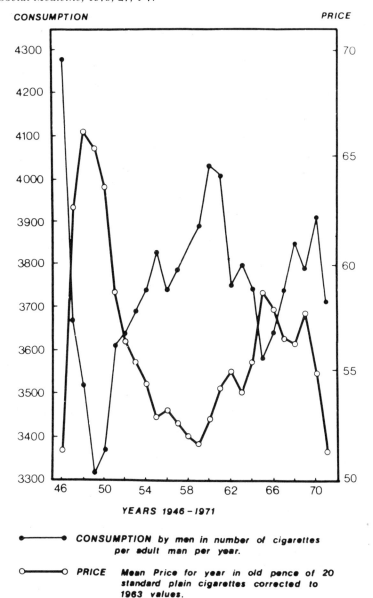

replaced with other, incompatible responses. Future work must attempt to develop such responses.

PREVENTION

Primary prevention is the second major approach to eliminating smoking behavior. Smoking usually begins in adolescence and such variables as parental modeling, peer pressure, and advertising are usually cited as causative factors (Russell, 1971). Education about smoking hazards in the preteenage and teenage years is one method to counteract these influences and demonstration projects with this goal have shown promising results. In one such study, a five-year program led to decreasing incidence of adolescent smoking in the participating schools at a time when adolescent smoking was increasing nationally (Gritz, 1977). Clearly, intervention in the adolescent population is of the utmost importance and health education within the framework of the schools is an obvious avenue to pursue. Such efforts should include systematic study of teaching methods to determine which sorts of information and methods of delivery offer the greatest yield in keeping adolescents off cigarettes.

Government has a role to play in primary prevention. Although the placement of cigarette advertisements is now regulated, the ads themselves continue to portray smoking as glamorous. Restrictions on content raise freedom of speech concerns but truth in advertising is a relevant issue here. The cost of tobacco is a variable that seems to affect consumption, and it could be argued that if cigarettes were extremely expensive that might discourage people from beginning to smoke. Fig. 13-3 (Russell, 1973) shows the essentially reciprocal relationship between cost and per capita consumption, suggesting that raising the price of tobacco might serve a useful purpose in discouraging cigarette use. A potential government role via taxation or soil banking is possible. Government could also prohibit smoking in public places. Such restrictions protect the right of nonsmokers to be in an environment free of tobacco smoke and help shift popular opinion in the direction of viewing smoking as an unacceptable behavior. Given the importance of modeling and peer pressure, it seems likely that a shift toward public disapproval of smoking would have preventive yield.

## Poly Drug Abuse

The abuse of illicitly obtained narcotics receives a great deal of publicity. The intensity of this public awareness may be in excess of the actual health threat that narcotics abuse entails, though intense concern is merited by the social consequences of narcotics addiction. On the other hand, the abuse of prescription medication receives little publicity unless a celebrity is found dead from an overdose of sedatives; yet there is a professional consensus that such abuse represents a major health hazard.

Poly drug abuse, the use of multiple drugs, which may be legally or illegally obtained, is distinguished from both opiate addiction and alcohol abuse, though this behavior may coexist with either or both of these problems. The federal government acknowledged poly drug abuse to be a distinct form of substance abuse in allocating funds for a poly drug project within the Special Action Office for Drug Abuse Prevention (SAODAP). A major study of poly drug abuse involving 12 centers located around the country followed and was reported in *Poly Drug Abuse: The Results of a National Collaborative Study* (Wesson et al., 1978).

Defining poly drug abuse is difficult. Because the category includes legally prescribed drugs, a judgment is required in deciding when medical indications are exceeded. With illicit substances, the tendency is to equate use and abuse, though this leads to some absurd groupings of people who have different drug use patterns and attendant problems. Finally, misuse of legally obtained nonprescription drugs bears only an informal relationship to doctor-patient transactions, rendering it difficult to define nonmedical use. Granting these definitional problems, however, there is a widespread professional perception that people are using psychoactive substances in nonmedical ways with increasing frequency and with negative consequences in many cases (Lennard et al., 1972). Though some challenge this view (Mellinger et al., 1974), it is probably fair to say that concern is increasing over misuse of psychoactive drugs.

Who are poly drug abusers? How many are there? These questions are difficult to answer. Surveys of emergency room contacts in which drugs play a role reveal that the problem crosses racial, social, and economic boundaries in a promiscuous fashion. Likewise, study of patients referred to poly drug programs from a variety of sources shows heterogeneity both between and within groups (Keegan & Schooff, 1978). There is evidence that women are more likely than men to be involved with misuse of prescription medication, but the stereotype of the bored middle-class housewife as the paradigm case in this regard does not withstand scrutiny (Dammann & Ousley, 1978). In short, poly drug abusers are exceedingly varied.

The incidence question also is not easy to resolve. Because the poly drug abuser obtains substances from a variety of sources, it is impossible to evaluate incidence on the basis of supply. Supplies of illegal drugs are not accurately known and prescription drugs find both legitimate and illegitimate use. The Drug Abuse Warning Network (DAWN) keeps national statistics on emergency room drug related events, but these involve only a portion of abusers. Narcotic analgesics and heroin account for only about 10% of these events, while prescription tranquilizers, barbiturates, sedatives, and these drugs in combination with alcohol are seen in about 40% of such patients (Beschner et al., 1978). These data suggest that abuse of prescription drugs is a problem of very large proportions. Lau and Benvenuto employed several statistical and survey techniques to obtain approximations of the prevalence of poly drug abuse, concluding that in excess of 2 million Americans are involved (1978).

OVERPRESCRIPTION

As we have seen, poly drug abuse is a major problem in our society. What causes it? An understanding of etiology facilitates preventive efforts; hence, a search for causal factors is of importance. Several variables have been suggested as pertinent in the etiology of poly drug abuse, and one of them is the prescribing habits of American doctors.

Traditionally, the physician is the arbiter of appropriate use of medication. Therefore, it seems likely that the attitude of physicians toward drug taking may shape attitudes toward the practice in society at large. To the extent that prescription is casual and frequent, patients may come to adopt an accepting attitude toward drug taking. DiMascio outlined several physician behaviors that might contribute to a social view of drug taking as an acceptable way to solve problems or to enjoy oneself (1972). When psychoactive drugs are prescribed for nontreatment reasons, the attitude is conveyed that "drugs are magic means of immediately modifying undesirable behavior and states" (p. 133). In a related vein, prophylactic prescription that has only marginal treatment indication suggests that drugs are an easy way to prevent or avoid unpleasant events.

A number of studies have reported that psychoactive drugs tend to be prescribed more frequently and for longer duration than is necessary (Ray et al, 1980) again, fostering overly optimistic and casual attitudes toward drug taking. Fejer and Smart surveyed Canadian adults who had been prescribed tranquilizers, finding that over 26% of them appeared to be remarkably well (1974). The patients reported good or excellent health with no serious health problem in the preceding 12 months either in themselves of in family members. They had never consulted a psychiatrist or other mental health professional for psychological problems and had not, in fact, seen a doctor during the preceding year. DiMascio also noted that to the extent that doctors prescribe at the suggestion of nonphysicians, be they social workers, psychologists, or patients, a message is conveyed that drug taking is not a matter of much concern (1972).

The tendency to overprescribe is probably nowhere more common than in the area of sleep disturbance. The prevalence of sleep complaints is high, with an estimated 13% of men and 26% of women complaining of insomnia (Hammond, 1964). "In 1977, about four and a half million prescriptions were written for barbiturate hypnotics, . . . twenty one million for non barbiturate hypnotics, [and] this does not include medication given in hospitals" (Institute of Medicine, 1979: 48). Since these drugs figure prominently in suicide attempts and accidental overdose, particularly when used along with alcohol, and since there is increasing evidence that they have a cumulative negative effect on a number of motor performances, a broad range of negative consequences may eventuate from the widespread use of these preparations.

After reviewing the question of sleep medications, a presidential commission made a series of recommendations regarding their use (Institute of Medicine, 1979). In the area of clinical practice, the commission concluded that such drugs are currently overprescribed, often without adequate diagnostic study in either the medical or the psychosocial realm: "As a class of drugs, hypnotics should have only a limited place in contemporary medical practice; it is difficult to justify much of the current prescribing of sleeping medication" (p. 138). Specifically, the drugs should be prescribed only in very limited quantity, say, for a few nights, and refills should be avoided. Patients should also be given much more detailed written information about the hazards and contraindications of these drugs, particularly vis-à-vis their effect on motor abilities (driving), their combined action with alcohol, and the dangers of habituation.

Prescribers should be acutely aware of suicide prevention, particularly in patients with a history of attempts. The inclusion of a small quantity of emetic in sleeping pills to induce vomiting following overdose has been suggested as one method of suicide prevention. From an epidemiologic perspective, much more careful toxicological analysis should be undertaken in drug deaths and motor vehicle deaths to obtain a better picture of the effect of these substances on the public health.

The report also noted that with the introduction of the benzodiazepines (Dalmane, Valium) an overly sanguinous attitude has appeared regarding the hazards of these drugs. While death from overdose is much less likely with these preparations as compared to the barbiturates, their longer half-life and toxic metabolites present other hazards that the barbiturates lack. Furthermore, in combination with alcohol they can be lethal. A more conservative attitude in prescription is clearly warranted; for example, the most frequently prescribed drug, Dalmane, is usually given in 30mg tablets although there is little evidence that this dosage is any more effective than 15mg.

Several factors seem to play a role in the tendency to overprescribe psychoactive drugs. First, physicians are generally reluctant to deal with psychological problems in their patients through psychological means. If a patient seems somewhat anxious, it is much easier to write a prescription for Valium than to explore verbally what the source of the anxiety is and to try to help the patient psychotherapeutically to cope. Many doctors protest that they do not have time to do psychotherapy with every patient, and there is certainly some merit in this argument. Listening takes time. One must note, however, that if a physician is really so busy that he has no time to listen to his patients, he would do well to examine his practice. Perhaps he is seeing too many people either because there are too few doctors in the locale or because he is striving to earn vast amounts of money. Perhaps he is hustling patients in and out of the office in order to avoid dealing with psychological problems—and needs better training in psychology. Given the technological thrust of American medicine currently one cannot be optimistic that the soft side of the curriculum will see expansion. However, it should be possible to counteract the dangerous idea that Valium is an acceptable alternative to psychotherapy and to teach doctors to refer, rather than prescribe, when they sense psychological problems in patients.

The tendency to overprescribe has other roots. For one thing, patients reinforce this physician behavior by taking the drugs and coming back for more. For another, drug companies spend vast sums of money advertising their products, putting on tax deductible conferences in romantic places, and in other ways encouraging physicians to use (prescribe) their products. The unending flood of advertising for non-prescription drugs further encourages drug taking from the perspective of both doctor and patient. If we are, as has been suggested, an overmedicated society, the responsibility is widely shared and corrective action will perforce be multidimensional. Far better health education for the public seems an integral part of this effort.

TEENAGE DRUG TAKING

The adolescent poly drug abuser is of special interest for two reasons. First, adolescents are the responsibility of their parents; hence, their illicit behavior inevitably involves persons other than themselves. This factor acts synergistically with normal parental concern for their children to focus attention on the drug taking behaviors of teenagers. Adolescent drug abuse is additionally troublesome because patterns of behavior established in this period tend to persist in adulthood.

Kandel outlined two general approaches to the question of why adolescents take drugs (1974). The first is intrapsychic in character and emphasizes traits like anxiety or depression, which drugs are supposed to relieve, or impulsiveness, which is supposed to cause drug taking. The second approach is social and looks for contextual events that lead to drug abuse in teenagers. In this regard two groups have been singled out as particularly significant—parents and peers.

A number of writers have argued that a major determinant of adolescent drug taking is the pill taking, alcohol drinking behavior of their parents (Mellinger, 1971). Others have been impressed with the influence of peers as sources of drugs and as models of drug taking behavior. This view describes a drug subculture with distinct values among which drug taking plays a prominent role (Goode, 1972). These points of view conflict in that the first sees parents as models who are imitated while the latter sees parents as persons against whom the adolescent rebels in joining a subculture deviating from parental values.

Kandel surveyed over 8000 high school students in a two-wave format that employed subjects and their best friends (1974). Surveys were also made of the parents of the selected children. Both groups were asked about their own and the significant other's drug and alcohol use. The survey found that parent and peer influence had synergistic effects, though peers exercised far greater influence. About 25% of adolescents whose mothers never used psychoactive drugs smoked cannabis, while over 35% of adolescents whose mothers used three psychoactive drugs smoked cannabis. By contrast over 60% of adolescents whose best friend used the drug also did so, while only about 15% of adolescents whose best friend did not use the drug did so. Summarizing the study, Kandel noted:

> A necessary condition for the appearance of adolescent illegal behavior may be the use of illegal drugs by friends. Parental use of psychoactive drugs, or alcohol, may be neither necessary nor sufficient for such adolescent behavior to develop. But given a situation in which peers use drugs, parental behavior becomes important in modulating peer influence. (p. 235)

PREVENTION

The unimodal approach discussed in relation to alcohol has also been applied to the problem of drug abuse (Smart, 1977). The unimodal approach, it will be recalled, posits a continuum ranging from no use through varying degrees of increasing use to abuse, the last involving a relatively small number of persons. Data in support of this model have been produced in the area of alcohol consumption and similar data can be shown for drugs. Smart described a series of studies on Canadian high school students that found continuous use distributions that roughly fit the distribution seen with alcohol. Furthermore, abuse and general frequency of use correlated highly. The implication is clear: to decrease abuse it may be necessary to shift the entire curve in the direction of less drug use. For alcohol, price increases are a possible answer. Alternative tactics may be needed in the area of drug abuse.

Establishment of prices for illicit drugs is obviously outside direct governmental control. It may be possible indirectly to raise prices by enforcing distribution constraints and thus driving up price through the normal supply and demand mechanism. However, crime tends to increase as narcotic prices rise; that is, the demand for narcotics is less elastic than the demand for alcohol so that altering price has less effect on consumption. As regards prescription drugs, manipulation of price would serve to discourage use but might be viewed as inhumane given the fact that these drugs have legitimate applications. All this would suggest that control of the problem requires modification of the demand side of the equation. Better drug education and tighter physician prescribing practices might be expected to decrease somewhat the propensity for using drugs. Such efforts would have to proceed in the context of a virtually continual barrage of advertising that encourages the use of drugs for a vast array of problems, including pain, nervousness, sleep difficulty, and overeating. As with tobacco advertising, freedom of speech concerns would be raised in response to any attempt to control advertising that encourages pill taking, issues of truth and falsity of claims aside. From the unimodal perspective, even veridical advertising may have a negative effect because it fosters attitudes that lead to increased use and thus inevitably to abuse of medications. This issue is obviously not easily resolved, but policy regarding drug dispensing and advertising should be made with an awareness that a general phenomenon like social attitude toward drug taking may systematically translate into use and abuse patterns.

## Conclusion

In this lengthy chapter we looked at alcoholism, smoking, and poly drug abuse. The problem of substance abuse is not easily summarized because we are dealing with a heterogeneous collection of specific problems that have to be addressed individually. Nevertheless, several general statements have relevance to at least a significant subsample of patients and problems. First, economic incentives to producers and dealers encourage use of these substances legally or illegally and therefore play a role in beginning and maintaining use patterns. Second, high relative cost discourages consumption; hence, social manipulation of this variable through taxation deserves more serious attention than it has yet received. Third, there is a very long history of either total failure or only marginal success in treating persons with abuse problems. While treatment efforts should and must continue, it is probable that substance abuse will be significantly altered only via preventive strategies. Certainly, substance abuse reflects deep-seated disaffection from the social order generally and/or one's place in it particularly. Ultimately, prevention may entail a restructuring of important aspects of political, economic, and social life, rendering less prevalent the feelings of anxiety and alienation from which drugs offer so costly an escape.

# 14

# Health Maintenance

In this chapter, the health maintenance organization system of care delivery will be discussed because of the HMO's preventive emphasis, as will behavioral dimensions relevent to preventive health care. Programs in prevention focus on modifying lifestyle, the goal being to help people live in a way that reduces their risk of disease and thus increases both quality of life and longevity.

It is important to distinguish between risk factor and cause in relation to the incidence of disease. In science, cause is conventionally used only when it is possible to show experimentally a temporal relationship between one category of event and another so that the introduction of one leads to the occurrence of the other. Because experimental manipulation and control are essential to this definition of cause, cause is inevitably demonstrated under more or less artificial circumstances. The demonstration that introduction of a particular microorganism into the body of a laboratory animal leads to the manifestation of symptoms labeled cholera is a causal demonstration. However, interpretation of this causal sequence in terms of the operation of interorganism relationships outside the laboratory must be tentative. The demonstration of risk is achieved by observation of what occurs in the natural environment. The statement that high blood pressure is a risk factor in stroke means that among large numbers of victims of this disorder, high blood pressure is seen with greater frequency than it is seen in matched groups of persons who do not have stroke. This is not the same as saying that high blood pressure causes stroke; in fact, it is difficult to see how one would go about demonstrating such a causal relationship, even theoretically, since such a procedure would require comparing two samples of people, inducing high blood pressure in one group, comparing the incidence of stroke, and controlling a host of confounding variables. Thus, in this chapter when I talk about efforts to change life style or control diet, it is not cause but risk factors that are at issue.

## Health Maintenance Organizations

As we saw in chapter 2, the central feature of HMO care is prepayment for total or nearly total coverage (Gumbiner, 1975). The economic incentive for the HMO is to avoid use of expensive services such as hospitalization, which goal can be best achieved by keeping the membership healthy. Accordingly, careful annual monitoring of health status is encouraged and is, of course, free to the subscriber, as are inoculations and screening for particular conditions such as cardiovascular disease, breast cancer, or venereal disease. Screening programs can be directed to patients in high-risk occupations or to those with high-risk demographic characteristics, and the HMO's complete data base on all members facilitates this process. Finally, HMOs have been leaders in patient education. While all of organized medicine pays lip service to this function, very little of it goes on in fee-for-service settings because it takes time and is less lucrative than delivering service. Because of the HMO's economic structure, patient education can be cost effective to the extent that it keeps people well and causes them to use fewer services. Physicians' assistants and nurse practitioners can play an increasing role in this educational activity (Rosser & Mossberg, 1977).

Service utilization in HMOs as compared with traditional service delivery models has been studied by a number of workers. Overall results point to more economical health care delivery by the HMOs, due in the main to fewer annual days of hospital utilization in HMO as compared to either indemnity or nonprofit insurance plans (Luft, 1978). Roemer found a lower freqeuncy of elective surgery such as hysterectomy, tonsillectomy, and appendectomy in HMO as opposed to fee-for-service settings, a result that makes perfect sense from the point of economic incentive (1974). He also found that patient satisfaction with service was generally high and that expressed dissatisfactions were not much different from those identified by patients receiving care in other settings.

Overall, then, the HMO appears to be a successful alternative model for health care delivery that is making some contribution to the preventive point of view. However, one must be careful not to overstate the case. As Havighurst commented:

The expression "health maintenance organization" probably promises too much. Medical care is primarily a remedial service, and, while there are some preventive measures . . . that are worthwhile, preventive medicine practiced by providers cannot achieve health benefits even remotely approaching those obtainable from public health measures, over which HMOs will have no direct influence. (1970:71)

While it is true that water purification has a vastly greater effect on disease incidence than anything HMOs currently do, for many diseases that seem to be a consequence of more subtle and individual lifestyle variables, cigarette smoking and overly rich diets being examples, the HMO offers an institutional structure within which to begin work. Furthermore, though medical care is now primarily a remedial service, the HMO provides an institutional framework within which to rethink the meaning of health care. The role of the physician may remain essentially remedial, but the role of the health care system as a whole may shift to preventive concerns.

## Diet

Life insurance acturial data show clearly that the lean live longer than the fat, other things being equal (U.S.D.HEW, 1967). For example, obesity is a risk factor in cardiovascular disease. For such reasons doctors have tried to get patients to lose weight. The usual method for getting weight off is conceptually very simple—one must reduce the number of calories consumed and increase the number used so that there is an intake deficit. When that happens, calories stored in the form of body fat will be used and one will lose weight. When we look at the cumulative professional and nonprofessional effort to control obesity, however, we cannot help noticing that the problem, while theoretically so simple to solve, has turned out to be complicated and intractable. The key difficulty is long-term maintenance of weight loss. As Schachter and Rodin commented: "Almost any fat person can lose weight: very few can keep it off" (1974:1). Behavioral techniques constitute one approach to long-term maintenance.

Behavior modification studies in diet have focused largely on obesity. However, obesity is but one problem in which control of eating is critical. Other conditions in which dietary control is crucial include diabetes mellitus, phenylketenuria, a wide range of allergies, kidney disease, and stomach ulcers. For these conditions, the issue is not simply calories but specific food types that must be either avoided or utilized. But in any dietary regime, the fundamental problem is to translate the doctor's (or nutritionist's or psychologist's or physiologist's) instructions about what to eat and what not to eat into appropriate behavior. Principles emerging from the study of obesity might thus have useful applications in a wide range of health problems.

The literature on behavioral methods in obesity is voluminous. Interested individuals are referred to the reviews by Leon (1976) or Stunkard (1977) and to the excellent chapters by Stuart (1980) and Bellack (1977). M. Mahoney and K. Mahoney (1976) and Stuart and Davis (1978) described specific behavioral programs in detail, and the reviews cite many others more briefly described in journals or chapters, for example, Jeffrey (1976) or Hall (1972). The following pages identify major theoretical and practical issues and outline several behavioral approaches to weight control.

Behavioral methods in obesity initially generated great enthusiasm, followed by a sobering reevaluation that suggested less dramatic success. Presently, more careful analysis of technique is ongoing and there is reason for guarded optimism. On balance, there is convincing evidence that behavioral methods can help people lose weight and keep it off, but great attention to methodologic detail is necessary, as is a commitment to long-term treatment and follow-up. Perhaps the single most important lesson that the history of these interventions teaches is that weight control programs cannot be one-shot affairs. Perhaps the second most important lesson is that the focus of intervention needs to be broad, including obesity related behaviors and not simply pounds lost. Obesity is complexly determined by a variety of factors that differ from case to case. Effective long-term modification of the condition requires attention to at least a part of this range of factors.

## ETIOLOGIC FACTORS IN OBESITY

Gambrill described some of the factors that play a role in obesity (1977). Weight gain and maintenance is a metabolic process determined by calories consumed, calories burned, and a host of poorly understood characteristics of the individual person. Obesity present since childhood is more difficult to modify than adulthood onset obesity and there is evidence that this difference reflects a relative increase during development in the number of adipocytes, or fat cells (Hirsch & Knittle, 1971). Obesity tends to run in families, suggesting a genetic aspect. Moreover, caloric use differs among people, with the obese tending to use calories less readily than do normal weight persons (Passmore et al., 1963). There may be further differences between overweight and normal weight people in the sense of taste. Goldman and associates reported that obese college students were more likely than their normal weight peers to abandon dormitory food in favor of restaurant fare (1968).

Nisbett hypothesized that overweight people suffer from a homeostatic shift in the upward direction of a mechanism sensitive to the proportion of body fat (1972). He suggested that among obese people weight loss and dietary control will eventuate in chronic hunger and discomfort as the hypothesized mechanism fights to regain lost fat.

## BEHAVIORAL TREATMENT OF OBESITY

Perhaps the first question which occurs as one begins to look at behavioral treatment for obesity, or any other treatment for the problem for that matter, is, Does it work? Yes or no? This simple sounding question has a complicated answer and really cannot be pertinently answered asked in this way.

Behavioral treatment of obesity includes many techniques; some are more effective than others. For practical purposes, sustained weight loss is the only meaningful criterion in technique evaluation. Following Mahoney's criticism of studies purporting to address the effectiveness of behavioral techniques (1976), Stuart recommended "inclusion of non-treated controls; inclusion of attention-placebo controls; accurate and complete procedural description; complete recording of outcome data for all subjects; inclusion of adequate follow-up periods; and exploration of potential contributors to change such as beliefs and attitudes" (1980:177, 179).

Placebo effects are ubiquitous in clinical settings and may be particularly important in weight control because of the volatility of the early stages of weight reduction—people can reduce poundage in a great many ways and for a great many reasons and attribution of cause to the technique cannot safely be made without appropriate controls. The use of group averages also has considerable hazard in terms of inference to general utility. A technique that causes some subjects to lose dramatic amounts of weight while not affecting others has different practical implications from one that reliably leads to modest weight loss across most subjects. The former sort of outcome raises questions concerning subject characteristics, for example, which is relevant to Stuart's last recommendation. At our present level of understanding, it makes sense to keep an open mind and to explore in any study other factors besides the experimental manipulation that have an effect on outcome. Such evaluation is greatly facilitated by examining weight loss trends on a case-by-case, as well as a group mean, basis. With these criteria in mind, let us look at specific programs.

### AVERSIVE TECHNIQUES

Many of the earliest behavioral efforts to control weight employed aversive conditioning. In such procedures, specific problem foods might be paired with electric shock (Meyer & Crisp, 1964) or the aroma of food paired with noxious odors (Kennedy & Foreyt, 1968). Morganstern employed cigarette smoking in a single subject for whom this behavior was highly aversive (1974). When eating high-calorie foods, the subject was to smoke a cigarette simultaneously. The procedure led to a reduction in consumption of these foods and to gradual weight loss over six months after cessation of the treatment. Mann used a response-cost format in which subjects deposited valuables with him, which were returned contingent upon weight loss (1972). The approach led to significant weight loss initially, but this result was not maintained (Bellack, 1977). Furthermore, undesirable patterns of weight loss were seen, with patients using diuretics or laxatives in an attempt to drop pounds prior to weigh-in. A number of investigators have used covert sensitization as an alternative to more cumbersome aversive conditioning methods: Cautela reported success in a series of single cases (1972), but Foreyt and Hagen found no difference between covert sensitization and placebo controls (1973).

Reviewing the aversive techniques as a whole, Bellack concluded that the results have not been positive (1977). Gambrill likewise stressed the limitations of purely aversive approaches and added that the character of the aversive stimulus may play a critical role (1977). Odors, for example, seem to be more effective than electric shock (Stunkard & Mahoney, 1976), a finding that makes heuristic sense since the aversive and positive stimuli in the former situation affect the same modality. This argument may also be relevant to Morganstern's report of the successful use of smoking as an aversive stimulus since smoking has both gustatory and olfactory sitmulus elements and involves placing something in the mouth (1974). Many writers charge that aversive methods fail to address alternative behaviors. Yet most cases of obesity reflect a complex interplay of variables, sedentary lifestyle being a primary one (Chirico & Stunkard, 1960). Furthermore, aversive techniques often lead to high attrition from treatment and thus to inflated estimates of success.

STIMULUS CONTROL

A number of programs have focused on modification of the antecedents of eating behavior. The logic is that the obese not only eat more than the nonobese but also eat in different situations and in response to different stimuli (Schachter, 1971). In operant terms, the obese have a wider range of SDs for eating than do the nonobese. In interventions proceeding from this model, subjects are encouraged to alter the situations in which they eat, for example, by limiting eating to only one room. Eating is to be done in the absence of all other activities (such as reading the paper or watching TV), thus breaking the SD contingency in relation to this behavior. The availability of food is also altered: prepared foods and snacks are not purchased, high-calorie foods are kept frozen, and foods are not left around the house since the sight of the candy dish is an SD for eating. All these maneuvers, and there are many others, are designed so that eating becomes conditioned to a new and much more limited range of stimulus events.

Results from studies using stimulus control variables have been mixed. Penick and associates found no significant difference between a stimulus control and a traditional psychotherapy condition in overall weight loss; however, the behavioral condition led to a greater percentage of patients losing significant amounts of weight (1971). Follow-up at six months showed good maintenance of weight loss among those who had lost during treatment. Nevertheless, the one-year follow-up showed relapse of the behaviorally treated patients to a level rendering them equal to the psychotherapy group (Stunkard, 1977). Wollersheim compared a stimulus control procedure with psychotherapy, social pressure–self-control, and a waiting list control group (1970). Weight loss was greatest in the stimulus control group but, as Bellack observed (1977), the procedure was confounded in this study with two other possible sources of behavior change—social reinforcement and self-monitoring—since therapists encouraged compliance and subjects recorded their adherence to the stimulus control contingencies. Self-monitoring has been repeatedly shown to lead to initial but unsustained weight reduction (Stuart, 1971) and social reinforcement affects almost all categories of behavior at least to some degree.

A very frequently cited study compared stimulus control with a well-known self-help method, TOPS (Take Off Pounds Sensibly) (Levitz & Stunkard, 1974). This study also examined the effect of professional versus lay status of the therapist on weight loss among clients. The stimulus control method was more effective than the TOPS procedure and had lesser attrition. The professional therapists also were more effective than the lay therapists, when both groups used the stimulus control procedure. At the one-year follow-up, only the group treated with behavioral methods by professionals showed sustained weight loss.

Bellack summarized the results of stimulus control studies, finding them encouraging but requiring more careful evaluation (1977). A major problem is confounding with other factors, particularly social reinforcement. One of the best known of these methods, that of Stuart and Davis (1978), uses stimulus control but also emphasizes calorie counting and reduction, exercise, and modification of the eating response. While this multifaceted approach is certainly appropriate for a commercial treatment package, it sets some limits on evaluation with regard to mechanism. At present, the most cogent conclusion appears to be that stimulus control procedures alone have limited utility but are important as part of a broader approach (Bellack, 1977; Gambrill, 1977).

## SELF-MONITORING

Another major category of behavioral technique places great emphasis on the patient as his own behavioral engineer. The treatment involves training the patient in monitoring his eating behavior. Part of the rationale for this approach is that obese people are often unaware of how much they eat. Through self-monitoring, some of their eating habits may come to light, and monitoring itself seems initially to reduce the frequency of such behaviors (Kazdin, 1974).

Researchers study self-monitoring in various ways. Patients may be asked to write down what they eat and where they eat each time they consume anything. Calories can also be counted after each meal. Alternatively, weight may be self-monitored, with daily weighings and charting of the results over time. Patients may be asked to monitor their thoughts about eating during the course of the day. Finally, patients may be asked to monitor their plans for eating, recording the data before they eat; such records list calories, foodstuffs, or both. A number of researchers have assessed the effects of different self-monitoring techniques.

Bellack looked at the effect of self-monitoring before eating, self-monitoring after eating, and two other conditions—stimulus control and a no contact control group (1974). The self-monitoring before eating was the most effective condition and remained so over a six-week follow-up. Romanczyk and colleagues found self-monitoring of calories to be more effective than monitoring of weight (1973). Furthermore, the calorie monitoring group did as well as a stimulus control group whose intervention was considerably more complicated and thus presumably more costly. This study was seriously weakened, however, by a relatively brief duration (four weeks) and no follow-up.

Bellack concluded that the self-monitoring studies overall suggest that precisely what is monitored may have a critical effect (1977). Certainly the pre-eating method has the face valid advantage of forcing the patient to evaluate what he is doing before he does it, which ought to affect what he eats. Post-eating monitoring, on the other hand, might be viewed as allowing for positive reinforcement if the number of calories or the quantity of food is low and for punishment if it is high. The temporal proximity of such events ought, from an operant point of view, to have some effect and indeed several studies have had success with post-eating self-monitoring (Stollak, 1967). One would expect self-monitoring of weight to be the least effective because of the remote relationship between what is being monitored and the events to be modified. Indeed, this seems to be what happens most frequently in the natural environment—one climbs on the bathroom scale, sighs, and then has a donut.

### Reinforcement Methods

The rationale for reinforcement techniques is familiar. The operant point of view holds that behavior is controlled at least in part by its consequences. When the behavior in question is eating, special problems arise. In the typical operant experiment, food is the reinforcer; thus, the opportunity to eat is made contingent on some behavior and the frequency of that behavior increases. The reinforcer that maintains the eating response itself seems inherent in the act—food reinforces eating. A reinforcement strategy to modify eating, therefore, needs a contingency that reinforces avoidance of eating, or the absence of eating behavior. Alternatively, what may be reinforced is the eating of allowed low-calorie foods rather than the consumption of preferred fattening foods, which apparently supply their own reinforcing consequences.

Viewing the problem in this way, one might well ask how it is that not everyone is obese. If food reinforces eating, what stops eating so long as food is available, as it is for the large majority of Americans? To answer the question one must hypothesize an internal mechanism of satiety that causes food no longer to be reinforcing. Food takes on its reinforcing property in response to another internal stimulus, hunger. Both these mechanisms reflect metabolic and neural events that have been studied in detail by physiologists. The specifics of this process need not concern us, but it is worth noting that the precise nature of the hunger-satiety phenomenon is unknown. Likewise, we know little about differences in this area between obese and nonobese persons (Wooley & Wooley, 1978). Lacking practical techniques for modifying the internal events of hunger and satiety, behaviorists have focused on what is manipulable, the consequences of eating.

In studies employing self-reinforcement, self-monitoring is obviously implicit. In fact, it might be argued that self-monitoring is effective to the extent that self-reinforcement is occasioned by monitoring procedures (Bellack, 1977). Studies using self-monitoring might thus be confounded by self-reinforcement effects. To test the unique contribution of overt self-reinforcement, Bellack employed two self-monitoring procedures, one supplemented by self-reinforcement (1976). Monitoring took the pre-eating approach in both groups, but the self-reinforcement group was instructed to assign a letter grade to the plan. The self-reinforcement procedure led to greater weight loss during treatment and over a six-week follow-up, suggesting that if self-reinforcement is operative in the self-monitoring condition, it is less effective than an explicitly arranged contingency involving overt behavior.

A number of studies have employed social reinforcement contingent on such parameters as weight loss, food intake, consumption of specific foods, or exercise. Social agents of reinforcement may be family members, others in treatment, or the therapist. Because of their presence in the natural environment, family members are viewed by some authorities as critical agents of change and are actively recruited to participate (K. Mahoney & M. Mahoney, 1976). Programs vary widely in the specification of the contingency, which ranges from general support of weight loss, through group congratulatory rituals as in Weight Watchers, to token systems (Stuart & Davis, 1978). At the heart of all these programs, however, is the basic operant principle that behavior is controlled by its consequences and that by modifying those consequences, obesity related behaviors can be modified.

Financial contingencies have been widely applied in weight control studies. One can turn the issue around conceptually and view recovery of deposited money as a form of positive reinforcement. Rozensky and Bellack used this method and compared it with a self-control and a no treatment control (1976). At the outset all subjects deposited money, which was returned in a noncontingent lump sum to all but the financial contingency group. These subjects were paid back at a rate of $2.00 per pound per week. Both treatment groups did better than the controls, but there was an interaction between a preassessed personality variable and success in the financial contingency condition. Subjects who were high in self-control did especially poorly in the financial contingency condition, while those low in self-control did well: "These results strongly suggest that there is an interaction between treatment form and subject style. . . . [C]aution is advised in the application of programs which place a premium on external management" (Bellack, 1977:16). This study highlights the point made earlier that subject variables may critically alter the effects of particular procedures.

Castro and Racklin reported an interesting study comparing self-reward, self-punishment, and self-monitoring in a procedure designed to equate the salience of the stimulus events in each method (1980). At weekly weigh-ins self-reward subjects received money in an amount of their choosing but limited to a total of $16.00 for weight loss. They had previously deposited the $16.00 with the experimenters. Self-punishment subjects donated money contingent on weight loss, also in an amount of their choosing and with a $16.00 upper limit for the study. Self-monitoring subjects paid $2.00 at each weigh-in no matter whether they had lost or gained. All three groups lost weight over the eight weeks of treatment and maintained weight loss over an eight-week follow-up. There were no significant differences among the groups. A waiting list control group gained weight during the eight weeks of treatment. The authors interpreted the outcome as suggesting that the self-reward procedure may be irrelevant to the success of programs that employ it since self-reward and self-monitoring of some sort are inevitably confounded. Perhaps the most perplexing finding was the successful weight loss for patients who were punished for weight loss by being made to pay. From an operant point of view one must simply conclude that in this study paying was by definition not a punishing stimulus since it did not suppress the behavior on which it was contingent. This study serves again to remind us that calling something either a reinforcer or a punisher does not make it so.

At this juncture one must conclude with Stuart that

> services to the overweight must offer constructive interventions that are systematically evaluated as they are offered, through use of optimal techniques of service delivery over an extended period of time. So long as behavior researchers and therapists continue to regard their technology as a powerful brand of magic . . . and so long as program plans omit consideration of the essential nature of the disorders that are the target of intervention, less than satisfying outcomes will be the norm rather than the exception. (1980:188)

The implications for future work seem eminently clear and involve attention both to procedural and to subject variables. On the procedural side it is obvious that sophisticated, longitudinal study of sizable groups using differing combinations of multiple treatments is essential. A number of promising methods are being studied, but much basic work remains to be done. As regards subject variables, the emerging picture of the obese patient grows more foggy the more we learn. Efforts at defining eating style differences have met largely with failrue, but several recent studies do suggest differences in appetite regulation among obese and nonobese subjects. It seems highly likely that a variety of obese types will emerge as more detailed study proceeds and that treatment strategies will be most effective if they are tailored to type.

## Health Education

The area of health education is broad, and the current ballooning interest in the topic is a manifestation of changing social expectations. The traditional way of practicing medicine, what Breslow and Somers termed complaint-response medicine (1977), is coming under increasing attack partly because of spiraling costs but also because there is growing awareness that this way of doing medicine does not work very well. During the 1960s every index of provision of traditional services rose, yet the overall death rate remained constant. This constancy, however, obscures a number of alarming trends, the most important of which is that the death rate for all groups between the ages of 15 and 74 actually rose, apparently a reflection of lifestyle variables. Clearly, preventive strategies are urgently needed and target groups, as well as the general public, require education in health maintenance.

When we talk about health education, several questions immediately arise: what should be taught, what is the best way to teach it, and what should be the result—the verbal and motor behavior change resulting from the educational process?


REDUCING RISK OF CARDIAC DISEASE
IN THE COMMUNITY

An interesting effort at community education was undertaken in 1972 by a group at Stanford University, the purpose being to modify behavior related to risk of cardiovascular disease (Farquhar et al., 1977). This work is especially important because it constituted a serious attempt to employ experimental methods in different communities and to compare results in populations given the educational package with control populations not so treated. Much educational research lacks control groups, and evaluation characteristically is pre–post, with change scores the dependent variable, rendering identification of the relevant independent variables suspect. The educational effort might account for observed changes, but so might either the passage of time or placebo effects. The Stanford group offered data that are at least partially free of these defects and the data suggest that educational efforts can modify population risk factors.

The study was conducted in three comparable northern California communities, roughly matched in size and age distribution. In each town a stratified random sample was obtained and interviewed once at the beginning and again at the end of each year of the study. The interviews assessed knowledge about heart disease and risk and allowed for estimation of the interviewee's behavioral status vis-à-vis major risk factors such as smoking and poor dietary habits. Also, plasma cholesterol and triglyceride concentrations, blood pressure, and body weight were assessed. A variable combining these parameters to yield an estimate of 12-year risk (the relative risk of heart disease in the coming 12 years) was employed as a summary index. In each of the towns a high-risk group was identified. Data on these people were separately analyzed and a subsample of them were given additional educational experience in one of the towns. Specifically, the experimental high-risk subgroup received one-to-one counseling in addition to the media methods used in the two experimental towns. The design thus allowed evaluation of media versus no media on the population as a whole by comparing experimental and control towns, along with a comparison of media versus media plus one-to-one counseling on the identified high-risk group.

The media campaign focused on the risk factors for heart disease and the specific behavioral steps to be taken to reduce those risks. Thus, for example, the information might be conveyed that cholesterol is a risk factor. Related behavioral messages might be recommendations to substitute fish for meat, margarine for butter, and skim for whole milk. The media campaigns were extensive, including "about fifty television spots, three hours of television programming, over 100 radio spots, several hours of radio programming, weekly newspaper columns, newspaper advertisement and stories, billboards, posters, and printed material posted to participants" (Farquhar et al., 1977:1193). The counseling sessions for high-risk people presented similar material but added personal contact. Spouses were invited to participate and the patient's physician was informed of the results of the screening tests. The counseling program for the first year lasted 10 weeks and included group and individual home sessions. During the second year, less intensive instruction focused on specific problems like reducing cigarette consumption and reinforcing gains.

The Farquhar study yielded impressive results. Comparing overall population risk in the experimental and control towns, at the end of the two-year study statistically significant relative improvement in the two experimental towns was seen in knowledge of risk factors, plasma cholesterol, systolic blood pressure, saturated fat intake, and the summary risk measure. Decreased cigarette consumption was found in one town but not in the other, but the intervention had no success in weight reduction. Similar results emerged for the high-risk subgroups. The one-year outcome demonstrated that the intensive intervention with personal contact led to much more rapid decline in risk, the high-risk experimentals showing lower risk at year one than the media-only group in their own or the other experimental town. By the end of the second year, these two groups had reached a level statistically equal to that of the intensively treated group except in two variables—knowledge of risk factors and cigarette consumption. In these two areas, the intensively treated high-risk subjects maintained superiority.

This study is very important in that it suggests that mass media efforts, properly designed, can have discernible effects on risk factors in a population experiencing no other intervention and that in high-risk subjects media supplemented by personal contact can have dramatic effects on even so recalcitrant a dependent variable as cigarette smoking. This interpretation must be tentative, however, because of the possible confounding of the evaluation process, the three interviews, with the media exposure. While the use of a control group allows confident conclusion that the evaluation process itself did not yield significant improvement, the evaluation method may have sensitized those participating in the project to the media messages, thus potentiating their effects. (One way to address this possibility would be to evaluate only at posttesting a matched sample of nonparticipants who ought theoretically to look more like participants in their own town than participants in the control town. Such a solution in turn raises problems of its own, which need not detain us here.) This concern aside, the Farquhar study is certainly among the best efforts of its kind.

The successful outcome of the attempt to modify population risk through education stands in stark contrast to a raft of disappointing results (Mendelsohn, 1973). In a discussion of the California study, McAlister and Berger mentioned three elements of the media intervention that may be important in differentiating successful from unsuccessful utilization (1979). First, the Farquhar media campaign stressed teaching of specific skills in addition to general information designed to modify attitudes or to induce motivation to change. Second, the techniques for behavior change were selected from among validated approaches then in use. Finally, the media program was tailored to fit the information deficits and the pattern of media consumption characteristic of the targeted population.

## FORMAL MODELS OF HEALTH EDUCATION

In concluding this discussion of health education, mention should made of the work of Jacard, who attempted to relate research on the social psychology of behavior change to health concerns (1975). Jacard applied Fishbein's model for predicting behavior (1967) to modifying health related behavior. The basic premise of the model is that a person will perform a behavior if he intends to perform it. In turn, the best way to predict what a person will do is to ask him what he intends to do: "Viewed in this manner, behavioral prediction reduces to a self-report by the individual of behavioral intent" (Jacard, 1975:153). Fishbein's model implies that behavior is guided by plans and expectations and to the extent that these can be accurately assessed behavior can be predicted. Several variables affect the accuracy of behavior prediction based on intention assessment. First, the more remote in time the two assessments, the less accurate the prediction since the passage of time allows for events, for example, new information, to occur that may change the intention. Second, the number of steps, or behavioral hurdles involved in carrying out the intention will affect the likelihood of the intended behavior. Related to this category of variable is ability—the subject must be able to do the things required to fulfill his intention. Finally, the more specific the assessment of intention, the more accurate is prediction likely to be. For example, assessment of an intention to "improve my diet" is less specific than assessment of an intention "not to eat dessert tonight."

This approach has been applied in a variety of experimental arrangements and the literature was reviewed by Ajzen and Fishbein (1973). Fishbein's model is relevant to health education because the relationship between imparting information and changing behavior is central in the latter. The model suggests several places where information might have an effect. Creation of an intention to do the behavior is the first. Presumably, if the goal is to reduce smoking behavior, for example, the subject must reach an intention to do so and this might be achieved by giving information on the deleterious effects of smoking. On the other hand, if the intention to quit smoking is already present, information of a very different kind is needed. Insight into the determinants of the subject's intention can guide educational efforts.

The model includes two categories of determinants of intention, attitudinal and normative, which refer respectively to one's beliefs about the behavior and one's impression of the beliefs of relevant others about the behavior. Attitudes toward the behavior have both evaluative (good versus bad) and strength dimensions, while the normative component addresses the quality of the perceived beliefs of relevant others and the degree of motivation the subject has to comply with the wishes of relevant others. Research with this model reveals that different intentions are variably determined by these two categories, some seeming to reflect personal beliefs in the main, while others are determined maximally by perceived social expectations. Jacard reported a study on the intention to smoke wherein intention seemed to be determined largely by personal attitudes rather than the perceived evaluations of relevant others (1975). Within the belief system, however, smokers and nonsmokers could be distinguished on several notions having to do with the effect of smoking on psychological function; for example, smokers believed that smoking relieves tension and helps in social intercourse, while nonsmokers denied these effects. This would imply that educational efforts might be better directed at changing attitudes about the psychological benefits of smoking rather than at its health consequences since there is consensus between smokers and nonsmokers in the latter regard.

In summary, Fishbein's model offers a structure within which to study subjects' intentions regarding health related behavior. Comparison of demographic groups may reveal disparate determinants of intentions and thus lead to more nicely tailored educational efforts with the goal of modifying behavioral intention in healthy directions. Translation of these intentions into action remains the critical issue, of course, but the evaluation and modification of intention is a reasonable place to begin.

## Conclusion

This chapter described a heterogeneous collection of strategies for preventing illness, ranging from educational efforts to modify risk of heart disease in populations to one-to-one treatments for obesity designed to reduce risk in a particular person. The HMO is an alternative structure for health care delivery, and some relationships between this type of institution and risk reduction methods were noted. These preventive approaches are all behavioral in that they require modification of the way people live as a method of improving their health. They deserve continued study and application.

# References

## Chapter 1. History and Logic of Medicine

ALLPORT, G. W. *The Nature of Prejudice.* Reading, Ma: Addison-Wesley, 1954.

BECKER, H. S., GEER, B., HUGHES, E. C., and STRAUSS, A. L. *Boys in White: Student Culture in Medical School.* Chicago: University of Chicago Press, 1961.

BURCH, G. E., and GILES, T. D. Coronary artery bypass operation requires further therapeutic evaluation. In R. L. Varco and J. P. Delaney (eds.), *Controversy in Surgery.* Philadelphia: Saunders, 1976.

CRISP, A. H. Psychosomatic research today: a clinician's overview. In Z. J. Lipowski, D. H. Lipsitt, and P. C. Whybrow (eds.), *Psychosomatic Medicine.* New York: Oxford University Press, 1977.

DuBos, R. *Mirage of Health.* New York: Doubleday Anchor, 1959.

ESPER, E. A. *A History of Psychology.* Philadelphia: Saunders, 1964.

FREIDSON, E. *Profession of Medicine: A Study of the Sociology of Applied Knowledge.* New York: Dodd, Mead, 1972.

HEMPEL, C. G. *Philosophy of Natural Science.* Englewood Cliffs: Prentice-Hall, 1966.

HUNTINGTON, G. On chorea. *Medical and Surgical Reporter,* 1872, *26,* 317–321.

MANN, W. N. (ed.). *Conybeare's Textbook of Medicine.* 7th ed. London: Churchill Livingstone, 1975.

MEEHL, P. E. Why I do not attend case conferences. In P. E. Meehl (ed.), *Psychodiagnosis: Selected papers.* Minneapolis: University of Minnesota Press, 1973.

METTLER, C. C. *History of Medicine.* Philadelphia: Blackiston, 1947.

MURPHY, E. A. *The Logic of Medicine*. Baltimore: Johns Hopkins Press, 1976.

POWLES, J. On the limitations of modern medicine. In R. L. Kane (ed.), *The Challenges of Community Medicine*. New York: Springer, 1974.

# Chapter 2. Medicine as a Social Institution

AMERICAN MEDICAL ASSOCIATION. *Socioeconomic Issues of Health*. Chicago: American Medical Association, 1973.

BLUM, R. H. Malpractice suits—why and how they happen: a summary of a report to the Medical Review and Advisory Board of the California Medical Association, 1958.

BUDDE, N. W. Specialty distribution of physicians. In *Socioeconomic Issues of Health*. Chicago: American Medical Association, 1973.

DERBYSHIRE, R. C. *Medical Licensure and Discipline in the United States*. Baltimore: Johns Hopkins Press, 1969.

FORD, A. S. *The Physician's Assistant: A National and Local Analysis*. New York: Praeger, 1975.

FREIDSON, E. *Profession of Medicine: A study of the Sociology of Applied Knowledge*. New York: Dodd, Mead, 1972.

GUMBINER, R. *HMO: Putting It All Together*. St. Louis: Mosby, 1975.

GROSS, S. J. The myth of professional licensing. *American Psychologist*, 1978, *33*, 1009-1016.

HETHERINGTON, R. W., HOPKINS, C. E., and ROMER, M. I. *Health Insurance Plans: Promise and Performance*. New York: Wiley, 1975

KASS, L. R. Regarding the end of medicine and the pursuit of health. *The Public Interest*, 1975, *40*, 11-42.

KENNEDY, E. M. *In Critical Condition: The Crisis in American Health Care*. New York: Simon & Schuster, 1972.

KRAUSE, E. A. *Power and Illness: The Political Sociology of Health and Medical Care*. New York: Elsevier, 1977.

MOORE, T. G. The purpose of licensing. *Journal of Law and Economics*, 1961, *4*, 93-117.

MEULLER, M. S. Private health insurance in 1973: a review of coverage, enrollment, and financial experience. *Social Security Bulletin*, 1975, *38*, 21-40.

NIXON, R. M. *Towards a Comprehensive Health Policy for the 1970's: A White Paper*. Washington, D.C.: U.S. Government Printing Office, 1971.

PARKER, A. W. The dimensions of primary care: blueprints for change. In S. Andreopoulos (ed.), *Primary Care: Where Medicine Fails*. New York: Wiley, 1974.

ROSSER, J. M., and MOSSBERG, H. E. *An Analysis of Health Care Delivery*. New York: Wiley, 1977.

SOMERS, A. R. Professional licensure: is it effective? In A. R. Somers and H. M.

Somers (eds.), *Health and Health Care: Policies in Perspective.* Germantown: Aspen, 1977. (a)

————. Who's in charge here? Alice searches for a king in mediland. In A. R. Somers and H. M. Somers (eds.), *Health and Health Care: Policies in Perspective.* Germantown: Aspen, 1977. (b)

SOMERS, H. M., and SOMERS, A. R. The changing doctor-patient relationship. In A. R. Somers and H. M. Somers (eds.), *Health and Health Care: Policies in Perspective.* Germantown: Aspen, 1977.

STEIN, L. The doctor-nurse game. *Archives of General Psychiatry,* 1967, *16,* 699–703.

WORTHINGTON, N. E. National health expenditures, 1929–74. *Social Security Bulletin,* 1975, *38,* 3–20.

## Chapter 3.  Behavioral Theory

BLOUGH, D. S. Spectral sensitivity in the pigeon. *Journal of the Optical Society of America,* 1957, *47,* 827–833.

CARNAP, R. The methodological character of theoretical concepts. In H. Feigle and M. Scriven (eds.), *Minnesota Studies in the Philosophy of Science,* Vol. I Minneapolis: University of Minnesota Press, 1956.

COOPER, A. J. A case of bronchial asthma treated by behavioral therapy. *Behavior Research and Therapy,* 1964, *1,* 351–356.

HEMPEL. C. G. *Philosophy of Natural Science.* Englewood Cliffs: Prentice-Hall, 1966.

LUDWIG, A. M., and OTHMER, E. O. The medical basis of psychiatry. *American Journal of Psychiatry,* 1977, *134,* 1087–1092.

MACK, T. M. General epidemiology: a guide to understanding biologic information. In R. L. Kane (ed.), *The Challenges of Community Medicine.* New York: Springer, 1974.

PREMACK, D. Toward empirical behavioral laws: I. Positive reinforcement. *Psychological Review,* 1959, *66,* 219–233.

SKINNER, B. F. *The Cumulative Record: A Selection of Papers.* New York: Appleton-Century-Crofts, 1972.

WOLPE, J. *The Practice of Behavior Therapy.* Elmsford, NY: Pergamon Press, 1969.

## Chapter 4.  Medicine I: Cardiology

ADSETT, C. A. and BRUHN, J. G. Short-term group psychotherapy for post-myocardial infarction patients and their wives. *Canadian Medical Association Journal,* 1968, *99,* 577–584.

BEIMAN, I., GRAHAM, L. E., and CIMINERO, A. R. Self-control progressive relaxation training as an alternative non-pharmacologic treatment for essential hypertension: therapeutic effects in the natural environment. *Behavior Research and Therapy*, 1978, *16*, 371–375.

BENSON, H., HERD, J. A., MORSE, W. H., and KELLEHER, R. T. Behaviorally induced hypertension in the squirrel monkey. *Circulation Research* (supp. 1), 1970, *26/27*, 21–25.

BENSON, H., SHAPIRO, D., TURSKY, B., and SCHWARTZ, G. E. Decreased systolic blood pressure through operant conditioning techniques in patients with essential hypertension. *Science*, 1971, *173*, 740–742.

BLANCHARD, E. B., and YOUNG, L. D. Clinical applications of biofeedback training: a review of evidence. *Archives of General Psychiatry*, 1974, *30*, 573–589.

BLEECKER, E. R., and ENGEL, B. T. Learned control of ventricular rate in patients with atrial fibrillation. *Psychosomatic Medicine*, 1973, *35*, 161–175.

BRENER, J. A general model of voluntary control applied to the phenomena of learned cardiovascular change. In P. A. Obrist, A. H. Black, J. Brener, and L. V. DiCara (eds.), *Cardiovascular Psychophysiology*. Chicago: Aldine, 1974.

BRENER, J. and HOTHERSALL, D. Heart rate control under conditions of augmented sensory feedback. *Psychophysiology*, 1966, *3*, 23–27.

BRENER, J., and KLEINMAN, R. A. Learned control of decreases in systolic blood pressure. *Nature*, 1970, *266*, 1063–1064.

CASSEM, N. H., and HACKETT, T. P. Psychiatric consultation in a coronary care unit. *Annals of Internal Medicine*, 1971; *75*, 9–14.

CROOG, S. W. and LEVINE, S. After the heart attack: social aspects of rehabilitation. *Medical Insight*, 1973, *5*, 10–15.

DiCARA, L. V. Learning in the autonomic nervous system. *Scientific American*, 1970, *5*, 15–20.

DiCARA, L. V., and MILLER, N. E. Instrumental learning of systolic blood pressure responses by curarized rats: the association of cardiac and vascular changes. *Psychosomatic Medicine*, 1968, *30*, 489–494.

———. Heart-rate learning in the non-curarized state, transfer to the curarized state, and subsequent retraining in the non-curarized state. *Physiology and Behavior*, 1969, *4*, 621–624.

EASON, R. G., and DUDLEY, L. M. Physiological and behavioral indicants of activation. *Psychophysiology*, 1970, *7*, 223–232.

ELDER, S. T., and EUSTIS, N. K. Instrumental blood pressure conditioning in out-patient hypertensives. *Behavior Research and Therapy*, 1975, *13*, 185–188.

ELDER, S. T., RUIZ, Z. R., DEABLER, H. L., and DILLENKOFFER, R. L. Instrumental conditioning of diastolic blood pressure in essential hypertensive patients. *Journal of Applied Behavior Analysis*, 1973, *6*, 377–382.

ENGEL, B. T. Operant conditioning of cardiac function: a status report. *Psychophysiology*, 1971, *9*, 161–177.

FORDYCE, W. *Behavioral Methods for Chronic Pain and Illness*. St. Louis: Mosby, 1976.

FREIS, E. D., and the Veterans Administration Cooperative Study Group on Anti-hypertensive Agents. Effects of treatment on morbidity in hypertension, results in patients with diastolic blood pressure averaging 115 through 129mm Hg. *Journal of the American Medical Association*, 1967, *202*, 1028–1034.

———. Effects of treatment on morbidity in hypertension, II, Results in patients with diastolic blood pressure averaging 90 through 114mm Hg. *Journal of the American Medical Association*, 1970, *213*, 1143–1152.

FRUMKIN, K., NATHAN, R. G., PROUT, M. F., and COHEN, M. C. Non-pharmacologic control of essential hypertension in man: a critical review of the experimental literature. *Psychosomatic Medicine*, 1978, *40*, 294–320.

GARRITY, T. F. Morbidity, mortality, and rehabilitation. In W. D. Gentry and R. B. Williams (eds.), *Psychological Aspects of Myocardial Infarction and Coronary Care*. St. Louis: Mosby, 1975.

GENTRY, W. D. Preadmission behavior. In W. D. Gentry and R. B. Williams (eds.), *Psychological Aspects of Myocardial Infarction and Coronary Care*. St. Louis: Mosby, 1975.

GOLDSTEIN, S., MOSS, A. J., and GREENE, W. Sudden death in acute myocardial infarction. *Archives of Internal Medicine*, 1972, *129*, 720–724.

GROEN, J. J. Psychosomatic aspects of ischaemic (coronary) heart disease. In O. Hill (ed.), *Modern Trends in Psychosomatic Medicine*, Vol. 3. London: Butterworths, 1976.

GULLEDGE, A. D. The psychological aftermath of myocardial infarction. In W. D. Gentry and R. B. Williams (eds.), *Psychological Aspects of Myocardial Infarction and Coronary Care*. St. Louis: Mosby, 1975.

GUYTON, A. C. *Textbook of Medical Physiology* 5th ed. Philadelphia: Saunders, 1976.

HACKETT, T. P., and CASSEM, N. H. Psychological intervention in myocardial infarction. In W. D. Gentry and R. B. Williams (eds.), *Psychological Aspects of Myocardial Infarction and Coronary Care*. St. Louis: Mosby, 1975.

JACOB, R. G., KRAEMER, H. C., and AGRAS, W. S. Relaxation therapy in the treatment of hypertension. *Archives of General Psychiatry*, 1977, *34*, 1417–1427.

JACOBSON, E. *Progressive Relaxation*. Chicago: University of Chicago Press, 1938.

JENKINS, C. D. Psychological and social precursors of coronary disease. *New England Journal of Medicine*, 1971, *284*, 244–255.

KELLNER, R. Psychotherapy in psychosomatic disorders. *Archives of General Psychiatry*, 1975, *32*, 1021–1028.

KIMMEL, H. D. Instrumental conditioning of autonomically mediated responses in human beings. *American Psychologist*, 1974, *29*, 325–335.

KRISTT, D. A., and ENGEL, B. T. Learned control of blood pressure in patients with high blood pressure. *Circulation*, 1975, *51*, 370–378.

LACEY, B. C., and LACEY, J. I. Studies of heart rate and other bodily processes in sensory motor behaviors. In P. A. Obrist, A. H. Black, J. Brener, and L. V. DiCara (eds.), *Cardiovascular psychophysiology*. Chicago: Aldine, 1974.

LACHMAN, S. J. *Psychosomatic Disorders: A Behavioristic Approach*. New York: Wiley, 1972.

LUTHE, W. and SCHULTZ, J. H. *Autogenic Therapy: Vol 2 Medical Applications.* New York: Grune & Stratton, 1969.

MANN, W. N. (ed.). *Conybeare's textbook of medicine.* 7th ed. London: Churchill Livingstone, 1975.

MILLER, N. E. Postscript. In D. Singh and C. T. Morgan (eds.), *Current Status of Physiological Psychology.* Monterey: Brooks/Cole, 1972.

MILLER, S., and KONORSKI, J. On a particular type of conditioned reflex. *Proceedings of the Biological Society (Polish Section, Paris),* 1928, *99,* 1155–1157.

OBRIST, P. A., HOWARD, J. L., LAWLER, J. E., GALOSY, R. A., MYERS, K. A., and GAEBELEIN, C. J. The cardiac-somatic interaction. In P. A. Obrist, A. H. Black, J. Brener, and L. V. DiCara (eds.), *Cardiovascular Psychophysiology.* Chicago: Aldine, 1974.

OLIN, H. S., and HACKETT, T. P. The denial of chest pain in 32 patients with acute myocardial infarction. *Journal of the American Medical Association,* 1964, *190,* 977–981.

PRANULIS, M. F. Coping with an acute myocardial infarction. In W. D. Gentry and R. B. Williams (eds.), *Psychological Aspects of Myocardial Infarction and Coronary Care.* St. Louis: Mosby, 1975.

REISER, M. F. Psychoanalysis in patients with psychosomatic disorders. In T. B. Karasu and R. I. Steinmuller (eds.), *Psychotherapeutics in Medicine.* New York: Grune & Stratton, 1978.

SCHWARTZ, G. E. Voluntary control of human cardiovascular integration and differentiation through feedback and reward. *Science, 1972, 175,* 90–93.

———. Toward a theory of voluntary control of response patterns in the cardiovascular system. In P. A. Obrist, A. H. Black, J. Brener, and L. V. DiCara (eds.), *Cardiovascular Psychophysiology.* Chicago: Aldine, 1974.

SCOTT, R. W., BLANCHARD, E. B., EDMUNSEN, E. D., and YOUNG, L. D. A shaping procedure for heart-rate control in chronic tachycardia. *Perceptual Motor Skills,* 1973, *37,* 327–338.

SKELTON, M.. and DOMINIAN, J. Psychological stress in wives of patients with myocardial infarction. *British Medical Journal,* 1973, *2,* 101–103.

STONE, R. A., and DeLEO, J. Psychotherapeutic control of hypertension. *New England Journal of Medicine,* 1976, *294,* 30–84.

TITCHENER, J. L., SHELDON, M. B., and ROSE, W. D. Changes in blood pressure of hypertensive patients with and without group psychotherapy. *Journal of Psychosomatic Research,* 1959, *4,* 10–12.

TJOE, S. L., and LURIA, M. H. Delays in reaching the cardiac care unit: an analysis. *Chest,* 1972, *61,* 617–621.

WEINER, H. *Psychophysiology and Human Disease.* New York: Elsevier, 1977.

WEISS, T., and ENGEL, B. T. Operant conditioning of heart rate in patients with premature ventricular contractions. *Psychosomatic Medicine,* 1971, *33,* 301–321.

WOLF, S. The end of the rope: the role of the brain in cardiac death. *Canadian Medical Association Journal,* 1967, *97,* 1022–1025.

————. Cardiovascular disease. In E. D. Wittkower and H. Warnes (eds.), *Psychosomatic Medicine: Its Clinical Application.* New York: Harper & Row, 1977.

# Chapter 5. Medicine II: Renal Disease

ABRAM, H. S. Survival by machine: the psychological stress of chronic hemodialysis. In R. H. Moos (ed.), *Coping with Physical Illness.* New York: Plenum, 1977.

ADLER, M. L. Kidney transplantation and coping mechanisms. *Psychosomatics,* 1972, *13,* 337–341.

BARGER, S. L. Personal-professional support: from a patient's point of view. In C. A. Garfield (ed.), *Psychosocial Care of the Dying Patient.* New York: McGraw-Hill, 1978.

BEARD, B. H. Fear of death and fear of life: the dilemma in chronic renal failure, hemodialysis, and kidney transplantation. *Archives of General Psychiatry,* 1969, *21,* 373–380.

BLAGG, C. R. Home dialysis. *American Journal of Medical Science,* 1972, *264,* 168–182.

————. Objective quantification of rehabilitation in dialysis and transplantation. In E. A. Friedman (ed.), *Strategy in Renal Failure.* New York: Wiley, 1978.

BLAGG, C. R., DALY, S. M., ROSENQUIST, B. J., JENSEN, W. W., and ESHBACK, J. W. The importance of patients training in home dialysis. *Annals of Internal Medicine,* 1970, *73,* 841–847.

CRAMOND, W. A. Renal transplantation: experiences with recipients and donors. In P. Castelnuovo-Tedesco (ed.), *Psychiatric Aspects of Organ Transplantation.* New York: Grune & Stratton, 1971.

DELANO, B. G. Home dialysis. In E. A. Friedman (ed.), *Strategy in Renal Failure.* New York: Wiley, 1978.

DENOUR, A. K., and CZACZKES, J. W. Emotional problems and reactions of the medical team in a chronic hemodialysis unit. *Lancet,* 1968, *2,* 987–991.

————. Personality factors in chronic hemodialysis patients causing noncompliance with medical regimen. *Psychosomatic Medicine,* 1972, *34,* 333–344.

DE-NOUR, A. K., SHALTIEL, J., and CZACZKES, J. W. Emotional reactions of patients on chronic hemodialysis. *Psychosomatic Medicine,* 1968, *30,* 521–533.

FELLNER, C. H. Selection of living kidney donors and the problem of informed consent. In P. Castelnuovo-Tedesco, *Psychiatric Aspects of Organ Transplantation.* New York: Grune & Stratton, 1971.

FOSTER, F. G., COHEN, G. L., and McKEGNEY, F. P. Psychophysiological factors in individual survival in chronic renal hemodialysis: a two-year follow-up (part 1). *Psychosomatic Medicine,* 1973, *35,* 65–82,

FRIEDMAN, E. A. Introduction. In E. A. Friedman (ed.), *Strategy in Renal Failure.* New York: Wiley, 1978.

GOMBOS, E. A., LEE, T. H., HARTON, M. R., and CUMMINGS, J. W. One year's experience with an intermittent dialysis program. *Annals of Internal Medicine,* 1964, *61,* 462-469.

GREENBERG, I. M., WELTZ, S., SPITZ, C., and BIZZOZERO, O. J. Factors of adjustment in chronic hemodialysis patients. *Psychosomatics,* 1975, *16,* 178-183.

GUYTON, A. C. *Textbook of Medical Physiology.* 5th ed. Philadelphia: Saunders, 1976.

HOLCOMB, J. L., and MACDONALD, R. W. Social functioning of artificial kidney patients. *Social Science and Medicine,* 1973, *7,* 109-119.

LEVY, N. B. Sexual adjustment to maintenance hemodialysis and renal transplantation: national survey by questionnaire; preliminary report. In N. B. Levy (ed.), *Living or Dying: Adaptations to Hemodialysis.* Springfield: Thomas, 1974.

LEVY, N. B., and WYBRANDT, G. D. The quality of life on maintenance hemodialysis. *Lancet,* 1975, *1,* 1328-1330.

REICHSMAN, F., and LEVY, N. B. Problems in adaptation to maintenance hemodialysis. *Archives of Internal Medicine,* 1972, *130,* 859-865.

REICHSMAN, F., and MCKEGNEY, F. P. Psychosocial aspects of maintenance hemodialysis. In E. A. Friedman (ed.), *Strategy in Renal Failure.* New York: Wiley, 1978.

ROBINSON, B. H. Intermittent hemodialysis in the home. *British Medical Bulletin,* 1971, *27,* 173-180.

SAND, P., LIVINGSTON, G., and WRIGHT, G. Psychological assessment of candidates for a hemodialysis program. *Annals of Internal Medicine,* 1966, *64,* 602-610.

SCRIBNER, B. H. Proceedings, conference to consider the treatment of patients with chronic kidney disease with uremia. New York City, June 1963.

SHAE, E. J., BOGDAN, D. F., FREEMAN, R. B., and SCHREIVER, G. E. Hemodialysis for chronic renal failure: IV. Psychological considerations. *Annals of Internal Medicine,* 1965, *62,* 558-563.

SHAMBAUGH, P. W., and KANTER, S. S. Spouses under stress: group meetings with spouses of patients on hemodialysis. *American Journal of Psychiatry,* 1969, *125,* 928-936.

SHORT, M. J., and WILSON, W. P. Roles of denial in chronic hemodialysis. *Archives of General Psychiatry,* 1969, *20,* 433-437.

SHUPACK, E. Discussion. In C. R. Blagg, J. DePalma, P. Jacobberger, A. Remmers, E. Schupack, and G. W. Stinson, Home dialysis. *Dialysis and Transplantation,* 1973, *2,* 10-35.

SIMMONS, R. G., HICKEY, K., KJELLSTRAND, C. M., and SIMMONS, R. Donors and non-donors: the role of the family and the physician in kidney transplantation. In P. Castelnuovo-Tedesco (ed.), *Psychiatric Aspects of Organ Transplantation.* New York: Grune & Stratton, 1971.

STINSON, G. W., CLARK, M. F., SAWYER, T. K., and BLAGG, C. R. Home dialysis training in three weeks. *Transactions of the American Society for Artificial Internal Organs,* 1972, *18,* 66-69.

TAYLOR, T. R., AITCHISON, J., PARKER, L. S., and MOORE, M. F. Individual differences in selecting patients for regular hemodialysis. *British Medical Journal*, 1975, *2*, 380–381.

WRIGHT, R. G., SAND, P., and LIVINGSTON, G. Psychological stress during hemodialysis for chronic renal failure. *Annals of Internal Medicine*, 1966, *64*, 611–621.

## Chapter 6. Surgery

AUERBACH, S. M. Trait-state anxiety and adjustment to surgery. *Journal of Consulting and Clinical Psychology*, 1973, *40*, 264–271.

BANDURA, A. *Principles of Behavior Modification*. New York: Holt, Rinehart & Wilson, 1969.

BECKER, M. C., ZUCKER, I. R., PARSONNET, V., and GILBERT, L. Rehabilitation of the patient with permanent pacemaker. *Geriatrics*, 1967, *22*, 106–111.

BLACKER, R. S., and BASCH, S. H. Psychological aspects of pacemaker implantation. *Archives of General Psychiatry*, 1970, *22*, 319–323.

COHEN, F., and LAZARUS, P. S. Active coping processes, coping dispositions, and recovery from surgery. *Psychosomatic Medicine*, 1973, *35*, 375–389.

EGBERT, J. D., BATTIT, G. E., WELCH, C. E., and BARTLETT, H. M. K. Reduction of post-operative pain by encouragement and instruction of patients: a study of doctor-patient rapport. *New England Journal of Medicine*, 1964, *270*, 825–827.

GOLDEN, D. A., and DAVIS, J. G. Counseling parents after the birth of an infant with Down's syndrome. In R. Moos (ed.), *Coping with Physical Illness*. New York: Plenum, 1977.

GREEN, W. A., and MOSS, A. J. Psychosocial factors in the adjustment of patients with permanently implanted cardiac pacemakers. *Annals of Internal Medicine*, 1969, *70*, 897–902.

HACKETT, T. P., and WEISMAN, A. D. Psychiatric management of operative syndromes: I. The therapeutic consultation and the effect of noninterpretive intervention. *Psychosomatic Medicine*, 1960, *22*, 267–282. (a)

————. Psychiatric management of operative syndromes: II. Psychodynamic factors in formulation and management. *Psychosomatic Medicine*, 1960, *22*, 356–372. (b)

HEALY, K. N. Does pre-operative instruction make a difference? *American Journal of Nursing*, 1968, *68*, 62–67.

HESSE, K. Meeting the psychosocial needs of pacemaker patients. *International Journal of Psychiatry in Medicine*, 1975, *6*, 359–372.

JACKSON, P. L. Chronic grief. In R. Moos (ed.), *Coping with Physical Illness*. New York: Plenum, 1977.

JANIS, I. L. *Psychological Stress: Psychoanalytic and Behavioral Studies of Surgical Patients*. New York: Wiley, 1958.

JOHNSON, J. E., DABBS, J. M., and LEVENTHAL, H. Psychosocial factors in the welfare of surgical patients. *Nursing Research*, 1970, *19*, 18–29.

JOHNSON, J., and LEVENTHAL, H. Effects of accurate expectations and behavioral instructions on reactions during a noxious medical examination. *Journal of Personality and Social Psychology*, 1974, *29*, 710–718.

KIMBALL, C. P. A predictive study of adjustment to cardiac surgery. *Journal of Thoracic and Cardiovascular Surgery*, 1969, *58*, 891–896.

LEVENTHAL, H. Findings and theory in the study of fear communications. In L. Berkowitz (ed.), *Advances in Experimental Social Psychology*, Vol. 5. New York: Academic, 1970.

LEVENTHAL, H., JONES, S., and TREMBLY, G. Sex differences in attitude and behavior change under conditions of fear and specific instructions. *Journal of Experimental Social Psychology*, 1966, *2*, 387–399.

MELAMED, B. G. Psychological preparation for hospitalization. In S. Rachman (ed.), *Contributions to Medical Psychology*, Vol. 1. Oxford: Pergamon, 1977.

MOOS, R. The crisis of illness: stillbirth and birth defects. In R. Moos (ed.), *Coping with Physical Illness*. New York: Plenum, 1977.

PATON, A. Life and death: moral and ethical aspects of transplantation. In P. Castelnuovo-Tedesceo (ed.), *Psychiatric Aspects of Organ Transplantation*. New York: Grune & Stratton, 1971.

VERNON, D. T. A., and BIGELOW, D. A. Effect of information about a potentially stressful situation on responses to stress impact. *Journal of Personality and Social Psychology*, 1974, *29*, 50–59.

WOLFNER, J. A., and DAVIS, C. E. Assessment of surgical patients' pre-operative emotional condition and post-operative welfare. *Nursing Research*, 1970, *19*, 402–415.

YERKES, R. M., and DODSON, J. D. The relation of strength of stimulus to rapidity of habit-formation. *Journal of Comparative Neurology and Psychology*, 1908, *18*, 459–482.

# Chapter 7.  Pain

ADAMS, R. D., and VICTOR, M. *Principles of Neurology*. New York: McGraw-Hill, 1977.

BEECHER, H. K. Relationship of significance of wound to the pain experienced. *Journal of the American Medical Association*, 1956, *161*, 1609–1613.

————. The measurement of pain. *Pharmacologic Review*, 1957, *9*, 59–209.

————. *Measurement of Subjective Responses*. New York: Oxford University Press, 1959.

BLITZ, B., and DINNERSTEIN, A. J. Role of attentional focus in pain perception: manipulation of response to noxious stimulation by instructions. *Journal of Abnormal Psychology*, 1971, *77*, 42–45.

BUSS, A. H., and PORTNOY, N. W. Pain tolerance and group identification. *Journal of Personality and Social Psychology*, 1967, *6*, 106–108.

CRAIG, K. D., and WEISS, S. N. Verbal reports of pain without noxious stimulation. *Perceptual Motor Skills*, 1972, *34*, 943–948.

DALESSIO, D. J. *Wolff's Headache and Other Head Pain.* 3d ed. New York: Oxford University Press, 1972.

EVANS, W., and HOYLE, C. The comparative value of drugs used in the continuous treatment of angina pectoris. *Quarterly Journal of Medicine,* 1933, *2,* 311–338.

FRIAR, L. R., and BEATTY, J. Migraine: management by trained control of vasoconstriction. *Journal of Consulting and Clinical Psychology,* 1976, *44,* 46–53.

FORDYCE, W. *Behavioral Methods for Chronic Pain and Illness.* St. Louis: Mosby, · 1976.

GOUGH, H. G. Diagnostic patterns on the MMPI. In G. S. Welsh and W. G. Dahlstrom (eds.), *Basic Readings on the MMPI in Psychology and Medicine.* Minneapolis: University of Minnesota Press, 1956.

HAZOURI, L. A., and MUELLER, A. D. Pain threshold studies in paraplegic man. *Archives of Neurology and Psychiatry,* 1950, *64,* 607–613.

HEINZ, P. L., COHEN, S. I., and SHMAVONIAN, B. M. Perceptual mode and cardiac conditioning. *Psychophysiology,* 1966, *3,* 101–107.

HENRYK-GUTT, R., and REESE, W. L. Psychological aspects of migraine. *Journal of Psychosomatic Research,* 1973, *17,* 141–153.

HILL, H. E., KORNETSKY, C. H., FLANARY, G. H., and WIKLER, A. Studies on anxiety associated with anticipation of pain: I. Effects of morphine. *Archives of Neurology and Psychiatry,* 1952, *67,* 612–619.

HUNGERFORD, G. D., DuBOULAY, G. H., and ZILKHA, K. J. Computerized axioltomography in patients with severe migraine. *Journal of Neurology, Neurosurgery, and Psychiatry,* 1976, *39,* 990–994.

KANFER, F. H. and PHILLIPS, J. S. A survey of current behavior therapies and a proposal for classification. In C. M. Franks (ed.) *Behavior Therapy: Appraisal and Status.* New York: McGraw-Hill, 1969.

KRUGMAN, A. D., ROSS, S., and LYERLY, S. B. Drugs and placebos: effects of instructions upon performance and mood under amphetamine sulphate and chloral hydrate with younger subjects. *Psychological Reports,* 1964, *15,* 925–926.

LYERLY, S. B., ROSS, S., KRUGMAN, A. D., and CLYDE, D. J. Drugs and placebos: the effects of instructions upon performance and mood under amphetamine sulphate and chloral hydrate. *Journal of Abnormal and Social Psychology,* 1964, *68,* 321–327.

MARSHALL, J. Cerebral blood flow in migraine. In R. Greene (ed.), *Current Concepts in Migraine Research.* New York: Raven, 1978.

MELZACK, R., and LOESER, J. D. Phantom body pain in paraplegics: evidence for a central "pattern generating mechanism" for pain. *Pain,* 1978, *4,* 195–210.

MELZACK, R., and WALL, P. D. Pain mechanisms: a new theory. *Science,* 1965, *150,* 971–979.

MERRITT, H. H. *A Textbook of Neurology.* Philadelphia: Lea & Febiger, 1973.

MITCHELL, K. R., and MITCHELL, D. M. Migraine: an exploratory treatment application of programmed behavior therapy techniques. *Journal of Psychosomatic Research,* 1971, *15,* 137–157.

MODLIN, H. C. A study of the MMPI in clinical practice. In G. S. Welsh and W. G. Dahlstrom (eds.), *Basic Readings on the MMPI in Psychology and Medicine*. Minneapolis: University of Minnesota Press, 1956.

NASH, H. The double blind procedure: rationale and empirical evaluation. *Journal of Nervous and Mental Disease*, 1962, *134*, 34–47.

PETRIE, A. *Individuality in Pain and Suffering*. Chicago: University of Chicago Press, 1967.

PHILLIPS, C. Headache and personality. *Journal of Psychosomatic Research*, 1976, *20*, 535–542.

SARGENT, J. D., WALTERS, E. D., and GREEN, E. E. Psychosomatic self-regulation of migraine headaches. *Seminars in Psychiatry*, 1973, *5*, 415–428.

SCHACHTER, S. *The Psychology of Affiliation*. Palo Alto: Stanford University Press, 1959.

SCHALLING, D., and LEVANDER, S. Ratings of anxiety-proneness and responses to electrical pain stimulation. *Scandinavian Journal of Psychology*, 1964, *5*, 1–9.

SHAPIRO, A. K. A contribution to a history of placebo effect. *Behavioral Science*, 1960, *5*, 109–135.

SNYDER, S. Opiate receptors and internal opiates. *Scientific American*, 1977, *236*, 44–56.

STERNBACH, R. A. *Pain: A Psychophysiological Analysis*. New York: Academic, 1968.

SWEENEY, D. R., and FINE, B. J. Note on pain reactivity and family size. *Perceptual Motor Skills*, 1970, *31*, 25–26.

TURSKY, B., and STERNBACH, R. A. Further physiologic correlates of ethnic differences in responses to shock. *Psychophysiology*, 1967, *4*, 67–74.

WATERS, W. E., and O'CONNOR, P. J. Epidemiology of headache and migraine in women. *Journal of Neurology, Neurosurgery, and Psychiatry*, 1971, *34*, 148–153.

WINSBERG, B., and GREENLICK, M. Pain responses in Negro and white obstetrical patients. *Journal of Health and Social Behavior*, 1967, *8*, 222–228.

WITKIN, H. A., LEWIS, H. B., HERTZMAN, M., MACHOVER, K., MEISSNER, P. B., and WAPNER, S. *Personality through Perception*. New York: Harper, 1954.

WOODROW, K. M., FREIDMAN, G. D., SIEGLAUB, A. B., and COLLEN, M. F. Pain tolerance differences according to age, sex, and race. *Psychosomatic Medicine*, 1972, *34*, 548–556.

ZBOROWSKI, M. Cultural components in responses to pain. *Journal of Social Issues*, 1952, *8*, 16–30.

# Chapter 8. Compliance

BALES, R. F. *Interaction Process Analysis*. Reading: Addison-Wesley, 1950.

BECKER, M. H. Sociobehavioral determinants of compliance. In D. L. Sackett and R. B. Haines (eds.), *Compliance with Therapeutic Regimes.* Baltimore: Johns Hopkins Press, 1976.

BERGMAN, A. B., and WERNER, R. J. Failure of children to receive penicillin by mouth. *New England Journal of Medicine,* 1963, *268,* 1334–1338.

BLACKWELL, B. The drug defaulter. *Clinical Pharmacology and therapeutics,* 1972, *13,* 841–848.

BOYLE, C. M. Differences between doctor's and patient's interpretations of some common medical terms. *British Medical Journal,* 1970, *2,* 286–289.

BRADSHAW, P. W., LEY, P., KINCEY, J. A., and BRADSHAW, J. Recall of medical advice: comprehensibility and specificity. *British Journal of Social and Clinical Psychology,* 1975, *14,* 55–62.

CARON, H. S., and ROTH, H. P. Patient's cooperation with a medical regimen: difficulties in identifying the non-cooperator. *Journal of the American Medical Association,* 1968, *203,* 922–926.

CHARNEY, E., BYNUM, R., ELDREDGE, D., FRANK, D., MACWHINNEY, J. B., MCNOBLE, N., SCHEINER, A., SUMPTER, E., and IHER, H. How well do patients take oral penicillin: a collaborative study in private practice. *Pediatrics,* 1967, *40,* 188–195.

DAVIS, M. S. Variations in patients' compliance with doctors' advice: an empirical analysis of patterns of communication. *American Journal of Public Health,* 1968, *58,* 274–288.

DIXON, W. M., STRADLING, P., and WOOTON, I. D. Outpatient PAS therapy. *Lancet, 1957, 2,* 871–872.

DONABEDIAN, A., and ROSENFELD, L. S. Follow-up studies of chronically ill patients discharged from hospital. *Journal of Chronic Disease,* 1964, *17,* 847–862.

EPSTEIN, L. H., and MASEK, B. J. Behavioral control of medicine compliance. *Journal of Applied Behavior Analysis,* 1978, *11,* 1–9.

FRANCIS, V., KORSCH, B. M., and MORRIS, M. J. Gaps in doctor-patient communication: patients' response to medical advice. *New England Journal of Medicine,* 1969, *280,* 535–540.

FREEMAN, H. Long acting neuroleptics and their place in community mental health services in the United Kingdom. In F. J. Ayd (ed.), *The Future of Pharmacotherapy: New Drug Delivery Systems.* International Drug Therapy Newsletter, Baltimore: Ayd Medical Communications, 1973.

FREEMON, B., NETRETE, V. F., DAVIS, M., and KORSCH, B. M. Gaps in doctor-patient communication: doctor-patient interaction analysis. *Pediatric Research,* 1971, *5,* 298–311.

GATLEY, M. S. To be taken as directed. *Journal of the Royal College of General Practitioners,* 1968, *16,* 39–44.

HAMMEL, R. W., and WILLIAMS, P. O. Do patients receive prescribed medication? *Journal of the American Pharmacological Association,* 1964, *NS 4,* 331–334.

HAYNES, R. B. A critical review of the "determinants" of patient compliance with therapeutic regimens. In D. L. Sackett and R. B. Haynes (eds.), *Compliance with therapeutic regimens.* Baltimore: Johns Hopkins Press, 1976. (a)

————. Strategies for improving compliance: a methodological analysis. In

D. L. Sackett and R. B. Haynes (eds.), *Compliance with Therapeutic Regimens.* Baltimore: Johns Hopkins Press, 1976. (b)

Joyce, C. R. B., Caple, G., Mason, M., Reynolds, E., and Mathews, J. A. Quantitative study of doctor-patient communications. *Quarterly Journal of Medicine,* 1969, *38,* 183–194.

Korsch, B. M., Gozzi, E. K., and Francis, V. Gaps in doctor-patient communication: I. Doctor-patient interaction and patient satisfaction. *Pediatrics,* 1968, *42,* 855–871.

Lane, M. F., Barbarite, R. V., Bergner, L., and Harris, D. Child resistant medicine containers: experience in the home. *American Journal of Public Health,* 1971, *61,* 1861–1868.

Ley, P. Memory aspects of doctor-patient communication. University of Liverpool, doctoral dissertation, 1969.

————. Primacy, rated importance, and recall of medical information. *Journal of Health and Social Behavior,* 1972, *13,* 311–317.

————. The measurement of comprehensibility. *Journal of the Institute of Health Education,* 1973, *11,* 17–20.

————. Psychological studies of doctor-patient communication. In S. Rachman (ed.), *Contributions to Medical Psychology.* Oxford: Pergamon, 1977.

Ley, P., Bradshaw, P. W., Eaves, D. E., and Walker, C. M. A method for increasing patients' recall of information presented to them. *Psychological Medicine,* 1973, *3,* 217–220.

Ley, P., Bradshaw, P. W., Kincey, J., and Atherton, S. T. Increasing patients' satisfaction with communication. *British Journal of Social and Clinical Psychology,* 1976, *15,* 403–413.

Ley, P., Jain, V. K., and Skilbeck, C. E. A method for decreasing patients' medication errors. *Psychological Medicine* 1976, *6,* 599–601.

Ley, P., and Spelman, M. S. Communications in an out-patient setting. *British Journal of Social and Clinical Psychology,* 1965, *4,* 114–116.

————. *Communicating with the Patient.* St. Louis: Green, 1967.

Luntz, R. W. N., and Austin, R. New stick test for P.A.S. in urine. *British Medical Journal,* 1960, *1,* 1679–1682.

Malahy, B. The effect of instruction and labelling on the number of medication errors made by patients at home. *American Journal of Hospital Pharmacy,* 1966, *23,* 283–292.

Michaux, M. W. Side effects, resistance, and dosage deviations in psychiatric out-patients treated with tranquilizers. *Journal of Nervous and Mental Disease,* 1961, *133,* 203–212.

Reynolds, E., Joyce, C. R. B., Swift, J. L., Tooley, P. H., and Weatherall, M. Psychological and clinical investigation of the treatment of anxious out-patients with three barbiturates and placebo. *British Journal of Psychiatry,* 1965, *111,* 84–95.

Sackett, D. L. The magnitude of compliance and non-compliance. In D. L. Sackett and R. B. Haynes (eds.), *Compliance with Therapeutic Regimens.* Baltimore: Johns Hopkins Press, 1976.

SACKETT, D. L. and HAYNES, R. B. (EDS.) *Compliance with Therapeutic Regimens.* Baltimore: Johns Hopkins Press, 1976.

SCHWARTZ, D., WANG, M., LEITZ, L., and GOSS, M. E. W. Medication errors made by elderly chronically ill patients. *American Journal of Public Health,* 1962, *52,* 2018-2029.

SOUTTER, R. B., and KENNEDY, M. C. Patients compliance in drug trials: dosages and methods. *Australian and New Zealand Journal of Medicine,* 1974, *4,* 360-364.

SPELMAN, M. S. and LEY, P. Knowledge of lung cancer and smoking habits. *British Journal of Social and Clinical Psychology,* 1966, *5,* 207-210.

STEWART, R. B., and CLUFF, L. E. A review of medication errors and compliance in ambulant patients. *Clinical Pharmacology and Therapeutics,* 1972, *13,* 463-468.

STIMSON, G. B. Obeying doctor's orders: a view from the other side. *Social Science and Medicine,* 1974, *8,* 97-104.

WATKINS, J. D., ROBERTS, D. E. WILLIAMS, T. F., MARTIN, D. A., and COYLE, V. Observation of medication errors made by diabetic patients in the home. *Diabetes,* 1967, *16,* 882-885.

WILCOX, D. R. C., GILLAN, R., and HARE, E. H. Do psychiatric patients take their drugs? *British Medical Journal,* 1965, *2,* 790.

WYNN-WILLIAMS, N., and ARRIS, M. On omitting P.A.S. *Tubercle,* 1958, *39,* 338-342.

ZIFFERBLATT, S. M. Increasing patient compliance through applied analysis of behavior. *Preventive Medicine,* 1975, *4,* 173-182.

# Chapter 9.  Psychiatry

AMERICAN PSYCHIATRIC ASSOCIATION. *Diagnostic and Statistical Manual of Mental Disorders.* 2d ed. Washington, D.C.: American Psychiatric Association, 1968.

————. *Diagnostic and Statistical Manual of Mental Disorders.* 3d ed. Washington, D.C.: American Psychiatric Association, 1980.

COX, S. M., and LUDWIG, A. M. Neurological soft signs and psychopathology. *Canadian Journal of Psychiatry,* 1979, *24,* 668-673.

DAHLSTROM, W. G., WELSH, G. S., and DAHLSTROM, L. E. *An MMPI Handbook* Vol. 1: *Clinical Interpretation.* Minneapolis: Lund, 1972.

DAVISON, G. C., and NEALE, J. M. *Abnormal Psychology: An Experimental Clinical Approach.* New York: Wiley, 1978.

DIDERICHSEN, B. *Formelle Karakteristika ved Associations-forlobet hos en gruppe born med hoj risiko for schizophreni.* Kobenhavns Universitet, Copenhagen, 1967. Unpublished thesis.

FEIGHNER, J. P., ROBINS, E., GUZE, S. B., WOODRUFF, R. A., WINOKUR, G., and MUNOZ, R. Diagnostic criteria for use in psychiatric research. *Archives of General Psychiatry, 1972, 26,* 57-63.

FINNEY, J. C. Programmed interpretation of MMPI and CPI. *Archives of General Psychiatry,* 1966, *15,* 75–81.

FREUD, S. *The Question of Lay Analysis.* New York: Norton, 1950.

GILBERSTADT, H., and DUKER, J. *A Handbook for Clinical and Actuarial MMPI Interpretation.* Philadelphia: Saunders, 1965.

HATHAWAY, S. R., and MCKINLEY, J. C. *The Minnesota Multiphasic Personality Inventory Manual.* New York: Psychological Corporation, 1951.

HESTON, L. L. Psychiatric disorders in foster home reared children of schizophrenic mothers. *British Journal of Psychiatry,* 1966, *112,* 819–825.

KETY, S. Genetic and biochemical aspects of schizophrenia. In A. M. Nickoli (ed.), *The Harvard Guide to Modern Psychiatry.* Cambridge: Belknap, 1978.

LUDWIG, A. M. *Treating the Treatment Failures: The Challenge of Chronic Schizophrenia.* New York: Grune & Stratton, 1971.

————. The psychiatrist as a physician. *Journal of the American Medical Association,* 1975, *234,* 603–604.

————. The proper domain of psychiatry. *Psychiatry Digest,* 1976, *37,* 15–24.

LUDWIG, A. M., and OTHMER, E. O. The medical basis of psychiatry. *American Journal of Psychiatry,* 1977, *134,* 1087–1092.

MARKS, P. A., and SEEMAN, W. *The Actuarial Description of Personality: An Atlas for Use with the MMPI.* Baltimore: Williams & Wilkins, 1963.

MEDNICK, S. A. Breakdown in individuals at high risk for schizophrenia: possible predispositional perinatal factors. *Mental Hygiene,* 1970, *54,* 50–63.

MEDNICK, S. A., and SCHULSINGER, F. Some premorbid characteristics related to breakdown in children with schizophrenic mothers. In D. Rosenthal and S. Kety (eds.), *The Transmission of Schizophrenia.* London: Pergamon, 1968.

OTHMER, E. O., and PENICK, E. C. Structured diagnostic interview for clinical practice. Paper presented at the annual meeting of the American Psychiatric Association, San Francisco, May 1980.

OTHMER, E. O., PENICK. E. C., and POWELL, B. J. *Psychiatric Diagnostic Interview.* 8th rev. ed. Los Angeles: Western Psychological Services, 1982.

ROSENTHAL, D. *Genetic Theory and Abnormal Behavior.* New York: McGraw-Hill, 1970.

SALZINGER, K. *Schizophrenia: Behavioral Aspects.* New York: Wiley, 1973.

SHAGASS, C. Neurophysiological studies. In N. Bellak and L. Loeb (eds.), *The Schizophrenic Syndrome.* New York: Grune & Stratton, 1969.

SLATER, B., and SHIELDS, J. *Genetical Aspects of Anxiety.* Ashford: Headley, 1969.

STERNBACH, R. A., ALEXANDER, A. A., and GREENFIELD, N. S. Autonomic and somatic reactivity in psychopathology. In J. Zubin and C. Shagass (eds.), *Neurobiological Aspects of Psychopathology.* New York: Grune & Stratton, 1969.

WENDER, P. H., ROSENTHAL, R., KETY, S. S., SCHULSINGER, S., and WELNER, J. Cross-fostering: a research strategy for clarifying the role of genetic and experiential factors in the etiology of schizophrenia. *Archives of General Psychiatry,* 1974, *30,* 121–128.

WOODRUFF, R. A., GOODWIN, D. W., and GUZE, S. *Psychiatric Diagnosis.* 2d ed. New York: Oxford University Press, 1979.

## Chapter 10. Terminal Illness

ANONYMOUS. The blocked bed. *Lancet,* 1972, *2,* 221–222.

BOWERS, M. K., JACKSON, E. N., KNIGHT, J. A., and LeSHAN, L. *Counseling the Dying.* New York: Nelson, 1964.

CARTWRIGHT, A., HOCKEY, L., and ANDERSON, J. L. *Life before Death.* London: Routledge & Kegan Paul, 1973.

CASSELL, E. J. Treating the dying: the doctor versus the man within the doctor. *Medical Dimensions,* 1972, *1,* 6–11.

DRIVER, C. What a dying man taught doctors about caring. *Medical Economics,* 1972, *50,* 80–86.

GARFIELD, C. A. Elements of psychosocial oncology: doctor-patient relationships in terminal illness. In C. A. Garfield (ed.), *Psychosocial Care of the Dying Patient.* New York: McGraw-Hill, 1978.

GARFIELD, C. A., and CLARK, R. O. The SHANTI project: a community model of psychosocial support for patients and families facing life-threatening illness. In C. A. Garfield (ed.), *Psychosocial Care of the Dying Patient.* New York: McGraw-Hill, 1978.

HOLMES, T. H., and RAHE, R. H. The social readjustment rating scale. *Journal of Psychosomatic Research,* 1967, *11,* 213–218.

KALISH, R. A. A little myth is a dangerous thing: research in the service of the dying. In C. A. Garfield (ed.), *Psychosocial Care of the Dying Patient.* New York: McGraw-Hill, 1978.

KALISH, R. A., and REYNOLDS, D. K. *Death and Ethnicity: A Psychocultural Study.* Los Angeles: University of Southern California Press, 1976.

KASTENBAUM, R. Is death a life crisis: on the confrontation with death in theory and practice. In N. Daton and G. H. Ginsberg (eds.), *Life-Span Developmental Psychology: Normative Life Crises.* New York: Academic, 1975.

KERSTEIN, M. D. Help for the young physician with death and grieving. *Surgery, Gynecology, and Obstetrics,* 1973, *137,* 479–480.

KÜBLER-ROSS, E. *On Death and Dying.* New York: Macmillan, 1969.

LERNER, M. When, why, and where people die. In O. G. Brim, H. E. Freeman, S. Levine, and N. A. Scotch (eds.), *The Dying Patient.* New York: Russell Sage, 1970.

MALKIN, S. Care of the terminally ill at home. *Canadian Medical Association Journal,* 1976, *115,* 129–130.

MERVYN, F. The plight of the dying patient in hospitals. *American Journal of Nursing,* 1971, *71,* 1988–1990.

MOUNT, B. M. The problem of caring for the dying in a general hospital: the palliative care unit as a possible solution. *Canadian Medical Association Journal,* 1976, *115,* 119–121.

MOUNT, B. M., AGEMIAN, I., and SCOTT, J. F. Use of the Bromptom mixture in treating the chronic pain of malignant disease. *Canadian Medical Association Journal,* 1976, *115,* 122–124.

MOUNT, B. M., JONES, A., and PATTERSON, A. Death and dying: attitudes in a teaching hospital. *Urology,* 1974, *4,* 741–747.

PARKES, C. W. The first year of bereavement: a longitudinal study of the reaction in London widows to the death of their husbands. *Psychiatry,* 1970, *33,* 444–467.

PATTISON, E. M. *The Experience of Dying.* Englewood Cliffs: Prentice-Hall, 1976.

————. The living-dying process. In C. A. Garfield (ed.), *Psychosocial Care of the Dying Patient.* New York: McGraw-Hill, 1978.

QUINT, J. C. Obstacles to helping the dying. *American Journal of Nursing,* 1966, *66,* 1568–1571.

SAUNDERS, C. Terminal care. In K. D. Bagshane (ed.), *Medical Oncology: Medical Aspects of Malignant Disease.* Oxford: Blackwell, 1975.

SONTAG, S. *Illness as Metaphor.* New York: Farrar, Straus & Giroux, 1978.

THOMAS, L. Notes of a biology watcher: the long habit. *New England Journal of Medicine,* 1972, *286,* 825–826.

WEISMAN, A. D. *The Realization of Death.* New York: Arnson, 1974.

WOODSON, R. Hospice care in terminal illness. In C. A. Garfield (ed.), *Psychosocial Care of the Dying Patient.* New York: McGraw-Hill, 1978.

# Chapter 11.  Geriatric Health Care

BALTES, P. B. and LaBOUVIE, G. V. Adult development of intellectual performance: Description, explanation, modification. In C. Eisdorfer and M. P. Lawton (eds.), *The Psychology of Adult Development and Aging.* Washington, D.C.: American Psychological Association, 1973.

BIGOT, A., and MUNNICHS, J. M. A. Psychology of aging, long term illness and care of the older person. In J. C. Brocklehurst (ed.), *Textbook of Geriatric Medicine,* 2d ed. London: Churchill Livingstone, 1978.

BLUM, J. E., FORSHAGE, J. L., and JARVIK, L. F. Intellectual changes and sex differences in octogenarians: A twenty-year longitudinal study of aging. *Developmental Psychology,* 1972, *7,* 178–187.

BOTWINICK, J. Intellectual abilities. In J. E. Birren and K. W. Schaie (eds.), *Handbook of the Psychology of Aging.* New York: Van Nostrand, 1977.

BOTWINICK, J., and STORANDT, M. Vocabulary ability in later life. *Journal of Genetic Psychology,* 1974, *125,* 303–308.

BOURESTOM, M. C., and PASTALAN, L. Death and survival. *Relocation Report,* No. 2. Ann Arbor: University of Michigan, Institute of Gerontology, n.d.

BRODY, S. J., BALABAN, D. L., PICKAR, G., and VERMERIEN, J. C. A diagnostic and treatment center for the aging: a program of pre-placement intervention. *Gerontologist,* 1976, *16,* 47–51.

CATTELL, R. B. Fluid and crystallized intelligence. *Psychology Today,* 1968, *3,* 56–62.

DOPPELT, J. E. and WALLACE, W. L. Standardization of the Wechsler Adult Intelligence Scale for older persons. *Journal of Abnormal and Social Psychology,* 1955, *51,* 312–330.

GREEN, R. F. Age-intelligence relationship between ages sixteen and sixty-four: A rising trend. *Developmental Psychology,* 1969, *1,* 618–627.

HORN, J. L. Organization of data on life-span development of human abilities. In L. R. Goulet and P. B. Baltes (eds.), *Life-span Developmental Psychology.* New York: Academic Press, 1970.

ISAACS, B. *Studies of Illness and Death in the Elderly in Glasgow.* Edinburgh: Scottish Home and Health Department, 1971.

JARVIK, L. F., KALLMAN, F. J., and FALEK, A. Intellectual changes in aged twins. *Journal of Gerontology, 1962, 17,* 289–294.

JEFFEREY, M. The elderly in society. In J. C. Brocklehurst (ed.), *Textbook of Geriatric Medicine and Gerontology.* 2d ed. London: Churchill Livingstone, 1978.

KAHANA, E. A consequence model of person-environment interactions. In P. G. Windley and G. Ernst (eds.), *Theory Development in Environment and Aging.* Washington, D.C.: Gerontological Society, 1975.

KLODIN, V. M. *Verbal Facilitation of Perceptual Integrative Performance in Relation to Age.* Doctoral Dissertation, Washington University, St. Louis, 1975.

LAWTON, M. P. The impact of the environment on aging and behavior. In J. E. Birren and K. W. Schaie (eds.), *Handbook of the Psychology of Aging.* New York: Van Nostrand, 1977.

LINDSLEY, O. R. Geriatric behavioral prothetics. In R. Kastenbaum (ed.), *New Thoughts on Old Age.* New York: Springer, 1964.

MARLOWE, R. A. Effects of environment on elderly state hospital relocatees. Paper presented at the annual meeting of the Pacific Sociological Association, Scotsdale, 1973.

NEWCOMER, R. J. Housing, services, and neighborhood activities. Paper presented at the annual meeting of the Gerontological Society, Miami Beach, November, 1973.

NORTON, J. C. Wechsler variables as a function of age and neurologic status. *Journal of Clinical Psychiatry.* 1979, *40,* 217–219.

OWENS, W. A. Age and mental abilities: A second adult follow-up. *Journal of Educational Psychology,* 1966, *51,* 311–325.

PRINSLEY, D. N. Effects of industrial action by the ambulance service on the day hospital patients. *British Medical Journal.* 1971, *3,* 170–171.

REGNIER, V. A., ERIBIES, R. A., and HANSEN, W. Cognitive mapping as a concept for establishing neighborhood services delivery locations for older people. Paper presented at the annual meeting of the Association for Computing Machinery, Atlanta, August 1973.

SANFORD, J. R. A. Tolerance of debility in elderly dependents by supporters at home: its significance for hospital practice. *British Medical Journal,* 1975, *3,* 471–473.

SCHAIE, K. W. Cross-sectional methods in the study of psychological aspects of aging. *Journal of Gerontology,* 1959, *14,* 208–215.

SCHAIE, K. W., ROSENTHAL, F., and PERLMAN, R. M. Differential mental deterioration of factorially "pure" functions in later maturity. *Journal of Gerontology,* 1953, *8,* 191–196.

SHANAS, E., TOWNSEND, P., WEDDERBURN, D., FRIES, H., STENHOUWER, J., and MILHOJ, P. *Old People in Three Industrial Societies.* London: Routledge & Kegan Paul, 1968.

SOMERS, A. R. Geriatric care in the United Kingdom: an American perspective. In A. R. Somers and H. M. Somers (eds.), *Health and Health Care: Policies in Perspective.* Germantown: Aspen, 1977.

TOBIN, S. S. Community to institution. Paper presented at the annual meeting of the Gerontological Society, Houston, October 1971.

U.S. SENATE, SPECIAL COMMITTEE ON AGING, SUBCOMMITTEE ON LONG TERM CARE. Nursing home care in the United States: failure in public policy, introductory report. 93d Congress, 2d session. Report 93-1420, December 19, 1974.

WECHSLER, D. *The Measurement and Appraisal of Adult Intelligence,* 4th ed. Baltimore: Williams and Wilkins, 1958.

# Chapter 12. Stress

ADER, R. Effects of early experience and differential housing on behavior and susceptibility to gastric erosions in the rat. *Journal of Comparative and Physiological Psychology,* 1965, *60,* 233–238.

————. The role of developmental factors in susceptibility to disease. In Z. J. Lipowski, D. R. Lipsitt, and P. C. Whybrow (eds.), *Psychosomatic Medicine: Current Trends and Clinical Applications.* New York: Oxford University Press, 1975.

ADER, R., and PLAUT, S. M. Effect of prenatal maternal handling and differential housing on offspring emotionality, plasma corticosterone levels, and susceptibility to gastric erosions. *Psychosomatic Medicine,* 1969, *30,* 277–286.

ANDERSON, N. H. Toward a quieter city: a report of the Mayor's Task Force on Noise Control. New York City, January 1970.

ARGUELLES, A. E., MARTINEZ, M. A., PUCCIARELLI, E., and DISISLO, M. V. Endocrine and metabolic effects of noise in normal, hypertensive, and psychotic subjects. In B. L. Welch (ed.), *Physiological Effects of Noise.* New York: Plenum, 1970.

BARNETT, S. A., EATON, J. C., and McCALLUM, H. L. Physiological effects of "social stress" in wild rats: II. Liver glycogen and blood glucose. *Journal of Psychosomatic Research,* 1960, *4,* 251–260.

BEN-ISHAY, D., and WELNER, A. Sensitivity to experimental hypertension and aggressive reactions in rats. *Proceedings of the Society for Experimental Biology and Medicine,* 1969, *132,* 1170–1173.

BERNARD, C. *Introduction to the Study of Experimental Medicine.* New York: Macmillan, 1927.

BOURNE, P., ROSE, R., and MASON, J. Seventeen-OHCS levels in combat: special forces "A" team under threat of attack. *Archives of General Psychiatry,* 1968, *19,* 135–140.

BRETT, G. Z., and BENJAMIN, B. Housing and tuberculosis in a mass radiography survey. *British Journal of Preventive and Social Medicine,* 1957, *11,* 7–9.

BUELL, T., and BRESLOW, L. Mortality from coronary heart disease in California men who work long hours. *Journal of Chronic Disease,* 1960, *11,* 615–626.

BULLOUGH, W. S. Stress and epidermal mytotic activity: I. The effects of adrenal hormones. *Journal of Endocrinology,* 1952, *8,* 265–274.

CANNON, W. B. Stresses and strains of homeostasis. *American Journal of Medical Science,* 1935, *189,* 1–14.

CARLESTAM, G., KARLSSON, C., and LEVI, L. Stress and disease in response to exposure to noise: a review. In *Proceedings of the International Congress on Noise as a Public Health Problem.* Washington, D.C.: U.S. Environmental Protection Agency, 1973.

CARRUTHERS, M. A. Aggression and atheroma. *Lancet,* 1969, *2,* 1170–1171.

CASSEL, J. Health consequences of population density and crowding. In *Rapid Population Growth,* Baltimore: prepared by the National Academy of Sciences, Johns Hopkins Press, 1971.

————. Psychosocial factors in the genesis of disease. In R. L. Kane (ed.), *The Challenges of Community Medicine.* New York: Springer, 1974.

CASSEL, J., and TYROLER, H. A. Epidemiological studies of cultural change: I. Health status and recency of industrialization. *Archives of Environmental Health,* 1961, *3,* 25–33.

CHRISTIAN, J. J. Endocrine adaptive mechanisms and the physiologic regulation of population growth. Lecture and Review Series, No. 60-62. Bethesda: Naval Medical Research Institute, 1960.

————. The potential role of the adrenal cortex as affected by social rank and population density in experimental epidemics. *American Journal of Epidemiology,* 1968, *87,* 255–264.

COBB, S., and ROSE, R. Hypertension, peptic ulcer, and diabetes in air traffic controllers. *Journal of the American Medical Association,* 1973, *224,* 489–492.

COHEN, A. Effects of noise on psychological state. In W. D. Ward and J. E. Frick (eds.), *Noise as a Public Health Hazard.* American Speech and Hearing Association Reports, No. 4. Washington, D.C.: American Speech and Hearing Association, 1969.

————. Industrial noise, medical absence, and accident record data on exposed workers. In *Proceedings of the International Congress on Noise as a Public Health Problem.* Washington, D.C.: U.S. Environmental Protection Agency, 1973.

CONGER, J. J., SAWREY, W. L., and TURRELL, E. S. The role of social experience in the production of gastric ulcers in hooded rats placed in a conflict situation. *Journal of Abnormal and Social Psychology,* 1958, *57,* 214-220.

DAHL, L. K. Discussion: mechanisms of hypertension. *Circulation Research Supplement,* 1970, *27,* I-32-I-39.

DAHL, L. K., HEINE, M., and TASSINARI, L. J. Effects of chronic excess salt ingestion; role of genetic factors in both DOCA-salt and renal hypertension. *Journal of Experimental Medicine,* 1963, *118,* 605-617.

—————. Effects of chronic salt ingestion: further demonstration that genetic factors influence the development of hypertension. *Journal of Experimental Medicine,* 1965, *122,* 533-545.

DAVIDSON, W. J. Psychotropic drugs, stress, and cardiomyopathies. In D. Wheatley (ed.), *Stress and the Heart.* New York: Raven, 1977.

ENGEL, G. L. Sudden and rapid death during psychological stress: folk lore or folk wisdom? *Annals of Internal Medicine,* 1971, *74,* 771-782.

ENTERLINE, P. E. RIKLI, A. G., SAUER, H. I., and HYMAN, M. Death rates for coronary heart disease in metropolitan and other areas. *Public Health Reports,* 1960, *75,* 759-766.

FARRIS, E. J., YAEKEL, E. H., and MEDOFF, H. Development of hypertension in emotional gray Norway rats after air blasting. *American Journal of Physiology,* 1945, *144,* 331-333.

FOX, K. M., CHOPRA, M. P., PORTAL, R. W., and ABER, C. P. Long term beta-blockade: possible protection from myocardial infarction. *British Medical Journal,* 1975, *1,* 117-119.

FRIEDMAN, M. *Pathogenesis of Coronary Artery Disease.* New York: McGraw-Hill, 1969.

FRIEDMAN, M., and ROSENMAN, R. *Type A Behavior and Your Heart.* New York: Knopf, 1974.

FRIEDMAN, M., ROSENMAN, R. H., and CARROLL, V. Changes in the serum cholestrol and blood clotting time in men subjected to cyclic variation of occupational stress. *Circulation,* 1958, *17,* 852-861.

FRIEDMAN, R., and DAHL, L. K. The effect of chronic conflict on the blood pressure of rats with a genetic susceptibility to experimental hypertension. *Psychosomatic Medicine,* 1975, *37,* 402-416.

—————. Psychic and genetic factors in the etiology of hypertension. In D. Wheatley (ed.), *Stress and the Heart.* New York: Raven, 1977.

FRIEDMAN, R., and WEISS, K. R. Avoidance behavior of two strains of rats with opposite genetic susceptibility to experimental hypertension. *Psychophysiology,* 1974, *11,* 222-223.

GLASS, D. C., and SINGER, J. E. *Urban Stress: Experiments on Noise and Social Stressors.* New York: Academic, 1972.

GOLDBERG, D. P. *The Detection of Psychiatric Illness by Questionnaire.* New York: Oxford University Press, 1972.

GROEN, J. J. Psychosomatic aspects of ischaemic (coronary) heart disease. In O. Hill (ed.), *Modern Trends in Psychosomatic Medicine,* Vol. 3. London: Butterworths, 1976.

GROEN, J. J., DREYFUSS, F., and GUTMAN, L. Epidemiologic, nutritional, and sociological studies of atherosclerotic (coronary) heart disease among different ethnic groups in Israel. In C. H. Miras, A. N. Howard, and R. Paoletti (eds.), *Progress in Biochemical Pharmacology: Vol. 4, Recent Advances in Atherosclerosis.* Basel, Switzerland: S. Karger, 1968.

GROEN, J. J., and DRORY, S. Influence of psychosocial factors on coronary heart disease: a comparison of autopsy findings with the results of a sociological questionnaire. *Pathologia et Microbiologia,* 1967, *30,* 779–788.

HAENZEL, W., LOVELAND, D. B., and SIRKEN, M. G. Lung cancer mortality as related to residence and smoking history. *Journal of the National Cancer Institute,* 1962, *28,* 947–1001.

HARBURG, E., SHULL, W. J., ERFURT, J. C., and SHOCK, M. A. A family set method for estimating heredity and stress: I. A pilot survey of blood pressure among Negroes in high and low stress areas, Detroit, 1966–67. *Journal of Chronic Disease,* 1970, *23,* 69–81.

HILDEBRAND, J. L. *Noise Pollution and the Law.* New York: Hein, 1970.

HINKLE, L. E. The concept of "stress" in the biological and social sciences. In Z. J. Lipowski, D. R. Lipsitt, and P. C. Whybrow (eds.), *Psychosomatic Medicine: Current Trends and Clinical Applications.* New York: Oxford University Press, 1975.

HOLMES, T. H., and RAHE, R. H. The social readjustment rating scale. *Journal of Psychosomatic Research,* 1967, *11,* 213–218.

HOWARD, J. H., CUNNINGHAM, D. A., and RECHNITZER, P. A. Health patterns associated with type A behavior: a managerial population. *Journal of Human Stress,* 1976, *2,* 24–33

JANSEN, G. Adverse effects of noise on iron and steel workers. *Stahl. Eisen.,* 1961, *81,* 217–220.

JENKINS, C. D. Psychological and social precursors of coronary disease. *New England Journal of Medicine,* 1971, *284,* 244–255.

————. The coronary prone personality. In W. D. Gentry and R. B. Williams (ed.), *Psychological Aspects of Myocardial Infarction.* St. Louis: Mosby, 1975.

JENKINS, C. D., ROSENMAN, R. H., and FRIEDMAN, M. Development of an objective psychological test for the determination of the coronary prone behavior pattern in employed men. *Journal of Chronic Disease,* 1967, *20,* 371–379.

————. Replicability of rating the coronary behavior pattern. *British Journal of Preventive and Social Medicine,* 1968, *22,* 16–22.

JENKINS, C. D., ROSENMAN, R. H., and ZYZANSKI, S. J. Prediction of clinical coronary heart disease by a test for the coronary prone behavior pattern. *New England Journal of Medicine,* 1974, *290,* 1271–1275.

KESSLER, A. Interplay between social ecology and physiology, genetics, and population dynamics of mice. Rockefeller University, doctoral dissertation, 1966.

KRISTIANSEN, E. S. Cardiac complications during a treatment with imipramine. *Acta Psychologica Neurologica Scandinavica,* 1961, *36,* 427–442.

KRYTER, K. D. *The Effects of Noise on Man.* New York: Academic, 1970.

————. Extraauditory effects of noise. In D. Henderson, R. P. Hamernik, D. S. Dosanjh, and J. H. Mills (eds.), *The Effects of Noise on Hearing.* New York: Raven, 1976.

LACEY, J. I. Somatic response patterning and stress: some revisions of activation theory. In M. H. Appley and R. Turnbull (eds.), *Psychological Stress.* New York: Appleton-Century-Crofts, 1967.

LANG, P. J., RICE, D. G., and STERNBACK, R. A. The psychophysiology of emotion. In N. S. Greenfield and R. A. Sternbach (eds.), *Handbook of Psychophysiology.* New York: Holt, Rinehart & Winston, 1972.

LAZARUS, R. S. Psychological stress and coping in adaptation and illness. In Z. J. Lipowski, D. R. Lipsitt, and P. C. Whybrow (eds.), *Psychosomatic Medicine: Current Trends and Clinical Applications.* New York: Oxford University Press, 1975.

LEWIS, B., CHAIT, A., OAKLEY, C. M. O., WOOTON, T. D. P., KIRCKLER, D. M., ONITIN, A., SIGURDSSON, G., AND FEBRUARY, A. Serum lipoprotein abnormalities in patients with ischemic heart disease: comparisons with a control population. *British Medical Journal,* 1974, *3,* 489–493.

LONG, R. T., LAMONT, J. H., WHIPPLE, B., BANDLER, L., BLOM, G. E., BURGIN, L., and JESSNER, L. A psychosomatic study of allergic and emotional factors in children with asthma. *American Journal of Psychiatry,* 1958, *114,* 890–899.

MASON, J. W. A re-evaluation of the concept of "non-specificity" in stress theory. *Journal of Psychiatric Research,* 1971, *8,* 323–333.

MILLER, R. G., RUBEN, R. T., CLARK, B. R., CRAWFORD, W. R., and ARTHUR, R. J. The stress of aircraft carrier landings: I. Cortical steroid responses in naval aviators. *Psychosomatic Medicine,* 1970 *32,* 581–588.

MOOS, R. H. Determinants of psychological responses to symbolic stimuli: the role of the environment. In Z. J. Lipowski, D. R. Lipsitt, and P. C. Whybrow (eds.), *Psychosomatic Medicine: Current Trends and Clinical Applications.* New York: Oxford University Press, 1975.

MOSS, G. E. Biosocial resonation: a conceptual model of the links between social behavior and physical illness. In Z. J. Lipowski, D. R. Lipsitt, and P. C. Whybrow (eds.), *Psychosomatic Medicine: Current Trends and Clinical Applications.* New York: Oxford University Press, 1975.

OSTFELD, A. M., and D'ATRI, D. A. Psychophysiological responses to the urban environment. In Z. J. Lipowski, D. R. Lipsitt, and P. C. Whybrow (eds.), *Psychosomatic Medicine: Current Trends and Clinical Applications.* New York: Oxford University Press, 1975.

PURCELL, K., BRADY, K., CHAI, H., MUSER, J., MOLK, L., GORDON, N., and MEANS, J. The effect on asthma in children of experimental separation from the family. *Psychosomatic Medicine,* 1969, *31,* 144–164.

RAHE, R. H. Epidemiologic studies of life change and illness. In Z. J. Lipowski, D. R. Lipsitt, and P. C. Whybrow (eds.), *Psychosomatic Medicine: Current Trends and Clinical Applications.* New York: Oxford University Press, 1975.

RAHE, R. H., BIERSNER, R. J., RYMAN, D. H., and ARTHUR, R. J. Psychosocial predictors of illness behavior and failure in stressful training. *Journal of Health and Social Behavior,* 1972, *13,* 393–397.

RAHE, R. H., McKEAN, J., and ARTHUR, R. J. A longitudinal study of life change and illness patterns. *Journal of Psychosomatic Research,* 1967, *10,* 355–366.

RATCLIFFE, H. L., YERASIMIDES, T. G., and ELLIOTT, G. A. Changes in the character and location of arterial lesions in mammals and birds in the Philadelphia Zoological Garden. *Circulation,* 1960, *21,* 730–738.

REES, L. The significance of parental attitudes in childhood asthma. *Journal of Psychosomatic Research,* 1963, *7,* 181–190.

ROSENMAN, R. H., FRIEDMAN, M., STRAUS, R., WURM, M., KOSITCHECK, R., HAHN, W., and WERTHESSEN, N. T. A predictive study of coronary heart disease: the western collaborative group study. *Journal of the American Medical Association,* 1964, *189,* 15–22.

ROSKIES, E., SPEVACK, M., SURKIS, A., COHEN, C., and GILMAN, S. Changing the coronary-prone (type A) behavior pattern in a non-clinical population. *Journal of Behavioral Medicine,* 1978, *1,* 210–216.

RUSSEK, H. I. Emotional stress and coronary heart disease in American physicians. *American Journal of the Medical Sciences,* 1960, *240,* 711–721.

————. Emotional stress and coronary heart disease in American physicians, dentists, and lawyers. *American Journal of the Medical Sciences,* 1962, *243,* 716–725.

RUSSEK, H. I., and ZOLMAN, B. L. Relative significance of heredity, diet, and occupational stress in coronary heart disease in young adults. *American Journal of Medical Science,* 1958, *235,* 266–275.

SCOTCH, N. Sociocultural factors in the epidemiology of Zulu hypertension. *American Journal of Public Health,* 1963, *53,* 1205–1213.

SELYE, H. A syndrome produced by diverse nocuous agents. *Nature,* 1936, *138,* 32.

————. Introduction. In D. Wheatley (ed.), *Stress and the Heart.* New York: Raven, 1977.

SYMINGTON, T., CURRIE, A. R., CURRAN, R. S., and DAVIDSON, J. N. The reaction of the adrenal cortex in conditions of stress. In G. E. W. Wolstenholme (ed.), *Ciba Foundation Colloquia on Endocrinology.* Vol. 3: *The Human Adrenal Cortex.* Boston: Little, Brown, 1955.

TACHE, J., and SELYE, H. On stress and coping mechanisms. In C. D. Spielberger and I. G. Sarason (eds.), *Stress and Anxiety,* Vol. 5. New York: Wiley, 1978.

TAGGART, P., and CARRUTHERS, M. Endogenous hyperlipidemia induced by emotional stress of racing driving. *Lancet,* 1971, *1,* 363–369.

————. Behavior patterns and emotional stress in the etiology of coronary disease: cardiological and biochemical correlates. In D. Wheatley (ed.), *Stress and the Heart.* New York: Raven, 1977.

TAGGART, P., CARRUTHERS, M., and SOMERVILLE, W. Electrocardiogram, plasma cathecolamines, and lipids, and their modification by oxprenolol when speaking before an audience. *Lancet,* 1973, *2,* 341–346.

TARNOPOLSKY, A., and MCLEAN, E. K. Noise as a psychosomatic hazard. In O. Hill (ed.), *Modern Trends in Psychosomatic Medicine* Vol. 3. London: Butterworths, 1976.

THOMAS, A., CHESS, S., and BIRCH, H. G. *Temperament and Behavior Disorders in Children.* New York: New York University Press, 1968.

TRYER, P. J., and LADER, M. H. Effects of beta-andrenergic blockade with sotalol in chronic anxiety. *Clinical Pharmacology and Therapeutics,* 1973, *14,* 418–426.

TYROLER, H. A., and CASSEL, J. Health consequences of cultural change: the effect of urbanization on coronary heart mortality in rural residents of North Carolina. *Journal of Chronic Disease,* 1964, *17,* 167–177.

WARD, W. D., and FRICK, J. E. (eds.), *Noise as a Public Health Hazard.* American Speech and Hearing Association Reports, No. 4. Washington, D.C.: American Speech and Hearing Association. 1969.

WELNER, A., BEN-ISHAY, D., GROEN, J. J., and DAHL, L. K. Behavior patterns and sensitivity to experimental hypertension in rats. *Proceedings of the Society for Experimental Biology and Medicine,* 1968, *129,* 886–890.

WOLF, A. The dynamics of selective inhibition of specific functions in neurosis: a preliminary report. *Psychosomatic Medicine,* 1943, *5,* 27–38.

WOLFF, C. T., FRIEDMAN, S. B., HOFER, M. A., and MASON, J. W. Relationship between psychological defenses and mean urinary 17-hydroxycorticosteroid excretion rates. *Psychosomatic Medicine,* 1964, *26,* 576–609.

YEAKEL, E. H., SHENKIN, H. I., ROTHBALLER, A. B., and MCCARN, S. Blood pressure of rats subjected to auditory stimulation. *American Journal of Physiology,* 1948, *155,* 118–127.

# Chapter 13. Substance Abuse

AMERICAN PSYCHIATRIC ASSOCIATION. *Diagnostic and Statistical Manual of Mental Disorders.* 3d ed. Washington, D.C.: American Psychiatric Association, 1980.

AZRIN, N. H., and POWELL, J. Behavioral engineering: the reduction of smoking behavior by a conditioning apparatus and procedure. *Journal of Applied Behavior Analysis,* 1968, *1,* 193–200.

BALES, R. Cultural differences in rates of alcoholism. *Quarterly Journal of Studies in Alcoholism,* 1946, *6,* 480–499.

BESCHNER, G., ADAMS, K. M., WESSON, D. R., CARLIN, A. S., and FARLEY, E. Introduction. In D. R. Wesson, A. S. Carlin, K. M. Adams, and G. Beschner (eds.), *Poly Drug Abuse: The Results of a National Collaborative Study.* New York: Free Press, 1978.

BIGELOW, G., LIEBSON, I., and GRIFFITHS, R. R. Alcoholic drinking: suppression by a behavioral time-out procedure. *Behavior Research and Therapy,* 1974, *12,* 107–115.

BOWERS, J. Z. *An Introduction to Medicine, 1975.* Washington, D.C.: U.S. Department of Health, Education, and Welfare, 1977.

CADORET, R. J. Genetic determinants of alcoholism. In R. E. Tarter and A. A. Sugarman (eds.), *Alcoholism: Interdisciplinary Approaches to an Enduring Problem.* Reading: Addison-Wesley, 1976.

CAHALAN, D. *Problem Drinkers: A National Survey.* San Francisco: Jossey-Bass, 1970.

CAHALAN, D., and ROOM, R. *Problem Drinking among American Men.* New Brunswick: Rutgers Center for Alcohol Studies, 1974.

CAUDILL, B. D., and MARLATT, G. A. Modelling influences in social drinking: an experimental analogue. *Journal of Consulting and Clinical Psychology,* 1975, *43,* 405–415.

COLE, J., and RYBACK, R. S. Pharmacologic therapy. In R. E. Tarter and A. A. Sugarman (eds.), *Alcoholism: Interdisciplinary Approaches to an Enduring Problem.* Reading: Addison-Wesley, 1976.

DAMMANN, G., and OUSLEY, N. Female poly drug abusers. In D. R. Wesson, A. S. Carlin, K. M. Adams, and G. Beschner (eds.), *Poly Drug Abuse: The Results of a National Collaborative Study.* New York: Free Press, 1978.

DANAHER, B. G. Research on rapid smoking: interim summary and recommendations. *Addictive Behavior,* 1977, *2,* 151–166.

DAVIES, D. L. Definitional issues in alcoholism. In R. E. Tarter and A. A. Sugarman (eds.), *Alcoholism: Interdisciplinary Approaches to an Enduring Problem.* Reading: Addison-Wesley, 1976.

DAVISON, G. C., and NEALE, J. M. *Abnormal Psychology: An Experimental Clinical Approach.* 2d ed. New York: Wiley, 1978.

DI MASCIO, A. The role of the physician in reinforcing and inhibiting drug abuse. *International Pharmacopsychiatry,* 1972, *7,* 131–137.

FEJER, D., and SMART, R. G. *Tranquillizer Users: How Many Are without Physical or Psychological Problems?* Toronto: Addictive Research Foundation, 1974.

FRANKS, C. M., FRIED, R., and ASHEM. B. An improved apparatus for the aversive conditioning of cigarette smokers. *Behavior Research and Therapy,* 1966, *4,* 123–124.

FREDERIKSEN, L. W., and SIMON, S. J. Modifying how people smoke: instructional control and generalization. *Journal of Applied Behavior Analysis,* 1978, *11,* 431–432.

GOLDMAN, M. S., TAYLOR, H. A., CARRUTH, M. L., and NATHAN, P. E. Effects of group decision-making on group drinking by alcoholics. *Quarterly Journal of Studies on Alcohol,* 1973, *34,* 807–822.

GOODE, E. *Drugs in American Society.* New York: Knopf, 1972.

GRIFFITHS, R., BIGELOW, G., and LIEBSON, I. Suppression of ethanol self-administration in alcoholics contingent time-out from social interactions. *Behavior Research and Therapy,* 1974, *12,* 327–334.

GRIMALDI, K. E., and LICHTENSTEIN, E. Hot, smokey air as an aversive stimulus in the treatment of smoking. *Behavior Research and Therapy,* 1969, *7,* 275–282.

GRITZ, E. R. Smoking: the prevention of onset. In M. E. Jarvik, J. W. Cullen, E. R. Gritz, T. M. Vogt, and L. J. West (eds.), *Research on Smoking Behavior.* National Institute on Drug Abuse Research Monograph No. 17. Washington, D.C.: U.S. Department of Health, Education, and Welfare, 1977.

HAMMOND, E. C. Some preliminary findings on physical complaints from a prospective study of 1,064,004 men and women. *American Journal of Public Health,* 1964, *54,* 11-23.

HUNT, G. M., and AZRIN, N. H. The community-reinforcement approach to alcoholism. *Behavior Research and Therapy,* 1973, *11,* 91-104.

HUNT, W. A., and MATARAZZO, J. D. Habit mechanisms in smoking. In W. A. Hunt (ed.), *Learning Mechanisms in Smoking.* Chicago: Aldine, 1970.

INSTITUTE OF MEDICINE. *Report of a Study: Sleeping Pills, Insomnia, and Medical Practice.* Washington, D.C.: National Academy of Sciences, 1979.

JARVIK, M. E. Biological factors underlying the smoking habit. In M. E. Jarvik, J. W. Cullen, E. R. Gritz, T. M. Vogt, and L. J. West (eds.), *Research on Smoking Behavior.* National Institute on Drug Abuse Research Monograph No. 17. Washington, D.C.: U.S. Department of Health, Education, and Welfare, 1977.

JELLINEK, E. M. *The Disease Concept of Alcoholism.* Highland Park: Hill House, 1960.

KANDEL, J. Interpersonal influences on adolescent illegal drug use. In E. Josephson and E. E. Carroll (eds.), *Drug Use: Epidemiological and Sociological Approaches.* New York: Wiley, 1974.

KEEGAN, J., and SCHOOFF, K. Referral sources and outreach: critical variables in understanding the poly drug-abusing sample. In D. R. Wesson, A. S. Carlin, K. M. Adams, and G. Beschner (eds.), *Poly Drug Abuse: The Results of a National Collaborative Study.* New York: Free Press, 1978.

KELLER, M. The oddities of alcoholics. *Quarterly Journal of Studies on Alcohol,* 1972, *33,* 1147-1148.

KESSLER, M., and GOMBERG, C. Observations of barroom drinking: methodology and preliminary results. *Quarterly Journal of Studies on Alcohol,* 1974, *35,* 1392-1396.

KLINE, N. S., WREN, J. C., COOPER, T. B., VARGA, E., and CANAL, O. Evaluation of lithium therapy in chronic and periodic alcoholism. *American Journal of the Medical Sciences,* 1974, *268,* 15-22.

LAU, J. P., and BENVENUTO, J. Three national estimates of prevalence of nonopiate drug abuse. In D. R. Wesson, A. S. Carlin, K. M. Adams, and G. Beschner (eds.), *Poly Drug Abuse: The Results of a National Collaborative Study.* New York: Free Press, 1978.

LENNARD, H. L., EPSTEIN, L. J., BERNSTEIN, A., and RANDSOM, D. C. *Mystification in Drug Misuse.* New York: Harper & Row, 1972.

LICHTENSTEIN, E., HARRIS, D. E., BIRCHLER, G. R., WAHL, J. M., and SCHMAHL, D. P. Comparison of rapid smoking, warm smokey air, and attention placebo in the modification of smoking behavior. *Journal of Comparative and Clinical Psychology,* 1973, *40,* 92-98.

LUBLIN, J., and JOSLYN, L. Aversive conditioning of cigarette addiction. Paper presented at the annual meeting of the American Psychological Association, Los Angeles, August 1968.

LUDWIG, A. M. Personal communication, 1980.

MANN, M. *New Primer on Alcoholism.* 2d ed. New York: Holt, Rinehart & Winston, 1968.

MELLINGER, G. D. Psychotherapeutic drug use among adults: a model for young drug users? *Journal of Drug Issues,* 1971, *1,* 274–285.

MELLINGER, G. D., BALTER, M. B., PERRY, H. J., MANHEIMER, D. I., and CISIN, I. H. An overview of psychotherapeutic drug use in the United States. In E. Josephson and E. E. Carroll (eds.), *Drug Use: Epidemiological and Sociological Approaches.* New York: Wiley, 1974.

MELLO, N. K., and MENDELSON, J. H. The effects of prolonged alcohol ingestion on the eating, drinking, and smoking patterns of chronic alcoholics. In W. A. Hunt (ed.), *Learning Mechanisms in Smoking.* Chicago: Aldine, 1970.

————. Drinking patterns during work-contingent and non-contingent alcohol acquisition. *Psychosomatic Medicine,* 1972, *34,* 139–164.

MENDELSON, J. H. (ed.), Experimentally induced chronic intoxication and withdrawal in alcoholics. *Quarterly Journal of Studies on Alcohol* (supp. 2), 1964, *25,* 1–29.

MILLER, P. M. The use of behavioral contracting in the treatment of alcoholism: a case report. *Behavior Therapy,* 1972, *3,* 593–596.

————. A comprehensive behavioral approach to the treatment of alcoholism. In R. E. Tarter and A. A. Sugarman (eds.), *Alcoholism: Interdisciplinary Approaches to an Enduring Problem.* Reading: Addison-Wesley, 1976.

NATHAN, P. E., and LISMAN, S. A. Behavioral and motivational patterns of chronic alcoholics. In R. E. Tarter and A. A. Sugarman (eds.), *Alcoholism: Interdisciplinary Approaches to an Enduring Problem.* Reading: Addison-Wesley, 1976.

NATHAN, P. E. and O'BRIEN, J. S. An experimental analysis of the behavior of alcoholics and non-alcoholics during prolonged experimental drinking: a necessary precursor of behavior therapy? *Behavior Therapy,* 1971, *2,* 455–476.

NATHAN, P. E., O'BRIEN, J. S., and LOWENSTEIN, L. M. Operant studies of chronic alcoholism: interactions of alcohol and alcoholics. In M. K. Roach, W. M. McIsaac, and P. J. Creaven (eds.), *Biological Aspects of Alcohol.* Austin: University of Texas Press, 1971.

NATHAN, P. E., TITLER, N. A., LOWENSTEIN, L. M., SOLOMON, P., and ROSSI, A. M. Behavioral analysis of chronic alcoholism. *Archives of General Psychiatry,* 1970, *22,* 419–430.

NIETZEL, M. T., WINETT, R. A., MacDONALD, M. L., and DAVIDSON, W. S. *Behavioral Approaches to Community Psychology.* Oxford: Pergamon, 1977.

NOBLE, E. P. *Alcohol and Health.* Washington, D.C.: U.S. Department of Health, Education, and Welfare, 1978.

NORTON, J. C., POWELL, B. J., PENICK, E. C., and SAUERS, C. A. Screening alcoholics for medical problems with the Cornell Medical Index. *Journal of Studies on Alcohol,* 1977, *38,* 2193–2196.

PATTISON, E. M. A critique of alcoholism treatment concepts, with special reference to abstinence. In E. M. Pattison, M. B. Sobell, and L. C. Sobell (eds.), *Emerging Concepts of Alcohol Dependence.* New York: Springer, 1977.

PATTISON, E. M., HEADLEY, E. B., GLESER, G. C., and GOTTSCHALK, L. A. Abstinence and normal drinking: an assessment of changes in drinking patterns in alcoholics after treatment. *Quarterly Journal of Studies on Alcohol,* 1968, *29,* 610–633.

PECHACEK, T. F. An overview of smoking behavior and its modification. In N. A. Krasnegor (ed.), *Behavioral Analysis and Treatment of Substance Abuse.* National Institute on Drug Abuse Research Monograph No. 25. Washington, D. C.: U.S. Department of Health, Education, and Welfare, 1979.

PECHACEK, T. F., and McALISTER, A. Strategies for the modification of smoking behavior: treatment and prevention. In J. Ferguson and C. B. Taylor (eds.), *The Comprehensive Handbook of Behavioral Medicine.* Vol. 3. New York: Spectrum, 1979.

POPE, J. W., and MOUNT, G. R. The control of cigarette smoking through the application of a portable electronic device to dispense an aversive stimulus in relation to the subject's smoking frequency. *Behavioral Engineering,* 1975, *2,* 52–56.

POPHAM. R. E., SCHMIDT, W., and deLINT, J. The prevention of alcoholism: epidemiologic studies of the effects of government control measures. *British Journal of Addictions,* 1975, *70,* 125–144.

RAW, M. The psychological modification of smoking. In S. Rachman (ed.), *Contributions to Medical Psychology,* Vol. 1. Oxford: Pergamon, 1977.

RAY, W. A., FEDERSPIEL, C. F., and SCHAFFNER, W. A study of antipsychotic drug use in nursing homes: epidemiologic evidence suggesting misuse. *American Journal of Public Health,* 1980, *70,* 485–491.

RUSH, B. An inquiry into the effects of ardent spirits upon the human body and mind: the first American medical work on the effects of alcohol. *Quarterly Journal of Studies on Alcohol,* 1943, *4,* 321–341.

RUSSELL, M. A. H. Cigarette smoking: natural history of a dependence disorder. *British Journal of Medical Psychology,* 1971, *44,* 4–16.

———. Changes in cigarette price and consumption by men in Britain, 1946–71: a preliminary analysis. *British Journal of Preventive and Social Medicine,* 1973, *27,* 1–7.

———. Smoking problems: an overview. In M. E. Jarvik, J. W. Cullen, E. R. Gritz, T. M. Vogt, and L. J. West (eds.), *Research on Smoking Behavior.* National Institute on Drug Abuse Research Monograph No. 17. Washington, D.C.: U.S. Department of Health, Education, and Welfare, 1977.

SCHAEFER, H. H., SOBELL, M. B., and MILLS, K. C. Baseline drinking behavior in alcoholics and social drinkers: kinds of drinks and sip magnitude. *Behavior Research and Therapy,* 1971, *9,* 23–27.

SHAPIRO, D., TURSKY, B., SCHWARTZ, G. E., and SHNIDMAN, S. R. Smoking on cue: a behavioral approach to smoking re-education. *Journal of Health and Social Behavior,* 1971, *12,* 108–113.

SIPICH, J. F., RUSSEL, R. K., and TOBIAS, L. L. A comparison of covert sensitization and "non-specific" treatment in the modification of smoking behavior. *Journal of Behavior Therapy and Experimental Psychiatry,* 1974, *5,* 201–203.

SMART, R. G. Social policy and the prevention of drug abuse: perspectives on the unimodal approach. In M. M. Glatt (ed.), *Drug Dependence: Current Problems and Issues.* Baltimore: University Park Press, 1977.

SOBELL, M. B., SCHAEFER, H. H., and MILLS, K. C. Differences in baseline drinking between alcoholics and normal drinkers. *Behavior Research and Therapy,* 1972, *10,* 257–268.

SOBELL, M. B., and SOBELL, L. C. Individualized behavior therapy for alcoholics. *Behavior Therapy,* 1973, *4,* 49–72.

————. Second year treatment outcome of alcoholics treated by individualized behavior therapy: results. *Behavior Research and Therapy,* 1976, *14,* 195–215.

SPIEGEL, H. A single-treatment method to stop smoking using ancillary self-hypnosis. *International Journal of Clinical Hypnosis,* 1970, *18,* 235–250.

STRAUS, R. Drinking in college in the perspective of social change. In G. L. Maddox (ed.), *The Domesticated Drug.* New Haven: College and University Press, 1970.

————. Alcohol and society. *Psychiatric Annals,* 1973, *3,* 9–103.

————. When it comes to alcohol, equal is different. *Accent on Alcohol,* 1979, *8,* 3.

————. Alcoholism and problem drinking. In R. K. Merton and R. Nisbet (eds.), *Contemporary Social Problems.* New York: Harcourt Brace Jovanovich, 1976.

TARTER, R. E., and SCHNEIDER, D. U. Models and theories of alcoholism. In R. E. Tarter and A. A. Sugarman (eds.), *Alcoholism: Interdisciplinary Approaches to an Enduring Problem.* Reading: Addison-Wesley, 1976.

TRACEY, D. A., and NATHAN, P. E. Behavioral analysis of chronic alcoholism in four women. *Journal of Consulting and Clinical Psychology,* 1976, *44,* 832–842.

VAN LANCKER, J. L. Smoking and disease. In M. E. Jarvik, J. W. Cullen, E. R. Gritz, T. M. Vogt, and L. J. West (eds.), *Research on Smoking Behavior.* National Institute on Drug Abuse Research Monograph No. 17. Washington, D.C.: U.S. Department of Health, Education, and Welfare, 1977.

VANNICELLI, M. Mood and self-perception of alcoholics when sober and intoxicated. *Quarterly Journal of Studies on Alcohol,* 1972, *33,* 341–357.

WESSON, D. R., CARLIN, A. S., ADAMS, K. M., and BESCHNER, G. (EDS.). *Poly Drug Abuse: The Results of a National Collaborative Study.* New York: Free Press, 1978.

WEST, L. J. Hypnosis in the treatment of the smoking habit. In M. E. Jarvik, J. W. Cullen, E. R. Gritz, T. M. Vogt, and L. J. West (eds.), *Research on Smoking Behavior.* National Institute on Drug Abuse Research Monograph

No. 17. Washington, D.C.: U.S. Department of Health, Education, and Welfare, 1977.

WILDE, G. J. S. Behavior therapy for addicted cigarette smokers. *Behavior Research and Therapy*, 1964, *2*, 107–110.

WILLIAMS, R. *Alcoholism: The Nutritional Approach*. Austin: University of Texas Press, 1959.

WOLFF, P. Ethnic differences in alcohol sensitivity. *Science*, 1972, *175*, 449–450.

WYNDER, E. L. Interrelationships of smoking to other variables and preventive approaches. In M. E. Jarvik, J. W. Cullen, E. R. Gritz, T. M. Vogt, and L. J. West (eds.), *Research on Smoking Behavior*. National Institute on Drug Abuse Research Monograph No. 17. Washington, D.C.: U.S. Department of Health, Education, and Welfare, 1977.

# Chapter 14.  Health Maintenance

AJZEN, I., and FISHBEIN, M. Attitudinal and normative variables as predictors of specific behaviors. *Journal of Personality and Social Psychology*, 1973, *27*, 41–57.

BANDURA, A. *Principles of Behavior Modification*. New York: Holt, Rinehart & Winston, 1969.

BELLACK, A. S. A comparison of self-monitoring and self-reinforcement in weight reduction. *Behavior Therapy*, 1976, *7*, 68–75.

———. Behavioral treatment for obesity: appraisal and recommendations. In M. Hersen, R. M. Eisler, and P. M. Miller (eds.), *Progress in Behavior Modification*, Vol. 4, New York: Academic, 1977.

BELLACK, A. S., ROZENSKY, R. H., and SCHWARTZ, J. A comparison of two forms of self-monitoring in a behavioral weight reduction program. *Behavior Therapy*, 1974, *5*, 523–530.

BRESLOW, L., and SOMERS, A. R. The lifetime health monitoring program: a practical approach to preventive medicine. *New England Journal of Medicine*, 1977, *296*, 601–608.

CASTRO, L., and RACKLIN, H. Self-reward, self-monitoring, and self-punishment as feedback for weight control. *Behavior Therapy*, 1980, *11*, 38–48.

CAUTELA, J. R. The treatment of overeating by covert conditioning. *Psychotherapy: Theory, Research, and Practice*, 1972, *9*, 211–216.

CHIRICO, A. M., and STUNKARD, A. J. Physical activity in human obesity. *New England Journal of Medicine*, 1960, *263*, 935–946.

FARQUHAR, J. W., MACCOBY, N., WOOD, P. D., ALEXANDER, J. K., BREITROSE, H., BROWN, B. W., JR., HASKLE, W. L., McALISTER, A. L., MEYER, A. J., NASH, J. D., and STERN, M. P. Community education for cardiovascular health. *Lancet*, 1977, *1*, 1192–1195.

FISHBEIN, M. Attitude and the prediction of behavior. In M. Fishbein (ed.), *Readings in Attitude Theory and Measurement*. New York: Wiley, 1967.

FOREYT, J. P., and HAGEN, R. Covert sensitization: conditioning or suggestion. *Journal of Abnormal Psychology,* 1973, *82,* 17–23.

GAMBRILL, E. D. *Behavior modification: Handbook of Assessment, Intervention, and Education.* San Francisco: Jossey-Bass, 1977.

GOLDMAN, R., JAFFA, M., and SCHACHTER, S. Yom Kippur, Air France, dormitory food, and the eating behavior of obese and normal persons. *Journal of Personality and Social Psychology,* 1968, *10,* 117–123.

GUMBINER, R. *HMO: Putting It All Together.* St. Louis: Mosby, 1975.

HALL, S. M. Self-control and therapist control in the behavioral treatment of overweight women. *Behavior Research and Therapy,* 1972, *10,* 59–68.

HAVIGHURST, C. C. Health maintenance organizations and the market for health services. *Law and Contemporary Problems,* 1970, *35,* 616–695.

HIRSCH, J., and KNITTLE, J. L. Cellularity of obese and non-obese human adipose tissue. *Federation Proceedings,* 1971, *29,* 1516–1521.

JACARD, J. A theoretical analysis of selected factors important in health education strategies. *Health Education Monographs,* 1975, *3,* 152–167.

JEFFREY, D. B. Behavioral management of obesity. In W. E. Craighead, A. E. Kazdin, and M. J. Mahoney (eds.), *Behavior Modification: Principles, Issues, and Applications.* Boston: Houghton Mifflin, 1976.

KAZDIN, A. E. Self-monitoring and behavior change. In M. J. Mahoney and C. E. Thoresen (eds.), *Self-control: Power to the Person.* Monterey: Brooks/Cole, 1974.

KENNEDY, W. A., and FOREYT, J. Control of eating behavior in an obese patient by avoidance conditioning. *Psychological Reports,* 1968, *22,* 571–576.

LEON, G. R. Current directions in the treatment of obesity. *Psychological Bulletin,* 1976, *83,* 557–578.

LEVITZ, L. S., and STUNKARD, A. J. Therapeutic coalition for obesity: behavior modification and patient self-help. *American Journal of Psychiatry,* 1974, *131,* 423–427.

LUFT, H. S. How do health-maintenance organizations achieve their "savings"? *New England Journal of Medicine,* 1978, *298,* 1136–1343.

MAHONEY, K., and MAHONEY, M. J. Cognitive factors in weight reduction. In J. D. Krumboltz and C. E. Thoresen (eds.), *Counseling Methods.* New York: Holt, Rinehart & Winston, 1976.

MAHONEY, M. J. The behavioral treatment of obesity: a reconnaissance. *Biofeedback and Self-regulation,* 1976, *1,* 127–133.

MAHONEY, M. J., and MAHONEY, K. *Permanent Weight Control: A Total Solution to Dietary Management.* New York: Norton, 1976.

MANN, R. A. The behavior-therapeutic use of contingency contracting to control an adult behavior problem: weight control *Journal of Applied Behavior Analysis,* 1972, *5,* 99–109.

MCALISTER, A., and BERGER, E. D. Media for community health promotion. In P. M. Lazes (ed.), *The Handbook of Health Education.* Germantown: Aspen, 1979.

MENDELSOHN, H. Some reasons why information campaigns can succeed. *Public Opinion Quarterly*, 1973, *1*, 50–61.

MEYER, V., and CRISP, A. Aversion therapy in two cases of obesity. *Behavior Research and Therapy*, 1964, *2*, 143–147.

MORGANSTERN, K. P. Cigarette smoking as a noxious stimulus in a self-managed aversion therapy for compulsive eating: technique and case illustration. *Behavior Therapy*, 1974, *5*, 255–260.

NISBETT, R. E. Hunger, obesity, and the ventromedial hypothalamus. *Psychological Review*, 1972, *79*, 433–453.

PASSMORE, R., STRONG, A., SWINDELLS, Y. E., and EL DIN, N. The effect of overfeeding on two fat young women. *British Journal of Nutrition*, 1963, *17*, 373–383.

PENICK, S. B., FILION, R., FOX, S., and STUNKARD, A. J. Behavior modification in the treatment of obesity. *Psychosomatic Medicine*, 1971, *33*, 49–55.

ROEMER, M.I. Can prepaid care succeed: a vote of confidence. *Prism*, 1974, *2*, 14–67.

ROMANCZYK, R. G., TRACEY, D., WILSON, G., and THORPE, G. Behavioral techniques in the treatment of obesity: a comparative analysis. *Behavior Research and Therapy*, 1973, *11*, 629–640.

ROSSER, J. M., and MOSSBERG, H. E. *An Analysis of Health Care Delivery.* New York: Wiley, 1977.

ROZENSKY, R. H., and BELLACK, A. S. Individual differences in self-reinforcement style and performance in self- and therapist-controlled weight reduction programs. *Behavior Research and Therapy*, 1976, *14*, 357–364.

SCHACHTER, S. Some extraordinary facts about obese humans and rats. *American Psychologist*, 1971, *26*, 129–144.

SCHACHTER, S., and RODIN, J. *Obese Humans and Rats.* Potomac: Lawrence Erlbaum, 1974.

STOLLAK, G. E. Weight loss obtained under different experimental procedures. *Psychotherapy: Theory, Research, and Practice*, 1967, *4*, 61–64.

STUART, R. B. A three-dimensional program for the treatment of obesity. *Behavior Research and Therapy*, 1971, *9*, 177–186.

————. Weight loss and beyond: are they taking it off and keeping it off? In P. O. Davidson and S. M. Davidson (eds.), *Behavioral Medicine: Changing Health Lifestyles.* New York: Brunner/Mazel, 1980.

STUART, R. B., and DAVIS, B. *Slim Chance in a Fat World.* Rev. and condensed ed. Champaign: Research Press, 1978.

STUNKARD, A. J. Behavioral treatments of obesity: failure to maintain weight loss. In R. B. Stuart (ed.), *Behavioral Self-management.* New York: Brunner/Mazel, 1977.

STUNKARD, A. J., and MAHONEY, M. J. Behavioral treatment of the eating disorders. In H. Leitenberg (ed.), *Handbook of Behavior Modification and Behavior Therapy.* Englewood Cliffs: Prentice-Hall, 1976.

U.S. DEPARTMENT OF HEALTH, EDUCATION, AND WELFARE. *Obesity and Health: A*

*Source-book of Current Information for Professional Health Personnel.* Arlington: U.S. Public Health Service, 1967.

WOLLERSHEIM, J. P. Effectiveness of group therapy based upon learning principles in the treatment of overweight women. *Journal of Abnormal Psychology,* 1970, *76,* 462–474.

WOOLEY, S. C., and WOOLEY, O. W. Methods and findings in study of food regulation in obesity. In N. A. Krasnegor (ed.), *Self-administration of Abused Substances: Methods for Study.* National Institute for Drug Abuse Research Monograph No. 20. Washington, D.C.: U.S. Department of Health, Education, and Welfare, 1978.

# Index